Fugitive States

Justice, Power, and Politics

Heather Ann Thompson and Rhonda Y. Williams, editors

The Justice, Power, and Politics series publishes new works in history that explore the myriad struggles for justice, battles for power, and shifts in politics that have shaped the United States over time. Through the lenses of justice, power, and politics, the series seeks to broaden scholarly debates about America's past as well as to inform public discussions about its future.

A complete list of books published in Justice, Power, and Politics is available at https://uncpress.org/series/justice-power-politics.

Fugitive States

The Life of Charlie Hill, a Black Radical Exile in Socialist Cuba

TEISHAN A. LATNER

The University of North Carolina Press
Chapel Hill

Set in Minion Pro by Westchester Publishing Services

Library of Congress Cataloging-in-Publication Data
Names: Latner, Teishan author
Title: Fugitive states : the life of Charlie Hill, a Black radical exile in socialist Cuba / Teishan A. Latner.
Other titles: Justice, power, and politics (bcp47)
Description: Chapel Hill : The University of North Carolina Press, [2026] | Series: Justice, power, and politics | Includes bibliographical references and index.
Identifiers: LCCN 2026018180 | ISBN 9781469693477 cloth | ISBN 9781469693484 paperback | ISBN 9781469686417 epub | ISBN 9781469693491 pdf
Subjects: LCSH: Hill, Charlie, 1949– | Black nationalism—United States—History—20th century | Radicalism—United States—History—20th century | Exiles—Cuba—History | Americans—Cuba—History | Cuba—History—1959–1990 | Cuba—History—1990– | BISAC: HISTORY / Caribbean & West Indies / Cuba | HISTORY / United States / 20th Century | LCGFT: Biographies
Classification: LCC E185.615 .L296 2026
LC record available at https://lccn.loc.gov/2026018180

Cover art: *Charlie in Havana*, by Dudley M. Brooks. Used by permission.

For product safety concerns under the European Union's General Product Safety Regulation (EU GPSR), please contact gpsr@mare-nostrum.co.uk or write to the University of North Carolina Press and Mare Nostrum Group B.V., Doelen 72, 4831 GR Breda, The Netherlands.

Contents

Preface

The Last Hijacker of the Sixties

At the center of Parque Central in Havana stands a white marble statue of José Martí, the iconic nineteenth-century poet and apostle of Cuba's long independence struggle against foreign domination. I am standing in its shadow, a history graduate student doing my best not to be mistaken for some kind of CIA agent or bounty hunter.

It's a muggy June morning in 2012, and I am looking for Charlie Hill, an American political exile in Cuba. I want to interview him to better understand Havana's small community of radical émigrés from the United States. I know that this is a delicate line of investigation. After all, the presence of the foreign exiles is a matter of national security interest in Cuba. Their safety falls under the purview of the government's capable state intelligence service. To make matters worse, I have no idea how to make contact with Hill. For lack of a better idea, I have been hanging around Parque Central, where I hear he sometimes comes to offer his services to tourists in need of a local guide.

I approach a group of middle-aged men who look like park regulars. I explain who I am looking for. He is an *estadounidense*—a person from the United States. Once he was a member of a 1960s-era Black nationalist and Pan-African organization. Accused of killing a police officer in New Mexico, he hijacked an airplane to Cuba in 1971 and was granted sanctuary by the revolutionary government. He has been living in Havana ever since.

At the time, American exiles in Cuba were objects of international intrigue. Assata Shakur, a former member of the Black Panther Party who was imprisoned on dubious charges of killing a police officer in New Jersey, was granted political asylum in Cuba in 1984 following a dramatic prison escape. I met her in 2004, less than a year before she withdrew from public life following the State of New Jersey's announcement of a $1 million reward for information leading to her capture and return to US custody. In Havana, rumors had swirled about foreign bounty hunters showing up, perhaps posing as tourists (or graduate students?). But Hill, who was not the subject of a bounty, remained free to move about. And tranquil Cuba, still one of the most secure societies in the world, was an improbable locale for a kidnapping.

To the Cuban government, Shakur and Hill were political activists, not criminals. Their alleged crimes decades ago had occurred amidst a context of militant antiracist struggle and state repression in the United States. Throughout the 1960s era, the Cuban press had grimly chronicled a litany of petty harassment, trumped-up charges, and political violence against civil rights organizers and Black Power radicals at the hands of police, the FBI, and ordinary racists. Against the backdrop of the global Cold War, Cuban journalists and artists had lampooned Washington's claims that the United States was a beacon of freedom and democracy for all. Shakur and Hill, Cuban officials argued, would be unlikely to receive fair trials. Rejecting extradition requests, the Cuban government pointed to its right as a sovereign nation, codified by the 1948 Universal Declaration of Human Rights and the 1951 Refugee Convention, to provide asylum to foreigners whom it deemed to be politically persecuted.

The right of nations to grant asylum also allowed Washington to decline extradition requests from Havana. At the time that I met Hill in Havana, the most wanted Cuban exile living in the United States was Luis Posada Carriles. Charged with orchestrating the 1976 bombing of a Cuban civilian airliner, Cubana de Aviación flight 455—an event that would stand ignominiously as the deadliest act of aviation terrorism in the Western Hemisphere until September 11, 2001—the CIA-trained Posada Carriles had been residing in Miami. Posada Carilles's alleged crimes constituted terrorism under internationally accepted definitions. Those of Hill and Shakur, accused of murdering police officers during racially charged traffic stops but not political violence carried out against civilians, did not.[1]

Washington would continue to rebuff Havana's calls for Posada Carilles's extradition until his death in 2018. Instead, it used Cuba's harboring of fugitives from the United States as a pretext for maintaining the State Department's 1982 designation of Cuba as a state sponsor of terrorism. The extradition of American exiles, including Shakur and Hill, now ranked among Washington's preconditions for the normalization of diplomatic relations and the end of decades of economic sanctions.[2] The failure of Washington since 1959 to honor a multitude of Cuban extradition requests for fugitives, including those accused of hijacking, murder, and other serious offenses on the island, was one reason for Havana's dogged provision of sanctuary to Americans.[3] Cuba's historical support for the Black freedom movement in the United States was another. Both impulses, I would soon discover, were outgrowths of the Cuban Revolution's enduring commitment to sovereignty, social justice, and internationalism.

It is now high noon. Everyone in Parque Central has retreated to the shade of the trees. The park regulars, it turns out, know exactly who I'm looking for.

One of them walks to a payphone. An hour later, a graying but sinewy man in his early sixties ambles into the park. He smiles and introduces himself: "Hey, man, good to meet you."

This is how I met Charlie Hill.

Leaving the park, we retreat to the deeper shade of an Old Havana bar. We order strong *cafecitos*. Hill obliges my interview questions, cautiously at first, then more animatedly as he realizes that I've studied up on the people and events that have shaped his life. We order more coffee. I scribble notes. I joke that, despite peppering him with questions, I'm not an FBI agent. "I don't care if you are!" he sasses back. His informal, amiable charm is not that of the nervous fugitive I half expected to meet. The conversation lasts almost six hours.

When I met him, Hill was the longest remaining US political exile in Cuba. A Vietnam veteran who had been expelled from the US Army for refusing to fight against the communist liberation forces, Hill joined the Republic of New Afrika, a dynamic Black nationalist movement that called for reparations for slavery and audaciously campaigned for the creation of a sovereign nation-state for Black people in the American South. Hill would spend less than a year in the organization. On November 27, 1971, accused of killing a white New Mexico state trooper, Hill hijacked an airplane from Albuquerque to Havana. Now a political exile, he hoped to make connections with African revolutionary movements and to reach Angola or Guinea-Bissau to join the armed struggle against colonialism and white supremacy. Instead, he would spend the next five decades in exile in Cuba.

My own routes to the island were far less dramatic. I first became involved with US-Cuba policy as an undergraduate intern at Global Exchange, a San Francisco–based international human rights organization, in 1998. I traveled to the island for the first time in 2004, arriving in the city of Santiago de Cuba with the Venceremos Brigade, a US anti-imperialist project that has engaged in people-to-people educational exchanges and volunteer work in support of Cuban self-determination since 1969. I returned to Havana on my own in July 2006, just in time to learn from people on the street that Fidel Castro, the historical leader of the still ongoing Cuban Revolution, had fallen ill and was stepping back from the presidency. But it was not until 2012 that I began spending extended periods of time on the island. As I conducted dissertation research for a doctorate in history, American exiles in Havana became valuable research contacts. Dozens of trips to Cuba later, that first interview with Hill in Old Havana became one of well over a decade of conversations.

It was Hill who proposed this biography. At first, I declined. I knew that a book about his life would present peculiar methodological and ethical dilemmas. It was not clear that such a book could even be written—or *should* be written. Hill is not a celebrated figure. His fame is owed largely to his notoriety, not his political activism. And social history is filled with people whose stories urgently need to be told: obscure protagonists of social change movements, lost architects of bygone freedom struggles, unstudied visionaries who changed the world but are now lost to time—most will never be the subjects of full-length biographies. Why not write about one of *them*?

Yet as many scholars can attest, some research is not chosen—it chooses you, and then it captures your imagination. Hill is an improbable choice for a biography. He does not always fit the exemplar of the inspiring figure, however multifaceted, who is the subject of most biographies. But *Fugitive States* is not a celebration of a hero or an icon. It is a gritty account of a US political exile in Cuba. I became fascinated by the power of Hill's story, told as social biography, to illuminate forgotten encounters within the transnational history of Cuba and the United States. To understand Hill's surprising life is to glimpse the hidden currents of radicalism that swirl around both nations.

To write this book, I conducted hundreds of hours of interviews, communicating with Hill, often daily, for six years. I traveled to Cuba regularly, sometimes staying for months at a time. I visited historical archives and obtained declassified US government documents. I tried to understand the maelstrom of history that was Hill's world. This biography does not purport to tell the whole story. It contains many silences, owing to both the choices I made in crafting a narrative and the limitations of archival and oral history. Some of Hill's claims are impossible to corroborate. He, too, undoubtedly made authorial choices. My biography of him is faithful to the truth as I understand it. *Fugitive States* is my attempt to follow Charlie Hill through the whirlwind.

Fugitive States

Introduction

Hothouse of Revolution

Havana in the 1970s was a symbolic capital of the insurgent third world. The streets of the city's Vedado district, with its foreign embassies, nightclubs, and columnated university, buzzed with international intrigue and mysterious foreigners. Waiting to enter Coppelia, the city's iconic socialist ice cream palace, where Cubans went to enjoy ice cream for a few pennies, patrons could find themselves queueing with Algerian medical students, chatting with members of a political delegation from Jamaica or Palestine, or sharing a communal table with exiled leftists from Chile or anticolonial guerrillas from Guinea-Bissau. "In that hothouse of revolution and charged hope," one foreign journalist wrote of the city's frenetic atmosphere, "all kinds of people meet and form relationships that would be unlikely to occur almost anywhere else in the world."[1] Although a poor country, Cuba's commitment to universal education and health care, its support for anticolonial insurgency in Africa, its dispatch of doctors beyond its shores, and its defiance of US imperialism had given the Caribbean nation an outsized place in the political imagination of the Global South.[2]

This was the radical milieu that Charlie Hill encountered when he hijacked a commercial airliner from Albuquerque to Havana with two comrades—activists Michael Finney and Ralph Goodwin—on November 27, 1971. Accused of murder in the killing of a New Mexico state trooper, the three men—with unexpected help from Chicano and Black youth in Albuquerque, where a major urban rebellion against police brutality had rocked the city just months earlier—eluded a massive manhunt during a period of acute popular anger at law enforcement. Granted political asylum by the Cuban government on the grounds that he and his friends, although claiming self-defense in the slaying of the officer, would be unlikely to receive a fair trial in the United States, Hill soon found himself among a multifarious community of foreigners in Havana. Cuba was a beacon of third world liberation, and North Americans, even airplane hijackers accused of serious crimes, were permitted to reside on the island as guests—so long as they were willing to contribute to Cuban society and respect its sovereignty.

Hill's flight into exile occurred at a time when large sectors of the multiracial American left were still deeply internationalist. Denouncing US interventionism and proclaiming solidarity with movements for self-determination in the third world, American leftists looked hopefully beyond the borders of the United States for models of resistance to imperialism and white supremacy and alternatives to the exploitation of capitalism. A Vietnam veteran who had been jailed for deserting the US Army while deployed near Huế, Hill's opposition to the war, and his sympathy for the historical Vietnamese struggle against foreign domination, had become refracted through the prism of his life in America. Growing up in the shadow of Jim Crow in Illinois, Alabama, and New Mexico, Hill had watched his parents, the grandchildren of slaves, eke out a meager living and battle racism and exploitation. Returning from the jungle combat zones of Vietnam, Hill embraced the Black nationalist vision of the Republic of New Afrika (RNA) movement. Offering a bold reimagining of the political subjectivity of Black Americans, members of the RNA proposed that the descendants of enslaved Africans were a captive Black nation inside the entrails of America who had the right to reparations, freedom—and land.

Havana in the early 1970s was already home to other Americans—voluntary expatriates whose stories were as surprising as Hill's. Lorna Burdsall, a ballet dancer from Connecticut, fell in love with Cuban revolutionary Manuel Piñeiro Losada and moved to Havana in 1955. Participating in the urban theater of the Cuban Revolution, Burdsall went on to become an important figure in modern dance in Cuba, while Piñeiro Losada—then her husband—headed the Departamento de América, which sought to export the Cuban Revolution by supporting armed struggle against US-backed Latin American rightwing dictatorships.[3] German-born Connie Veltfort arrived in 1962 with her American stepfather, a communist veteran of the Abraham Lincoln Brigade who had accepted a job working for the Cuban government alongside other American supporters of the revolution.[4] Oakland-born Musician Pablo Menéndez, son of American folk singer and activist Barbara Dane, moved from California to Cuba in 1966 as a teenager, living for the next five decades in Havana, where he became a household name as a producer and band leader.[5] New York–born feminist poet Margaret Randall moved to Havana following the 1968 massacre of university students in Mexico City, where she had been living, and raised her four children in Cuba for the next decade.[6] Jane McManus, daughter of a New England corporate executive who became radicalized through her participation in the civil rights movement, moved to Havana in 1969 to work as a translator for Cuba's famed Organization of Solidarity of the Peoples of Asia, Africa and Latin America.[7]

Americans continued arriving as émigrés throughout the 1970s and 1980s. CIA agent turned whistleblower Philip Agee, who exposed Washington's covert operations to overthrow leftwing governments in Latin America, sought asylum in Cuba after the US government revoked his passport, then wrote his best-selling 1975 memoir, *Inside the Company*, in Havana.[8] Black Panther Party cofounder Huey P. Newton sought political asylum in Cuba in 1974, spending nearly three years on the island. Other American exiles followed. Assata Shakur, persecuted in a series of high-profile trials for acts attributed to the Black Liberation Army, sought asylum in Cuba in 1984. William Morales, a bomb maker for the Puerto Rican nationalist organization Fuerzas Armadas de Liberación Nacional, which sought to free the island of Borikén—Puerto Rico's Indigenous name—from US colonial control, escaped from a New York prison hospital and obtained asylum in Cuba in 1988. Harlem activist Nehanda Isoke Abiodun, accused of political crimes that included aiding Shakur's escape from prison, followed in 1990.[9]

Yet the most enigmatic group of Americans in Havana was undoubtedly the hijackers. Between 1968 and 1973, as Cuba became the world's most frequent destination for commandeered aircraft, Havana's foreign population was augmented by a curious group of North Americans. Some staged their hijackings as acts of political protest, while others expressed their desire to escape life in the United States or to join Cuba's unfolding revolution. Still others, describing themselves as victims of political repression, sought asylum. A few of these radical sanctuary seekers, such as William Lee Brent, a former Black Panther who hijacked a plane to Cuba in 1969 and later became a schoolteacher in Havana, successfully made lives for themselves in exile. Most, though, became a nuisance for the Cuban government.

Together, these Americans in Cuba—left-wing émigrés, voluntary expatriates, formal political exiles, and airplane hijackers—made up an eclectic community of foreigners in Havana. As they made lives for themselves, they quietly made history, becoming part of the saga of US-Cuba relations in unexpected ways. The presence of the hijackers, for instance, compelled Havana and Washington to temporarily overcome their diplomatic stalemate and negotiate an agreement to end the scourge of air piracy in 1973, yet Cuba's protection of some as political asylees enabled US officials, forgetful of America's juridically identical protection of hijackers from Cuba, to demonize the island's leaders. American expatriate writers such as McManus and Randall helped to translate, literally and figuratively, the lived experience of revolutionary Cuba to audiences stateside. Black political exiles, especially Abiodun and Shakur, became important bridges between the Cuban Revolution and the African American freedom struggle. Yet their presence in Havana—above all Shakur, who became the subject of a second $1 million reward for her apprehension in 2013, bringing the total to $2 million—provided Washington with an additional pretext for the maintenance of diplomatic hostility toward Cuba long after the Cold War.

American political émigrés in Havana may appear, at first glance, to be outliers. Most political expatriates crossing the Straits of Florida after 1959 have been Cubans moving northward toward the United States. Yet when viewed through wider temporal and geographic lenses, American political expatriation to Cuba comes into the frame again as part of an older phenomenon. Throughout the history of the United States, dissenters and political sojourners have crossed borders and oceans to evade political pressure. In the twentieth century, amid the ideological regime of the Cold War, American left-wing activists highlighted the distance yet to be traveled between the soaring rhetoric of American freedom and the lived realities of racism, exclusion, and inequality. Some did so by leaving American shores. Whether Black Americans seeking refuge in the Soviet Union, Ghana, and France from Jim Crow and anticommunist persecution; American leftists and artists living in Mexico City to evade McCarthyism and red scares; draft resisters fleeing to Canada during the Vietnam War; or Black radicals evading politicized legal charges or seeking Pan-African horizons in Tanzania and Algeria—all arguably challenged American exceptionalism.[10] As they made lives for themselves in foreign lands, they troubled Cold War truisms that US liberal capitalist democracy had produced a free society for all, one from which no citizen need ever seek political refuge. Many became permanent expatriates. Some went to Cuba.

Hill's life encourages us to think about these transnational encounters—and about the progression of history and social change—in new ways. Like most historical actors swept into the currents of radical upheaval, Hill is neither a movement icon nor a celebrated activist. In many ways he is not a traditional historical protagonist at all. He played no major role in any organization or social movement, and while he retained a consistent political radicalism through the years, he has been more gadfly than spokesperson. Yet it is precisely because of the obscurity of figures such as Hill within standard accountings of the past that his biography reveals a hidden social history of his time. The same historical forces that created the iconic figures of the global 1960s era also created Hill. Protagonists like him, one might say, live their lives, but not "just as they please"; they live them, as Marx wrote of a different place and epoch, "under circumstances directly found, given and transmitted from the past."[11] To understand Hill and the other forgotten historical actors who populate this book is to glimpse a buried archive of transnational encounter. It is also to glimpse, in the end, a more universal story, for in their human experiences of dislocation, loss, adaptation, and longing, their lives resonate with exiles the world over.

Between Homeland and Humanity

When Hill hijacked a commercial airliner to Cuba in November 1971, he did so with the expectation that Havana could serve as a gateway to anticolonial movements on the African continent. But as Hill and his companions settled into a government-run halfway house for foreign hijackers in Havana, their dreams of joining the struggle in Africa were dashed. A stream of self-made American revolutionaries, some of dubious credibility in the eyes of the Cuban government, had arrived in recent years. Many were regarded as little more than naive adventurers. Hill and his American comrades in Havana would have to prove themselves to their Cuban hosts.

It was also clear that despite the Cuban government's support for Black liberation movements in the United States—above all the socialist and internationalist Black Panther Party—there was little room for independent Black politics in Cuba itself. The ambivalence extended well beyond the state. In the *cafeterías* and nightclubs of Havana and the sugar cane fields of the countryside, the Afro-Cubans that Hill met embraced figures such as Stokely Carmichael and Angela Davis, whom the Cuban press had lionized and whose affirmations of Black pride had captivated *afrodescendiente* Cubans during the activists' visits to the island. But these same Afro-Cubans, pointing to the dramatic leveling effects of the Cuban Revolution, also insisted that racism was being vanquished by the unfolding process of constructing socialism.

Indeed, few Cubans seemed to identify strongly with race at all. Cuban national identity, Hill discovered, was distinctly multiracial. Premised on *mestizaje*, or racial mixture, to be Cuban, national narratives suggested, was to be of mixed European and African ancestry. Since the nineteenth century, Cuba's national mythology of amalgamation had produced racial hierarchies, to be sure, but also identities far less rigid than those of its US counterparts, where citizenship had historically been predicated on narrow notions of whiteness and racial purity. The intellectual architects of Cuban nationalism had long proposed that unity was key to securing independence from foreign domination. Cubans of all colors fought and died together in nineteenth-century wars against Spanish colonialism. Stark inequality persisted after independence, however, and racism remained a defining feature of national life. With the Cuban Revolution of 1959, new revolutionary ideologies emerged to proclaim that racial equality was fundamental to defending national self-determination and to building socialism for all Cubans. Antidiscrimination campaigns were mounted, and key bulwarks of exclusion were dismantled. The state poured massive resources into universal access to education, health, nutrition, and social welfare and aggressively redistributed wealth. Social inequality, including that associated with race, declined to levels unprecedented in Cuban history. But in the early 1960s, the revolutionary state declared racism eliminated, foreclosing further public debate. Under this mantle of official silence, racism, particularly in its cultural and attitudinal forms, was allowed to continue.[12]

The contrasts between the Black nationalism of the RNA, premised on a fundamental pessimism about the prospects for racial equality in the United States, and Cuban revolutionary nationalism, premised more optimistically on the conviction that equality was being achieved through the collective struggle to build socialism, could hardly have been more striking. By the 1970s, Cuba had undoubtedly become the most equal nation in the Western Hemisphere. By the 1980s, racial inequality in several key indicators of population health, educational attainment, and life expectancy had become statistically insignificant. This astonishing leveling of society, including in key material indicators of racial inequality, accomplished largely through a structural approach of enshrining education, health care, nutrition, jobs, and housing as social rights for all, stands as one of the great achievements of Cuba's socialist experiment. Nothing in United States history comes close to Cuba's antiracist accomplishments in these areas. Yet racism was not uprooted. Racial inequities remained in important areas of national life. This paradox, of the persistence of racism in a society that had become remarkably egalitarian by global standards, one that celebrated its African roots but avoided public discussion of racial prejudice, would be a recurring theme of Hill's efforts to understand Cuba.

During the coming years, Hill's life in exile would intersect repeatedly with Black political movements in the United States, some of whose members were also traveling to Cuba, not as hijackers but as journalists, political sojourners, researchers, and members of solidarity brigades. The Black radical traffic to Cuba had begun more than a decade earlier. Cuba's revolution triumphed at an apex of anticolonialism on the African continent and civil rights organizing in the United States. Fidel Castro's rhetorical battles with the Eisenhower administration—friend to neither civil rights nor anticolonialism—caught the attention of civil rights activists stateside.[13] The Cuban leader's trip to New York to attend the UN General Assembly in September 1960 made Castro a Harlem legend after the Cuban delegation, snubbed by a midtown hotel, moved their headquarters uptown to the Hotel Theresa. "Some 2,000 brown New Yorkers," as the *New York Citizen-Call* put it—including ten-year-old Nehanda Abiodun and her Garveyite father—congregated outside in the pouring rain as Malcolm X met with Castro inside.[14]

Transnational radical encounters such as these propelled the Cuban Revolution into the imagination of US third world leftists during the tumultuous era when Hill, a member of the pivotal Black Power generation, came of age in New Mexico and California.[15] Years before he read about the Cuban Revolution in the *Black Panther* newspaper in Oakland, Hill had encountered the stylized likeness of Che Guevara in murals painted by Chicano activists in Albuquerque. Cuba's provision of political asylum in 1961 to North Carolina civil rights activists Mabel and Robert F. Williams set the precedent of sanctuary for US Black radicals but hinted at future disappointments. By 1965, Robert Williams had lost faith in the Cuban state, which he viewed as hostile to Black nationalism, and traveled on to China.[16]

Yet contact between luminaries of the US Black freedom struggle and the Cuban Revolution was just beginning. When Student Nonviolent Coordinating Committee activist Stokely Carmichael attended the Latin American Solidarity Organization conference in Havana in 1967, he was feted as a guest of honor and appeared at huge rallies with Castro, electrifying audiences with his calls to wage a hemispheric war on racism and exploitation.[17] The Black Panther Party sent a delegation in 1968, and the Cuban government granted asylum to one of its leaders, Eldridge Cleaver, later that year. Like Williams, Cleaver became critical of the Cuban government, but the affinity between Cuba and the Panthers continued. While Cleaver had little contact with everyday Cubans during his six months in Havana, Huey P. Newton lived on the island for almost three years, sometimes in residential neighborhoods, concluding that socialist Cuba was an inspiration for the kind of society the Black Panthers wanted to build in North America.[18]

But many of the American hijackers in Havana were not like the formal asylees or invited activists. In fact, many were not activists at all, with some fleeing crimes that had no obvious political import. With little knowledge of Cuba but expecting a warm welcome, some hijackers were surprised to find themselves confined to immigration jails while the Cuban government tried to figure out what to do with them. Even Hill and the other American hijackers who supported the Cuban Revolution—young Black, white, and Latino radicals who labored to win the respect of their Cuban hosts, attempting to differentiate themselves from "opportunists who turned into counterrevolutionaries," as Hill later put it, "who hijacked planes to Cuba and then blamed the government when they didn't like Cuba"—sometimes stumbled themselves. Petty crimes earned Hill stints in prison. During international events, state security twice sent him to live outside Havana as a precaution.

For a while, Cuba's socialist revolution advanced. The 1980s were years of optimism. Health care and education had long become universal. Food and clothing were social rights; the arts and entertainment became the birthright of all Cubans. The island's scientific and athletic achievements were the envy of the Global South. Hill marveled at the nation's internationalist commitments, from global medical brigades to support for revolutionary movements across the third world. Cuba's participation in anticolonial insurgencies reached epic proportions in Africa, where hundreds of thousands of Cuban soldiers and civilians worked, fought, and died. A massive Cuban military intervention in Angola eventually contributed to the fall of racist apartheid in nearby South Africa. But storm clouds darkened the horizon. With the dissolution of the Soviet Union in 1991, Cuba was plunged into a severe economic depression. The future of the global socialist project—on the island and everywhere else—was suddenly in question.

Years became decades. Hill became a father in Cuba, then a grandfather. Washington's regime of economic warfare against Cuba had cost the island billions of dollars. Cautious market reforms, which legalized some small businesses and created new entrepreneurial opportunities, increased inequality—paradoxes of the island's compulsory new dance with capitalism that had no simple solutions. That Cuba remained among the most equal nations in the world was little consolation to a younger generation of Cubans facing an uncertain future. Therefore, the historic efforts of Barack Obama to normalize diplomatic relations in 2014 and remove the shackles of economic sanctions provoked an infectious optimism on the island.

It would, however, be short-lived. The first presidency of Donald Trump coincided with—indeed, helped initiate—an economic crisis in Cuba that would eventually assume historic proportions. The Trump administration appointed foreign policy hawks, rolling back the Obama-era détente. Normalization of US-Cuba relations became a dream deferred. Then came the COVID-19 pandemic. Tourism disappeared, beaches closed, sanitary curfews were enforced for months on end. As the Cuban government waged an all-out battle to keep the virus at bay, serious shortages of food and medicine arose on the cash-strapped island.

These scenes were the context for unprecedented street protests for two days in July 2021. Amid the worst weeks of the pandemic, as a health crisis finally overwhelmed the island's vaunted health system and power outages in the summer heat stretched tempers to the breaking point, several thousand Cubans took to the streets in popular demonstrations. Throughout the decades, Hill had remained a dedicated supporter of the revolutionary process. The Cuban socialist dream of an egalitarian society based on principles of solidarity, social rights, and internationalism, which had fired his imagination as a young man, still held his heart in old age. Sitting at home as the demonstrations spread, however, Hill caught himself wondering whether this might be the beginning of the end of the Cuban Revolution. If that day eventually came, what would be its final legacy?

Protests continued the next day. Hill's thoughts strayed to his own life. Now seventy-two years old, he had spent most of his life in exile. He had been many things in Cuba: a laborer and an organic intellectual; a student of history and of the streets; a fugitive sought by the FBI and a guide for American tourists; a spiritual devotee of Santeria and a nightmare-prone war veteran; a prison inmate and a homesick expatriate dreaming of his childhood. He had been away from his country for half a century. What would be *his* legacy?

The Social History of Social Movements

Hill is an unusual choice for a biography of an activist. Social movement biographies have primarily examined the lives of celebrated figures: trailblazing political crusaders, defenders of the dispossessed, agitators against oppression. These are the subjects of history who changed the world, whose lives hold educational, even inspirational, value for contemporary social justice movements.[19] Social movement biographies are especially vital when they illuminate consequential figures who have been overlooked by historical memory. Historian James N. Green describes his book about Brazilian writer and guerrilla Herbert Daniel, for instance, as a "recuperative biography," one that "focuses on a person who was important but has not been recognized as such."[20] Scholar Carole Boyce Davies's biography of pioneering Black communist and feminist Claudia Jones recovers the legacy of a key political figure who inexplicably "disappeared from major consideration."[21] Biographical scholarship in this tradition is the labor of recovery and reconceptualization, of restoring to historical memory key protagonists of social movements past.

Hill does not fit neatly into these frames. Briefly a political activist, he led no organization, published no writing, and gave no acclaimed speeches. While rank-and-file actors populate all grassroots movements, most have eluded long-form biographical treatment. Some of the most innovative biographies are therefore those that have written into this historiographical void by examining the lives of lesser-known grassroots activists.[22] Yet even in this company, Hill is an outlier, for virtually all such biographies remain portraits of people engaged in conventional political activity, even if they did so in relative obscurity. By contrast, Hill's engagement is not so clearly definable. Indeed, it is difficult to argue that Hill has consistently been an activist at all. He was a member of the Republic of New Afrika for less than a year in California. In Cuba, Hill's political engagement has been uneven or assumed nontraditional forms. He has maintained little contact with movements in the United States. In contrast to two of his contemporaries in exile in Cuba—Assata Shakur and Nehanda Abiodun—whose deep political engagement on and off the island is well known, and whose ability to maintain connections with movements stateside made them widely known, even beloved figures in exile, Hill has remained on the margins.

Most social movement biographies are also not about subjects accused of murder. *Fugitive States* is not a defense of Hill, who has never denied his involvement in the death of New Mexico state trooper Robert Rosenbloom in 1971. Rosenbloom's killing, which left two children without a father and a young woman widowed, was a tragedy. Hill has expressed no remorse for the slaying, which he portrays as an act of self-defense during a confrontation between three Black activists and a white police officer who had racially profiled them. In an era of epidemic police lawlessness and violence in Black and Brown communities, and as the FBI waged a campaign of surveillance, disruption, false arrests, frame-ups, and dirty tricks to "neutralize" Black radical organizations in the United States, Hill saw the police as the enforcers of state-sponsored repression—and vowed to resist by any means necessary. Hill's refusal to claim innocence sets him apart from some activists of the Black Power era who have faced captivity or exile. Unlike imprisoned writer Mumia Abu-Jamal, for instance, a former Black Panther who maintains that he was framed for the killing of a Philadelphia police officer in 1981, or Pete O'Neal, a former Panther who contends that he was wrongfully convicted on a weapons charge in 1969 prior to seeking political exile in Tanzania, or Assata Shakur, who maintained her innocence in the killing of a New Jersey state trooper in 1973, Hill acknowledges playing a role in the death of Rosenbloom.[23]

Yet innocence and guilt are fraught categories for interpreting historical figures who challenged entrenched systems of power and oppression. From John Brown to Leila Khaled, and from Lolita Lebrón to Georges Ibrahim Abdallah to Nelson Mandela, radical history is replete with subalterns and insurrectionists whose politically motivated acts in the context of liberation struggles were recast as acts of terrorism or criminality by the regimes they challenged. Hill asserts that his actions must be similarly read in political terms. Legacies of imperialism, white supremacy, and American exceptionalism, Hill points out, influence "commonsense" notions about which lives matter and which political violence is considered legitimate within and beyond US borders.[24] Asked by a CNN reporter in 2015 whether he was a "cop killer," for instance, Hill denied the charge but pointed out, "I'm a Vietnam veteran. People don't ask me, did I kill Vietnamese."[25]

Social history abounds with ordinary people whose lives reveal profound insights about the world. The subjects of biographies need not be simplistic for their lives to be windows onto the world. As a social biography, one that situates the life of a grassroots figure within broad historical forces, *Fugitive States* takes up Howard Zinn's exhortation to write history through the lives of protagonists who exist in the shadows, outside the gaze of conventional historical imagination.[26]

Fugitive States

While this book is primarily the story of an American expatriate, in a more modest way it traces the outlines of post-1959 Cuba itself. A fugitive from the Washington-led world order, a neo-colony that escaped from the political and economic control of the United States at the height of the global Cold War, socialist Cuba was a fitting refuge for US political exiles who embraced the island's revolutionary process as their own.[27] Yet the power of their perspectives lie not simply in their proximity to Cuba's *longue durée* struggle for national self-determination but also in their quiet sharing of the quotidian experience of its internal life. Few US-born Americans have lived as much of Cuba's modern history as has Charlie Hill.[28]

The Cuba that is portrayed in this book is the nation seen through Hill's eyes. After more than fifty years on the island, Hill remains a revolutionary and a socialist, radical partisan who feels deeply connected to the ideals of the Cuban revolutionary project and continues to support the one-party state. Like a great many Cubans on the island, he also advocates reforms "*within the revolution*," in ways that seek to strengthen its radical aspirations and defend its once expansive socialist system.[29] In this, Hill is not unique, for even amid the contemporary dislocation of economic crisis and popular disenchantment, the bedrock ideals of the Cuban Revolution, rooted in social rights, sovereignty, and solidarity, retain deep wells of support on the island. Calls for reform emanating from within Cuba, including those that are critical of some state policies, are frequently calls for deepening social and economic rights, not replacing them with free markets.

Commentary about Cuba in the United States often uncritically foregrounds the perspectives of dissidents on the island, positioned to speak for all Cubans, and those who live elsewhere, especially in Miami, where the political influence of the right-wing exile community in that onetime electoral swing state could once explain some of the durability of Washington's implacable bipartisan hostility to Cuban sovereignty. Yet despite the drumbeat that has portrayed Cuba as little more than a totalitarian state, that dark vision replaces complexity with its own simplistic narratives and media-ready tropes. Hill's unique perspective, that of a North American who has lived in Cuba for half a century, encourages us to move beyond hackneyed binaries that imagine post-1959 Cuba as either a revolutionary nation without blemishes or an authoritarian regime without freedom, but rarely something else entirely. Hill's life in Cuba is bound to both the shifting tides of US-Cuba relations and the ebb and flow of change within Cuba itself, a nation whose dynamic internal life belies travelogue cliches of an island "frozen in time."

"The history of Cuba," historian Ada Ferrer writes, "lends itself to monumental and epic tellings" populated with great figures and driven by magisterial historical forces. Yet this approach, Ferrer cautions, obscures the ordinary people who "serve as guides through this history."[30] In *Fugitive States*, it is Hill and his comrades who are the guides through a saga of modern Cuba and the United States. Hill and the American political exiles of Havana have lived as permanent guests for more than half a century. They have doggedly made lives for themselves against the odds, and sometimes even thrived. They have variously been part of the complex relationship between the US anti-imperialist Left and the Cuban Revolution, and sometimes even the intrigue of US-Cuba diplomacy. Inscrutable and often contradictory, they nonetheless set out to become citizens of Cuba's revolutionary world.

Chapter 1

Daydreams of Childhood

As family legend tells it, Charlie Hill's great-grandfather Alford was born in slavery in Alabama. Escaping captivity as a young man, Alford Hill went to live in the Appalachian Mountains among the scattered remnants of Cherokee, Chickasaw, and Choctaw communities that still remained in the years after the 1830 Indian Removal Act and the ethnic cleansing of the Southeastern United States. While there, Alford met Fannie Willis, a woman reputedly of significant Cherokee ancestry. They married and settled in rural Randolph County in east-central Alabama, where the town of Wadley would later be founded. James A. Hill—Charlie Hill's grandfather, whom everyone called Jack—was born to them in 1875.[1] Grandmother Mollie, Jack's wife, was also said to have had Cherokee ancestry. That entire side of the family—the Hills—seemed to have Indigenous as well as African features, including freckles and black wavy hair.

Randolph County—formed in 1832, after the Creek Nation was forced to cede its lands in the Treaty of Cusseta following years of illegal settlement by white squatters—had a human history reaching back at least eleven thousand years.[2] But the Hill family legend of Indigenous lineage would eventually unravel. When one of Jack's granddaughters submitted a genetic ancestry test, no Native American heritage was in evidence at all. Instead, the autosomal DNA indicated only African and European genetic origin.[3] In the absence of Native American ancestry, it now seemed probable that Alford's children had derived their light features from his master. Indeed, great-grandfather Alford, it had long been suspected, had been the son of the white man who enslaved his mother. Neither is it certain how Jack and Mollie acquired their farm in Wadley, but by 1910 the couple owned it and were living there with their seven children.[4] The youngest, James William Hill—Charlie's father—was born in Wadley in 1909.[5]

Charlie would later have vivid memories of Jack and Mollie's farm in Alabama. A patchwork of forest and fields set on the banks of the Tallapoosa River, rural Wadley was paradise to a youngster. Blackberries and hawthorn grew in thickets shaded by tall pecan trees. Charlie and his sisters would throw rocks to knock down the delicious nuts. The household grew or raised nearly everything they ate, save for a few staples procured from the local store, bought with money made selling their sugarcane and cotton in town. Grandmother

Mollie cooked on a cast-iron stove, and Charlie recalls mealtimes as feasts: corn bread with freshly churned butter, biscuits and meat gravy, stews of wild game or meat cured in the smokehouse, pies filled with apple, sweet potato, or blackberries. "I miss a lot of things about those early years," Charlie would later reminisce. "The food and camaraderie. Family, Christmas, Thanksgiving. I had a happy childhood."[6]

The Great Migration, which would shape the fortunes of the tens of thousands of Black Southerners who moved northward in search of jobs and an escape from Jim Crow, also swept up the Hills. Leaving Alabama as a young man, James W. Hill made his way to Michigan, settling in Detroit and working as a bricklayer around the time that the second World War transformed the city into a foundry of military production. Dorethea Betty Mooring, Charlie's mother, had been born in Savannah, Georgia, in 1922 but spent much of her childhood in Harlem, New York.[7] When the war came, Dorethea moved to Detroit, taking a job as a bar server. There she met James. They married and moved to Illinois, settling in the town of Olney. Not long after, their first child, Charlie, was born on December 15, 1949, at the Olney Sanitarium.[8] A family practice hospital run by three generations of doctors, all brothers, the sanitarium was locally renowned for its treatment of anyone who arrived at its doors, often free of charge—"medical care for all," as the *Herald and Review* in Decatur later put it—regardless of their ability to pay.[9]

Olney, set in the downstate farm country of Richland County, had a population of around eight thousand residents, nearly all of them white. When the Hills arrived, they rented a wood-frame house. Much of the surrounding land was owned by a local white family that had become wealthy by rural standards, raising livestock, sheep, and hogs. Charlie remembers the two families being on amicable terms, and he and the family's son, Kenneth, a boy several years his senior, became fast friends. James was a mason who specialized in the construction of chimneys, and Dorethea was a housewife.[10] When Charlie's sisters were still toddlers, Dorethea taught him how to sew and crochet so that he could help her in the house. As Charlie got older, his father took him fishing in the Wabash River and taught him how to hunt rabbits and squirrels for the supper table. The family grew corn, tomatoes, cucumbers, okra, and beets, which they canned for the winter. Decades later, Charlie's memories of childhood in Olney often lingered happily in the kitchen: "It seemed like we always had huge tables of food: wild turkey and pheasant, sweet potato pie, corn bread."[11]

Although they were the only Black family in the area, the Hills initially had no trouble. Along with Kenneth's family, the Hills counted as friends a white family down the road. The Hills were also friendly with the local sheriff, whose son became Charlie's playmate. Nonetheless, Charlie would later scrutinize these carefree memories. His parents, he recalled, kept a .22 Remington rifle above the door. It was true that the family hunted. Charlie had grown up with guns, learning how to clean and maintain them and how to use them to put food on the table. But his parents also kept two handguns close at all times: his mother's Derringer and his father's .22 long-barreled pistol.

Charlie's sense of carefree security was jarred when he entered the first grade. As the oldest child, Charlie was the first of his siblings to traverse the racial gauntlet of public education in rural Illinois. He was later told that he had been the first Black child to attend Central Elementary School in Olney. On the first day, Charlie was nervous. "Son," his dad told him somberly, "just remember everything I taught you." Walking onto the school grounds, all Charlie could see were white faces. "It was very intimidating. I remember them calling me a nigger. And I remember my neighbor Kenneth putting his arm around me and saying, 'Don't touch him.' He took me inside the building."[12] The school was not segregated, however, and so Charlie attended classes with the other students. "The segregationists were not active in Richland County," he later speculated, "but only because there were almost no Black people to defend against."[13]

Charlie survived the school year, yet the experience had changed him. "I knew that day, probably for the first time in my life, that there was a distinction between me and the rest of the people in that area," Charlie recalls. "Being the only Black kid in an all-white county made me realize in a hurry that I was Black, and that the discrimination I was facing was racial. It was a very intimidating experience." In later years, Charlie would wonder why his family moved to a virtually all-white county in the first place. "I'll never know. They must have had a reason. I assume Daddy had found work there that he needed." Over time, Charlie made friends. "The kids realized that I was not stupid. They had not known me before. They also saw that I wasn't just going to take a beating." His school experience, Charlie later realized, marked a watershed in his racial consciousness. "The next time that we traveled south to visit my grandparents, I realized that the bathrooms said 'white-only.' I was old enough to read by then."[14]

The tranquility of Olney was finally shattered for good one dark October night. At home with his mother while his dad was away on a work trip, he heard a car pull up in the dark. He went to the window and saw three white men by the barn, their faces illuminated by a torch that one of them was jabbing against the barn. Charlie seized the .22 rifle above the door. His mother shouted at him not to go outside, but she did not object when Charlie opened the window, leveled the rifle, and fired over their heads. The men ran to their car and sped away. With buckets of well water, he and his mother doused the flames. Charlie no longer held illusions about his white neighbors.[15]

The Hills left Illinois not long afterward, the visit by motorized night riders almost certainly playing a role. The year prior, Charlie's father had been shot at while driving, the bullet coming right through the windshield of his Chevy panel truck; James Hill never saw who fired at him. Still, Charlie's clearest memory from this period is his parents' separation, coming just around the time he finished the sixth grade. It was their divorce that appears to have compelled his father to leave the state. James moved to New Mexico, settling in the village of Pojoaque, just north of Santa Fe. Dorethea moved to Albuquerque with Charlie and his siblings a year later, so that they could be near their father.[16]

If rural Illinois was where Charlie first began to understand himself in relation to the simmering racial cauldron of America, the Southwest was where he sought to understand what the family still believed was their Indigenous heritage. Charlie's father proudly identified with it. "He used to say, 'We're both; we're Black and Indian.'"[17] Some twenty Indian reservations dotted New Mexico, from small Pueblo communities to the sprawling Navajo Nation that covered the state's northwest corner and a vast swath of Arizona. Charlie and his father hunted on a nearby Pueblo reservation, and Charlie was surprised to discover that the primary languages spoken were Indigenous, not English or Spanish. Running water and electricity were rare. Thousands of people lived in isolated communities connected by dirt roads. "By my teenage years," Charlie recalls, "I had seen poverty. . . . In some ways, it was more comparable to what I saw later in Vietnam than in any US city. I knew poor Black people in New Mexico, but none who had dirt floors or lived in the middle of the desert without electricity or running water. The poorest people in the Southwest were Native."[18]

The nascent Black Power movement was rising from Mississippi to California, but in 1966, the Southwest was an epicenter of the burgeoning Chicano movement. Like the Black nationalist organization that Charlie would later join, whose dream of a territorial nation in the heart of the former Confederacy would fire the imaginations of Black radicals, Chicano activists in New Mexico had long focused on the political question of land in a region whose history mingled legacies of conquest and land theft.[19] In the preceding decades, thousands had joined campaigns to return land to the heirs of community land grants made by the Spanish and Mexican governments. With the founding of the New Mexico–based Alianza Federal de Mercedes—the

Federal Alliance of Land Grants—by Reies López Tijerina in 1963, campaigns to repatriate land to the heirs increased in militancy.[20]

In October 1966, hundreds of Alianza members occupied the Echo Amphitheater, a natural rock formation of multicolored sandstone in Carson National Forest, which lay within the historical boundaries of the San Joaquín del Río de Chama land grant. A key legal battleground in the land repatriation movement, activists proclaimed the site the sovereign Republic of San Joaquín. On June 5, 1967, armed Alianza members led by Tijerina invaded a courthouse in the small town of Tierra Amarilla in an audacious attempt to capture the district attorney. In the shoot-out that followed, a state police officer and a county jailer were wounded. The Alianza raiders took hostages and fled to Kit Carson National Forest until New Mexico's governor sent Army National Guard troops in after them.[21]

Yet it was not the Chicano struggle to free the land that Charlie would ultimately remember most vividly about Albuquerque but rather Chicanos' struggle with the city's police. Albuquerque's poor neighborhoods, largely Chicano, experienced unemployment at levels far surpassing national averages, and police relations were frequently strained. "Police brutality was not a buzz word at the time. People just knew that the police kicked their asses, and nothing was done about it."[22]

Within a few short years, simmering tensions between Chicano communities and Albuquerque's police would become intertwined with the rise of the multifaceted Brown Power movement. A local chapter of the Brown Berets was founded in the city, and it adopted a ten-point program inspired by the Black Panther Party. Chicano activists organized community health and education programs and campaigned against police brutality. In 1969, activists formed a new organization called Las Gorras Negras—the Black Berets—its name a nod to Che Guevara. The organization admired the Argentine revolutionary, one activist later explained, as "a person who was working for all poor communities throughout the world."[23] Renderings of Che, adopted by Chicano activists as an emblem of Latino pride and Pan–Latin American militancy, were conspicuous in murals and political ephemera. Stylized images of Che, his complexion sometimes darkened to suggest Indigenous ancestry, were ubiquitous in the iconography of the Brown Berets and Las Gorras Negras. A rendering of the Argentine revolutionary appeared on the masthead of *Venceremos*, the latter's newspaper, and posters of him adorned the group's free community health clinic in Albuquerque.[24]

Cuba's revolutionaries, Charlie notes, were symbols of third world nationalism, emblems of racial pride, and agents of resistance to hemispheric US power. It was in a Brown Beret pamphlet that he first saw a reference to the

Cuban Revolution. Las Gorras Negras was internationalist in orientation, drawing inspiration from the Global South and forging coalitions with a wide array of communities inside the United States. "We will not be free," the organization wrote in its "12 Point Platform and Program," "until our Puerto Rican, Black, Indian, and Asian brothers are also free from the oppressive and colonial rule of this system. We are not free until our brothers in Latin America, Africa, and Asia are liberated."[25]

The anticolonial and anticapitalist political imagination of Las Gorras Negras became central to the group's community programs in Albuquerque's public schools, aiming to transform an education system that the Alianza had described as "intentionally ruining the lives of hundreds of thousands of Indo-Hispano, Black and Indian kids" with its racist, Anglo-centric curriculum.[26] Speaking at a community meeting organized after aggressive policing at a park in Albuquerque sparked three days of riots in June 1971, one member of Las Gorras Negras described his radicalization: "The day I became a priest was not as sacred a day as the day I became a [B]lack Beret. . . . I do not want our children to be taught that his ancestors landed on Plymouth Rock. I do not want Indian children to be taught Columbus discovered America."[27]

Police violence in Albuquerque took center stage in 1968 with a spate of police killings of unarmed Chicano men. The shooting death of Tommy Valles on August 13 resulted in an explosion of community organizing and protest in the city.[28] Interrupting a city commission meeting on August 19, Brown Beret activist Gilberto Ballejos, accompanied by Reies López Tijerina, told the room that the killing of Valles was the spark that "brought to light a history of abuse and brutality by Albuquerque police. This abuse had been directed mainly against the poor and minority groups who until now have had no power to control the police and fight back."[29]

The ferment of the multifaceted Chicano movement in New Mexico was the backdrop—sometimes nascent, sometimes immediate—of Charlie's years in Albuquerque. He had no personal contact with the movement; he was not yet politicized, nor was he particularly aware of the social upheaval churning around him. Yet it is notable that the political trajectory of his life, defined first in Vietnam, where he came to identify with the Vietnamese struggle to free the land from foreign occupation, and later through the Republic of New Afrika's campaign for Black territorial autonomy in the American South, and finally through the saga of Cuba's centuries-long struggle to claim its independence, first from Spanish colonialism and then from US imperialism, came to be defined by the question of land and sovereignty as the material basis of freedom.[30] These early political currents, swirling inchoately but perceptibly in Charlie's formative years, helped seed the fertile ground in which his worldview would take root.

Chapter 2

East Oakland to West Germany

Charlie completed the ninth grade in Albuquerque and then went to live with his uncle Aubrey in East Oakland, California, in the summer of 1964. Oakland was a city transformed by Black migration. The youth who would define California's pivotal "Black Power generation," in the words of historian Donna Murch, were largely Southern transplants, like Charlie.[1] Thousands migrated to the Bay Area during the second World War to work in the shipping and federal defense industries. The absence of de jure segregation allowed the rise of a Black middle class. Postwar deindustrialization and urban renewal would eventually hollow out Oakland, yet it retained all its metropolitan cultural vitality.[2]

Charlie was dazzled by the city. "Black people with cars, nice houses, and businesses. Oakland was something."[3] Uncle Aubrey had been a police officer in New York. A lover of music and "a reader, a guy who liked books," Uncle Aubrey was "a conscious Black man, very intelligent, a progressive guy," although not politically active. In Olney, the Hills had been the only Black people in the area. Albuquerque was defined by its Anglo and Chicano communities. Now, attending Oakland's Castlemont High School, Charlie was surrounded by Black students. The Bay Area was a political hub of Black California, and Charlie's guides to this world were Uncle Aubrey and his son, Aubrey Jr. Several years Charlie's senior, his cousin Aubrey had spent most of his life in Harlem, where he had become a Pan-Africanist.[4]

By the mid-1960s, the Bay Area had become fertile ground for progressive social movements—and a magnet for youth who wanted to be part of them. "I was fortunate to live in that part of the West Coast, the Bay Area, during the time of progressive ideas and social movements. The hippies were there, the civil rights movement was there, and soon, the Black Panthers were there. I came of age under the influence of all of that."[5] Yet the Bay Area was bifurcated by inequality that was inscribed onto the geography of urban space. For activists in Oakland, the concept of colonialism became a way to conceptualize, in both metaphorical and material terms, the ways in which regional race and class disparities produced local microcosms of global power relations.

Across the bay, many community activists perceived the spatially inflected power relations of San Francisco's Mission District in similar terms. The neighborhood's "colonial status," as *Ramparts* magazine had described the culturally vibrant neighborhood in an article about seven Latino youth accused of killing a police officer in 1969—including one who would later hijack a plane to Cuba and became Charlie's housemate in Havana—was shaped by deindustrialization. The influx of Latin American immigrants and the departure of white residents and their capital created a Latino urban enclave whose economy was dominated largely by outside interests, and whose political terrain was controlled by white city officials. "The Latin immigrants who came to San Francisco to escape the deprivations and indignities of colonialism," *Ramparts* wrote, "found them again, more subtly, within the Mission."[6]

Nowhere was the quasi-colonial status of Black and Latino communities in the Bay Area more palpable than in their relationship with the police. In September 1966, a series of urban rebellions that would become known as the Hunters Point Uprising unfolded in San Francisco after a police officer shot an unarmed Black teenager who had run from police after stealing a car. Hunters Point, a Black enclave characterized by crippling unemployment born of systematic job discrimination, was the section of the city that James Baldwin had once described as the "San Francisco Americans pretend does not exist."[7] It exploded in fury. As the Hunters Point rebellion got underway, young Black men engaged in shoot-outs with National Guardsmen. The *Black Panther* lionized the "unknown Freedom Fighters of Hunters Point" who gave the "occupying army a taste of their own medicine."[8] Students rioted in several high schools in support. President Lyndon B. Johnson ordered an investigation into Black unemployment in the city.[9]

A month later, when Oakland erupted, Charlie's high school was at the epicenter. Black students, supported by parents and community activists, had organized a boycott of three predominantly Black junior and high schools, including Castlemont, to protest de facto school segregation within the city resulting in substandard education and callous white school officials. Tensions had also been inflamed by years of episodic police violence against students. In October 1966, police attempting to disburse students congregating outside a school clubbed a fifteen-year-old girl, then choked and detained her.[10] As the boycott went into effect and students attended alternative "Freedom Schools" organized by volunteers, students rebelled in what became known as the Castlemont Riots.[11] Youth smashed car windows, destroyed school property, and attacked teachers. In the surrounding streets, some hurled Molotov cocktails at the police.[12] One of them was Charlie. "Everyone knew that this young girl had been assaulted. We vented anger at the whole system. The police were the enforcers."[13]

As social unrest engulfed American cities in 1966, local events played out against a backdrop of global ones. Television coverage had noted the curiously named Operation Birmingham. But when footage of American troops and helicopters appeared on Charlie's family's television screen, the setting was not the one they had expected—central Alabama, a perennial focus of Southern civil rights organizing—but rather South Vietnam.

The war in Indochina would have a curious effect on Charlie. Lurid images of helicopter gunships and men with guns running through rice paddies flickered through his thoughts all summer. Although still more than a year away from his eighteenth birthday, Charlie had become preoccupied with the draft. Older schoolmates had already received their induction notices. "At the time, at this stage in my political development, going to Canada would have felt like being a traitor. I had an analysis of racism, and I was against the war, but I had not yet taken that final turn in my politics."[14]

But the army, Charlie later admitted, exerted a curious psychic pull. His older brother, Truman, had been an infantryman during the Korean War. "He was a very charming, handsome guy," Charlie recalls.[15] Truman was full of stories about army life, but of the war itself, he spoke little. The skin on his feet was scarred by frostbite on the Korean Peninsula. Other wounds were less visible. Truman suffered from severe post-traumatic stress. When he drank, he became so inebriated that he would lose consciousness and wet himself. "The war got my boy like this," their father would say sadly.[16] Despite his wariness, however, Charlie had considered enlisting. Since he was not yet eighteen, he reasoned, he would not be sent to the front lines. Instead, he would earn a wage and learn a trade.

Youthful impulsivity won out. While visiting his mother in Albuquerque, Charlie walked into a recruiting office on the day after his seventeenth birthday and, on December 16, 1966, enlisted in the army.[17] Arriving at Fort Bliss in Texas, Charlie received two months of basic combat training.[18] Then it was on to Fort Dix in New Jersey for instruction in records administration. In May 1967 he was sent to Stuttgart, West Germany, to begin a two-year tour of duty. Working as a clerk typist, he eventually moved up to personnel specialist in the army records division at the rank and pay of specialist fifth class.[19]

Charlie joined the United States Army during a period of transition that would shape the experiences of thousands of Black GIs. The army that fought the Vietnam War was America's first racially integrated military force. In the years following the desegregation of the US armed forces by executive order in 1948, Black Americans had joined the military in large numbers and reenlisted at double the rate of white Americans.[20] Excluded from the civilian labor market, many viewed the institution as a ladder out of poverty and segregation, realities that conditioned Charlie's zeal to enlist, even as he knew that Black GIs were significantly overrepresented on the front lines.[21] Charlie's unit in Germany, which performed administrative duties, he noted wryly, contained only six Black GIs.

Racial tension was a fixture of life on American military bases in West Germany. White soldiers were known to display Confederate flags, and some even started chapters of the Ku Klux Klan. Crosses were burned in front of Black GIs' barracks, and tensions often escalated into physical confrontation.[22] So frequent were violent incidents between Black and white GIs in Germany that in 1970, the Pentagon took the unusual step of sending a fact-finding team to investigate.[23] Racism and rebellion continued. In August 1972, Stuttgart finally erupted. "About 100 black US soldiers armed with knives, fence staves, broken bottles and stones clashed with police for five hours," as the *Los Angeles Times* reported it, after German police arrested several Black GIs inside a bar.[24]

Of all the American military bases spread across the globe, those in West Germany would witness some of the highest levels of GI resistance to the war. Black GIs organized the Black Action Group in Stuttgart to resist racism on bases.[25] Contrary to perceptions among military brass and the white public about professional "Black militants" within army ranks, most antiwar resistance was carried out by ordinary people: GIs who opposed the war or wanted to leave the army.[26] While Charlie found German anti-Black racism to be less overt than that emerging out of the roiling racial dynamics of the United States, Germany had its own deep caverns of ethnic hatred. Indeed, Stuttgart was the site, in August 1967, of one of the trials of Albert Widmann, a German SS officer, chemist, and Stuttgart native who had participated in the Nazi euthanasia program in occupied Eastern Europe.[27] Charlie's relationship with his girlfriend, a white woman of French German background, seemed to draw attention in the neighborhoods around the base, a zone known for discrimination against Black US GIs.[28]

To escape Stuttgart, Charlie and other Black GIs headed for cosmopolitan Frankfurt or the port city of Hamburg, with its sizable Black population of North American and African extraction. During leave, Charlie took the opportunity to see as much of Europe as he could, visiting Sanremo on the Italian coast with his girlfriend and hanging out in Denmark with his army buddies. In Copenhagen, "there seemed to be no racial tension, that we could sense," Charlie later recalled. "It was almost strange. There were a lot of Black GIs living there. Racism existed in Europe, of course, but it was nowhere near as overt as what we had experienced in America. The tension was not as acute. It was not a post-slavery society. Europeans seemed more accepting of Blacks, and there was a lot more mixing."[29]

Charlie was a soldier in an army at war, and in January 1968, the course of the war changed. Vietnamese liberation forces launched the Tet Offensive, attacking US and South Vietnamese positions in dozens of cities before being pushed back. In the barracks at Stuttgart, rumors flew of an American buildup in Vietnam. Sure enough, on March 10, General William Westmoreland requested twenty thousand more American troops.[30]

Pressure seemed to be building. In May, American troops endured the deadliest month of the war. Graphic media coverage of the conflict, unburnished in the United States, was even starker in the German press. Antiwar sentiment was rising on military bases. On April 4, 1967, Martin Luther King Jr., speaking in Harlem, made his strongest condemnation of the war, lambasting "this business of burning human beings with napalm, of filling our nation's homes with orphans and widows, of injecting poisonous drugs of hate into the veins of peoples normally humane."[31]

King's words had little effect on Charlie. War and battle, he later admitted, held a potent siren fascination. "I had met people in Germany who had come back from Vietnam. People who had been in combat. I knew one guy who was a cook on a fire base. But the base was always under attack. He was a cook, but he walked around with an M16. He wound up having to fight. And so my curiosity was magnificent. I couldn't control it. What did the guys see? What is it like?"[32] Charlie, now eighteen, was eligible for combat. Caught in this sea of conflicting feelings, he impulsively volunteered to be transferred to Vietnam.

He would regret his decision almost immediately.

Chapter 3

Vietnam

Decades later, Charlie would sometimes try to explain the Vietnam War through the story of Geronimo Pratt. A Louisiana teenager who enlisted in the US Army and completed two combat tours in Vietnam, earning a Purple Heart for his bravery, Elmer Gerard "Geronimo" Pratt had returned to study political science at the University of California, Los Angeles, on the GI Bill. Not long after, he joined the Southern California chapter of the Black Panther Party. A natural leader and pragmatic strategist, Geronimo served the organization with legendary distinction, earning him the ire of the FBI, which eventually framed him for a murder they knew he did not commit. Imprisoned for twenty-seven years—a victim of the FBI's Counter Intelligence Program, which sought to destroy Black radical movements in the United States—Geronimo would have plenty of time to reflect. "I go through Watts, I go through Chicago, I go through Harlem," Geronimo later said, "and I see that the people in what's called the ghetto, the Black community, the colonies or whatever you want to call them, were treated almost exactly the way we just got through treating Viet Cong, or Vietnamese people, in Vietnam. So I began to draw parallels that the police departments in these various situations, in these cities, were actually the same thing we were in Viet Nam: occupying forces."[1]

Like other radicalized Black GIs returning home, Charlie would eventually reach a similar conclusion. And, like Geronimo, who had enlisted in the army of his own free will and who had fought, by all accounts, as a deadly member of his unit, Charlie's political transformation was not immediate.[2] It probably helped that by the time he got to Vietnam, Charlie was already a conflicted soldier. On leave in July 1968, Charlie visited family in Harlem before taking a Greyhound bus cross-country back to Oakland. Somewhere along the way he decided that he did not want to go to Vietnam. The date on which he was scheduled to report to Oakland Army Base came and went, but Charlie failed to report for duty. He contemplated trying to find a way out of the army. "I didn't know how to go to Canada. I had no family or connections there. . . . If I had more political guidance, I would have been able to make a better decision and just stayed in Germany."[3]

Perhaps. But it had been his decision to go to Vietnam. He had not been drafted, no one had pressured him, and he had certainly not been impelled by any sense of patriotic duty. Like legions of other foolish young men,

Charlie had been motivated, he later insisted, by something more visceral: the desire to experience war and battle. There was no time to ponder all this, however, because a few days later, military officials knocked on Uncle Aubrey's door looking for him. They escorted him to the Oakland Army Base, and on August 31, 1968, he was on a chartered flight to Vietnam.[4]

Charlie arrived at Bien Hoa Air Base in South Vietnam, where he would spend the fall as a typist in the base's records division continuing at the rank of specialist fifth class.[5] He had been assigned to an administrative unit of the 101st Airborne Division—the renowned "Screaming Eagles"—which specialized in air assault and had sustained some of the highest casualties of any US division during the war. Charlie had not come to Vietnam to be a clerk, however, and so in January 1969 he volunteered to be sent to Camp Eagle, an American army base near the city of Huế in central Vietnam. There he could volunteer for combat.[6]

He soon got his opportunity. On February 14, 1969, Charlie transferred to E Company of the Second Battalion, 502nd Infantry Regiment of the 101st Airborne.[7] He boarded a helicopter and flew to a fire support base called Anzio, a fortified infantry and artillery position in the jungle. Bristling with barbed wire and armed with 105 mm and 155 mm howitzers pointing in all directions, Anzio was part of a network of US firebases throughout occupied Vietnam that functioned like forts in hostile territory. Charlie volunteered for E Company's reconnaissance platoon. Led by a bold sergeant named Fletcher, the platoon was tasked with local patrolling in the forest, tracking enemy units, and laying ambushes.[8] Traveling light, armed only with their M16s, they relied on helicopters and artillery from Anzio for fire support but were otherwise alone in enemy territory. Carrying everything on their backs and bivouacking in the jungle at night, the reconnaissance platoon was often away for two or three days at a time.

The Vietnamese guerrilla units they were hunting—or being hunted by—were also in those hills. The American and Vietnamese forces circled each other in the jungle in a terrifying game of cat and mouse. "Combat was excruciating," Charlie later recalled.[9] And so was its aftermath. The land was littered with the remains of Vietnamese dead. Shallow graves marked the forlorn spots where Vietnamese fighters had been forced to leave fallen comrades when they could not be retrieved during battle. The Americans exhumed the graves and added the corpses to their body count tallies, which served as Washington's metric for measuring military progress. But of what he had seen in the forest, Charlie would later say little.[10]

Less than a week after leaving Anzio, Charlie was at the rear of his platoon as they were picking their way down a ravine in heavy undergrowth. They had just begun crossing a creek when the lead man almost bumped into a dwelling, just a crude thatched hut of wood and woven grass. Beside it was a fire pit, still smoking. Everyone froze. "Sergeant Fletcher, he never shied back. He motioned me to keep on looking behind, and then he went down to the creek first, and I see him sticking the barrel of his M16 into the hut. And then I take a sharp glance behind me again and see a Vietnamese with an AK-47, and I don't say nothing, man, I just shoot. And there's AK fire that I don't know where it's coming from. And I sort of jumped over this embankment and fired again. . . . I was scared shitless. But you have to sort of learn how to handle fear, you have to react."[11]

It was Charlie's first experience of combat. No one in the platoon was injured. With night falling, they were forced to halt for the night. They bivouacked on the ridge above the creek and posted guard. Of course, the Vietnamese fighters they had just shot at knew where they were. Charlie tried to conquer his fear. "You make a circle, set up your Claymore mines, you have a little dinner in your tin can, and you wait for the next morning." Charlie began to entrust his life to his platoon. "Fletcher, my man knew what he was doing. He was a badass, and he made you into a badass by training you. He would say, 'Don't do that again, you'll get yourself killed, and I can't have anyone killed on my watch!' He was an expert. You had to respect him."[12]

But Charlie could not take his mind off the Vietnamese fighters, young men and young women, sometimes in gender-integrated units, who were trying to shoot him in the hills around Anzio. The liberation forces—the communist guerrillas of the National Liberation Front, known in popular parlance as the Viet Cong, and the North Vietnamese army regulars—had learned to move in close to the American invaders to negate their deadliest advantage: the massive firepower that the Americans could rain down from aircraft and artillery. Combat in the forest was up close and intimate, and in that closeness emerged Charlie's sympathy for the historical Vietnamese freedom struggle.

> We constantly had to throw up smoke bombs to make sure our own helicopters did not strafe us. But mostly we just waited. We would spend hours just staring at the jungle, wondering if that leaf that had just moved, or that sound in the brush, was actually a Vietnamese. We were in their territory. They were super dangerous, and we feared them. They were hard fighters, and they were fighting for the freedom of their country. I was just a few miles from where the B-52s were dropping those enormous bombs. I saw what those planes could do, what artillery did when it tore up an area. How anyone could survive that was amazing to me. And still the Vietnamese were there, resisting, sometimes just with their AKs. I learned to appreciate and admire the people that I was

> fighting against. Maybe other soldiers felt that the Vietnamese were the devil or something, but I didn't feel that way. These people were fighting for their homeland. But I was out there, and I still had to fight in order to stay alive. It was a matter of survival. I tried to stay aware and not make any mistakes.[13]

Dread of combat—and a sickening sensation that he had joined the wrong side of a war of liberation—was augmented by other realizations that hit like thunderbolts. "Our platoon was one big family, Black, white, and Latin, but that didn't mean it wasn't a racist war."[14] Although he was unaware of the longer history of the epithet "gook" by US soldiers to describe racialized enemies—from the Philippines to Nicaragua to Haiti—it was not difficult for Charlie to recognize its kinship to the slurs for the internally colonized of America. Geronimo Pratt had noticed this too. "I caught two of my guys trying to hang an enemy soldier. Had a rope around his neck, threw it over a tree," he later recounted. "They were pulling him up when I turned the corner. You can imagine what I thought, being black and from the South. . . . After a while I began to see the war as another kind of racism. In boot camp and advanced infantry training all we ever heard was 'gooks,' 'Buddha-heads,' 'slopes,' same way our daddies heard 'Krauts' and 'Japs.' You got to make people subhuman before you kill 'em."[15]

It was this sense that racism played a central animating role in the logic of American imperialism in Asia that finally solidified Charlie's identification with Vietnam's struggle for national liberation even as its patriots were trying to kill him. The more he thought about them, the more he began to admire them.

> I began to see Vietnamese people much like I saw Black and oppressed people in America. The Native Americans on reservations, who had been kept down. How racism had affected all of us. . . . I saw so many youngsters in Vietnam fighting for their freedom. It's incalculable how many Vietnamese were killed between the French and the Americans. And the Vietnamese kept fighting until they finally won. After a while, I began to feel like one of them. These people were struggling for their freedom. To be treated equal. It was like the Black neighborhoods in the US are occupied by the police and national guard, or Native American land being invaded centuries ago, creating reservations. MLK had been assassinated. Malcolm had been assassinated. Activists were in prison. All of these things accumulated in my head. It didn't make any sense. I was in this foreign land, fighting for reasons that I didn't understand. Vietnam was the turning point in my political thinking. The Vietnamese pushed me all the way left.[16]

After three months of jungle missions, Charlie had seen enough. He resolved to find a way out of Vietnam. When an old knee injury suddenly flared up after a long trek, Charlie was sent back to Camp Eagle and prescribed painkillers and rest.[17] The brief respite cleared his head. The swelling in his knee subsided, but when his platoon's helicopter arrived in Camp Eagle to resupply, Charlie refused to get on it. The first sergeant at Camp Eagle warned that he would be considered AWOL and subject to court-martial if he did not board the next helicopter out. Charlie again refused. He was ordered to wait in an empty E Company tent for court-martial.[18]

Charlie became paranoid. Afraid to fall asleep in the tent, he spent the night in the fortified trench behind it. The next morning, Charlie was peering out the tent's flap when he saw the first sergeant and two soldiers, armed, advancing up the hill. The sergeant motioned for one soldier to approach from the left, the other from the right. "I didn't know what they were going to do, but I was scared." Charlie hid himself in the shadows as the men entered the tent. Then he emerged behind them, gripping his M16. "I think I was a little crazy by that point. I told them to not turn around, and to drop their weapons." And they did.[19]

Charlie fled. Hiding out in the base's labyrinth of bunkers and trenches, he sought out a friend of his from Berkeley, Raymond, who was also serving in Vietnam and had been stationed at Camp Eagle. Raymond, who delivered mail between the base and the nearby city of Huế in an army jeep, told Charlie that he could hide out in a house in the city where American GIs went to score drugs. The next morning, Charlie, hidden among the mail, rode to Huế. They stopped in front of a concrete block house. Raymond presented him to the occupants: a Vietnamese family.

The house, Charlie realized, was an opium den and a brothel. The clients were American GIs. The family spoke no English so Raymond communicated using hand gestures. The family agreed to hide Charlie in exchange for some C rations and US military payment certificates, which had become currency in the zones around the US bases. Raymond assured Charlie that he would be safe and promised to check on him in a few days. Then he got in his jeep and drove back to Camp Eagle. Sitting in silence with the family, Charlie began to feel apprehensive. The family, he realized, might be collaborating with the Viet Cong. "We never knew who was who. They could have just cut my throat and left me in the street, just another dead American soldier that the enemy had found." But there was no turning back. Charlie slept fitfully, his head propped up on his backpack, his M16 across his chest.[20]

Nothing happened. The next morning, one of the women in the house filled a wooden tub so that Charlie could bathe. Nervous, he took the M16 with him. Halfway through his bath, the woman rushed in whispering, "MP! MP!" Military police from the US Army had stopped in front of the house. The woman waved at Charlie to go out the back door. Jumping out of the tub, he rushed into the bushes behind the house and, stark naked, stumbled into a water-filled ditch. Charlie heard someone get out of the jeep. He crouched down into the knee-deep water. It smelled awful. The MPs eventually left. The whole family came out of the house, laughing uproariously as Charlie waded out of the ditch, which turned out to be the neighborhood's open sewer.[21]

Charlie stayed with the family in Huế for three days, and his apprehension faded. The family addressed him using an English phrase cannily popularized by the Vietnamese communists: "soul brother." The children coaxed him into playing games with them. "We were in the middle of a war zone, but these people were smiling and cracking jokes constantly. The kids were tugging on me and playing. It really got to me. That interaction with them, of them not trying to kill me and me not trying to kill them, laughing and bonding with their children, sealed it. We were not enemies." The experience finally made clear to him the basic inhumanity of the war. "One of the things I remember most clearly about Vietnam was how well that family treated me and how it made me feel. I knew I had done the right thing by going AWOL. But it wasn't enough just to refuse to fight and go back to being a typist. I wanted to leave Vietnam, because everyone there was contributing to killing Vietnamese, who were fighting against the most powerful military on earth."[22]

Hiding out in Huế only postponed the inevitable. On the third day, Charlie returned to Camp Eagle and turned himself in. He was court-martialed and stripped of rank.[23] He was sentenced to serve time in a military prison and put on a C-131 transport plane to Bien Hoa Air Base, whereupon he would be taken to jail. Upon arriving at the base, however, Charlie decided he was not yet ready for a cell. With fake papers prepared for him by his old friends in the base's records division, he caught a ride in a military transport truck to the nearby city of Saigon, a renowned hideout for deserting American soldiers. So many Black GIs lived in the city that one strip of the city was dubbed "Soul Alley," a collection of bars, restaurants, and clubs operated by Black former GIs and their Vietnamese partners.[24]

But Saigon was no oasis. Although nominally controlled by US forces and the South Vietnamese, the Viet Cong operated clandestinely in the city, supported by a network of spies and civilian supporters. Off-limits to US soldiers unless they had a pass, Saigon was patrolled by edgy American MPs. Wanted posters of GIs accused of desertion, fragging, and murder were posted on trees. The tension in the city was palpable. Charlie became nervous. After a few days, Charlie returned to Bien Hoa Air Base and turned himself in. He was taken into custody, and on May 14, 1969, he became a prisoner of the US military.[25]

Of all the US military prisons in Vietnam, Long Binh Jail, nicknamed "LBJ," was the most notorious. Overcrowded to almost double capacity by 1968, approximately 50 percent of the prisoners were Black, a figure far exceeding the numerical representation of Black Americans within the US armed forces in Vietnam. The prison's guards were disproportionately white. LBJ became notorious as a hothouse of racial animus.[26] In August 1968, Black prisoners launched a major rebellion, freeing Black prisoners, attacking guards and white prisoners, and destroying buildings. Grievances ranged from bad food, infrequent mail, and preferential treatment of white prisoners, yet "most of them," one army psychologist at the scene wrote, "just wanted out of the Army and out of Vietnam" and "felt they faced the same kind of prejudice that they had in the ghettoes of the U.S."[27] While the army later attempted to co-opt tensions by instating Black officers, reports of racism and brutality emanated from LBJ for years.[28]

Prisoners admitted to LBJ were subject to a medical examination and evaluation by an army psychiatrist. When Charlie's turn came, he explained that he had gone AWOL because of his moral opposition to the war. The white psychiatrist asked whether he felt patriotism for his country. "Patriotism?" Charlie was incredulous. "There is no patriotism on the American side!" He was almost shouting now. "This country has been occupied by the French, and Japanese, and now the Americans. They're the ones who were patriotic, not us!"[29]

Inmates at LBJ were housed in cells with tin roofs, which produced a stifling heat. Charlie was ordered to fill sandbags in the hot sun and repair flat tires on military trucks. When a Black officer yelled in his face for not stopping on command, Charlie yelled back. He was confined to his cell. He would be released, he was informed, if he apologized to the officer. Charlie was escorted into the officer's quarters to make amends. Instead, Charlie lunged at him. Guards beat him almost unconscious. After being injected with Thorazine, he was thrown into the dark pit of an isolation cell, barely able to move from the effects of the drug.[30] His health deteriorated. Transferred to the prison's hospital ward, Charlie was eventually diagnosed with hepatitis.[31] Looking at himself in the mirror, Charlie was alarmed to see that his skin had turned yellow from jaundice.

Charlie was confined to bed rest. His physical deterioration, he realized, had been accompanied by a psychological break. Lying in the hospital cot, his thoughts drifted to his brother, Truman, who had been tormented by nightmares after returning from the Korean Peninsula. Mostly, though, Charlie thought about the Vietnamese jungle. "There were a lot of messed-up kids in that jail," he would later reflect. "Including me. A lot of people [were] burned out by what they had seen. Everybody was young. A few were there for fragging, trying to shoot officers, but most were there for going AWOL. People saw things in war that messed them up. Everyone handles it in a different way. I handled it in my own way. One of the ways was trying to forget what I had seen."[32]

Charlie was discharged "under honorable conditions" from the armed forces of the United States for reasons of "unfitness" due to "character and behavior disorders." And so, after forty-three days of incarceration at LBJ, he was sent back to the United States, arriving at Oakland Army Base on July 26, 1969.[33] Like so many others of the Black Power generation, Charlie's experience in Vietnam was a watershed in his life. The war had finally made plain to him what it meant to be part of a world born of colonization, racism, and empire. Now, for the first time, he wanted to do something about it. He was not alone. As he became more politically aware, he began to meet activists and radicals—"Black brothers who had been in the war, and Chicanos, and a few white cats"—who were veterans. All of them had been changed by their experience of war.[34]

The personal transformation wrought by Vietnam, he later reflected, had changed the course of his life. "I began to question everything. When I returned, I was not in the best state of mind, but I was now clear about my values. Vietnam was my left turn."[35]

Chapter 4

New Afrikans

While Charlie had been soldiering in Germany and Vietnam, the Bay Area had emerged as an epicenter of the bourgeoning Black Power movement. What began as a local Oakland organization—the Black Panther Party for Self Defense—gained national attention after its cofounder and principal theoretician, Huey P. Newton, was imprisoned in October 1967 following an exchange of gunfire with an Oakland police officer during a traffic stop. The campaign to secure Newton's freedom eventually exploded into an international cause célèbre. Drawing into its ranks an unusually wide array of progressive forces, the Free Huey movement launched the Panthers as the most iconic organization of the Black Power era. But other radical movements were vying for space and national influence. One of the most dynamic was the Republic of New Afrika (RNA).

Founded in 1968 in Detroit by associates of the martyred Malcolm X, the RNA grew out of the city's wellspring of Black political activity and drew on broad Black nationalist and Pan-African traditions.[1] The organization—officially known as the Provisional Government of the Republic of New Afrika—was notable during the Black Power era for its emphasis on the centrality of land to the question of Black freedom in America. Its political platform, unabashedly revolutionary, was formed around a central pillar: the creation of a territorial nation-state for Black people in the American South. RNA cofounder and main theorist Imari Obadele articulated this emancipatory vision as "the Malcolm X doctrine." Territory, Obadele contended, constituted the true basis for Black self-determination in America: "Land and power," Obadele wrote, "on *this* continent, in *our* time."[2]

The RNA's dream of a territorial Black republic was premised on an argument with a long lineage within Black freedom movements: reparations for slavery and the century of Jim Crow, racial violence, and discrimination that followed the Civil War. Carved from five states in the former Confederacy—Louisiana, Mississippi, Alabama, Georgia, and South Carolina—the country's establishment could be financed, the RNA argued, through the payment of long-overdue recompense for generations of unpaid labor and by contributions from Black Americans—and anyone else—willing to support Black self-determination. The new nation would be called the Republic of New Afrika, and its citizens would be all the Black people in America who chose to pledge their citizenship. Members of the RNA symbolically remade their subjectivities as "New Afrikans": members of a captive Black nation inside the entrails of America that had a right under international law to determine its future with a plebiscite.[3]

Never a large organization, the RNA nonetheless attracted a talented and disciplined membership. Gaidi Obadele, the elder brother of Imari, had been a member of the Tuskegee Airmen during World War II. Earning his law degree from Yale University, Gaidi Obadele launched a career as an indefatigable civil rights attorney. He was an associate of Malcolm X, whom he accompanied to Egypt and whose casket he later bore. While the RNA's initial voted leadership was honorific and held little governing power, the predominance of Black nationalist luminaries suggested the organization's hallowed standing. Robert F. Williams became the first president of the RNA's provisional government; Betty Shabazz, widow of Malcolm X, served as vice president; the legendary activist Queen Mother Moore was the minister of health and welfare and the first signatory of the New Afrikan Declaration of Independence; and firebrand Student Nonviolent Coordinating Committee leader H. "Rap" Brown was the minister of defense. The acclaimed writer Amiri Baraka served as co-minister of culture with Ron Karenga, leader of US Organization and creator of the Kwanzaa holiday.

Whereas mainstream civil rights organizations called for the opportunity, long denied, for Black Americans to participate as equals in American capitalism, the RNA called for Ujamaa, or African-inspired cooperative economics, in which the territory of New Afrika would be organized around a socialist "national economy" that would produce for the collective good of all, ensuring that each citizen had the "five essentials of decent human life": food, housing, clothing, health services, and education.[4] "Ujamaa Economics, based on African communal living," as the RNA's national leadership put it in December 1970, "rests on cooperative ownership, cooperative work, and equal sharing of the surplus wealth created by the community."[5]

But Charlie evinced little interest in politics. He had arrived in Oakland straight from the stockade in Vietnam. He was suffering, he later realized, from post-traumatic stress. "I would go to bars, and I would be standing with my back to the wall, uncomfortable around so many people. I couldn't relax. I felt very nervous. I couldn't sleep. . . . I knew I was sick. I still had not gone to Albuquerque to see my mother because I felt I was ill, and I didn't want to let her see me like that."[6] Wanting to be around kin, however, he moved back to Uncle Aubrey's house in East Oakland, where his cousin was also living. Aubrey Jr. had recently returned from a stint living in Harlem, where the neighborhood's vibrant world of Black politics and culture had turned him into a Black nationalist. The house in East Oakland reverberated with the sounds of the Last Poets and the recorded speeches of Malcolm X and Kwame Nkrumah.[7]

When Charlie finally began to overcome the trauma of Vietnam, it was due to both the emotional nurturing of family and the fount of critical analysis and historical self-awareness that is Black radical thought. "My uncle, and my cousin Aubrey, they spent a lot of time with me. My uncle did not condemn me for what I did in Vietnam. They began talking to me, and my cousin started giving me books to read, trying to focus my attention. He also started talking to me about political things, gave me things to study. He gave me RNA literature. The movement's platform was an understanding of power as based in land. In order to have power, you had to have control of your land. . . . The more I listened to Aubrey, the more it made sense."[8] As the summer of 1969 waned, Charlie began to feel better. He started running and lifting weights, and he reconnected with high school buddies in Oakland.

Recovery from the psychic wounds of war was short-lived. In late September, Charlie received a chilling telephone call from his mother in Albuquerque, who told him that his close childhood friend, James, had been killed in Vietnam. He was just nineteen years old.[9] Born in Colbert, Oklahoma, James Monroe Willard had moved to Albuquerque with his family as a youngster. Enlisting at the age of eighteen, James had become a sergeant in the Ninth Infantry Division, Third Battalion.[10] There would be a funeral service in Albuquerque. Packing a change of clothes, Charlie caught a bus to New Mexico that very day.

The teenager's death in battle in Vietnam would haunt Charlie for the rest of his life. "I was shaken by that," Charlie would later remember. "That could have been me. It confirmed that I had done the right thing in refusing to go back. James was the first close personal friend that I had who was killed in Vietnam. He had only been there a few months. Even thinking about it now, after all these years, is really hard for me."[11] The Willard family held a service at their home. Approaching the open casket, Charlie looked down at the face of his friend. "His family held me, and they cried. I cried. I couldn't believe it. He looked like he was alive, but he was dead."[12]

In a daze of sadness, Charlie returned to Oakland. The cover art for that week's issue of the *Black Panther* was fitting. In it, the transparent helmet of a weeping Black soldier provides a view into a nightmarish collage of images in his head: white police officers with clubs beating civil rights activists, a bloodied Black student protester at the 1968 San Francisco State strike being arrested, and Black men being lynched. A protest sign depicts a uniformed Black man holding an AK-47—the weapon of the Vietnamese, not the American occupiers—with the words "Our Fight Is Not in Vietnam." The title reads "Free the GI's [*sic*]."[13]

Charlie was still trying to free himself from the memory of Vietnam. Eager for a change of scenery in the spring of 1970, he accepted an invitation from Aubrey to try his hand at seasonal employment in Fairbanks, Alaska, where Uncle Aubrey worked during the summers. Although the city leaned right-wing, Fairbanks was also a college town. Antiwar rallies, while rarely boasting more than a hundred people, were still the largest protests in the city's memory.

Charlie was welcomed into the local antiwar movement. "These activists told me that the movement in the city had few veterans, and that I should stay and help organize."[14] Charlie tried to use his personal experience of the war to convince others to oppose it. Never much of a public speaker, Charlie nonetheless read the names of dead American GIs at rallies and told his story of going AWOL at antiwar meetings. His activism was cut short only by a recurrence of hepatitis. Confined to bed rest at a Veterans Affairs clinic at Eielson Air Force Base, Charlie passed the time reading.[15]

What was supposed to be a brief sojourn to Alaska lasted almost a year. Charlie bought a beat up '59 Chevy Bel Air, moved into a small apartment, and started dating a woman named Kathy. Soon they were falling in love. "It was really good for me, being around her. Fairbanks was also good for me. It was a small, quiet city. There was a gym there that I worked out at."[16] Charlie enrolled at the University of Alaska Fairbanks on the GI Bill, and a friend convinced him to follow his interests in history and politics. His transcript for the fall 1970 semester lists his courses as Western Civilization, History of Afro-American People, Intro to American Government and Political Science, and Elementary English, although he ultimately failed or withdrew from all of them.[17] As the semester set in, so did the subarctic freeze. It snowed in September, and temperatures plunged below zero in October.

Charlie's time in Alaska was not without wrinkles. In November, he was arrested for attempted burglary, but the charges were eventually dropped. Officially, the Fairbanks District Attorney's Office had insufficient staff to prosecute all of its cases. For his part, Charlie maintains that the police arrested him on a pretext, and that the DA was forced to drop the charges due to lack of evidence.[18] Then, in February, Charlie was arrested again, this time for marijuana possession. It's not clear whether he was ever charged.[19] Nonetheless, Charlie left the state shortly afterward. Returning to California in February 1971, he moved in with Aubrey Jr. at his apartment on Bush Street in San Francisco.

The sojourn to Alaska had cleared his mind. From then on, Charlie spent all his time with his cousin. Accompanying Aubrey around the Bay Area, Charlie met his friends in the Nation of Islam and hung out with the Panther cadre in San Francisco. When Aubrey invited him to a meeting of the RNA in Oakland, Charlie accepted. Chairing the meeting was Jim Nabors, the organization's western regional vice president. Like Charlie, Nabors had been in the army.[20] As a student at UC Berkeley, Nabors became a campus leader of the third world student strike in 1969 and, as a Berkeley Police Department surveillance file on local activists disdainfully put it, "a hotshot on campus in radical movements."[21] The more Charlie listened to Nabors and the New Afrikans describe their plans, the more he wanted to be part of them.

Skeptics would regard the RNA's quixotic dream of a breakaway Black nation, founded on land ceded by the United States government, as hopelessly implausible. Charlie would later marvel at the group's audacity. "Given how little we had to work with, we had to be some outrageously bold, idealist thinkers to ever think we would be successful."[22] But the RNA's platform was appealing because it was aimed straight at the heart of the material foundations of Black unfreedom in America. "The RNA wanted reparations, forty acres and a mule. . . . They understood that in order to have power and freedom, you have got to have land."[23] Like the Nation of Islam, the RNA was fundamentally pessimistic on the question of collective white benevolence and the potential for racial equality in a nation that had yet to reckon with the legacy of slavery. "By that point in my life," Charlie would recall, "I had become convinced that Black people would never get a fair shake in white, capitalist, imperialist America. Black people in America were a nation within a nation."[24]

There were other critiques of the RNA's separatist territorial aspirations, including its clarion call to free the land. What of Indigenous nations, whose land claims obviously preceded those of the RNA and the settler colonial nation of the United States? One answer could be found in the Code of Umoja, the RNA's 1970 constitution, which pledged "to negotiate with the American Indian Nations the claims which conflict with the claims of the New Afrikan nation and to resolve these claims in the spirit of justice, brotherhood, and mutual revolutionary commitment."[25] The RNA's position of support for Indigenous land claims is clear in the organization's documents and public statements. Indigenous activists and intellectuals of the Red Power era, for their part, also repeatedly voiced support for the concept of land reparations for slavery for African Americans, belying claims that territorial Black nationalism in the United States was fundamentally incompatible with Indigenous self-determination.[26] Nonetheless, the dilemma of whether there could ever really be justice on stolen land—the very land where a settler colonial state now existed—would remain an open question within the RNA's political imaginary and an active debate within broader struggles for reparations and social justice in the United States and beyond.[27]

One of the ways that the RNA grappled with these questions, together with the contradictions inherent to a project of Black nationalism inside a multiracial state, was through frameworks of solidarity and internationalism. The RNA embraced a global emancipatory vision that sought common cause with peoples fighting for liberation across the globe. If the RNA's first duty was to free Black people in America, its second goal, the organization's Declaration of Economic Intent proclaimed, was "to wage the world revolution until all people everywhere are so free."[28] As the New Afrikan movement grew, it forged alliances with movements organized by other colonized racialized peoples within the confines of US territory, including Native American and Chicano movements, whose land-based struggles paralleled those of the RNA, as well as the Puerto Rican independence movement's anticolonial quest for independence from the United States.[29] A few non-Black revolutionaries, including the stalwart Japanese American civil rights activist Yuri Kochiyama, became RNA citizens of record. The RNA also had a small number of white supporters, at least in California. "We accepted support from anyone who was committed to aiding us," Charlie later explained. "We accepted the idea that in a movement, everyone has a different role to play."[30]

Charlie joined the Oakland chapter of the RNA—officially known as a consulate—in April 1971, adopting the organization's political cosmology. The RNA argued that Black Americans were "paper citizens": members of a colonized people that had been forced to adopt the citizenship of the United States, but with neither the full benefits of citizenship nor inclusion in the national community.[31] Now, as part of their symbolic conversion as citizens of New Afrika, a nation founded on inclusion and liberation, each member jettisoned their "slave name," which signified the severance of their African identity, and replaced it with an "Afrikan name," given during an RNA naming ceremony.[32] Charlie's ceremony was held at the apartment of Jim Nabors. Sitting in a circle, the assembled New Afrikans rose one by one, describing how they perceived Charlie's personality and psychological makeup. After consulting books of names in Swahili, Yoruba, and Arabic, they proclaimed Charlie's new name: Fela Sekou Olatunji.[33]

As the movement readied plans to launch pilot communities in the American South, its immediate goal, Imari Obadele wrote, was "simply *demonstrating* that our government, the *Republic of New Africa* [sic], does in fact have the consent of the people who live in the areas we claim as subjugated territory."[34] Preparations began for the creation of a fledgling Black community on purchased land in Mississippi. The RNA called for all New Afrikans to "come to the South and establish a better life through new communities, reparations and a plebiscite."[35]

Charlie threw himself into the labor of grassroots movement building. The Oakland consulate organized community aid programs in the Bay Area, modeled on the survival programs of the Black Panther Party, including an after-school program in San Francisco for mothers who could not afford day care. The program offered a curriculum of Black history, mathematics, reading, and martial arts. Charlie began working in support of it by soliciting donations from local businesses. "The idea appealed to me: helping our community, helping our people. My job was to keep the school running with paper, pencils, detergent to wash their clothes, schoolbooks, and food."[36] Many businesses contributed voluntarily; a few refused—and were "expropriated" by Charlie. The program was soon receiving a large quantity of donated and stolen goods. "I started to feel really good. I was doing important work in the community and was reading and exercising, and I was not thinking about Vietnam."[37]

Two weeks later, Charlie joined a security detail at a Berkeley concert by singer and musician Curtis Mayfield, who had tapped the RNA for the job because he did not trust the police. Swaying to the funky soul music, a loaded 9 mm Browning hidden in a shoulder holster under his jacket, Charlie was feeling positively swell. Standing next to him were two other members of the organization that Charlie had not seen before.

One of them introduced himself as Michael.

Michael Robert Finney, a nineteen-year-old San Francisco native from a middle-class family, was in fact the son of a police inspector, John Finney, who had broken the color line to become one of the first Black officers in the San Francisco Police Department. As a high school student in San Francisco, Michael was among the Black students who were bused to Lincoln High School, a formerly segregated, majority white high school in the city's Parkside District, where they were greeted by racist graffiti.[38] Fistfights broke out between Black and white students, and police were called to Lincoln repeatedly during the fall of 1968 and the winter of 1969.[39]

As the tide of student protest rose, Michael became an activist. Prompted by the efforts of a teacher, Black and white students formed an integrated student union at Lincoln. Inspired by the student movement at nearby San Francisco State College in the fall of 1968, led by the Third World Liberation Front and centering student demands to create a College of Ethnic Studies that would teach the history of Black, Latino, and Asian American students, Lincoln's Black Student Union launched its own protests. Boycotting classes until demands were met, members called for a Black history curriculum in the high school. Some white and Chicano students joined the protest, as did local organizations—including the Black Panther Party.[40]

Michael was fascinated by the Panthers. Emulating their iconic style and swagger, Michael started wearing a black leather jacket affixed with "Free Huey" buttons to school and read about the group's exploits in community newspapers. In 1968, when he was seventeen, Michael went to see a play about the trial of Huey P. Newton, then in prison following the October 1967 shootout in which Oakland police officer John Frey was killed. Halfway through the play, real Panthers—Michael says he recognized Bobby Seale among them—filed into the room behind the audience, watching the play silently from the shadows. Transfixed, Michael watched the Panthers instead of the actors.[41] Within a few weeks, Michael began attending meetings for Panther recruits in Oakland, although it is not clear whether he ever formally joined the organization.

Accepted to the University of California, Berkeley, in fall 1968, Michael declared a major in political science.[42] Around the same time, he married his girlfriend, Melani (Njeri) Jackson, with whom he became a father. UC Berkeley's campus was afire with student activism, and Michael threw himself into it. He was also active in the Third World Liberation Front student group, a Berkeley counterpart to the student movement that had been making headlines across the bay at San Francisco State College, leading to his arrest by University of California police on more than one occasion.[43]

Michael would later recall his activist days at UC Berkeley with a broad smile: "Picture in your mind tear gas dropping out of helicopters, police cars on fire, police shooting tear-gas canisters and students throwing 'em back at the police."[44] Activism ultimately won out over academics: "It seemed pointless." He dropped out of the university after two years. "It had a lot to do with the frustrations of being a young black rebel at that time. You don't want to go into the mainstream, and yet you don't know exactly what you're doing."[45] Joining the RNA in 1970, Michael was given the Mandinka-Swahili free name of Sundiata Macheo.[46]

Accompanying Michael in the security detail at the Curtis Mayfield concert was his friend Ralph Laurence Goodwin, who served as Oakland consul for the RNA's national organization.[47] He introduced himself to Charlie by his free name: Antar Ra.

Born into a middle-class family of activists, Antar's parents were stalwarts of the local civil rights movement. His mother, Joye Speights Goodwin, a nurse by training who had earned a master's degree in epidemiology from UCLA, was a formidable political activist who spent much of her life working for community causes.[48] As chair of the NAACP's Housing Committee in San Francisco for many years, Joye's activism during Antar's youth frequently focused on housing discrimination. Like the Finneys, the Goodwin family had been de facto race pioneers in a segregated world. As Antar's sister Hope would later remember it, "When I was a child, we never lived in a black neighborhood. We integrated every neighborhood we lived in; my parents believed in civil rights and integration."[49]

Luther Ambrose Goodwin, Antar's father, was also a racial justice pioneer. Attending UCLA, he befriended George E. Brown Jr., the future progressive congressman who was at that time involved in efforts to desegregate UCLA's student housing in Westwood. Brown invited Goodwin to be his roommate, and the two became the first Black-white roommates in UCLA's history.[50] Goodwin, however, left UCLA during World War II, completing flight school in 1944 and going on to become a member of the famed Tuskegee Airmen, flying a B-52 in bombing missions over Europe during World War II and serving again in the Korean War. After earning his degree and attending the University of California's Hastings College of Law, Luther Goodwin would eventually became San Francisco's deputy district attorney general.[51] Cofounding a law firm, attorney Goodwin earned national recognition when he successfully co-defended civil rights activist Fania Davis Jordan—the sister of Angela Y. Davis—after she and her husband exchanged gunfire with San Diego deputy sheriffs inside their own home in November 1969 after the deputies, accosting them on the street outside their house, followed them inside.[52]

Antar enrolled at the University of California, Berkeley, first majoring in physics, then mathematics. Graduating with his bachelor's degree in 1969, Antar enrolled in graduate studies at Berkeley, also in mathematics, but dropped out after one semester.[53] Antar's priority was the campus's Black Student Union (BSU). Growing out of the Third World Liberation Front, the BSU's politics embraced an internationalist political analysis that emphasized the linkages between local and global struggles against oppression. The problems facing Black communities in America, the group proclaimed in 1970, included not only "poor housing, high rent, police brutality, unemployment, [and] education in the school system" but also "the Southeast Asian war."[54] From its headquarters at 505 Eshleman Hall, the BSU launched efforts to expel military recruiters on campus, support jailed local Panthers, and educate people about the ongoing anticolonial struggle in Portuguese Guinea.[55]

Antar, well read in Pan-Africanism and Black history, was a few years older than Charlie and Michael, and both clearly admired him. "[Antar] was highly intelligent, well read, and willing to give up his life for what he believed in," Charlie later said.[56]

As the RNA's chapter in Oakland blossomed during the summer of 1971, the three young men—Antar, Michael, and Charlie—became friends, then comrades. Eventually, they would become like brothers.

The RNA maintained a military wing, the Black Legion. Created in the spirit of Malcolm X, its mandate was to defend the organization from attack, whether by police or by ordinary white racists.[57] In this sense, the RNA followed a storied tradition of Black armed defense and freedom struggle.[58] The opening chapter of Imari Obadele's 1967 treatise, *War in America*, sketches out the history of Black resistance to violent white supremacy in the bowls of America. The chapter, appropriately titled "Background of Violence," begins with words that echo the famous opening lines of Frantz Fanon's *The Wretched of the Earth*: "The black man's struggle for freedom in America has always been violent."[59] For the RNA, the Black Legion was central to these goals. "We knew that if we ever wanted to have an independent Black nation in the South," Charlie would later explain, "there would have to be a self-defense and military aspect of this movement."[60] With his military background, Charlie was an ideal recruit for the RNA's military wing.

Within the movement's spheres of activity, RNA leadership sought to keep the organization's political work separate from its quasi-military activities. The separation of spheres allowed the movement to develop footholds of support in a wider variety of places. Not everyone was willing to die for a cause. "There can be collaboration between people with different levels of commitment and skills," Charlie would later explain. "These people were called 'collaborators,' and they could go as far as they wanted to go. It was important not to push them. There were collaborators, teachers and unionists, for instance, who did various things. Sometimes they didn't know the full extent of what was happening. . . . It was important to accept people at the level that they were at and not push or judge them."[61]

The RNA had already suffered one violent confrontation. Police activity at the New Bethel Baptist Church in Detroit, where the RNA held its one-year anniversary conference in March 1969, resulted in two police officers shot, one fatally, under contested circumstances as they approached armed guards of the Black Legion outside.[62] Police then burst into the church, firing as they advanced, shooting 4 people and arresting 142.[63] Most were released the next day at the order of Judge George Crockett Jr., a pathbreaking Black jurist and later congressman, who condemned the killing of the officer but defended the rights of the accused. "Can any of you imagine the Detroit Police invading an all-white church and rounding up everyone in sight to be bused to a wholesale lockup in a police garage? . . . Can any of you justify the jailing of

32 women all night long when there was admittedly not the slightest evidence of their involvement in any crime? Can anyone explain in other than racist terms the shooting by police into a closed and surrounded church?"[64]

The New Bethel incident led to a wave of police harassment of RNA chapters. Now, two years later, Charlie suspected that they were being surveilled in the Bay Area. FBI surveillance files on the RNA confirm this suspicion.[65] Members of the organization reported being followed by patrol cars or tailed by suspicious vehicles. As the harassment increased, so did the organization's paranoia. Michael eventually took to wearing a concealed pistol under his shirt everywhere he went, vowing that "no ignorant racist pig is going to abuse me."[66] The certainty that they were under government surveillance but the lack of definitive proof before March 1971—when the FBI's Counterintelligence Program was revealed after antiwar activists broke into an FBI office in Media, Pennsylvania, and leaked documents about the program to national news agencies—created an eerie sensation. As Black Panther Party leader Ericka Huggins later described it, "We could all feel that there was something going on that was bigger than us."[67]

Armed confrontation between the RNA and the police eventually erupted in Jackson, Mississippi. Tensions had been palpable in the city for months. On May 15, 1970, Jackson had been the site of a mass shooting by police and highway patrolmen at historically Black Jackson State College. The officers, responding to reports of rioting amid student protests near the campus, had fired a fusillade of over 150 rounds at a student dormitory, killing two Black students and wounding twelve more, an action for which no police officer was ever criminally charged.[68]

It was in Mississippi, in the heart of the old slavocracy, a state where many counties were still majority Black, that the RNA sought to establish a territorial foothold. The organization attempted to purchase twenty acres of land from a local Black farmer, Lofton Mason, to build a model independent Black community. Under pressure from the FBI and local white residents, Mason abrogated the land sale.[69]

Amid these rising tensions between the RNA and law enforcement, police and FBI forces raided the organization's office at sunrise on August 18, 1971. The RNA activists, heavily armed, attempted to repel them, wounding a Jackson police officer and an FBI agent and killing police officer Louis Skinner. Police maintained that the RNA had fired the first shots, describing the captured residence's fortifications as "a Vietcong-type bunker and a tunnel with firing ports."[70] Other RNA activists, including Imari Obadele, were arrested at a nearby residence. The defendants would become known as the RNA 11, initiating a protracted and expensive legal battle.

Armed defense now became the RNA's national priority. In Oakland, activists stockpiled guns and procured stolen dynamite. But while members of the Oakland consulate had occasionally conducted target practice in the countryside, there had been no sustained training program. Antar, Jim Nabors, and other members of the local leadership decided to plan a wilderness retreat to combine weapons training with survival skills. "The RNA's goal was to build a Black nation on empty land," Charlie would later explain, "but many of the brothers and sisters in the movement were city people, and so the idea was to get them used to a rural environment, including camping out and cooking over fires."[71]

So, in late October 1971, thirty people packed into cars and drove south to Los Padres National Forest on the central California coast. The group camped out for the night at the Arroyo Seco campground in Monterey County. Charlie slept in a sleeping bag on the ground with his girlfriend Kathy, who was visiting from Alaska. On a wooded hillside deep inside the park, Charlie set up combat simulations based upon his experience in Vietnam. In one, the RNA soldiers arrayed themselves to defend a knoll. In another, they attacked a position, represented by tree stumps, with live fire. As one group advanced through the chaparral, another crept up from the right, out of the line of fire. A third group guarded the rear and left approaches. Gunfire echoed through the park.

The low thudding sound of a helicopter brought the paramilitary exercise to a halt. The helicopter landed, and a park ranger, a youngish white man, climbed out. "Good afternoon, gentlemen," the ranger said almost cheerily. "You guys got a permit for this?" They did not. "Well, you have to understand, this is not allowed here," the ranger explained, eyeing the guns. "There are people camping nearby. This is a state park!"[72] The RNA trainees agreed to stop. The ranger seemed satisfied and left in his helicopter. Upon returning to the campsite, however, they learned that the local sheriff and his deputies had showed up, issuing citations for illegal campfires and for "brandishing weapons and disturbing the peace."[73] As they were leaving the campground, they realized that there was a large police presence in the area. Miraculously, though, no confrontation ensued. Michael would later surmise that the police had been intimidated. "They didn't realize how well armed we were," he later told a reporter. "They set up a roadblock, they said we could leave the park but we had to turn in our weapons. We said fuck that. We had 30 barrels sticking out of those cars—they backed off."[74]

News of the incident was picked up by the media. Police had observed the group flying the Republic of New Afrika flag, doing group calisthenics, marching in formation, and engaging in target practice with rifles.[75] But the

Monterey County District Attorney's Office pressed no charges. Other than the citations issued, there had been no violations. "I can find nothing in the Penal Code," DA William D. Curtis explained, "that covers paramilitary activity."[76] Nor had the RNA been the first to engage in target practice in the area. As one of the park rangers told the *Oakland Tribune*, a different armed group had conducted target practice in the area the previous summer. "We were told by the FBI to take no action, so we left them alone."[77]

The RNA chapter in Mississippi was not so lucky. Costly legal battles loomed, police harassment continued, and armed white vigilantes lurked. Convinced that another attack was coming, the RNA posted guards outside their houses. It was now critical to save what was left of the organization's foothold in Jackson, and a call went out for volunteers to help. And so in early November 1971, Charlie, Michael, and Antar volunteered to travel to Mississippi. As they prepared to leave, they met with the RNA's national minister of defense, Alajo Adegbalola, in a restaurant in San Bernardino, where they agreed to provide security in Jackson.[78] Adegbalola instructed them to bring a cache of legally purchased rifles, handguns, and ammunition, together with a significant quantity of dynamite.[79] They did not hesitate. "We were soldiers, we were following orders," Charlie later explained. "I had military experience, had confidence in Antar and Michael. That was no problem."[80]

But there was another element to the mission—something secret. Adegbalola instructed them to travel to Mississippi by way of Louisiana, where they would receive instructions about the operation. The RNA commander gave Charlie an address in Louisiana. Some have speculated that the mission was, in fact, a plot to break Imari Obadele out of jail. Charlie, for his part, says he was told only that details would be forthcoming in Louisiana.[81]

Whatever the precise nature of the Jackson mission, Charlie, Michael, and Antar were unorthodox candidates for work in the organization's underground sphere. Two of them had public profiles: Michael was the minister of information for the RNA's Oakland consulate and, with Antar, had participated in the group's community work. Indeed, just a few days before their trip, the city's newspaper of record had listed Michael and Antar's scheduled appearance on KFOG's "Black Renaissance" radio program on 104.5 FM to "discuss the concepts and goals of the Republic of New Africa"[*sic*].[82] And all three had been linked by police to the ill-fated trip to Los Padres National Forest.

Planning began for the Jackson mission. The RNA comrades in the Bay Area assumed that the FBI and local police had them under surveillance. Harassment had continued all fall. In September, for instance, the apartment that Charlie shared with Aubrey on Bush Street had been raided. Acting on information provided by an informant that dynamite was being stored at the location, officers from the San Francisco Police Department Intelligence Detail kicked down the door.[83] "I was there when it was raided. It was very tense. We were not armed."[84]

With guns drawn, police searched the house while Charlie and the others sat on the couch under guard. But the officers found nothing. When the FBI eventually found what they were looking for, it was more than a thousand miles away in New Mexico.

Chapter 5

The Largest Manhunt

Charlie was awake before dawn on November 8, 1971. Dressing neatly, he loaded his suitcase and a duffel bag into a shiny new green Ford Galaxie sedan that a supporter of the RNA had rented for them using a stolen credit card. Then he drove to Oakland to pick up Michael and Antar. Packing the car quickly in the predawn fog, they departed the city and drove east. Making for the San Joaquin Valley, they picked up US Route 99 and drove south, stopping only for snacks and gas.

Stowed among their bags were the legally registered weapons: rifles, shotguns, handguns, and boxes of ammunition. Concealed underneath was a cache of dynamite—not legal at all. To avoid speeding or an inadvertent traffic infraction that could justify a police stop, the three comrades followed a system: whoever was driving would be accompanied by someone in the front seat who was always awake. Picking up Interstate 40 near Bakersfield, they crossed into Arizona as darkness fell.[1]

Charlie was at the wheel as the trio entered western New Mexico. Nearing Albuquerque a little after 10:30 p.m., about eight miles from city limits, Charlie noticed the glimmer of headlights appear in his rearview mirror, still in the distance but gaining rapidly. Antar, who was riding with him in front as Michael slept in the back, craned his head around to look, then leaned over to check the speedometer. "That guy's either crazy or it's a cop," he muttered as the headlights closed in. The car was flying. As it crossed into the parallel lane and began to pass them, they saw that it was a state police cruiser. Looking to the left, Charlie could make out a white officer's face peering back at him. The cruiser hesitated, then slowed and fell in behind them. The dome lights switched on.

The officer was New Mexico State Trooper Robert Rosenbloom, twenty-eight years old, who had been returning to Albuquerque after transporting a witness across state lines to Arizona. News accounts would later suggest that Rosenbloom initiated the traffic stop because he was suspicious that the green Galaxie, which he described to the police radio operator at 10:41 p.m. as containing "three negro subjects," had been stolen. According to the radio operator, Rosenbloom did not request a criminal check on California license plate 824-EDH. The radio operator ran the plate anyway, obtaining negative results on the NCIC search. But when he radioed back to Rosenbloom, the officer did not respond.[2] Rosenbloom may have already been dead.

News coverage would later skirt the matter of why the Galaxie had been pulled over. A late model car with California plates traveling east on the interstate, day or night, would not have been out of place. If the stop was initiated for some traffic violation, it was not noted by the police radio operator. Media reports described the stop as a "routine check" and sometimes referenced the suspicion that the car had been stolen, although no details were provided.[3] There was, of course, a more prosaic explanation. "I know we were not speeding," Charlie would later say. "He had been about to pass us, but it was as if once he saw who we were—three young Black guys with afros—he decided to pull us over."[4]

In the years that followed, neither Charlie nor Michael nor Antar would offer a full account of the shooting to foreign journalists visiting Cuba. The RNA comrades did not deny their involvement in Rosenbloom's death, but they never revealed who had pulled the trigger. In fact, they provided only scant details. Rosenbloom, they averred, had tried to search the car. Then, it all happened in an instant. The officer had pulled his gun on them. Fearing that he would open fire, one of the three shot Rosenbloom first. It had been self-defense.[5] According to the police homicide report, when Rosenbloom was found, face down and dead of a gunshot wound to the throat, the officer's Smith and Wesson .357 Magnum was found lying next to his right side, unfired. Six feet away lay a single spent .45-caliber casing.[6]

Decades later, however, Charlie would tell a somewhat different version of the story, one less congruent with any classical notion of self-defense. Rosenbloom, alone and without backup, had insisted on searching the car's trunk. Angry about the racially motivated stop and worried about the dynamite, Charlie, Michael, and Antar protested the search. "He had no cause to do that. It was an illegal search. But he went ahead anyway."[7] Rosenbloom pulled suitcases and bags out of the trunk, placing them on the ground, getting closer to the dynamite. A short distance away, where Rosenbloom had told them to wait, the RNA comrades shouted their objection. Then Charlie made toward the officer. "I was going to tussle with him, take his gun." Realizing what was about to happen, Rosenbloom dropped the suitcase that he had halfway out of the trunk and spun around, facing his attacker and reaching for his gun. There was a scuffle on the side of the highway. Charlie grabbed at the officer's wrist, preventing him from raising his weapon. Then a shot rang out. Someone had shot the officer at point-blank range. Rosenbloom fell forward. Then he lay still.[8]

The RNA comrades fled. Leaving the highway, they sped into the heart of South Valley, a historically Chicano neighborhood of Albuquerque bisected by the Rio Grande. They eased the car into a vacant lot and cut the engine. They yanked bags and suitcases out of the trunk. Then they abandoned the vehicle. Pausing in another overgrown lot a few blocks away, they fumbled through the luggage in the dark, taking the handguns but leaving everything else. Then, crouching through alleys, they made for a place that Charlie knew well.

An hour later, Dorethea Hill parted the shades to see who was softly knocking on her door in the middle of the night. Charlie had not informed his mother of the trip. As he would later recall, "She asked me what happened. I told her only that a police officer had pulled us over, and that the officer was now dead." Dorethea just stared at her son. But she allowed them to stay. The next morning, she made a phone call. An hour later, her friend Johnny Earl Vines, a twenty-nine-year-old father of four who worked at the airport, arrived to take them to another house.[9]

By daybreak, the killing of officer Rosenbloom was headline news. Roadblocks went up throughout the state in what one official described as the largest manhunt in New Mexico's modern history. The FBI cast their net wide, instructing the airport to keep a lookout for anyone matching the suspects' descriptions and to see "if any Negroes purchased tickets."[10] Charlie's first instinct after fleeing the highway had been to set fire to the car. But the vacant lot was in a residential neighborhood, and police would close off the area before they had a chance to get out. By the time police discovered the Galaxie the next morning, the suspects were long gone.

Yet the RNA comrades had already made mistakes. They had neglected to wipe down the car for fingerprints. In the frantic rush to abandon the vehicle, they had jettisoned personal effects, some of which yielded identifying information. Police cataloged the items, including camping gear, sleeping bags, clothing, binoculars, shoe polish, an apple and one "slice of pie (pumpkin)." There were also the guns, magazines, and ammunition: one US M1 carbine rifle, two Fabrique Nationale M-49 rifles, one 12-guage shotgun, and about three hundred rounds in various calibers.[11]

And then there was the dynamite, eighteen sticks in all, some, according to police, with fuses already attached.[12] A briefcase marked with the initials "MRF" contained a large amount of RNA literature together with sundry political pamphlets. Some were about the People's Movement for the Liberation of Angola, while another had been produced by the Liberation Front of Mozambique. There was also political literature about socialist China and Vietnam, editions of the English-language Chinese news magazine *Peking Review*, and notebooks from a Swahili language class.[13]

Indeed, MRF was apparently a voracious reader with tastes in Pan-Africanism, anticolonialism, and socialist theory. The briefcase was stuffed with books—forty-four in all—including Albert Memmi's *The Colonizer and the Colonized*; Julius K. Nyerere's *Ujamaa: Essays on Socialism*; George Jackson's *Soledad Brother*; three books by Che Guevara, including *Man and Socialism in Cuba* and *Guerrilla Warfare*, three volumes of the writings of Mao Tse-tung, and Vietnamese communist revolutionary Võ Nguyên Giáp's *The Military Art of People's War*.[14] "From literature located in the car," the FBI concluded on November 10, "occupants appear to be of a militant, racially orientated group with tendencies toward violence."[15]

So far, none of the suspects had been identified, but that would soon change. The discarded items connected at least two of the car's occupants to the Bay Area. No fancy detective work was necessary, for in the rush to abandon the car, Michael Finney had accidentally left his passport in a duffel bag.[16] And so, on November 16, news media reported that the New Mexico State Police had identified Michael and charged him with murder in the killing of officer Rosenbloom. Police also assisted the FBI in filing federal charges against Michael for having been in possession of "six homemade bombs" composed of sticks of dynamite with attached blasting caps, which police allegedly discovered in the suitcase with Michael's passport.[17]

The arrest warrant, which contended that Rosenbloom had been killed with a .45-caliber weapon, noted that a Llama .45-caliber automatic pistol had been legally purchased in Oakland by Michael's wife, Melani (Njeri) Jackson, and that an instruction manual for such a gun had been found in the abandoned car.[18] But this proved nothing, and the rifles were similarly legal. Investigating the M-49s, the FBI learned that its agents had encountered precisely these weapons, identified by their serial numbers, just a week prior in California. Summoned to an Oakland gun range on November 3 to investigate several individuals who had been "observed firing semi-automatic rifles," bureau agents found nothing illicit: the individuals were in possession of legally purchased firearms and were fully within their rights.[19]

On November 16, the New Mexico State Police issued a $1,000 reward, confidential and without conditions, for information leading to Michael's whereabouts.[20] Charges against Antar, identified by fingerprints found in the car, followed three days later.[21] Thus far, police had made no public mention of Charlie, nor did they appear to be aware that one of the suspects had ties to Albuquerque. Police units continued to scour South Valley. Acting on information provided by informants, police performed raids on at least three residences in the area, with negative results.

In the end, the RNA comrades evaded capture in Albuquerque for two and a half weeks, a feat owed almost entirely to the assistance of others. Johnny, of course, had been indispensable, but there were others. At least two of Charlie's childhood friends helped hide them or brought food and provisions. And there were several others, complete strangers, who aided them for unknown reasons. It was this support, most of it entirely unexpected, that allowed them to elude a massive urban manhunt.

Yet the aid that they received must also be viewed within the social and historical context of Albuquerque in the early 1970s. More than anything, it would be shaped by festering popular anger at the Albuquerque Police Department.

While Charlie had been away, long-simmering enmity between police and the city's Chicano communities had finally boiled over. *El Grito del Norte*—an Española-based community newspaper cofounded by Elizabeth "Betita" Martínez, a longtime civil rights activist and writer who had worked for the Student Nonviolent Coordinating Committee before moving to New Mexico—had repeatedly warned of rising popular anger about police misconduct. And there were allegations of even worse things. Left-wing activists in the state had been on edge for years. Killings of several Chicano activists in New Mexico, including the suspicious death in 1970 of Bobby Garcia, who had been found shot in the head outside Albuquerque—his death had officially been ruled a suicide—were feared to be part of a larger pattern of political violence in New Mexico.[22] "A series of police shootings and the deaths of almost a dozen Chicano activists from Taos to Albuquerque," scholar David Correia wrote, "some unarmed and shot in the back, produced rumors of death squads operating within the Albuquerque Police Department and the New Mexico State Police."[23] By the fall of 1971, the tension between law enforcement and citizens in Albuquerque was palpable.

Indeed, the biggest social conflagration in the city's modern history had erupted just months before the RNA comrades arrived. A series of riots and skirmishes between police and Chicanos and white youth in Albuquerque made national news in June 1971 after police, who had been attempting to arrest youth in Roosevelt Park after a canceled rock concert, "were suddenly set upon by parts of the crowd."[24] Members of the Las Gorras Negras organization tried to intercede by getting between the police and "hundreds of almost naked hippies and hundreds of teenagers from Albuquerque's Mexican-American barrios," as the *New York Times* described the scene, but to no avail. Police ignored the activists' pleas for calm.[25] In the rioting that followed over the next three days, the city incurred $3 million in property damage. Nine people were shot, the majority by police; businesses were looted; the Fraternal Order of Police lodge and a school were firebombed; several hundred people were arrested; and the National Guard was called in.[26]

The aggressiveness of the police during the Roosevelt Park Rebellion, as the events of the day came to be known, shocked bystanders. Some later attended a community meeting organized by Las Gorras Negras. "A kid went riding slowly by in a convertible," recounted a man who said he had been at the park with his wife and daughter. "All of a sudden a cop grabbed him and started beating on him. I told him to leave him alone and about five cops turned on me. I didn't believe police brutality existed, now I'm 100 per cent [*sic*] sure it does."[27] In a statement, La Alianza Federal de Mercedes, the organization founded by Reies López Tijerina, cited lack of employment opportunities for Chicano youth, the exclusion of Chicanos from political power in the city, police brutality, and lack of civilian police oversight as contributing to the community tensions underlying the unrest. Yet the deeper context, La Alianza wrote, was "123 years of racism and oppression in New Mexico of the Indo-Hispano by the Anglo since the signing of the Treaty of Guadalupe Hidalgo."[28]

It was this buried legacy of colonialism, the activists of Las Gorras Negras argued in the pages of their newspaper, *Venceremos*, that lay at the root of police repression and violence in Chicano and Indigenous communities in New Mexico.[29] And it had gone unchecked for years. In the aftermath of the Roosevelt Park Rebellion, *Venceremos* documented a litany of cases involving harassment, false charges, illegal searches, violence, and robbery of Chicanos at the hands of the Albuquerque police. Three weeks after the rioting, *El Grito del Norte* similarly traced the origins of the conflagration to a history of police violence, a scourge that the newspaper had documented repeatedly since its founding. "The Albuquerque Rebellion did not just happen on a hot Sunday afternoon," *El Grito* wrote in July 1971. "Its beginning goes back days, weeks, months and years . . . to other Sunday afternoons or Saturday nights or any time when a young Chicano lay dead on some hot, sticky, black-topped street."[30]

Nor was scorn for the city's police confined to Chicano communities. Albuquerque had recently witnessed public skirmishes between police and primarily white college students and counterculture youth. The previous year, members of the National Guard had clashed with striking students at the University of New Mexico who were protesting the United States invasion of Cambodia. In the resulting melees, guardsmen stabbed ten unarmed students and one local television reporter with their rifle-mounted bayonets, shocking normally impassive observers. Film footage aired nationally showed National Guardsmen knocking a student on crutches to the ground with a rifle butt and slashing a second with their bayonets. A third student retaliated with a specially prepared weapon—a cup of urine—which he flung at the guardsmen.[31]

This was the simmering social cauldron of police-community relations that Charlie, Michael, and Antar had stumbled into when they unexpectedly found themselves being aided in Albuquerque. "How is it possible," Charlie later mused, "that a cop is dead, but all of these people, Chicano and Black, who have been so oppressed and abused by the police, . . . feel that they have to help us get away? If the police had been working in the community, had been part of the community, had built trust, we would have gotten nowhere. The police in Albuquerque made enemies for themselves out of a whole neighborhood."[32]

Almost the whole neighborhood. A reward for information leading to the arrest of the suspects, initiated by the *Albuquerque Journal* and reaching $1,600 by November 16, incentivized tips.[33] At least one acquaintance of Dorethea Hill, who had previously been a "reliable" informant, according to the FBI, advised the bureau that Charlie had told his mother that he had been "in the car that was used by the persons who shot a New Mexico State Officer on November 8."[34] In any case, the RNA comrades, now accused murderers, were taking no chances. They made it clear to those who aided them that they would resist police capture by any means necessary. It would be freedom or death, but not prison. For three Black radicals accused of killing a white police officer, there would be no fair trial. It would be life in a cage—if they made it that far. "We knew that in all likelihood, if the cops caught up to us, there is a good chance that they would just shoot us. They could say we pulled a gun or tried to run."[35]

Escape from Albuquerque was therefore critical. As they watched the news coverage on television at the improvised safe house that Johnny had taken them to, mug shots of Michael and Antar flashed across the screen. Charlie became paranoid. Although he still had not been publicly named as a suspect, it was only a matter of time before his identity was uncovered. Once that happened, police would visit Charlie's mother. That would lead them to Johnny—and then to the house where they were staying. And so, after nightfall on Thanksgiving eve, someone drove them to another friend's house. To throw off the profile of three Black men, Michael, the slimmest, donned a borrowed wig, a pretty black dress, and high heels.

It was now November 25, 1971, Thanksgiving Day. The RNA comrades had been in hiding out for seventeen days. As they sat in a bedroom watching the news, they were thinking hungrily about the plates of turkey, dressing, mashed potatoes, and pie that one of Charlie's childhood friends had promised to bring them. As a security precaution, Charlie instructed the friend to park her car several blocks way, turn the corner, and then wait on a neighbor's porch to ensure that she had not been followed. But the friend arrived early—and without the food. She had learned something troubling. An acquaintance of hers, a man who worked at Albuquerque police headquarters as part of the maintenance staff, had overheard officers discussing one "Charles Hill." Originally believed to have been in Alaska, police now suspected that Charlie had been at the scene of Rosenbloom's killing.[36]

Forgetting their hunger, Charlie, Michael, and Antar resolved to slip out of the house that very night. Sure enough, an hour later, the television set confirmed the woman's warning. Charlie's fingerprints, lifted from a beer can found in the Galaxie, had been identified. An arrest warrant was issued on murder charges.[37] When Charlie's photograph flashed across the television screen, it was his mug shot from one of the arrests in Fairbanks the previous winter.

It was time to run. The destination seemed obvious—if they could make it. Although media accounts of the hijacking would later emphasize the men's initial demand to fly to Africa—"We *did* ask to go," Charlie would later confirm—he insists that the request was fanciful. "We knew the continent was a long ways."[38] Cuba, on the other hand, had in recent years received a steady stream of hijacked flights from the United States. Some of the perpetrators had sought political asylum from the government of Fidel Castro.

Indeed, Cuba's reputation as a sanctuary for beleaguered radicals on the lam had become a legend of the era. As Eldridge Cleaver was preparing to flee the United States to avoid returning to prison in 1968, for instance, his supporters had proposed that he board a commercial flight under the auspices of traveling to a speaking engagement out-of-state and then hijack the plane to Havana.[39] When over one thousand prisoners staged an uprising at Attica Correctional Facility in New York in September 1971, the inmates' demand for safe passage to a "non-imperialist country" was interpreted to mean Cuba or Algeria.[40] Back at the restaurant in San Bernardino, Alajo Adegbalola had pointedly advised them to try to reach Cuba if they found themselves facing prison or death during their mission to Mississippi. "We knew that Robert F. Williams and Eldridge Cleaver had been here," Charlie would explain years later in Havana. "Cuba was a multiracial society, and it was close to the US and well-connected with the rest of the world. . . . It was the best place to go into exile as a US revolutionary."[41]

Once again, Johnny proved his worth. Employed at Albuquerque International Airport as a fueler for Southwest Air Rangers, Inc., he was well acquainted with the airport's flight area, which had few security features.[42] Drawing up a map, Johnny indicated a place near the baggage claim where it was possible for someone to walk from the external pickup area onto the airport's main ramp where passengers boarded airliners.

That is, if they could get into the airport without being seen.

This part they would have to figure out themselves. Johnny dropped them off at a junkyard beside the airport and wished them good luck. They could hide out there, he told them, until they were ready. Behind the junkyard was a gas station. Beyond that, the lights of the runway blinked in the hazy darkness. Michael surveyed the scene skeptically. The three of them would be clearly visible once it got light. Charlie, however, was remembering how his platoon had protected themselves in Vietnam when they were pinned down by fire. He instructed Michael and Antar to scrape man-sized holes in the sand. Then they lay down, moving old furniture over the top for cover. There they lay all the next day, gnawed by hunger and thirst.

Sundown found the three comrades still hiding in their coffin-shaped holes. Once it was fully dark, the three men climbed stiffly out. Another cold night in the junkyard was out of the question. Squinting at a flight schedule, they settled on a target: a red-eye TWA flight to Chicago—flight 106—which was scheduled to depart around 2:00 a.m.—Saturday, November 27. But there was still the problem of getting to the airport's baggage claim without being noticed. Fatigued from thirst, Charlie risked walking down to the gas station to buy some sodas from the vending machine. Next to it was a payphone. An idea began to crystallize. Perhaps they could call a taxi to the airport? Michael demurred. A nighttime call for a taxi would be too suspicious. "What about a wrecker?" Charlie dialed a towing service and requested a tow truck to the intersection of San Jose Ave and Mulberry Street SE.

The headlights of the wrecker approached, moving slowly in the darkness. Charlie drew his .38 and pointed it at the startled driver. "I'm sure you can guess who we are."[43] Charlie beckoned Michael and Antar, and the three jumped into the cab. They ordered the driver to take them to the airport's baggage area. Just as Johnny had described, the airport's apron could be seen directly in front of them. There was no fence. The driver switched off the headlights. The four men sat in the darkness in silence.[44] As they watched the jet ramp, however, they could see two Boeing TWA airliners, both with mobile stairwells connected. Which was flight 106? Looking at the aircraft, Charlie saw that one of them had begun boarding. It had to be now.

The FBI later summarized the tow truck driver's statement: "Observing a TWA 727 being almost completely loaded, the one Negro individual who seemed to be in charge opened a valise which he was carrying, handed out a couple guns to the other two individuals, and then ordered [redacted] to move the truck in the vicinity of the TWA plane."[45] Only a curb stood between them. The hijackers ordered the driver forward. The wrecker "drove at full speed toward the curb, jumped same, and then entered onto the ramp area of Albuquerque International Airport."[46]

The tow truck halted beside the plane. Gripping their pistols, Charlie, Michael, and Antar jumped out. They hurried up the jet's boarding stairs—and came face to face with a flight attendant. She never missed a beat. "We must have looked like hell," Michael later recalled. "The stewardess got this big smile on her face and said, 'Don't get nervous, the plane is yours. Where do you want to go? Cuba? We'll take you. Don't get nervous.'"[47] Pushing past the flight crew, Charlie barged into the cockpit and leveled the pistol. "This plane is going to Cuba," he barked at the startled flight captain.[48] But the flight engineer had not yet arrived, so they were not going anywhere.

Through the cockpit windows Charlie now saw police cars, lights flashing, pouring onto the ramp around the airplane. "Get the pigs out of here and get the engineer up here right now," Charlie threatened the flight crew.[49] "I will start throwing people out of this plane."[50] The police retreated. The engineer boarded and confirmed fueling complete. TWA flight 106, with forty passengers aboard, pulled away, and by 2:07 a.m., it had sped down the runway and was airborne.[51]

By 1971, airplane hijackings in the United States had become so routine that they were a fixture of popular imagination. The passengers of the flight that Charlie, Michael, and Antar hijacked included uniformed US military personnel, a newspaper reporter, and Jerry McNerney, a West Point cadet who would go on to serve in the House of Representatives and the California State Senate. Arriving at the airport that night, McNerney later recalled, his mom had waved good-bye and said, "Now, don't get hijacked, Jerry."[52]

Gallows humor of the American hijacking era.

Indeed, one of the most storied acts of air piracy had unfolded the day before, when a man opened the rear door of a Boeing 727 flying at cruising altitude and, with $200,000 in ransom money, parachuted out somewhere over Washington state and vanished, never to be seen again.[53] When the *New York Times* reported the hijacking that Charlie, Michael, and Antar carried out in Albuquerque, their mug shots prominently displayed, the article appeared directly above one about the previous day's events over Washington. The facial composite sketch was of a hijacker who would become known as D. B. Cooper.[54]

The passengers of TWA flight 106 out of Albuquerque later recounted their ordeal. As the FBI would tell it, one of the hijackers "attempted to recruit a US Air Force enlisted passenger to join the Republic of New Africa [*sic*]," providing the Black man with a brochure about the organization, and "also afforded a white passenger an opportunity to go to Cuba which was declined."[55] Michael recalled it differently. Some "hippie" passengers, he later maintained, had passed the hijackers a handwritten poem celebrating the "three black warriors taking over the belly of a silver bird."[56] A newspaper reporter who happened to be aboard the hijacked flight characterized the perpetrators as "organized and incredibly calm," while a member of the flight crew told the FBI that the hijackers had been "firm, but friendly."[57]

So friendly that, abandoning caution, they allowed themselves a can of Michelob beer each and became chatty with the flight attendants to the point of carelessness. The next day, the *New York Times* printed flight attendant Elizabeth Caubre's claim that the men, who apparently had no intention of ever returning to the United States, had confessed to the shooting. "They told us the youngest one, Michael, who has now taken the African name Mancha [*sic*], had killed the officer in New Mexico."[58]

The hijacked TWA landed in Tampa to take on fuel. Charlie ordered the pilot to taxi to the far end of the runway—away from the police arrayed around the terminal. A single fuel truck would be permitted to approach the aircraft. Only after the fuel needle was up would the passengers be released.[59] Fearful of snipers, the RNA comrades stayed away from the cabin windows. FBI agents may well have been pointing rifles at the plane. "I have a secret signal," pilot John McGhee later told reporters. "If I make the designated movement, the FBI shoots out the tires. . . . I made darn sure not to give it." Having already shot a police officer, McGhee concluded, the three men "had nothing to lose" and were genuinely dangerous.[60] The airport sent a bus for the passengers. The crew remained, and the plane was soon airborne again.

The northern coast of Cuba is some 330 miles from Tampa, and so the plane had barely reached cruising altitude before it was descending again. Crouching in the cockpit behind the pilots, Charlie now heard air traffic controllers speaking in Spanish-accented English. They granted permission to enter Cuban airspace and issued landing instructions. Charlie had initially worried about being tricked into landing somewhere in Florida. He watched for any indication of a change in direction, but the plane flew only southwest, the early morning sun illuminating the cockpit from the left. Peering out, Charlie could see only ocean and sky, then the gray mass of land rushing toward them. The jet banked low. Plowed fields of bright rusty red earth appeared below. Now he could see red dirt roads, palm trees, and simple ramshackle homes with corrugated roofs. This was not Florida. On the horizon appeared an airport with a single runway.

The plane landed. Military jeeps approached. Cuban soldiers in green uniforms took up positions. A green-clad military officer ascended a mobile stairwell and stepped confidently into the aircraft. "Good morning," he said, looking at the flight crew and hijackers in turn. He was unarmed. Continuing to speak in accented English, the officer instructed Charlie and his companions to give him their weapons. They did. Then they followed him down the jet stairs, where another officer asked for their bullets. "Follow me," said the first officer. The hijackers had not been handcuffed.

The TWA flight crew was escorted into the airport separately, where Cuban officials questioned them briefly.[61] Then the Cubans switched to hospitality mode. Even by its critics, the government was credited for courteous and efficient treatment of foreign airline employees and passengers—whether from Colombia, Mexico, or the United States—who unwittingly found themselves hijacked to the island. Cuban officials facilitated the prompt return of aircraft, passengers, and crew to their country of origin. Foreign passengers and crew, now involuntary tourists in Cuba, were given refreshments, maybe even a round of strong mojitos or Cuba libres—made with rum and Canada Dry Cola, not American Coca-Cola, of course—and fed while aircraft were refueled. The guests were placed in hotels if the stay would be overnight, given dinner, sometimes a tour of Havana, and even invited back to Cuba for a vacation.[62] The crew of TWA flight 106 from Albuquerque fared no differently. Placed in suites in the Hotel Deauville beside El Malecón, Havana's picturesque seaside boulevard, the crew was taken on a personal tour of the city by Cuban officials before returning to Florida the next day.[63]

The RNA hijackers, however, were not taken to a seaside hotel. They were taken to an interrogation room inside the airport and then the questions began. Why had they hijacked a plane to Cuba? Why were they running from the police? The RNA comrades had decided to be as forthright as possible. "We are Black revolutionaries from the Republic of New Afrika. We are accused of killing a police officer. But it was self-defense. We are in solidarity with the Cuban Revolution."[64] The officers looked at them intently. There was more they wanted to know, the Cubans said, but first the hijackers had to be given a medical exam. The hijackers were given snacks and juice, then taken for a physical and asked about their health histories and vaccinations. Blood was drawn. Then they were put in the back seat of a new-looking Alfa Romeo, still uncuffed.

Driven deep into Havana, they arrived at some kind of guarded facility in a residential neighborhood. There they would be confined for the next six weeks. "It wasn't an iron-bar dungeon, it was like a room, with a porthole to pass food," Michael later recalled. "We played chess and cards. . . . We wrote a lot of letters. We sang Motown tunes, and when the Cuban guards told us to be quiet, we didn't understand."[65] They ate in the cell: rice, beans, chicken, something that resembled canned beef, and *tocinillo de cielo*, a flan-like dessert. Once each day, the three men were taken outside for sun and exercise.

The Cuban guards gave them books: Ernest Hemingway's *Old Man and the Sea*; a Spanish-English dictionary; a book in Spanish that appeared to be about Cuban history; and Jack Belden's *China Shakes the World*, which contained "Gold Flower's Story."[66] The story, which took place before the 1949 communist revolution, was about the life of a Chinese girl from an impoverished family who was forced into an arranged marriage. The book's description of poverty and the patriarchal control of women and girls made a deep impression on Charlie. "It was devastating for me," he remembers.[67]

Cuban officials knew that the three hijackers were accused murderers before their interrogation. Indeed, the legal charges had arrived in Havana before they did. The US State Department had filed an extradition request—facilitated by the Swiss embassy in Havana, since the United States had no embassy in the country—while the hijacked jet was still refueling in Tampa.[68] According to a State Department spokesperson in Washington, the Cuban government had been informed "that these men are charged with murder and we hope it will be possible to return them to the United States for trial."[69] In a note to the State Department dated November 29, two days after the hijacking, the Cuban government, communicating as always through the Swiss embassy in Havana, said only that the hijackers would be dealt with in accordance to Cuban law.[70]

But the Cubans were conducting their own investigation. Hijackers from the United States were as likely to be spies or common criminals, state security officials presumed, as persecuted political activists. The facility where they were being detained, Charlie later learned, was none other than Villa Marista, an important nerve center of La Seguridad del Estado—Cuban state security. Occupying an entire city block in a nondescript residential neighborhood called Sevillano in the heart of the Havana municipality of Diez de Octubre, complete with vegetable gardens and exercise areas, Villa Marista was operated by the Dirección General de Inteligencia, referred to in popular parlance as "G2," and fell under the purview of the Ministry of the Interior. The officers in the airport, of course, were also from state security. Now they interrogated the hijackers pointedly, returning to various elements of their story, cross-checking details, dates, and names. What exactly had occurred on the highway in New Mexico? Why had they been so heavily armed? What kind of mission were they taking part in? How did they escape the police dragnet in Albuquerque?

The questioning shifted to the RNA. The intelligence agents seemed unfamiliar with the organization, unlike the Black Panther Party, whose personalities and philosophy they appeared to know well. Who were the RNA's leaders? What was the organization's ideology? Why had they decided to come to Cuba? And, crucially, did they know anyone on the island? Charlie, Michael, and Antar answered the questions dutifully.

At times the officers appeared skeptical. As the RNA comrades would soon learn, the Cubans had plenty of prior experience with airplane hijackers. Dozens had arrived in recent years, with eclectic motivations and philosophies: activists and *lumpenproletariat*, idealistic radicals and apolitical criminals, lone actors and members of political organizations, all uninvited, all seeking sanctuary in Cuba.

Chapter 6

Free Territory of *América*

It was nighttime when Charlie, Michael, and Antar were released from the Villa Marista state security facility in Havana in early January 1972, some six weeks after their arrival in Cuba. Escorted out of the compound, they squeezed into the back seat of a wine-colored Alfa Romeo. Cruising through the humid darkness of Diez de Octubre, they could make out the gray forms of houses but little else. "It's just an *apagón* . . . a blackout," the Cuban officer riding in the front reassured them. "*No hay problema.*" The RNA comrades exchanged glances but said nothing. The car stopped in front of a building, what appeared to be a large house. A uniformed officer came out with a flashlight. They were shown to bunk beds in a small room and then abruptly left alone.

They awoke the next morning to find that they were in a mansion. La Casa de Los Transitos—or "Hijack House," as some of its occupants had dubbed it wryly—was a kind of halfway home for American hijackers in Havana who had been released from security detention. Located in Siboney—a neighborhood in the Playa municipality of Havana, which had been wealthy before the 1959 revolution—the area's columnated colonial mansions and nineteenth-century villas had been either converted into government offices and boarding schools or subdivided into apartments that were now occupied by working-class Cuban families. Two-stories high, its blue paint peeling, the mansion had spacious patios and a swimming pool, although with no water. Managed by Cuba's immigration department, under the purview of the Ministry of the Interior (MININT), and supervised by two live-in officers, the house provided each resident with a bunk in communal dormitories. The Americans were encouraged to study Spanish, learn about Cuban history, and acclimate while they decided what kind of work or education they wanted to pursue.

Like the RNA comrades, most of the American hijackers at the house had come to Cuba to escape legal charges. Over a spartan breakfast of coffee, bread, and milk, they introduced themselves. One was George 'Geo' López, who had been one of seven young men of Salvadorean, Honduran, and Nicaraguan descent who had been charged in the killing of a white San Francisco police officer in the city's Mission district on May 1, 1969, in a high-profile, racially charged case. The men would become known as Los Siete de la Raza.[1]

Charlie remembered the case well from the Bay Area. The slain officer and his partner had detained a group of Latino men on suspicion of burglary. A fight ensued and officer Joseph Brodnik was shot with the gun belonging to his partner, Paul McGoran. Credited with some four hundred burglary arrests, McGoran had been decorated by the police force. Witnesses interviewed by the defense characterized Brodnik as a quick-tempered racist, bitter at the influx of Latino immigrants into the Mission, a rogue cop known for intimidation and false arrests.[2] The movement to defend Los Siete de la Raza became a cause célèbre that intertwined the third-worldist and multiracial radical politics of the Bay Area.[3]

To their supporters, Los Siete symbolized "every Brown brother harassed on every street corner in this country."[4] Their legal defense became a social movement in its own right. Launching a free breakfast program for children and a community medical clinic—modeled on the programs of the Black Panther Party (BPP)—as well as a legal aid service formed in response to the death of a Latino man in police custody, the grassroots effort to free Los Siete proclaimed itself a "defense organization for the people."[5] The case galvanized the Bay Area's Latino communities, supported by members of the mostly white New Left and the Panthers, which provided logistical support and one of its star attorneys, Charles Garry.[6] All the defendants were eventually acquitted in November 1970.

But Geo, the only defendant not to stand trial, was long gone. As police officers kicked in doors in the Mission in the days after the shooting, the accused men, fearing for their lives, fled.[7] As the *Black Panther* explained, "Why did Los Siete run? They were fleeing a scene of mortal danger, a danger that had nothing to do with the facts of the incident. They were Brown, and a White cop had been killed."[8]

Geo left California and kept running. Traveling under pseudonyms, he made his way to Baja California, Mexico, before sneaking back into the United States. Never politically inclined, he had become radicalized by his experience of fugitivity and the solidarity of strangers. The summer of 1969 found Geo in Denver, where he became involved with the Chicano civil rights organization Crusade for Justice under the alias "Juan Gómez." One of the organization's activists would later describe the mysterious newcomer who arrived at their headquarters: "young, about 5 feet, 9 inches tall . . . shoulder-length black hair . . . barrio-accented English . . . softly spoken . . . looking like a barrio-bred Che Guevara . . . popular with young women in the growing social circle of youth activists."[9] Fall found Geo living with a collective of activists in the New Mexico countryside. On July 1, 1970, four months before the Los Siete defendants were acquitted, Geo hijacked a DC-8 airliner from Las Vegas to Havana.[10]

As hijackings from the United States to Cuba continued in 1970, Geo was joined at the MININT house in Siboney by several other Americans. Many were still living there when Charlie, Michael, and Antar arrived. One of them was James Cherry.

A former member of the BPP's chapter in Atlantic City, New Jersey, Cherry arrived in Cuba in fall 1970 to escape murder charges in the killing of a police officer.[11] Atlantic City, known in movement lore as the place where the spectacle of the Mississippi Freedom Democratic Party's fight to seat Black delegates at the 1964 Democratic National Convention unfolded, had witnessed a surge of civil rights organizing. By 1969, however, Black Power had come to the Jersey Shore. Black Panthers in Atlantic City opened an activist space called the Black Community Information Center, and in February 1970 launched a free breakfast program, supported by donations from local businesses, which was soon feeding five hundred neighborhood kids a day.[12]

That same month, Cherry and two other Atlantic City Panthers were arrested on misdemeanor charges. The *Black Panther* described their trial on "the fabricated charge of creating disorder in a public building" as political persecution.[13] The city's police department, community activists had long maintained, harbored racist white officers. Some Black officers agreed, signing a "list of grievances against alleged racism, segregation, and brutality within their own department" in August 1970.[14] A month later, however, the department closed ranks when a white police officer, John P. Burke, was felled by a shotgun blast to the throat while attempting to question two men on September 30, 1970.[15] Cherry, alleged to have been in the vicinity, was later implicated by witnesses. Cherry fled the city. He would later maintain his innocence, although it's not clear whether activists in Atlantic City shared this view. Curiously, neither the local Black Panthers nor the national organization appear to have taken up the case or supported his legal defense.[16]

There was also Edna Lee, one of three women at the MININT house in Siboney. A community activist of Chinese descent from San Francisco, Edna and her companion, Tyrone Won, had hijacked a single-engine Cessna from Ambergris Caye, a tourist paradise in British Honduras (later Belize), to Cuba on March 25, 1970. It is not clear whether Lee was fleeing from legal charges at the time of the hijacking, although Won was. Reputedly a member of the Red Guard Party, a Chinese American leftist organization founded in San Francisco's Chinatown that had arisen in the context of the Third World

Liberation Front struggle at San Francisco State College, Won had been accused of killing a Los Angeles police officer.[17] The pilot of the Cessna, who had been ferrying tourists, later recalled the hijacking: "There had been a lot of people around but suddenly they just melted away. Then a girl appeared with a double-barreled shotgun pointed at my ribs." Ordering the passengers off, Lee and Won directed the pilot to fly to Cuba. They eventually landed on a dirt road in the middle of sugarcane fields. Lee and Won were taken into state security custody. The pilot was taken to a hotel.[18]

And there was Richard Frederick Dixon, who had arrived a month before Charlie, Michael, and Antar. At thirty-one years old, Dixon was a veritable elder at the MININT house. A white man from Pontiac, Michigan, he had recently been paroled after serving prison time for bank robbery. His desire to reach Cuba was not precipitated by fresh legal trouble, however, but by political idealism. Inspired by the Cuban Revolution, Dixon decided that he wanted to join it. Nervous and clutching a .38 pistol in his pocket when he arrived at the Detroit airport on October 9, 1971, Dixon's demeanor was suspicious enough to alert Eastern Airlines staff, who had been profiling potential hijackers. Drawing the .38 as he was approached by airport security, Dixon took a flight attendant hostage and boarded a jetliner. It was the pilot's second hijacking to Cuba.[19] Dixon was talkative during the flight. Describing himself as a product of a "white middle-class establishment family," according to his flight attendant hostage, Dixon explained that he was opposed to the "American way of life" and admired the Black freedom struggle.[20] "He kept talking about Angela Davis and George Jackson and how he agreed with their philosophies."[21] As the plane refueled in Havana, crew and passengers were fed steak and French fries by their Cuban hosts while Dixon was led away by officers.[22]

Eager to taste free air in Cuba after weeks of confinement, Charlie, Michael, and Antar decided to explore Havana that very afternoon. The collective residence for hijackers, the MININT officers explained, was not house arrest. They could go anywhere they wanted. With Geo, James, Edna, and Richard leading the way, they caught a bus to downtown Havana.

The wide tree-lined boulevards of Siboney, Miramar, and Vedado gave way to a dense grid of narrow streets and maze-like *solares,* or subdivided tenement buildings, as they entered the Cayo Hueso neighborhood of Central Havana. The bus turned right onto a busy avenue lined with shops, long ago nationalized, some adorned with half-functioning neon signs from the prerevolutionary era. This was Galiano Street, Geo explained, the teaming heart of *el barrio.* Making their way back up to Vedado on foot, they glimpsed the famous Habana Libre hotel, which Fidel Castro and hundreds of shaggy guerrillas had occupied to use as a temporary headquarters after the revolution. Across the street, a line stretched halfway around the block as people waited to be seated at the wildly popular Coppelia, a huge subsidized ice cream parlor that took up half a city block. Below were the clubs and theaters of La Rampa, the final section of Calle 23 as it plunges down to El Malecón, the city's iconic seaside promenade.

They found a table in a state-run *cafetería*. Over Cuban-style pizzas and cold pineapple juice, Geo explained how things worked. "The Cuban government considers us guests, at least for now, so we don't have to work," he said. "They mainly want us to try to learn Spanish and adjust to Cuba." As wards of the state, Geo explained, the hijackers at the MININT house were guaranteed their basic needs: three meals a day at the house, a place to sleep, basic essentials such as socks and soap, if they were available, and a small cash living stipend. As guests in Cuba, however, the Americans would have to prove their willingness to contribute to society. They were encouraged to enroll in university, study Spanish, or do volunteer labor. A few of the hijackers had taken jobs for wages to supplement their stipends, allowing them to buy extra food, go out at night, or take weekend trips to the beach. Geo was working at a soap factory, while James was apprenticing as a welder.

Although the collective house for hijackers fell under the jurisdiction of MININT, their political contact with the Cuban government was the Instituto Cubano de Amistad con los Pueblos (ICAP)—the Cuban Institute for Friendship with the People. Founded in 1960, ICAP's role was to facilitate solidarity between the Cuban Revolution and its political supporters abroad from a variety of social movements and political formations, including those from the United States. By the early 1970s, ICAP had facilitated innumerable US delegations to Cuba, including the National Lawyers Guild, the American Civil Liberties Union, the Socialist Workers Party, and the Communist Party USA. As an intermediary between foreign leftists and the Cuban state, ICAP was also the gateway through which the foreign hijackers could participate in political activities in Cuba.

A few days after their arrival at the MININT house, ICAP sent a staff worker to visit Charlie, Michael, and Antar. Her name was Orlaida Cabrera, and she was a young Afro-Cuban revolutionary from Camagüey Province. Growing up, her family had been so poor that she often missed school because she had no shoes. Her whole family became revolutionaries. When the Batista government fell to Fidel Castro's grassroots rebel army on January 1, 1959, Cabrera would later explain, it was due in no small part to the energies of a multitude of Cubans from humble backgrounds who dedicated their lives to the cause of remaking society.[23] Studying sociology and English at the

University of Havana, which was now free for all Cubans, she was recruited into ICAP's North American division, the branch tasked with strengthening Cuban ties with the US Left. Cabrera also worked with some of the American hijackers and exiles. Charlie, Michael, and Antar, she later recalled, told her that they had come to Cuba because they feared for their lives after being accused of killing a police officer. Familiar with the horror stories about US police murdering Black people for lesser crimes, Cabrera needed no convincing.[24]

Cabrera asked them what they wanted to do in Cuba. "She was all business," Charlie recalled. "She was strict. But she was also kind, and she translated for us a lot once we joined the internationalist brigades."[25] Classes at the university had already begun for the semester. But the fabled sugar harvest, or *zafra*, which lasted from winter through late spring, was just beginning. North Americans, they knew, had already participated in it. In the Bay Area, the RNA comrades had read testimonies from members of the Venceremos Brigade: multiracial delegations of US solidarity activists, several hundred strong, who began traveling to the island annually in 1969, in violation of Washington's travel ban, to evaluate the Cuban Revolution with their own eyes and participate in volunteer labor.[26]

In Cuba, being a revolutionary meant working, including through the contribution of voluntary labor. Government officials were not exempt. The year before the RNA comrades arrived on the island, Cuba's annual sugar harvest had become a spectacle of revolutionary mobilization on an enormous scale, dramatizing the way in which volunteer labor was linked in national discourse to the development of the nation through collective sacrifice. The government had set a massive production goal for the harvest—ten million tons, or *la zafra de los diez millones*, as it was christened—which sought to mobilize the labor of the entire island in the service of the greater good. Despite Cuba's efforts to diversify its economy, sugar enabled the state to capture foreign exchange. The Soviet Union had supported its socialist ally in the Caribbean by paying above-market prices, providing a reliable subsidy that was insulated from the price fluctuations of global commodity markets.[27]

Cutting sugarcane was notoriously backbreaking work. Labor brigades from across the island, many of them augmented by foreign volunteers, worked continuously throughout the *zafra* of winter 1972, officially christened the Year of Socialist Emulation. The Cuban media chronicled the progress of the cane-cutting brigades as if covering the exploits of a national sports team at the Olympics. Photos of triumphant-looking young volunteers, some posing in groups with their machetes, others smiling in front of thickets of cane stalks, accompanied the wall-to-wall coverage of their progress in Cuban newspapers during the harvest season.[28]

It was into this war for the development of the new socialist nation that Charlie, Michael, and Antar enlisted in the winter of 1972, when they joined a labor brigade sponsored by ICAP. The volunteers, Cuban and foreign, lived and worked together in the countryside for several weeks at a time. And so it was that just a couple of weeks after their release from confinement at Villa Marista, the RNA comrades boarded a bus with Geo, Richard, and James and traveled east of Havana to the town of Jaruco, where they had been assigned to the Nuestra América Brigade, an international labor contingent composed of volunteers from the western hemisphere, primarily Latin America. They were given a lesson in the handling of the short cleaver-like machetes, called *mochas*. Then they were assigned to a sub-brigade of workers and turned loose to do battle with the endless hectares of cane.[29]

For the RNA comrades, voluntary labor in Jaruco would prove to be a singularly formative experience, one that would introduce them to the heady revelation of anti-imperialist internationalism. Hailing from Colombia, Uruguay, Brazil, Haiti, Guatemala, Mexico, and Argentina, many members of the Nuestra América Brigade were themselves political exiles. Indeed, Havana in the early 1970s seemed to throng with foreign *militantes*. The arrival of so many Latin American exiles—many fleeing violent repression under right-wing military dictatorships supported by Washington, others drawn by the radical allure of Cuba's unfolding revolution—imbued Havana with a palpable atmosphere of hemispheric insurgency. The city, in the words of one exiled Brazilian leftist guerrilla, Marília Guimarães, had become "*una América Latina completa*."[30]

Some of the Latin Americans, Charlie was surprised to learn, had also reached the island by hijacking airplanes.[31] One was Guimarães. A combatant in the Vanguarda Armada Revolucionária Palmares, a Marxist-Leninist formation engaged in armed struggle against the right-wing dictatorship that had risen to power with the US-backed 1964 coup d'état, Guimarães, her two small children in tow, hijacked a plane to Cuba in 1970 with five other comrades. Arriving in Havana during the enormous *zafra de los diez millones* mobilization, Guimarães noted the "deserted streets that announced the work in the countryside," augmented by internationalist volunteers: "Canadians, Americans, Brazilians swell the ranks of millions of Cubans determined to reach the goal of 10 million."[32]

Most of the Latin Americans, however, were formal political asylees who had been invited by the Cuban government to seek sanctuary from the anti-Left violence unfolding under Southern Cone dictatorships. Placed in collectives, or *colonias*, of several dozen people from the same political organization in shared houses and compounds around Havana—and, eventually, across the entire island—these political asylees found in Cuba not only sanctuary from acute danger but also training for what lay ahead. Combining regimented physical work with study of political theory, the Latin American exiles trained their bodies and their minds for their eventual return to the revolutionary struggle in their own countries.[33]

Darío Croc, a Uruguayan student activist who joined the Marxist-Leninist Movimiento de Liberación Nacional-Tupamaros and endured torture at the hands of government security forces, would later describe his elation upon arriving at Havana's José Martí airport in 1972 with other asylees aboard a Cubana de Aviación airliner. After undergoing a medical evaluation, the passengers were taken to a large collective house managed by MININT in a converted mansion in Siboney, remarkably like the nearby residence for American hijackers, complete with ample terraces, a pool without water, and bunk beds in dormitories. This was not a vacation, however, but a continuation of the political struggle in Uruguay. The exiles would have to maintain a rigorous schedule of work and study and abide by security protocols. "It is not going to be easy for you," the intaking Cuban officer had warned them. "Don't think this is a paradise. This is not easy. This is the dictatorship of the proletariat."[34]

But if revolutionary Cuba was a beacon for hemispheric leftists, not all who sought its shores were *militantes* from political parties and organized movements. Indeed, some of the airplane hijackers from Latin America, not unlike their US counterparts, defied neat classifications. The case of Colombia, where dozens of hijackings to Cuba originated—more than any other country in the hemisphere after the United States—was representative.[35] As scholar Massimo Di Ricco argues, far from being members of established political movements, a sizable percentage of the Colombians were ordinary people, some with inchoate leftist ideals, but whose acts of air piracy were motivated principally by the desire to leave behind poverty and lack of opportunity. For them, the radical hope embodied by the Cuban Revolution lay not in the possibility of forging connections with third world revolutionaries or of receiving guerrilla training but in the guarantee of universal social rights: access to employment, healthcare, and education, and the possibility of starting new lives in a society of opportunity for the poor.[36]

The material accomplishments and radical aura of the Cuban Revolution, which drew both political activists and everyday people from across Latin America, had also impressed visitors from the North. One of them was Black Panther activist George Mason Murray, whose dismissal from his position as an English instructor at San Francisco State College in 1968 had been one of the sparks that set off campus protests by the Third World Liberation Front that had so galvanized Michael Finney and his classmates at Lincoln High School. Upon his return from a trip to Havana at the invitation of the Cuban government in August of that year, Murray had described Cuba as a kind of "factory of revolution," marveling at the multitude of global radicals who seemed to be everywhere. "That was the thing that, I guess, had the strongest effect on me," Murray later reported of his visit to the island. "The whole country is geared toward the fomenting of the revolution, not just in Latin America but everywhere in the world. And there you meet people—we met people from Guinea, Congo, South Africa, comrades from North Vietnam, South Vietnam, . . . North Korea, comrades from China, other parts of the world where people are actively engaging in struggle."[37]

From the so-called Nordic Brigades of Scandinavia to the delegations from occupied Palestine, Cuba's volunteer camps in 1972 teemed with solidarity activists and militants from around the world. Yet it was undoubtedly the Latin American political refugees—whom everyone in Havana called Los Latinos—who most impressed Charlie, Michael, and Antar. "These guys were all guerillas, man, people fighting for liberation in their homelands," Charlie would later say of his subunit within the Nuestra América Brigade. "They were revolutionaries. It was very compelling for us to have contact with freedom fighters from around the world." Three Colombian brothers, all members of Las Fuerzas Armadas Revolucionarias de Colombia, a Marxist-Leninist guerrilla movement, particularly impressed him. "These guys had been in the mountains. You could tell by the toughness of their skins and hands that they were country people. Being around them was a complete awakening for us. We realized that we were not just some isolated cases, [that] we were not alone. In our minds, we were revolutionaries like them, who just happened to be North American, and we developed a strong kinship with each other. We exchanged political perspectives, taught each other about the political situations in our countries. There was a lot of camaraderie and solidarity."[38]

Inspired by the discipline of Los Latinos, who seemed to approach political education with the same zeal as voluntary labor, Charlie, Michael, Antar, Richard, and others formed a study group in the winter of 1972 that they called the Revolutionary Collective.[39] Meeting on Sunday mornings, its members read and debated texts on Cuban history, radical theory, and anticolonialism. The leadership rotated each week, so that each member was responsible for selecting texts, ensuring that people were reading them, and facilitating the debates. The Revolutionary Collective would ultimately play a decisive role in their socialization to Cuba. Where other American hijackers failed to adapt, the discipline and camaraderie of the collective allowed its members to make the most of their desire to succeed as guests in revolutionary Cuba.

The MININT house had accumulated a small collection of books and political literature, some of it donated by ICAP, which often received materials in English from visiting US organizations, such as the National Lawyers Guild. The members of the Revolutionary Collective now set about building a respectable radical library. As the group's studies progressed, reading was augmented by research assignments involving improvised ethnography. Armed with their halting knowledge of Spanish, the hijackers set out to interview people in the neighborhood about their experiences during the Cuban Revolution, the nature of Afro-Cuban religion, and the lived realities of socialism. The results of the interviews were then presented during study sessions for analysis and debate.[40]

Havana was home to at least one other political collective of North Americans. The Union of North Americans was an association of American expatriates in Havana, including journalists, translators, and other trusted professionals who had been invited to work for the Cuban government. The Union of North Americans was an officially sanctioned body that liaised directly with the Cuban government through ICAP. Members met to discuss issues related to US solidarity with Cuba, hold political study sessions, draft political resolutions, and march as a bloc in the annual May Day parade in Havana.[41] The Revolutionary Collective, by contrast, was more informal, yet it allowed the hijackers to demonstrate their political commitment to the Cuban revolutionary process and to show their desire to contribute to society. As the Revolutionary Collective became a cohesive unit that studied and worked together, it also gained the respect of MININT, which eventually placed the collective in their own two-story house in Miramar, a neighborhood that, they soon learned, was dotted with other collective houses that the Cuban government had assigned to foreign exiles from Latin America.

In the coming months, the MININT house for hijackers in Siboney would receive new arrivals from the United States. One of them was Patrick Dolan Critton. Born in Harlem, Critton had been a high school honors student and went on to study history and political science at Lehman College. One of only a handful of Black students on campus, Critton become an activist and a member of the Black Student Union. He graduated, got married, became a father, and took a post as a teacher and youth counselor for the City of New York while continuing his community activism. As the left-wing politics of the 1960s radicalized, so did Critton. At some point he joined the Republic of New Afrika, although whether in an official capacity or as an informal affiliate, it is not clear. Certainly, his activities in the coming months would not have been publicly sanctioned by the RNA's national leadership.

With a group of comrades, Critton organized a clandestine armed cell to fund the expansion of their community programs. Robbing banks to fund community programs, Critton felt, held a certain poetic justice. "We consider[ed] our armed expropriations as back payment for our 40 acres and mules," Critton later wrote.[42] Emboldened by Frantz Fanon's defense of anticolonial violence as a tool of both political and psychic liberation, Critton carried a copy of *The Wretched of the Earth* in his pocket during the heists.[43] "I've never felt in my heart and soul we were wrong to engage in armed struggle. . . . Being a student of History [*sic*] enabled me to trace the footprints of our peoples['] struggle throughout our four centuries in America."[44] The Black Revolutionary Assault Team, as Critton's group referred to itself, eventually launched a campaign of bombings targeting the New York consular facilities of apartheid South Africa, as well as Mobutu Sese Seko's right-wing post-Lumumba government in Zaire.

Hundreds of political bombings by insurrectionary left-wing groups, ranging from the Weather Underground to activists fighting for Puerto Rican independence, had shaken New York in recent years. In 1971, Critton's militants began contributing their own blasts. On the morning of April 12, 1971, for instance, the Associated Press office received a phone call: "This is the black revolution assault team," the caller allegedly stated. "We have just bombed the South African consul. More power to the people."[45] Although there were no injuries within the damaged Madison Avenue office—its employees were on leave following the Easter holiday—the symbolic attack was intended, Critton later wrote, as "a sign of solidarity with our brothers and sisters under demonic apartheid. The apartheid government got no peace even though they were in New York City."[46]

Then, in July, Critton's cell staged a bank robbery in Manhattan. A furious shoot-out with police ensued, resulting in the death of Critton's brother-in-law. Fearing that he would be identified, Critton went underground, living in one of the organization's safe houses. Eventually he fled to Canada. Purchasing a ticket aboard Air Canada flight 932 from Thunder Bay, Ontario, to Toronto for December 26, 1971, Critton waited until after takeoff and then handed a flight attendant a note: "Think," it read. "We have fragmentation grenades and a 38 calibre revolver. Take me to the captain in the cockpit. We are going to Havana, Cuba. This is no joke."[47] Described by one crew member as "very, very rational and rather calm," Critton allowed the unsuspecting passengers to deplane at the scheduled destination of Toronto—they learned that they had been hijacked only later—and directed the crew to refuel and fly to Havana.[48]

The hijacking of flight 932 would stand as the only successful act of air piracy to an international destination in Canada's history. Of course, other nations were not so fortunate. Upon landing in Havana, the crew of Critton's Air Canada flight discovered that two other hijacked aircraft were already present at the airport. Cuban officers boarded the plane and took Critton away.[49] "The tropical hot night air," he later wrote, "was the first thing that hit me when I emerged from the plane."[50] Critton, however, had done his research. From press accounts about the spate of recent hijackings from the United States, he had learned something of the experiences of those who had made it to Cuba. So confident was Critton of where he would soon be residing that he told the flight crew that if someone should need to contact him, he could receive mail at "Hijacker House in Havana."[51]

Together with Critton, there was Jimmy (James) Brewton of Chicago. Known to his comrades as Ali Shanna, he had helped found a chapter of the Black Panther Party in the downstate Illinois city of Carbondale, where he attended Southern Illinois University (SIU). A liberal college enclave that had witnessed a surge of student activism during the civil rights era, Carbondale nonetheless evinced deep racial divisions. The city's Black communities experienced widespread poverty. The Panthers and their supporters converted the first floor of a house in a residential neighborhood into a community center featuring a food cooperative, a free breakfast program for children, political education classes, a clothing giveaway, a youth after-school program, and a car service to bring people to a local prison to visit incarcerated family members.[52] The Panthers slept upstairs. Interviewed by a reporter, Brewton explained that the young activists had deep ties to the community. "We have no leaders; we have brothers and sisters here just working for the movement—this is an organization of the people, by the people, and for the people."[53]

The charismatic yet sensitive Brewton, with his talent for community organizing, was central to these efforts. And he had other qualities too. To those who knew him, Brewton exuded something intangible. He had been a member of the powerful Black P. Stone Nation street gang as a teenager in Chicago. "He was always carrying a lot of books," one of his comrades in the Carbondale Panthers, Reggie Brown, later wrote. Yet he guessed that the serious young man that he had seen around the SIU campus was "more than a studious intellectual."[54] Brown was not disappointed.

The Carbondale BPP had a tense relationship with the police from the start. When Chicago Panther chair Fred Hampton traveled to Carbondale to speak on the SIU campus in November 1969, Brewton, fearing that the Panther leader might be a target for the police, coordinated Hampton's security, secluding him in a safe house.[55] Three weeks later, however, Hampton and fellow Panther Mark Clark were assassinated—Hampton while he was asleep in his own bed—by Chicago police in the early morning hours of December 4, 1969.[56] Panther chapters throughout the United States mobilized to defend themselves, but police harassment and trumped-up charges continued. It was in this context that Brewton was arrested in July 1970 and charged with an unsolved local robbery. When police tried to apprehend him, a shoot-out erupted, and Brewton allegedly shot one of the officers in the leg before escaping.

Evading capture for two months, Brewton made his way to the southern Illinois city of Cairo, where he hoped to aid Black residents in defending themselves against a wave of racist violence.[57] A place notorious for white supremacist activity, by 1970 Cairo had become, in the words of the US Commission on Civil Rights, "synonymous nationwide with racial violence with a northern accent."[58] The epicenter of Cairo's race war was a group of Black housing projects that had been repeatedly subjected to sniper attacks by white vigilantes and the Ku Klux Klan. One photograph reproduced in the *Black Panther* in July 1970 depicted a Black man inspecting the side of his car, which was pockmarked with over sixty bullet holes.[59]

It was in this tense atmosphere in southern Illinois in the fall of 1970 that heavily armed police attempted to raid the Black Panther Party's community center in Carbondale on November 12, 1970. Remembering the Hampton-Clark assassination, the Carbondale Panthers had fortified the second floor of the house with sandbags and stockpiled ammunition and gas masks. "We weren't going to be ambushed and killed in our beds like the brothers in Chicago," one of the Carbondale Panthers later asserted.[60] In the ensuing gunfight, police shot some 778 rounds into the Panther house's walls and windows, but return fire succeeded in preventing the police from entering. Daybreak found police cars perforated and shell casings littering the ground. Miraculously, no one was killed. As daylight shined through bullet holes in the walls, neighbors surrounded the Panther house to prevent further police attack and mediated a ceasefire.[61]

Now facing charges of attempted murder, the Carbondale 3, as the Panther prisoners came to be called, were defended by the People's Law Office (PLO), the intrepid radical legal collective from Chicago that the Panthers had asked to lead the investigation of the Hampton-Clark assassination in December 1969. Opening a field office in Carbondale, the PLO lawyers developed a close relationship with the city's Panthers. "We were particularly impressed by the leadership of Jimmy Brewton, later known as Ali Shanna," the PLO later wrote.[62] "Ali radiated leadership and quiet charisma," PLO attorney Flint Taylor recalled decades later. "He was a Carbondale version of Fred Hampton."[63] The Carbondale 3 were eventually acquitted by a multiracial Carbondale jury that included "a young, white Vietnam veteran," Taylor later wrote, who "demonstrated to his fellow jurors how the Panthers had defended themselves against the police attack."[64]

But Brewton was taking no chances in court himself. His subsequent hijacking to Cuba appears to have been a bid to avoid standing trial. Joining forces with a former Panther named Joseph Terron Bennett, the two commandeered a Bahamas-bound Chalk's International Airlines seaplane out of Miami on March 7, 1972. Shooting the pilot and an airline mechanic in the process—both survived—Bennett and Brewton exchanged gunfire with police before forcing the co-pilot, who had never flown solo before, to take them to Havana.[65] They were released from Cuban state security custody and sent to the MININT house for hijackers in Siboney in the late spring of 1972. Brewton would become one of Charlie's close friends in Havana.

William Lee Brent, an ex-Black Panther, had already been living at the MININT collective house but had been away cutting sugar cane when Charlie, Michael, and Antar arrived. Now he returned to Siboney. Bill Brent, as he was known, had joined the Oakland chapter of the party in early 1968 during a period of rapid growth for the organization, which saw the Panthers evolve from a local organization into a major political force with dozens of chapters around the nation.[66] Disciplined, studious, and dedicated, Brent rose quickly through the ranks to become a trusted member of the Party's Oakland cadre, where he served as an armed bodyguard for Eldridge Cleaver and other Panther leaders and often inaugurated Panther rallies by reading aloud the organization's Ten-Point Program. His exhilarating months with the Panthers were cut short, however, when he was involved in a shoot-out with San Francisco police on November 19, 1968.

Brent would later write that he been severely sleep deprived and high after taking Dexedrine pills to stay awake for several days in a row in order to fulfill his Panther duties. Pulling up to a gas station in the marked van that the organization used to deliver the *Black Panther*, Brent says that he walked "half dazed" to the attendant's window to obtain change for a twenty-dollar bill. "My jacket was open and the handle of [the] automatic was sticking out of my waistband," Brent later wrote. "The attendant looked down at the gun, then up at my face. Whatever he saw there made him scoop up all the bills in the cash box and hand them to me. Without thinking, or even glancing at the money, I stuffed them into my jacket pocket, walked back to the truck, and climbed in."[67] San Francisco police, responding to the attendant's report of a robbery, pursued the van. Seeing police, guns in their hands, running toward him, Brent, believing that he was about to be killed, fired first, wounding two officers. The Panther organization, which was currently enmeshed in a high-stakes legal battle to secure Huey Newton's released from prison, summarily expelled Brent for the incident, branding him a government agent intent on tarnishing the already embattled public image of the Panthers.[68] Finding himself isolated and with no resources for a legal defense, Brent hijacked a New York–bound TWA flight out of San Francisco on June 17, 1969, and diverted it to Havana.[69]

Upon arriving in Cuba, however, Brent languished in state security detention for twenty-two months, apparently on suspicion of being a spy. The source of the allegation appears to have been Panther leader Eldridge Cleaver, who had come to Cuba the previous year as a formal political asylee and was in Havana at the time of Brent's hijacking.[70] Brent later described his security evaluation in Cuba to the *Black Scholar*:

> When I first got here I had to go through a period of investigation. I was treated with a certain amount of suspicion, which is natural and understandable. But I was also treated very kindly, very warmly. I wasn't greeted as being the great black liberator or the great black revolutionary who came from the States with all the answers to the problems of the people. I was treated as someone who had come here without permission and who had to be investigated so that the authorities would know whether that person was someone trustworthy, someone willing and able to contribute to the development of the revolution in some way, or whether I was an agent or some nut or someone who might be dangerous or harmful. But after the period of investigation was over, I was given a place to live. All my basic needs were provided for—food, clothing, housing, money to spend—and I was free to travel in any part of the country that I wanted to.[71]

Brent was finally released to the MININT house in Siboney in April 1971.[72] Despite his hurt feelings at having been expelled from the Panthers, an organization he deeply loved, Brent made a supreme effort to prove his willingness to adapt to Cuba. Joining voluntary labor brigades and becoming involved with the Union of North Americans, he worked at a soap factory and took other paid jobs, eventually graduating from the University of Havana and becoming a schoolteacher. Settling down in Cuba and marrying, Brent eventually won the lasting respect of his Cuban hosts.

Other American hijackers in Havana would not be so fortunate.

Chapter 7

Conflicting Solidarities

As they settled in at the Ministry of the Interior (MININT) residence for American hijackers in Siboney, Charlie, Michael, and Antar reflected on their efforts to adjust to socialist Cuba and to convince their hosts that they were legitimate political exiles, worthy of protection from extradition. Many of the other Americans, including Bill Brent, Geo López, Patrick Critton, Jimmy Brewton, and Richard Dixon, were doing the same. Although they were strangers in a foreign land, they tried to demonstrate their willingness to contribute to the nation's revolutionary project and to respect its sovereignty and political conventions.

The same could not be said of some of the other American hijackers. It had gradually become apparent that there was a split between those who wanted to be in Cuba, or at least were willing to adapt, and those who were disillusioned and wanted to leave. At first, these differences seemed rooted in unfulfilled expectations about what life in a revolutionary society would be like, as well as diverging ambitions about what they hoped to achieve outside the United States.

Many of the Americans saw Cuba as only a temporary way station. The island, some believed, could be a gateway to theaters of anticolonial struggle in Africa and to antiimperialist movements in Latin America. Charlie, Michael, and Antar initially counted themselves among this group. African anticolonialism had figured prominently within in the Black radical imagination stateside. The *Black Panther* had regularly covered national liberation movements on the continent, devoting special attention to Angola, Guinea-Bissau, Mozambique, Rhodesia, South Africa, and Zambia, and had made a point of noting Cuba's support for African anticolonial insurgency.[1]

Now, as guests on the island, Charlie, Michael, and Antar noted that coverage of African liberation movements was everywhere in the Cuban press. Indeed, in May 1972, as the RNA comrades were finishing their stint cutting sugarcane with the Nuestra América Brigade, Fidel Castro embarked on a two-month tour of African and Eastern European countries, eliciting continual media coverage. In *Granma*, the official organ of the Communist Party of Cuba and the island's most prominent newspaper, Charlie, Michael, and Antar gazed at the photo spreads of Fidel with African leftist leaders.[2] Hoping to be allowed to join the struggle on the continent, the RNA comrades asked MININT and Cuban Institute of Friendship with the Peoples (ICAP) to help them make connections with representatives of the movements.[3]

Nothing ever came of it. "The Cubans had promised to see what they could do, but so far nothing had happened," Bill Brent later wrote. "The general feeling among these brothers was the immigration officials weren't going to do anything for them because they didn't consider them real revolutionaries."[4] That was likely true; other hijackers had tried. Yet the government's reluctance to facilitate the American hijackers' participation in foreign theaters was also rooted in geopolitical considerations. Havana had little to gain and much to lose by training US citizens in guerrilla warfare, an act that would have been interpreted by Washington as a direct provocation.[5]

Nor was the situation unique to the Americans. The Cuban government had declined overtures from other foreign leftists. As Marília Guimarães recalled, some exiled Latin Americans in Havana, yearning to travel to the front lines of armed insurgencies in the hemisphere, had been similarly rebuffed after requesting military training.[6] Here, too, geopolitical factors intervened. By the early 1970s, Cuba had temporarily withdrawn its policy of direct support for armed left-wing movements in Latin America, which had suffered devastating defeats.[7] Cuba continued to provide sanctuary for political refugees from Latin America, most notably Chileans after the US-backed coup of September 1973 that overthrew the elected socialist government of Salvador Allende. Nonetheless, Cuban strategists initially counseled Allende's supporters against armed struggle with the Pinochet government, which Havana viewed as firmly entrenched. While Cuba provided critical support for the exiled Chilean leadership and the global resistance movement against Pinochet, this support was initially logistical, financial, and diplomatic. Only later did Havana provide military training to Chileans.[8]

The American hijackers were largely unaware of these geopolitical dynamics and strategic considerations. Meanwhile, Cuban cultural production continued to lionize armed struggle in the hemisphere. One example, Charlie recalls, was *Los comandos del silencio*, a wildly popular Cuban TV series depicting the urban guerrilla campaign of the Tupamaros in Uruguay, with an evocative theme song sung by Cuban music icon Silvio Rodríguez. The message of heroism and sacrifice was clear. For the RNA comrades, these images only compounded their frustration. Viewing themselves as legitimate revolutionaries, they chafed at the Cuban government's apparent disinclination to support their revolutionary dreams.

Yet it was also obvious that some of the Americans were neither political activists nor individuals with any particular interest in Cuba itself. Some rejected opportunities to adapt to the island altogether. Cubans expected foreigners, both invited formal political asylees and hijackers, to contribute to society, just like Cubans were expected to, and to participate in the construction of the socialist project. One member of the Communist Party of Uruguay later recalled the advice he received for proper revolutionary behavior as a political exile in Cuba: "In Cuba, to be a revolutionary is to work. . . . We are here to help move the [Cuban] economy forward."[9]

Some of the American hijackers saw it differently. Living at the MININT house, Brent became frustrated with what he saw as an attitude of entitlement among some of his American bunkmates. Some declined to participate in volunteer brigades arranged by ICAP. Others resisted adapting at all. "A number of the brothers in the house refused to learn Spanish," Brent later wrote. "They regarded Spanish as just another colonial slave language that would make it easier for the Cubans to brainwash them."[10] Exasperated, Brent opined that "the idea that you'd be recolonized because you learned a new language was taking things to extremes."[11] Brent's impatience may have been directed at hijackers like Richard Duwayne Witt, a nineteen-year-old former Marine, and Garland Grant, twenty, of Milwaukee. Both hijacked airplanes to Cuba citing a desire to escape life in the United States, and both regretted it. Interviewed by two US journalists for *Penthouse* magazine, Witt reported that he had been fed up with life in the United States and wanted to try living in an African country. It was "tension—and I guess pressure," Grant told them. "I just snapped. I'm an idiot, I admit it."[12] Neither youth was interested in settling in Cuba. When the Cubans tried to enroll Grant in a Spanish-language course, he declined. "I'd rather learn Swahili or Arabic. And they got pissed off."[13]

Geo López had also observed a distinction between the hijackers who appeared to be dedicated to adapting to the complex realities of Cuba and others who made demands on their hosts. Some refused to work, broke Cuban laws, or flouted cultural customs. Paul Harris, a cofounder of the pioneering San Francisco Law Collective, based in the Mission District, who represented both Geo and Huey P. Newton, traveled to Havana in 1977 to meet with his exiled clients. While "there are many revolutionary exiles in Cuba who try to study and plan their futures," Harris said Geo had told him, "there were a number of crazy American hijackers, some in prison and some on the streets hanging around the tourist hotels." These hijackers, according to Geo, had "no socialist beliefs and were just a problem for the Cubans."[14]

By 1972, dozens of airplanes had been hijacked to Cuba from the Western Hemisphere, including seventy-three successful hijackings from the United States and its territories.[15] Hijackers who were members of known political movements in the United States appear to have received a warmer reception. Indeed, one of the first questions that Cuban state security officers had asked Patrick Critton was whether he was a member of the Black Panther Party.[16] He was not, but the RNA was by that time known to the officers, whose colleagues had recently investigated Charlie, Michael, and Antar. "They never handcuffed me," Critton reported, "and I was put in a furnished room and given something to eat."[17] The Cuban government allowed most hijackers to prove themselves by demonstrating their commitment to adapt. Time and again, American hijackers who expressed a desire to work or study reported being given the opportunity to join Cuban society.

Nonetheless, the government evaluated hijackers warily. Many of Cuba's uninvited guests, officials believed, were little more than troubled youth, radical self-seekers, apolitical opportunists, common criminals, and potential spies.[18] Some behaved erratically or appeared mentally unwell, prompting Fidel Castro to lament to the Swiss ambassador to Cuba that "most of the hijackers are not completely normal people."[19] Cuban officials were especially unlikely to be sympathetic to hijackers who abused passengers and crew or stole from them. Hijackers who demonstrated a desire to adapt to Cuban society, on the other hand, were routinely given the opportunity to settle on the island permanently, including in cases where the hijackers had been accused of violent acts in the United States.[20]

American hijackers sometimes misread the Cuban government's motivations for providing sanctuary. "Many of the hijackers felt our being here was all political propaganda," Brent later wrote. "Having a bunch of Third World freedom fighters, especially those who hijacked airplanes to escape from the United States, made the Cuban government look good. The longer we stayed here, the more political mileage Cuba got out of us."[21] This perception was mistaken. The Cuban government considered few of the Americans to be "persons in real danger as a result of their political activities."[22] According to Cuba's Law No. 1226, passed in September 1969 to deter hijacking, the majority of hijackings from the United States were carried out by "common criminals, corrupt individuals, mentally unbalanced persons and socially unadapted persons anxious to change their country of residence or prompted by strictly personal motivations, which . . . cannot be considered as being of a revolutionary nature.[23]

Far from serving as propaganda assets to Havana, the presence of the hijackers, particularly those who appeared to be psychologically unwell or had been fleeing crimes that lacked obvious political import, were a public relations liability, not a boon. Their arrival risked complicating Cuba's deserved reputation as a haven for beleaguered revolutionaries seeking political asylum. The Cuban government's frustration with the scourge of hijackings from its northern neighbor eventually led it to enter into an antihijacking agreement with Washington in 1973, the first diplomatic accord between the two nations in over a decade.[24]

US hijackers arriving in Cuba were confined to immigration prisons for weeks or months while the Cuban intelligence system evaluated them. Eldridge Cleaver, who arrived in Havana in December 1968 and befriended some of the American hijackers during his stay in Havana, later explained the rationale: "Security. It's reasonable. . . . You get all kinds of people who come to Cuba. You get some kooks, real kooks. It's conceivable you could get a C.I.A. agent. So this is what they do: they try to find out what you are."[25]

To find out what they were, state security officials evaluated the hijackers' willingness to contribute to society. Revolutionary citizenship in Cuba hinged on civic participation. The construction of socialism required workers and volunteers, the Americans were told, not armchair revolutionaries. As uninvited guests, hijackers were expected to volunteer—just as Cubans did—for stints of agricultural labor in the countryside. Hijackers who refused this expectation quickly wore out their welcome. Gabor Louis Babler, a Hungarian American man who had hijacked a plane to Cuba in 1967 in the hopes of being trained in guerilla warfare and sent to Latin America, reported bouncing around Cuban prisons and enduring compulsory labor stints on the Isle of Pines, an island municipality off the southern coast, then aboard a Cuban ship, before finally being allowed to live in Havana with his Cuban girlfriend.[26]

As two Canadian journalists concluded in November 1971, Cuban officials appeared to divide hijackers into two groups: "those the Cubans believe are endangered in their own country because of their political views and those the Cubans feel are undesirables."[27] One anonymous young resident of Hijack House who was interviewed by the journalists—most likely Diane McKinney, a seventeen-year-old girl who had arrived in Cuba with her eighteen-year-old boyfriend aboard a hijacked airplane from Gastonia, North Carolina—captured the sense of disappointment shared by more than a few of the American hijackers. "My mother wouldn't believe it. We've got a swimming pool, we live in a house that used to belong to a millionaire and we have a cook and a gardener. The catch is that the pool never has any water, the house is falling apart and the cook and gardener are keeping us under surveillance."[28]

The colorful circumstances and diverse ideological predilections of the Americans were enough to befuddle Cuban officials. In January 1972, two students from Mayfair College in Chicago were arrested on charges of conspiring to poison the city's water supply with biological agents, including *Salmonella enterica* serotype Typhi, the bacterium that causes typhoid fever. The students, Allen C. Schwander, nineteen, and Steven Pera, eighteen, both of them white, had created an organization animated by a vaguely defined radical ecological ideology that they called RISE.[29] Their plot to contaminate the city's water, according to police, was intended as the opening salvo in a plan to depopulate the world, leaving a small group that would live in harmony with nature. An FBI investigation claimed that the organization had been producing the biological agents in a lab. Skipping bail and making their way to Jamaica, Schwander and Pera then hijacked a charter plane to Cuba, where they were sent to live at the MININT house in Siboney.[30]

Hijackers such as Schwander and Pera, of course, made ready fodder for the tabloids. Foreign journalists seemed to relish dramatizing the dashed revolutionary dreams of idealistic American youth who fell victim to their own unrealistic expectations of Cuba. Yet some of this reportage landed close to the mark. "Few of the American hijackers were genuinely seeking political asylum," *Penthouse* wrote in April 1973. "They are teenagers frustrated with the monotony or the discipline of their lives, hardened criminals seeking a final way out of the sentences that hang over them, black power activists with dreams of a truly egalitarian society where discrimination, poverty and prejudice are a thing of the past, unbalanced psychiatric cases who never think of the lives they are endangering or their own doomed fate, misguided idealists and men desperate to grab front-page headlines. They were men who felt trapped in the United States and wanted out. Now the lives they left do not seem so bad."[31]

In contrast to the Latin American émigrés in Havana, the majority of whom were members of disciplined Marxist political parties and were often invited by the Cuban government to seek political sanctuary on the island, the US hijackers had earned a reputation as unserious adventurers. As one American expatriate in Havana later put it, they were "common criminal[s] with political pretensions."[32] Charlie maintains that this reputation was often deserved. Some of them "had no ideology, and were basically apolitical." Worse, they behaved like "entitled Americans," contributing nothing to Cuban society but expecting the government to cater to their desires. This was a symptom, Charlie came to believe, of the insidious tendency of US Americans, regardless of their racial background or socioeconomic extraction, to expect the wider world to bend to their expectations. They were unprepared for the material realities of the third world. "They had . . . no concept of poverty or what underdevelopment meant, especially with the US blockade in effect on Cuba. A lot of them just hijacked planes because they were fed up with life in the United States. Many of these people got into trouble in Cuba, and some of them even turned into counterrevolutionaries."[33]

The propensity of disgruntled American hijackers to become embittered critics of the Cuban state would become a trope of foreign news coverage of the hijacking era. Michael later tried to explain the phenomenon to a foreign journalist: "The majority of hijackers were not strongly political people. Some of them were emotionally unbalanced. Some of them came here under strongly false impressions."[34] According to Charlie, this was an apt description of Richard Duwayne Witt and Garland Grant. Upon their release from Cuban immigration detention, they allegedly refused to join an agricultural brigade or enroll in university, spending most of their time on the street in Havana. There they became targets for the police, who were known to hassle Cubans who seemed to be "idle" as well as youth sporting "western" and "hippie" fashions—tight miniskirts on women, for instance, or long hair on men—or those displaying "Afrocentric" clothing and hair. "One time I had an Afro haircut and was wearing a dashiki," Grant told *Penthouse*, "and they thought I was a Cuban going back to Africa and so they arrested me."[35]

By the time the RNA comrades arrived at the MININT house in early 1972, the trope of the disillusioned American hijacker had become a cliché among Cubans in Havana. Charlie had gotten the distinct sense that Cuban officials had not been impressed with some of the house's previous occupants. These impressions, in turn, had been shaped by previous events in Vedado. Indeed, it was hijackers such as Witt and Grant—young, dispirited with Cuba, reluctant to participate in agricultural brigades and disinterested in Spanish instruction, outraged by perceptions of Cuban racism and uninterested in conforming to the nation's political norms—that Eldridge Cleaver had taken under his wing in Havana during the winter of 1969. The tensions that developed between Cleaver and the Cuban government would shape the dynamics between American hijackers and their Cuban hosts long after his departure. The Cuban government became warier of accepting Americans as formal political émigrés. This was especially true of those who seemed, to Cuban eyes, unwilling to respect Cuban sovereignty.

In contrast to the hijackers, Cleaver had arrived in Cuba by invitation. Granted political asylum to escape legal charges stemming from an April 1968 shootout with Oakland police, his relationship with the Cuban government began warmly enough. Arriving in Havana harbor aboard a Cuban cattle ship from Canada, the Panther leader was accorded a status akin to a foreign diplomat. Taken on an extended tour of the island, during which he visited schools, hospitals, and agricultural projects, he was later installed in a commodious high-rise apartment on L Street in Vedado. The Cuban government pointedly requested that Cleaver maintain a low profile during his asylum, however, and to refrain from public political activity.[36]

Cleaver eventually became bitterly disillusioned with his hosts. Initially, the Panther leader's disappointment owed to his perception that the Cuban government had reneged on promises of material and logistical support to the Panthers. Cleaver assumed that he would be able to operate openly in Havana in his full capacity as minister of information for the Black Panther Party. Cleaver also maintained that the Cuban government had assured him of access to Radio Havana Cuba in a manner similar to Voice of Vietnam, a shortwave program hosted by North Vietnamese revolutionaries living in Havana and audible as far away as Minnesota, and Robert F. Williams's earlier *Radio Free Dixie* program, whose broadcasts of news and political commentary had been audible throughout much of the continental United States.[37] According to Cleaver, the Cubans had also promised him "a permanent, well-organized facility," where Panthers would receive military training, from which they could be spirited back into the United States to participate in covert actions.[38] While this latter claim is uncorroborated, and there is little evidence that the Cuban government ever believed in the feasibility of armed struggle inside the United States, it is clear that Cleaver expected Havana to match its rhetorical support for Black revolution in North America with tangible material and military assistance.[39]

Indeed, the Cuban government's response to Cleaver's requests may have been influenced by its unease with the Panther leader's fixation on guerrilla warfare inside the United States. Cuban officials had long encouraged American radicals who sought their advice to focus on building mass-based, working-class, multiracial social movements, which they believed offered the most realistic path to achieving meaningful change in the United States.[40] Armed struggle, Cuba's revolutionaries believed, was unrealistic, because objective conditions to support a successful insurrection in the United States—namely a base of popular support—simply did not exist. These were not abstract debates; they had a direct relation to Cleaver's political exile in Cuba. Indeed, rumors had already called into question Cleaver's story about the shoot-out with Oakland police. Cleaver would later admit that his story had been a lie. He and a group of Panthers had ambushed Oakland police on April 6, 1968, not the other way around. The attack had been retaliation for the assassination of Martin Luther King Jr. two days earlier.[41] Whatever the merits of political violence against the police in 1968, Cleaver's small band had been massively outmatched. In the gun battle that followed, Oakland police murdered a young Panther, Bobby Hutton, as he tried to surrender.[42]

It is not clear how much Cuban officials knew when Cleaver arrived in Havana. What is clear is that the Panther leader's reception was cooler than he had anticipated. In marked contrast to Stokely Carmichael, who maintained a close relationship with Fidel Castro and was feted by the revolutionary government at public events, as Angela Davis would be during her visit to Cuba in the next few years, Cleaver met Fidel only briefly, and had almost no contact with other high Cuban officials, who left him primarily in the hands of low-level security officers for the entirety of his stay on the island.[43]

Already disappointed in the Cuban government, Cleaver noticed other things. Cuba, he concluded, was not the racially egalitarian society he had expected to find and that the revolutionary state had claimed existed. Cleaver noted the paucity of Afro-Cubans in the upper echelons of the government, whose ranks were largely composed of white Cubans.[44] When Cleaver went to the Biblioteca Nacional de Cuba José Martí, Cuba's most important library, and asked librarians to direct him to the writings of Antonio Maceo—the Afro-Cuban icon of Cuba's nineteenth-century independence struggle and a renowned military strategist—he was informed that no writings were available. Cleaver was now thoroughly suspicious of the government's claims to have forged a racially egalitarian revolutionary society.[45]

It was in this context that Cleaver's tensions with his Cuban hosts sharpened after talking with the most disillusioned among the Black American hijackers—those who wanted no part of Cuba's revolutionary project.[46] One of these was Byron Vaughn Booth. Imprisoned in juvenile and adult penal facilities in California for much of his life, Booth had gradually become politicized. Angered by the denial of his parole application at the California Institution for Men in Chino after prison officials intercepted his personal mail and discovered that prominent members of the Black Panther Party—including Cleaver and Bunchy Carter, both ex-prisoners themselves—had been sending him copies of the *Black Panther* newspaper, Booth resolved to escape. Together with a prisoner named Clinton Smith Jr., Booth liberated himself from Chino in January 1969. Obtaining a gun, the two men took over a commercial jetliner in mid-flight and instructed its pilot to head for the Caribbean. "Ladies and gentlemen," Booth recalled telling the passengers over the plane's intercom, "this is your new captain speaking. Just relax. We're gonna have a holiday in Cuba."[47]

Booth's trip to Cuba turned out to be anything but a holiday. Held in a Cuban detention facility, Booth and Smith were questioned by state security officers who seemed to be trying to determine if the two ex-prisoners were FBI informants. Perhaps, the Cubans seemed to suggest, the hijacking had been a cover to enter Cuba and infiltrate the solidarity activities that visiting delegations of leftwing Americans often participated in? Some of these organizations had indeed been infiltrated by US government agents and had suffered disruptions by suspected FBI agents provocateurs.[48] Upon his release from detention several weeks later, Smith was sent to join a sugarcane cutting brigade, while Booth was assigned to menial work at a dairy farm. They soon tired of the work.

Participation in volunteer brigades had long been standard for visiting foreign revolutionaries, solidarity brigades, and political exiles. Beyond the symbolism of demonstrating solidarity with the Cuban Revolution, voluntary labor allowed foreign visitors to support the process of constructing socialism, not with words and speeches but with their bodies and labor. For foreign hijackers, voluntarism allowed them to give something back to the nation that was protecting them from extradition. In later years, foreign volunteers in Cuba would primarily construct houses or perform less specialized agricultural work, as the skill required to correctly harvest sugarcane with a machete exceeded the ability of most newcomers. Nevertheless, Cuba's reputation for expecting visitors to contribute to society by cutting sugarcane lingered for decades. Honduran medical student Luther Castillo, who moved to Cuba in 1999 after accepting a scholarship to study medicine for free in Havana, later joked about his preconceptions. "Some people thought I was crazy.... They even told us we would have to work in the fields: work in the afternoon, study at night. So I brought my boots, to be able to cut cane.... I thought, well, if I have to cut cane, I'll do it! I had to take those boots back home, because I never did need them."[49]

Booth and Smith wanted no part of it. When the Cuban and foreign workers at the dairy farm volunteered for the cane cutting brigade, Booth flatly refused. "I didn't escape prison to come cut sugarcane or to even work in this factory," Booth later stated. "Everybody seemed very disappointed, very let down."[50] Booth left the farm and, following rumors that another US hijacker was working in a cane cutting brigade in the same province, Booth set out to see if it was Smith. It was. Under cover of darkness, the two friends abandoned the cane fields and eventually made their way to Havana, where they found Eldridge Cleaver's apartment on L Street in Vedado.[51]

That two Americans—men who had entered the country illegally seeking sanctuary—would refuse to conform to the norms of their host country offended the sensibilities of the Cubans, who regarded political exile as a relationship of reciprocity between guest and host. Booth did not see it that way. "I expected for them to connect me with those who were going into South America to lead revolution," he explained decades later.[52] The tensions that Booth experienced with the Cuban government were born of these differing expectations. "We wasn't [*sic*] that close to the Cubans," Booth noted. "We didn't give them enough credit. We had our own struggle to contend with. Like, for instance, when I was asked to join the sugarcane cutting brigades, and I didn't do it. That was enough to really make them angry."[53] Instead, Booth spent most of his time on the street with Smith. "In Havana, the other problem was our lifestyle," Booth went on. "I mean, here we are in Cuba, we got nothing to do except to liaise with our people in the U.S., therefore, what are we doing in Havana? Hey, we're trying to have a good time, trying to get something to eat, 'cause getting food was hard in Havana, chasing a lot of girls, having a lot of fun."[54]

Cleaver's interactions with the American hijackers were increasingly viewed by the Cuban government as violating that most sensitive of its principles, the one that was notoriously invisible to US Americans: respect for Cuban sovereignty. When several American hijackers deserted volunteer brigades in Camagüey Province, where they had been sent to cut sugarcane, Cleaver sent them his address in Havana. Defying Cuban officials, who wanted to arrest the hijackers, Cleaver sheltered the deserters. Organizing a chapter of the Black Panther Party in his apartment, in defiance of the Cubans' request that he refrain from political organizing on Cuban soil, Cleaver unilaterally baptized the young hijackers into the organization. Cleaver was also armed. He had his own pistol and two AK-47 rifles that had been left in the apartment by one of the Cuban security personnel. Cleaver brashly informed Cuban officials that they would have to take the American hijackers by force.

Tensions came to a head when a Reuters reporter, tipped off to the Panther leader's presence in Havana, filed a news report revealing that Cleaver was living in Cuba, making headlines and blowing the low profile that the Cuban government had requested.[55] They promptly forced Cleaver to leave the island. Placing him on a flight to Algiers, Cleaver was sent to join the International Section of the Black Panther Party, which the Algerian government had allowed to operate, for the time being, under what amounted to diplomatic status.[56]

Yet the saga of the disillusioned American hijackers was not over. The last one to find Cleaver's apartment in Havana was Raymond Johnson. A student at Southern University in Baton Rouge, Louisiana, who said that he had been framed by police on arson charges in the wake of the nationwide uprisings that followed the assassination of Martin Luther King Jr., Johnson hijacked a commercial flight to Havana on November 4, 1968, in order to ask for political asylum. But Johnson's relationship with Cuban officials turned sour almost immediately. When the plane landed in Havana, the flight crew reported that Johnson had robbed the passengers.[57] Cuban officials returned the stolen cash to the passengers before allowing the plane to return to the United States. Johnson was confined to an immigration prison, where he met other American hijackers jailed on various charges.[58]

With Cleaver in Algeria, the hijackers in Havana were left to fend for themselves. Interviewed by Fenton Wheeler, the Associated Press's last remaining correspondent in Cuba, Johnson, now conducting himself as a member of the Black Panther Party, asserted that "the Panthers have not been received in a revolutionary fashion" in Cuba.[59] Johnson provided a somber assessment of the island's racial climate. "We think there's racial discrimination in Cuba. It's a peculiar kind of racial discrimination. In some ways it's comparable to attitudes in the United States. White Cubans have a subconscious conspiracy to maintain control of the island."[60] Reporting that American hijackers had been arbitrarily arrested on the streets in Havana and "forced to work in labor camps," he appealed to the Panther leadership stateside for support. "We would like this information to reach the Black Panther Party in the United States so the party will know the unrevolutionary way we are being treated. We want them to protest at Cuban missions everywhere."[61]

Party leadership in California protested the next day, although not in the way that Johnson had hoped. In response to Wheeler's article, Panther chair Bobby Seale called a press conference in which he accused Johnson of being a CIA and FBI agent bent on discrediting the Cuban government and a hijacker who had been "disappointed because he came to Cuba to get guerrilla training." These apparently contradictory claims notwithstanding, Seale roundly condemned Johnson and affirmed the Black Panther Party's allyship with Cuba and "all progressive socialist governments that we find throughout the world."[62]

Cleaver and Johnson, Charlie learned, had not been the first US Black activists in Cuba to become disillusioned with the Cuban government. There was also Mabel Williams and Robert F. Williams, who had first arrived as political exiles in Cuba in 1961. Famed civil rights activists and advocates of Black armed self-defense in North Carolina, the Williamses had fled from trumped-up FBI kidnapping charges after confrontations with armed white mobs and the Ku Klux Klan in the town of Monroe. At first they were welcomed as revolutionaries in Havana and hailed by everyday Cubans as daring freedom fighters against Southern racist terror.[63]

Installing them in an apartment and giving them a private car and a chauffeur, the Cuban government invited the Williamses to broadcast a Friday evening radio program from the studios of Radio Havana Cuba on Infanta Street in Central Havana. Carried on the station's powerful shortwave signal, listeners as far away as the Great Lakes and the Pacific Northwest could pick up *Radio Free Dixie*, an hour of soul, jazz, and rock and roll interspersed with news from the Black freedom struggle stateside and punctuated by the Williamses' fiery excoriations of white supremacy.[64]

The Williamses eventually became embittered with the Cuban leadership's discomfort with Black nationalist ideology. The Cuban government, they believed, had embraced a reductive, myopically class-centric vision of social transformation. The US Black freedom struggle, the Cubans had argued, would be wise not to alienate white workers, who would be necessary to any social transformation in the United States on account of their sheer numbers. Change in the United States, Cuba's leadership insisted, would have to emerge from a broad multiracial movement. But Robert Williams was skeptical about the potential of interracial working-class allyship in the United States. "You keep talking about [white] workers and farmers. You know, when I left Monroe they had about 5000 workers and farmers howling after me like mad dogs out in the streets. How am I supposed to unite with *them*?"[65]

The Williamses left Cuba in 1965 for China and appear to have had no direct communication with the American hijackers in Havana. Nonetheless, the reports from Havana were alarming. In a statement published in the *Chicago Defender* in January 1969, near the peak of the hijacking epidemic, Robert Williams urged would-be Black US hijackers to consider the legal repercussions of air piracy and exile. And he warned against attempting to advocate for Black nationalism in Cuba:

> There are times when oppressive circumstances will force our people into exile. Under certain conditions, exile is a sensible and logical course of action, but above all, black youth should not inject felony into unnecessary exile. If our people feel they should go into exile, they should do it voluntarily if possible, without burning bridges behind themselves. The hijacking of planes by youth without serious charges against them is a first magnitude tragedy. It closes the door permanently. The drama and glamour soon wear off and those who have other interests are not as disposed to fighting racism as the brothers are. I weep for any Black Nationalist, not charged with a deadly felony, who hijacks a plane to Havana. Black Nationalism is the first order of business "only in America." At this time I elect not to be specific, but I hope that a hint to the wise is sufficient. For the sake of avoiding tragedy, I hope our nationalist brothers will think carefully before hijacking a plane as a "revolutionary" act. The world is not ready for a militant black nationalist colony yet. If the brothers force the issue it will ultimately lead to bitter disillusionment and some open racist reaction on the part of the "comrades" below the border.[66]

But Charlie felt little sympathy for the sense of betrayal that some of the American hijackers expressed. "It was absurd," he later fumed. "No one told them to hijack planes to Cuba, but once they got here they felt like the Cuban government owed them something. A lot of hijackers came here thinking that

Cuba would welcome them as revolutionaries, give them a house and money, like Rob Williams. They did not know anything about Cuba. . . . Some of the hijackers just couldn't handle the idea that their idealization had been false. I said to some of them, the contradictions in Cuban society are their problem. You have to be grateful to the Cubans for granting you asylum and protecting you and feeding you."[67]

Hijackers from the United States were not alone in running afoul of their Cuban hosts. Some among the multitude of Latin American visitors and formal asylees had also experienced tensions. Alberto Ulloa Bornemann, a Mexican leftist who traveled to Havana in 1967 on a tourist visa with the hope of receiving "military and political training," although he did not have the backing of any party or known organization in Mexico, was eventually deported from Cuba after state security officials became suspicious of him. His case, one official told him, was not exceptional. "Many other young men . . . from all over the world were attracted by the Cuban Revolution," Bornemann later wrote in his memoirs. "Some arrived on the island without luggage," creating a problem for the government, which had to figure out what to do with them, where to house them, and how to solve their basic needs.[68]

Less frequently, tensions had developed among the formal political asylees from Latin America as the Cuban government tried to provide housing and distribute resources equitably amid an acute national shortage of units. "Prolonged stays in hotels . . . caused a certain degree of resentment," historian Tanya Harmer notes, "leading to complaints and even a hunger strike among one group, while others who insisted on expressing gratitude to the island's revolutionary government watched with deep embarrassment."[69]

Dismayed by the behavior of their US compatriots, Charlie, Michael, and Antar insisted on expressing gratitude. The Cuban Revolution clearly had its share of imperfections, the RNA comrades decided, but as guests, they were in no position to make demands. "A lot of the hijackers, they had been daydreaming about what Cuba was," Charlie would later reflect. "They should have read more. They saw everything through their American eyes, with no notion of internationalism. They thought it was a place that had no problems. They thought there was no racism. Cuba has always had problems, and the revolution has not been perfect because they are human beings. All Cubans know that."[70]

For Brent, however, the apparent eagerness of foreign journalists and critics of the Cuban revolutionary process to propagate the grievances of the American hijackers in Havana signaled something more insidious. Interviewed in Havana by the *Black Scholar* in early 1973, Brent argued that the amplification of the negative perspectives of some Black American visitors in

Cuba played into hackneyed anticommunist tropes whose purpose was to simultaneously discredit socialism and Black radicalism—and, by extension, Black socialists in the United States:

> Our enemies felt that if they could convince black people that the Cuban Revolution was no good, that it was racist, that it was not beneficial to black people or not significant to black people, then they would effectively kill two birds with one stone. Cuba is socialist. Rather than making an out-and-out campaign among black people against socialism, they made an out-and-out campaign among black people in the area in which we ourselves were consciously struggling—racism. Convince us that Cuba is racist and the automatic conclusion is that socialism is also racist. . . . I think it's significant that some of our brothers and sisters understand that this is why a lot of real fucked up and bullshit propaganda is going back to the States through the mouths of some black revolutionaries (and I still consider them to be revolutionaries, I just think that they are mistaken and need to correct their position).[71]

Charlie, Michael, and Antar increasingly came to see their adjustment to Cuba as a matter of living up to their political commitments. As guests, they believed that they owed it to their hosts to learn Spanish, adapt to scarce material conditions, respect Cuba's sovereignty, and embrace the ethic of voluntary labor. These were the terms under which they had been invited to participate in the construction of socialism in Cuba. Charlie and the other RNA comrades would ultimately forge strong bonds with the Latin American exiles in Havana, most of whom were already socialists and all of whom, whatever their varied class extractions, hailed from the Global South and were familiar with underdevelopment. In the coming years, Charlie would have plenty of time to reflect:

> I had spent time on reservations in New Mexico. I had been in Vietnam, had slept on the ground in the rain. By the time I got to Cuba, I had experienced hardship. Michael and Antar and I didn't come with the same idealistic ideas of Cuba as a paradise as some of the other hijackers had. We had never been to Cuba, but we had read and studied revolutions in the third world, and we knew that building a different society was hard. And so that made us understand intuitively that Cuba was not going to be perfect, and it influenced how we adjusted to Cuba. You had to have a certain kind of attitude to live in a place where the lights might go out for hours at a time, or the tap water might not be running that day. Not everyone can accept that. I had grown up in poor parts of the

> United States, but this was a different reality. Cuba is a small country, with few natural resources, under an imperialist economic blockade. My grandparents in Alabama didn't have lights for most of their life, but even residents of the poorest ghettoes and barrios of the US had electricity. You can't compare an underdeveloped country to the United States. To us, it was amazing that the Cuban people, even with US imperialism staring them down for all of those years, had been able to stay positive and advance and maintain their independence.[72]

Of all the US hijackers, however, it was Patrick Critton who had acquired the most detailed knowledge of Cuba prior to his arrival. He had read *The Youngest Revolution: A Personal Report on Cuba*—a journalistic and ethnographic account of Cuba published in 1969—during his long hours of guard duty at one of the Harlem safe houses during his organization's bombing campaign.[73] Written by the acclaimed Chicana journalist and civil rights activist Elizabeth Sutherland, who had first visited Cuba in 1959 and returned in 1961—she would later drop the anglicized version of her name, which she had adopted to elude discrimination in New York's publishing world, and become known as Elizabeth "Betita" Martinez—*The Youngest Revolution* used interviews Sutherland conducted in 1967 with Cubans from all walks of life, in cities and villages across the island, together with striking photographs, to provide an intimate portrait of a rapidly changing society.[74] Sutherland would become a lifelong supporter of the Cuban Revolution. "When Cuba declared itself socialist" in 1961, she later wrote, "so did I."[75]

Knowledge of the quotidian realities of underdevelopment and the political complexities of Cuban socialism—including on questions of racial identity—gave Critton rare presence of mind. His reading, he later surmised, had prepared him to adapt to the conditions that he encountered, allowing him to transform his time in Havana into one of the great pedagogical experiences of his life. "Cuba for me was a master's degree in political science and development studies," Critton later wrote. Because he had prepared himself intellectually, he was able to assimilate this real-world education. He also understood what would be required of him as a foreigner. "'Attitude,'" Critton observed, "was everything in adjusting to the new reality of exile and Cuba."[76] It also helped that he found like-minded comrades. "I feel that for us black men to come to Cuba in exile and to meet in the early stage of [our] exile was god sent. . . . Each one of us sensed [that] what was to take place in the immediate future would be dependent to a great extent upon how well we proved ourselves to our hosts."[77]

Geo López, too, was determined to adjust to his new exilic reality. Joining the Nuestra América Brigade to cut sugarcane and later a "microbrigade" of volunteers who built houses for Cuban families, López also took a job at a soap factory and attended the study sessions of the Revolutionary Collective. Unlike some other Los Siete de la Raza defendants, however, López had not previously been politically conscious. The accused had been an eclectic group: young men who were as different as they were similar. Some had been college students and community organizers. Others were "irresponsible street people," as radical attorney Paul Harris would later affectionately describe the young men he defended in court.[78] López, apolitical, was the latter. He had come to Cuba, he told Harris, with a drug addiction.[79] Living a clandestine existence in the United States as he evaded the police dragnet, López experienced a political awakening as a result of his encounters with sympathetic community activists and movement lawyers, like Harris, who protected him. But it was in Cuba where López fully became a revolutionary and finally recovered from his addiction.[80] "There were no drugs in Cuba," Harris later recalled, "so getting clean was easy."[81] López enrolled in classes at the University of Havana, studied Marxism and third world liberation movements, and talked of his desire to travel to El Salvador, where he had relatives, in order to participate in the left-wing insurgency there against the military dictatorship.[82]

Political commitments were only a temporary balm for the pain of exile. Willpower alone could not spare the members of the Revolutionary Collective from the pangs of homesickness. Even amid the wonder and exhilaration of experiencing revolutionary Cuba, Charlie's thoughts often strayed to home. The events in Albuquerque had resulted in enormous police pressure on his parents. Charlie's first telephone call after his release from the Villa Marista state security facility in Havana in January 1972 had been to his mother.

Dorethea had been waiting anxiously for her son's call. Or any call. Weeks had gone by, and there had been no news. She assumed that her phone was tapped, but when the call finally came, Dorethea was so relieved that she did not care. Charlie reassured her that he was fine. Then he asked about her. The police had banged on her door in the middle of the night after the hijacking and interrogated her. Dorethea initially refused to cooperate.[83] It was only after police questioned her for approximately two hours, without a lawyer present, that she was taken to state police headquarters and finally read her rights. Dorethea was charged with harboring and aiding Antar and Michael, although not Charlie, since close familial relations were exempt from laws pertaining to aiding and abetting of fugitives. It was not until January 1972 that the district attorney's office dismissed the charges. Her coerced testimony to police interrogators, who never Mirandized her, was suppressed as unconstitutional.[84] As for Johnny, he had been arrested shortly after the hijacking. The FBI had visited his house and collected fingerprints.[85] Johnny was sentenced to five years in prison for his role in aiding the fugitives.[86] Dorethea told her son that she loved him. With a lump in his throat, Charlie hung up the phone.

Next, he dialed his girlfriend, Kathy, in Fairbanks. She had learned of the hijacking from Charlie's mother, who had called her to break the news. Now, Kathy had news of her own for Charlie: she was pregnant. She and Charlie had conceived a child during her visit to the Bay Area the previous October. The baby was due in July. She would raise the child alone if she had to. There was nothing else they could do. She was not coming to Cuba. They promised to keep in touch.[87]

Finally, Charlie called his dad. James Hill urged his son to return to the United States to turn himself in, promising to find a good criminal defense attorney. Charlie's heart sank. "Daddy, I'll think about it," he responded, not wanting to disappoint his father.[88] He had no intention of turning himself in. His parents, Charlie later admitted, had known almost nothing about his political activism or activities in the RNA prior to the hijacking. "The whole thing was a huge shock for them."[89]

Antar's parents were likewise taken by surprise. Longtime civil rights activists, Joye and Luther had known of Antar's student activism at the University of California, Berkeley, and were aware that he had joined the RNA. But they knew nothing of his involvement in clandestine activities. Following the hijacking, the Goodwins leapt into action. Looking up Dorethea Hill's home address, Joye traveled to Albuquerque unannounced to visit Charlie's mother. Charlie's teenage sister Janet opened the door to find Joye Goodwin standing there in the early morning light. The two women embraced and cried. Then they sat on the couch and talked about their sons.[90]

Joye helped Dorethea send care packages to her son in Cuba, entrusting small parcels to members of the National Lawyers Guild visiting Havana. In later years, Dorethea found ways to send money. But she never visited her son in Cuba. She had little money and, with Americans banned from legal travel to the island by the US Treasury Department, save for a brief period in the late 1970s during the détente of the Carter era, the prospect of a circuitous and expensive journey via Mexico, one that would probably draw police attention, was intimidating. Michael's mother, who had once been a journalist, managed to visit her son for the first time in Havana in 1976 as a credentialed member of a Black press delegation covering an international seminar about apartheid in South Africa.[91]

Dorethea and James Hill had no such political connections. And they faced other pressures, from which the friendship—and legal advice—of the

Goodwins could not shield them. Charlie later learned that his mother had been harassed regularly after the hijacking. Anonymous phone calls came in the middle of the night, and state police detectives had showed up at her door trying to glean information about her son in Cuba.[92] Charlie's sister, Janet, later recounted how Albuquerque police once followed her in a patrol car as she walked to Lincoln Junior High School. Assuming that her phone was tapped, Dorethea repeatedly told her daughter not to talk about Charlie on the telephone.[93]

For Joye and Luther Goodwin, however, the personal and professional fallout from the killing of officer Rosenbloom and the hijacking would eventually lead them to leave the United States. Heartbroken by their son's exile and yearning for a place where the family could reunite—and from which Antar's extradition to the United States would be unlikely—the Goodwins looked to Africa. Attracted to the Pan-Africanist developmental politics of Tanzania's Julius Nyerere, whose socialist concept of *Ujamaa* had fired the imaginations of the African diaspora and Black radical activists worldwide, the Goodwins moved to Tanzania in late 1972. There Luther took a post working for the nation's Ministry of Natural Resources, one of dozens of Black professionals from the United States who lived and worked in Tanzania in the 1970s in support of the Nyerere government.[94]

And so it was that the Goodwins, like dozens of other African American activists during the Civil Rights and Black Power eras, including several former members of the Black Panther Party, would unexpectedly come to live a version of their son Antar's political dream: to work in Africa for the development and liberation of the continent.[95] Antar began preparations to travel from Cuba to Tanzania. But there was no rush. He would have plenty of time to rejoin his family in Dar es Salaam when the time was right. And Cuba had taken Antar's heart—as had an American woman who was living in Havana at the time as a solidarity activist.

Indeed, despite gnawing homesickness, all three men were falling in love with Cuba. On days between stints of voluntary labor, Charlie, Michael, and Antar would hang out at Coppelia or on the Malecón, talking politics with *habaneros*, as people from Havana were called, for hours. On weekends, La Rampa became a mob scene. "Cubans back then liked to party, man, just like now," Charlie would later say with a grin. "On Saturday nights Vedado would be absolutely packed with people, dressed up and ready to have a good time. Workers, students, lines of people cueing up for Club Tokia and Karachi Club an hour before opening time. There was cheap food and good beer."[96] When the RNA comrades attended their first *carnaval* in July, they thought they had died and gone to some kind of Caribbean heaven filled with pretty women and raucous, colorful street celebrations. "*Carnavales* back in those days were really something. I loved going to the one in Santiago, and it was cheap to go. The train had a diner car, serving half a chicken for two pesos, 80 cents for a beer!"[97]

Havana's radical cosmopolitan milieu was the perfect place to meet political sojourners from around the world. "Cuba was fascinating because everything was political. There were revolutionaries everywhere. You could be . . . waiting to get into a club, [and] there would be some guerrillas from Zimbabwe or South Africa or Bolivia in line with you. We felt right at home."[98]

In an era in which Cuba was pivoting its anticolonial foreign policy toward Africa, Havana offered a glimpse of revolution on the continent—and of Cuba's role in it. "There were Africans everywhere, studying in Cuba, or political refugees, guerrillas who had been in wars, or regular people in African nations who had been injured or maimed and were here for treatment. I saw them everywhere. It was easy for me to communicate with those people, to get information about the struggles there. . . . Cuba was easy to adjust to because we believed that it was a revolutionary society."[99]

Chapter 8

We Are the Revolutionists!

Dawn was still two hours away when Charlie, Michael, and Antar stumbled out of their bunk beds in the darkness at the Ministry of the Interior (MININT) house on May 1, 1972. Bathing quickly, they ate dry bread, washing it down with sugary-sweet black Cuban coffee. Then they boarded a bus to the Plaza de la Revolución in the heart of Havana's government district. As they neared the open expanse that lay before the towering white marble monument to José Martí, Cuba's icon of national independence, the streets were completely choked with people. As dawn broke, they could see enormous brigades, organized by workplace, readying painted banners. Student associations and faculties congregated in huge formations carrying flags, while families, members of government ministries, neighborhood associations, and farmers from Havana Province were assembling in contingents. "Everyone to the Plaza with Fidel. Long Live the First of May!" the front page of the newspaper *Granma* proclaimed.[1] The May Day celebrations of 1972 had begun.

Recent years had witnessed almost a million people turn out for International Workers' Day marches, and this year would be no different. The crowds in the plaza swelled until the RNA comrades could go no farther. Off to the side were water trucks, ambulances, and medics. In rows of tents, food was being prepared. "We were stupefied by the size of the march," Charlie later recalled. "We had never seen that many people marching before. The energy was palpable."[2] The morning would mark the first of many such choreographed spectacles of patriotism and mass revolutionary fervor that the RNA comrades would participate in, all of them thrilling in their immensity and electric political atmosphere.

Yet for some of the Americans at the collective house, many of the most memorable—and politically transformative—experiences of their time in Cuba would occur not through the political pageantry of mass rallies but through the sweaty solidarity of the voluntary labor brigades. Eager to participate in the island's fabled sugar harvest, Patrick Critton had accompanied the other members of the Revolutionary Collective out to the countryside the previous winter to join the Nuestra América Brigade. The experience of working alongside so many revolutionaries from the Western

Hemisphere—including Colombia, Argentina, Mexico, Chile, Brazil, and Haiti, "all of us helping Cubans to produce their most important export crop"—made a lasting impression on Critton.[3] "I still remember the intense heat that comes off a burning cane field and the beauty of young green cane stems as they grew acre upon acre in the cool evening sun," he later wrote. "For us in the collective it was a badge of honor to work and work hard. We wanted to prove to our host that we were serious revolutionaries in work as well as in war."[4] Making day excursions in the rolling farmland around Jaruco, Critton and his new Latin American comrades shared meals with *guajiros*, as Cubans call people from rural areas; visited schools; and were greeted by village neighborhood associations.

As the seasonal sugar harvest wound down, they turned to their next revolutionary battle: the construction of proletarian housing with a Cuban workers' brigade that was building apartment blocks in San Agustín, an outlying area of Havana. Having proven themselves dedicated practitioners of socialist emulation in the cane fields, six members of the Revolutionary Collective accepted an invitation to work in a project overseen by Ramón Castro, an agricultural engineer and the elder brother of Fidel and Raúl. Launched in 1971 to address the island's housing shortage—a national shortfall estimated to be nearly one million units—the "microbrigades" were collectives of employees from existing workplaces, anywhere from factories to government ministries, who volunteered to build housing under the supervision of technicians and skilled laborers provided by the Ministry of Construction, which also supplied the building materials.

The *Black Panther* would later explain the *microbrigada* system to its North American readership. "Workers take time off from their regular jobs to work on housing projects and then rent one of the finished units for just six percent of their salary," which continued to be paid by their original employer during their stint with the microbrigade. Approximately 80 percent of the new housing units were allotted to the workers who built them. "When a worker gets his apartment he can go back to his old job and another comrade comes to take his place," a Cuban civil engineer told the *Black Panther*. "That way everyone gets a chance to have an apartment."[5]

Conceptualized as a way to utilize surplus labor while increasing productivity, Cuba's microbrigades ultimately built 100,000 units of housing across the island by 1983.[6] Like the sugar harvest, the progress of microbrigades across the island was chronicled in the Cuban press, which ran photo essays about the campaigns and interviews with the Cuban and foreign volunteers.[7] For the North American volunteers, the experience of building housing blocks for Cuban families—in many cases alongside the very people who would live in them—was a source of enormous satisfaction. "We, the Collective," Critton later wrote proudly, "completed a five story, thirty apartment building with 15 Cuban campesinos that would live in those apartments."[8]

The proletarian apartment blocks springing up around the city were not just for Cubans. Despite the shortage of housing resulting from Cuba's dramatic population growth during the baby boom decade of optimism that followed the 1959 revolution, housing for foreign political asylees was included in national planning goals. As Chilean political exiles received sanctuary in Cuba following the US-backed coup that toppled the government of Salvador Allende in September 1973, the Chilean presence in Havana and other cities became conspicuous. By mid-1974, over one thousand Chilean refugees had arrived, including Beatriz Allende, a Chilean Socialist Party leader and the daughter of former President Allende, who led the resistance to the dictatorship in exile with Cuban logistical support and funding.[9] Although Chilean exiles were the most numerous, the city thronged with other political asylees, termed "refugees" (*refugiados*). "In Havana, the Chilean accent was joined with that of Uruguayans, Paraguayans, Argentines, [and] Brazilians who escaped death," Brazilian political exile Marília Guimarães later wrote. "Cuba's solidarity, the one that we knew day-to-day, sheltered thousands of exiles."[10]

In the Alamar neighborhood of eastern Havana, some sixty Chilean children—sent abroad by their parents amid the waves of repression against leftists following the 1973 coup—were housed together in an apartment block under the care of surrogate Cuban parents.[11] Charlie marveled at the desire of everyday people to aid the political exiles who had come to the island to escape Pinochet's prisons and death squads. "A lot of Cubans felt it was their revolutionary duty to aid them, and we admired the Cubans for sacrificing on behalf of foreigners."[12] Many Cubans in microbrigades painted a white "T" for "Tupamaro" on their helmets in honor of the guerrilla movement in Uruguay. Placards at mass rallies in Havana captured this sentiment: "Para Chile, No Solo Nuestra Sangre: También Nuestro Pan" (For Chile, not only our blood, but also our bread).[13]

Airplanes carrying Latin American political exiles arrived in Cuba throughout the 1970s. Gregory Randall, an American-born youth who arrived in Cuba in 1969, where he would live for the next fourteen years, had been sent to the island with his three sisters by their mother, writer and activist Margaret Randall, when the family fled political repression in the aftermath of the Tlatelolco Massacre in Mexico City, where they had been living. "The streets of Havana were filled with militants from all over the continent," Gregory Randall later wrote of this period. "At the end of the seventies, for example, one could find many Central Americans, victims of land mines, roaming Miramar on crutches." Randall, like many of his classmates and friends in Havana, organized to aid the newcomers. "Cubans, and those like ourselves who identified with Cuba's ideology, looked at these people with admiration and gave them everything we could. Considering the scarcity of the times, we didn't have much, but this made it even more meaningful."[14]

Cuba's ethos of global solidarity also captured the imagination of Bill Brent. "Cuba is Cuba, but the international flavor of Cuba is noticeable to anyone who comes here." Newspapers produced a steady drumbeat of coverage about Cuban medical professionals and civil engineers working abroad, featuring photographs of proud-looking workers who were preparing to go on international missions and interviewing them about their reasons for participating.[15] While Cuban internationalists often worked in nations allied with Cuba, such as Vietnam—whose postwar reconstruction in the 1970s was aided by Cuban technicians—thousands of Cubans participated in humanitarian and development work in nations whose governments were at bitter political odds with Havana but were willing to accept humanitarian aid. Cuban specialists in agriculture, mining, construction, transportation, agronomy, and fishing were among those dispatched abroad.[16] All of them, from doctors to construction workers, were lionized as national heroes in the Cuban press.

One by one, the concrete apartment blocks—four- or five-story rectangular Soviet-style buildings—sprang up in Alamar and San Agustín, whole neighborhoods built by workers, for workers. The Cubans in the microbrigade that Geo López participated in voted to donate one apartment unit in every building they constructed to a Chilean refugee family, an idea first proposed by Fidel and then adopted on a voluntary basis by Cubans—"an act of autonomous sacrifice," historian Tanya Harmer argues, "rather than a provision of the Cuban state."[17] Students and volunteers from around the world joined the internationalist brigades, but the bulk of the labor came from Cubans in cities and villages across the nation. It was a significant gesture of solidarity and sacrifice, Geo later marveled, in a country experiencing a critical shortage.[18] As one Chilean who had been assigned an apartment in Santiago later told Harmer: "Imagine what it cost for a Cuban to give you houses, share all their achievements. . . . The Cubans gave us the little they were already working [to build]."[19]

During the first week of work, Ramón Castro came by to meet the Americans from the Revolutionary Collective. He inquired whether they needed anything back at the MININT house in Siboney—shoes, work clothes? Yes, the men replied: better food! Bread, milk, and coffee, they pointed out, were calorically insufficient for hard labor. Thereafter, Ramón saw to it that some eggs, cheese, and ham were sent over for their breakfasts, supplementing the hearty lunches already provided to Cuban workers at the construction sites: rice and black beans (*arroz congrí*) with a stew of chicken or pork or dried salted codfish, called bacalao. Sometimes it would be a picadillo of ground canned Russian beef or canned Chinese pork cooked with onions and spices, and meals were accompanied by fried smashed green plantains (tostones) and boiled sweet potato (boniato).

The hijackers threw themselves into the work, logging twelve-hour days for weeks on end. "We were young guys, and strong! Sometimes we worked from 7 a.m. to 9 or 10 at night," Charlie would later say gleefully. "You had to have heart to do that kind of work."[20] Arriving at the construction site in Alamar one day to find it occupied by "strange dudes" from other brigades and anticipation in the air, Critton was surprised to see Ramón Castro drive up in a jeep loaded with chests of ice and bottles of rum. As the workers passed around potent rum punch, both the work and the raucous laughter reached a frenzied pace as a hundred workers poured the foundation of a building. Critton, pushing a wobbling wheelbarrow full of cement up a wooden ramp, lost his balance and "fell off those planks, wagon and all." As he recalled, "There were hoots and yells telling me I couldn't drink, and that I shouldn't mess around with the 'guachipupa.'"[21]

Through their dedication to political education and voluntary labor in the service of Cuban socialism, Charlie and the comrades in the Revolutionary Collective hoped to demonstrate the earnestness of their revolutionary aspirations. But there were other dimensions to this proving ground. Physical labor, Charlie imagined, also trained their bodies and disciplined their minds for their greatest ambition: to be given the opportunity to join an anticolonial movement in Africa. Armed struggle, Charlie well knew, would require similar abilities of physical and mental discipline.

The hardest work in Cuba was indisputably harvesting sugarcane the traditional way. Bill Brent, who had worked hard his entire life—both for wages and for the State of California as an unpaid convict laborer—was no stranger to toil under the hot sun. "Topping and felling trees and fighting fires in Ben Lomond, working in lumber mills and light industry, farm labor—I had done them all," Brent would later write. "But for sheer hard, backbreaking work, none compared with cutting sugarcane in Cuba. I'd been on the verge of turning in my *mocha* [a heavy machete with a blade that's short and wide] many times, but now the harvest was over and I had made it through with flying colors. . . . I was pulling my own weight in Cuba and felt damned good about it."[22]

Their stint with the *microbrigada* managed by Ramón sometimes involved agricultural work on a farm near the town of Aguacate. The place, as it turned out, was El Plan Especial Genético, the famed experimental dairy farm at Valle de Picadura, which was also directed by Ramón. Initiated in 1969, the farm was part of a cutting-edge cow-breeding and research venture that crossed Canadian Holsteins—prized milk producers but ill-suited for tropical climates—with hardy Cebu cattle, prized for their quality meat. It was launched with the goal of developing new breeds of dairy cows capable of increasing the island's production of milk, a key source of protein that was rationed to ensure that children and expectant mothers had access to it. The scientists and the animals alike eventually became veritable celebrities in Cuba. As scholars Reinaldo Funes-Monzote and Steven Palmer write, "A famous Canadian stud bull was declared a hero of the revolution, and one of his thousands of descendants, Ubre Blanca (White Udder), would not only break the world record for milk production, but in a fitting ideological twist, unseat the reigning champion from the United States in the process."[23]

Many of the workers in the microbrigade and the dairy farm at Valle de Picadura had been employees in Holguín Province on the estate of Ángel Castro—late father of Ramón, Fidel, and Raúl—prior to the revolution.[24] The plantation was dismantled during the post-1959 nationalizations, and Ramón invited some of the workers to relocate to Valle de Picadura. It was these men from the old Castro family estate that Charlie and Patrick Critton now worked alongside as laborers. Clearing brush, digging out tree roots, and using oxen to move boulders, they prepared the land for planting with Pangola, a tropical grass native to southern Africa that was prized for its nutritive value for livestock. Charlie, who had always loved country settings, took an immediate liking to the bucolic rugged beauty of Valle de Picadura. The food, typical Cuban country fare, was delicious. Working at the dairy farm during the summers of 1972 and 1973, he slept in the barracks that housed both volunteers and the farm's paid workers. Charlie eventually became the latter. As a manual laborer, he qualified to receive the nation's lowest standardized salary grade of approximately 85 pesos per month. The hours were long, but he derived satisfaction from being part of a labor collective that was dedicated to producing sustenance for the population.[25]

Throughout all of it, the solidaristic adventure of voluntary labor proved to be a formative political education. "We were working with revolutionary Cubans," Charlie would later say, "learning Spanish, becoming revolutionaries in the Cuban sense, beyond our former identities."[26] Critton would later depict it as a kind of experiential radical pedagogy. "I cannot express in words what a 'proletarian education' working in physical hard labor in construction and cane cutting was for me in Cuba," Critton would later enthuse.[27] Decades later, Critton's excitement was still palpable. "All of this drama was acted out under the hot, yellow, punishing Caribbean sun. Now was the time to get it on, Revolution in process! Here was an opportunity to help the developing Cuban dairy industry. The work was hot and hard. It was a hump, you dig. We sang and jibed and discussed many things there in the fields. Everyone appeared pleased with our enthusiasm. 'We are the revolutionists!' and we wanted everyone to know it."[28]

As Charlie got to know the workers, his Spanish improved sufficiently to have detailed conversations, allowing him to ask questions about Cuba and to answer their endless queries about the United States. News items about police repression in Black communities in the United States had been regular fare in the Cuban media for years, and 1972 was no exception.[29] Charlie was shocked by the level of knowledge that these laborers from rural eastern Cuba had about the Black freedom struggle in the United States. Books by Malcolm X and Richard Wright, together with speeches by Martin Luther King Jr., had been translated into Spanish by Cuban publishers and were widely available at Havana bookstands. The workers knew all about the civil rights movement and the struggle to end the Vietnam War, and had followed the rise of the Black Panther Party in Oakland.

In the summer of 1972, media attention in Cuba was fixed on an "Afro-North American communist" and "young black revolutionary," as *Granma* described her, from the United States: Angela Davis.[30] State newspapers and periodicals such as *Granma*, *Verde Olivo*, *Bohemia*, and *Juventud Rebelde* printed a continual stream of coverage of Davis's legal battle on charges of murder, kidnapping, and criminal conspiracy, charges that at one point led Davis to consider political exile in Cuba herself. At Valle de Picadura, the Cuban workers peppered Charlie, Michael, and Antar with questions about American society, giving the RNA comrades opportunities to practice their Spanish. Charlie's Spanish-English dictionary, which he carried everywhere he went, eventually fell apart from use.

But the best way for Charlie to improve his Spanish, the workers mischievously advised, would be to find himself a Cuban girlfriend. Charlie wondered if romance between Cubans and people from the United States—the hostile nation to the north that was continually trying to overthrow their revolution—could carry a social stigma. But Cubans seemed unconcerned. Most were curious about the three young Americans. Political discourse on the island diligently distinguished between the American government and the American people. "Cubans were smart. They assumed that Americans walking around in Havana in the 1970s were probably anti-imperialists who were on Cuba's side. There was no tourism in those days."[31]

Cuban youths, in particular, were interested in the Americans. René Trujillo was a teenager from Central Havana who hung out on La Rampa. René, who identified as *afrodescendiente*, or of African descent, met Charlie in 1972 and was fascinated by the Black American radicals who had hijacked planes to the island and who "spoke English and had big hair," René later recalled, "and talked about Black Power."[32] Even in Vedado's hip youth culture scene, Charlie, Michael, and Antar stood out. "We were like a new breed to them. We were both . . . Americans and Black, and that made us interesting," Charlie later said. "We were not the foreigners they were used to seeing, like the Africans, Latin Americans, or Eastern Europeans you would see on the street in Havana. Cuba and the United States were completely cut off."[33] Charlie had arrived during a period when Moscow-Havana ties were deepening, yet the eastern bloc's cultural influence on the island was limited and uneven.[34] "You saw a lot of Russians, but you didn't really see them interwoven in Cuban society, inter-marrying."[35]

Charlie's first female acquaintance in Cuba, a dedicated young revolutionary, was clearly curious about him as a foreign radical. "She gave me a lot of information about the revolution. I believe she dated me because she believed I was a revolutionary from the US. Her family was revolutionary as well."[36] Charlie's Spanish improved exponentially. It was the beginning of a recurring dynamic, in which Charlie's early understandings of Cuban society—linguistically, politically, and culturally—would be shaped by the women who would become his romantic interests.

Charlie's first serious girlfriend, however, was a medical student named Delia. The two had met while cutting sugarcane. She was a member of the Unión de Jóvenes Comunistas (UJC)—the Union of Young Communists—a vanguard organization founded in 1962 that was dedicated to forging revolutionary consciousness among youth. Guided by Marxist-Leninist principles adapted to the Cuban context, the UJC required academic excellence, a commitment to voluntary work and to social solidarity, and a commitment to the defense of the nation through the all-encompassing "ideological battle" against imperialism and capitalist values.[37] Delia's older sister was dating Richard Dixon, the white man from Michigan who had hijacked a plane to Cuba and became a core member of the Revolutionary Collective. The four of them spent hours debating history and politics.

The women, Black Cubans to Charlie's North American eyes, self-identified as *mulata*, or of mixed African and European descent. Charlie was taken aback to hear them using terms such as "good hair" (*pelo bueno*). It was the beginning of years of debates about what he considered to be the internalization of Eurocentric beauty standards among Afro-Cubans. "This shocked us. In the US, hair had become part of Black revolutionary politics. But not in Cuba. We tried to convince them that 'good hair' didn't exist. 'Say "straight hair," don't say "good hair,"' we said."[38]

From Charlie's perspective, Cuba's racial logics were paradoxical. There was no question, he decided early on, that the Cuban Revolution had benefited Afro-Cubans. They had been active participants in the revolutionary process, he knew, and clearly remained among its strongest supporters. Nor was there any question that Cuba was a far more racially equal nation by material measures, including education, life expectancy, and population health, than the United States. Empirical evidence confirms his observations.[39]

Yet the egalitarian impact of the revolutionary process had not come about through targeted race-consciousness policies. Instead, Cuba had moved toward racial equality through a structural approach: by socializing the provision of social services, thereby raising living standards, changes that were skewed toward the most marginalized sectors of society. Afro-Cubans, disproportionately poor, benefited considerably from sweeping changes to the economic system. By 1981, a decade after Charlie's arrival, racial inequality had narrowed or become statistically insignificant in several key social indicators related to educational attainment, literacy, fertility, and—most significant of all from the standpoint of population health—overall life expectancy.[40] By the early 1980s, Cuba's achievements in creating a more racially equitable society, far surpassing the United States and Brazil—multiracial nations in the Americas with large Black populations—were nothing short of astonishing.[41]

This was not to say that racism had been eliminated in Cuba; far from it. Racial inequities and racist attitudes remained, made all the more intractable by the state's tendency to characterize them as epiphenomenal, a vestige of the prerevolutionary capitalist past, instead of realities that were reinforced by extant institutional practices, cultural discourses, and informal networks.[42] Yet the nation's socialist welfare system had allowed Cuba to become, without a doubt, the most equitable nation in the Western Hemisphere.[43]

In this respect, Cuba's achievements paralleled those of other state socialist nations. World Bank data for this period demonstrates that when compared to nations at similar levels of economic development, the physical quality of life in socialist nations, as measured by infant mortality, child death, overall life expectancy, per capita caloric intake, and physician-to-population ratio, as well as adult literacy and rates of enrollment in higher education, were superior in socialist countries versus their capitalist peers in the vast majority of global comparisons.[44]

As a postcolonial, postslavery, multiracial society with a significant Black population, Cuba's experience demonstrated the ability of socialism to increase racial equality. "The efficacy of the structural approach with which the revolution addressed the racial issue is proven by the fact that, with regard to several important social indicators, racial inequality has disappeared in Cuba," historian Alejandro de la Fuente wrote in 1995, using data from the 1970s and 1980s. "This is true with regard to education—measured not only in terms of literacy—as well as to some important demographic indicators, such as fertility and mortality. Cuba has achieved a degree of racial equality reached by no other country in the continent with a substantial black population."[45]

Yet it was also obvious that racism, most visibly in its cultural and attitudinal dimensions, had not been uprooted in revolutionary Cuba. For Charlie, the reluctance of many Cubans to acknowledge the existence of racist ideas suggested that culture was a neglected theater of political struggle in socialist Cuba. The island had witnessed no Black pride movement during the sixties. Traveling throughout the island in 1967, for instance, Elizabeth Sutherland described what she perceived as Eurocentric aesthetics of cultural production and art. "The Revolution had put the impoverished masses in power—and most blacks belonged to that class. The basic needs to which the state addressed itself were the basic needs of black Cubans," she wrote in *The Youngest Revolution*, the book Critton had read in New York.[46] "But something was still wrong. You could see it almost immediately, in the posters." Magazine fashion spreads featured almost exclusively white faces. "A typical sign was the big one on the road from the airport into the capital town of the Isle of Pines: 'Welcome,' it said, while a blond girl with Caucasian features waived her straw hat." In some cases, the artists creating the images were Black.[47]

"At first I saw them as victims of racism," Charlie later said, "like they believed in the subtle ideas that made Black people subordinate and inferior and didn't know any better. That may have been true. But later I came to understand that Cuba and the US also had different histories, and it was impossible to compare the two contexts. I had to adapt culturally to Cuba. It wasn't easy."[48]

Charlie had not been the only recent American exile in Cuba to perceive an absence of Black racial consciousness. Raymond Johnson, speaking to Associated Press journalist Fenton Wheeler in the June 1969 article that had triggered the condemnation of the Black Panther Party, had criticized the Cuban government for failing to acknowledge the psychic dimensions of racism. "We feel the Cubans have a misunderstanding of the political, cultural and revolutionary thinking of the black revolution," Johnson charged.[49] Cuba's revolution may have instituted policies that had benefited Afro-Cubans, Johnson implied, but Cubans, as he put it, were "lagging in the revolution of the mind." Like Charlie, Johnson had found Cubans reticent about racial consciousness. The cultural revolution of Black pride that had swept the United States in the 1960s, embodied in the "Black Is Beautiful" movement, had no clear equivalent in Cuba. "We found this is completely repressed by Cuba," Johnson observed. "We have talked to a number of Cuban women and they have started wearing natural hair styles, but to relate to one's African heritage in Cuba is looked down on."[50]

For Bill Brent, however, whose formative political education had occurred in the Black Panther Party in Oakland, as the organization explicitly embraced Black pride *and* socialism—and saw no contradiction between them—racial consciousness represented but one weapon in the multifaceted battle against white supremacy. In his interview with the *Black Scholar*, Brent explained his perception of Cuba's racial climate in ways that echoed the Marxist analysis of the Panthers. Exile in Cuba had confirmed Brent's belief that dismantling the most pernicious effects of racism required making a break with capitalism. "There are very definite signs of individuals here who still possess what could be interpreted as racist attitudes," Brent told the *Black Scholar*. Yet Cuba's approach to dismantling racism differed from the antiracist struggle in the United States, Brent opined, because it was rooted in a structural approach: the incorporation of all working-age Cubans into the labor force, and ensuring universal access to education, health care, and housing, which had been removed from the savage forces of the market.[51]

In a society where the private sector had all but disappeared, what remained was a vast public sector controlled by the revolutionary state. While individual Cuban racists certainly existed, Brent confirmed, he believed that such individuals no longer wielded significant power over the lives of others through public institutions. The material and biological consequences of racism in Cuba were limited because the ability of race prejudice to harm members of society had been undermined. "They are not going around with big signs. They are not going around condemning everybody, but they are incorporating everyone into the work force. There are no jobs that are restricted to anyone because of their color. Also if you look at the officials in the local committees, the CDR's, the mass organizations, etc., in all of the provinces you will find people of all hues and colors running those organizations—leading those organizations."[52]

A decade later, Assata Shakur, a former Panther like Brent, would write of her own first impressions of Cuban society in the mid-1980s. Like Brent, Shakur was optimistic that the structural changes wrought by the transition to socialism had weakened the material consequences of racism. In subsequent years, Shakur's convictions would deepen as she played important advisory roles in the revolutionary government on matters of race and Cuba's relationship with the Black freedom struggle stateside. Working with Cuban cultural and research institutes and with government officials, Shakur eventually became a bridge, symbolically and materially, between the Cuban Revolution and the Black freedom struggle in the United States.[53]

As a newcomer in Cuba, however, what struck Shakur most were the contrasts between the racial integration of her adoptive home and the de facto segregation of American cities. "I spent my first weeks in Havana walking and watching," she wrote in her memoir, *Assata*. "Nowhere did i find a segregated neighborhood, but several people told me that where i was living had been all white before the Revolution. Just from casual observation it was obvious that race relations in Cuba were different from what they were in the United States. Blacks and whites could be seen together everywhere—in cars, walking down streets. Kids of all races played together. It was definitely different.[54]

In the years to come, Shakur's impressions, like those of Bill Brent, would become more nuanced as the persistence of racism in Cuba became more apparent to her North American eyes. As the racial inequities occasioned by the economic contraction of the Special Period emerged after the fall of the Soviet Union in the 1990s, the challenges of fully eradicating racism—in Cuba or anywhere else—became clearer.[55] Brent eventually grew critical of the Cuban government's unwillingness to address racism through targeted race-specific initiatives despite Fidel's call for such a practice in 1986.[56] But the 1970s were heady years of optimism and radical possibility in Cuba, and Brent was still confident that the demonstrable successes of socialist redistribution in augmenting racial equality would continue to render race prejudice impotent. If the institutional basis for racism to cause material harm—through job and housing discrimination, through unequal access to education and health care, or through exclusion from civil and labor organizations—had been undermined, what kind of racism persisted? As Brent told the *Black Scholar*:

> The few incidents that I have seen or that I do have knowledge of concern individuals. . . . A brother took one of the white sisters to court and accused her of practicing racism against him and his family in the building that they were living in. The revolutionary court investigated and found out that there was some ground for him to suspect that the woman was practicing this, and they took action against her to forbid

> her from doing this. The big thing about it was that the community took up the cause and they began to talk to the woman and to find out exactly what her problems were, etc. This happened last year some time and right now there is no problem. I can't say that this woman still doesn't have some racist attitudes or racist ideas, but the big thing is that she is not allowed to express them either by the revolutionary government or by the people in the community.[57]

For Charlie, the survival of race prejudice in a society that had achieved significant progress in ameliorating the material markers of racial equality would remain one of the puzzles of his adjustment to Cuba. In later years, Charlie would often tell the story of a woman that he had been dating to illustrate the point. In the fall of 1972, Charlie met a tall, beautiful Black woman at Coppelia. Her name was Margarita, and she lived in the working-class Havana municipality of Cerro. She had natural hair and liked to hang out in Vedado. "People who were into the hippie thing or the Black thing, they would all come to Vedado. Vedado was the jet set. The hippie set. The Black set. There were a few Black Cubans with natural hair, dashikis. In those days, as a Cuban, you could still get funny looks for having an afro and dashiki."[58] The two hit it off. "Margarita was very free-minded. She had her own thoughts and ambitions."[59]

Most Cubans, including Afro-Cubans, insisted that institutional racism had all but disappeared in the decade after the 1959 revolution. What remained, they argued, was of little consequence to their daily lives. Indeed, upon arriving in Havana, Charlie had been surprised to find that the Afro-Cubans with whom he conversed in his still rudimentary Spanish did not seem particularly race conscious, at least in ways that were legible to his North American sensibility, which had been formed amid the Black–white binary of US racial logic. By contrast, racial classification in Cuba depended on an individual's appearance, not ancestry. As he would later explain: "In the United States, the struggle was definitely about race, you knew who was who, and what the rules were. Anyone who had some African in them was Black. That was the basis of our unity. But in Cuba race was highly classified. Cubans had so many different ways to describe someone's racial appearance, from *mulato* to *mulato claro*, *negro fino*, *jabao*, *maro*, [and] *negro azul*, it was so confusing. It was as if they hadn't quite decided what race was."[60] Eldridge Cleaver had made similar observations. "A lot of people they consider to be white, we wouldn't buy it," he told scholar Henry Louis Gates Jr. in 1975. "I think the colour spectrum in the US has a meaning only for the US. It loses its meaning in some other cultures."[61]

But the greater fluidity of Cuban racial categories did not mean that they lacked their own logics of racial hierarchy, in which proximity to whiteness connoted status.[62] Cubans clearly held firm opinions about phenotypical differences that they ascribed to race. Many vigorously defended the idea of a "raceless" Cuban national identity even as they appeared to embrace the linguistic trappings of Eurocentrism and white normativity. As Charlie later reflected,

> I learned early on that it wasn't worth debating whether it was okay to say "good hair" with Cubans, because they just wouldn't understand. We argued constantly about the idea of "good hair." I would try to explain that, historically, if the first human came from Africa, the first "good hair" was African hair. Eventually I just learned that I had to let it go, because I wasn't going to convince anyone. I remember in particular with some of the girls who were members of the UJC around 1972 or 1973. They were *mulata*. They would have been Black in America. But their revolutionary consciousness had nothing whatsoever to do with race consciousness. They didn't talk about race, and the political struggle was not about race in Cuba.[63]

Margarita talked about race, however, and was interested in the Black Power movement in the United States. When Stokely Carmichael visited Cuba in summer 1967 to attend the Organization of Latin American Solidarity (OLAS) conference, to great fanfare from the Cuban press, Margarita followed the news coverage with pointed interest.[64] During her state visit to Cuba in October 1972, Angela Davis similarly participated in a high-profile tour of the country with Cuban officials of the Communist Party, stirring a modest fashion sensation on the island as some Black Cubans—including Margarita—adopted Davis's natural hairstyle and took note of her simultaneous embrace of Marxism and Black pride.[65] But if Davis saw no contradiction between the two, the same could not be said for many Cubans. Davis had been embraced on the island—by state officials and the public alike—as a *foreign* North American Black revolutionary during the precise historical moment in which *indigenous* Cuban affirmations of Black racial identity were perceived as antithetical to the national ideology of racial integration and cultural amalgamation.[66]

It was this intersectional but amorphous status of being simultaneously foreign, Black, socialist, and racial nationalist that Charlie, Michael, and Antar seemed to embody for the Cubans they interacted with. Cubans seemed to regard the fashions and aesthetic sensibilities of the US Black exiles with mingled curiosity, trepidation, skepticism, and admiration: They were North American and therefore foreign yet also revolutionary. But while foreigners were granted latitude in their deviations from Cuban cultural norms, the same could not be said for Cubans. While some Afro-Cubans styled their hair naturally and wore dashikis, which were often handmade or procured from African students, their numbers were tiny. This was not a mass movement. The phenomenon was also confined almost entirely to Havana, yet these *habaneros*—those who embraced aesthetic markers associated with diasporic Black pride—could still face ostracization or outright hostility.

For Afro-Cuban *habaneras*, these dynamics were compounded by gendered expectations of dress and comportment, including the Cuban version of the sixties-era global panic over miniskirts, which came to Havana a decade late. Once, shortly after Charlie and Margarita had started dating, he met her in Vedado for a night out and found her crying. She said that someone had called her names because of her appearance. She was wearing an afro and a miniskirt, common in the United States but still risqué in Cuba. At first Charlie did not believe her and asked if she was exaggerating. She affirmed that she was not. To prove it, she walked a short distance away and told Charlie to observe the reactions of passersby. Sure enough, someone addressed her. "Whore, why are you wearing that short dress? Why are you wearing your hair like that?" Charlie overheard the man say. "It blew my mind. It never occurred to me that people in Cuba could be so closed-minded."[67]

Charlie, Michael, and Antar tried to understand what they were witnessing. "The Cubans supported the Black movement in the United States, but at that historical moment they felt that the Cuban Revolution had triumphed, and that maybe there was some leftover racist attitudes, but there was no need anymore to struggle against racism in Cuba because racism was going to be wiped out completely. Most of the government and the population didn't believe that racism existed in Cuba. Now today, that seems crazy, but that's how it was."[68] According to Afro-Cuban scholar Esteban Morales Domínguez, bringing *la problemática racial*—the race question—to the fore "meant we had to run the risk of being called 'racist' and 'divisive,' the worst piece of adverse criticism a revolutionary could get at the time."[69]

For some Afro-Cubans, the negation of their lived experiences of racism led to disillusionment with the revolutionary process itself. Since racism was supposed to have met its demise with the beginning of the construction of socialism and the elimination of de jure racial barriers, the suggestion that the germ of prejudice and institutional exclusion might be alive and well in revolutionary Cuba was treated as an indictment of the revolution itself, which had proclaimed itself not only to have eliminated racism but to be the natural ally of the Black freedom struggle in the United States. Scholar Danielle Pilar Clealand relates the story of a Cuban man whom she interviewed. Once, while in his twenties in the mid-1970s, he had tried to create his own Cuban chapter of the Black Panther Party in Havana. Questioned by state security, he was warned that political organizing of this kind would result in further detentions. The man recalled the words of the state security officer: "You wanna create the Black Panthers here? The only Black Panther in Cuba is Fidel Castro!"[70]

Charlie recalled these dynamics clearly: "Many of these people were well-read, had attended rallies for Stokely and Angela, related to the Black struggle in the US, and read the translations of Malcolm X's book that were now available in Cuba. They had become pan-Africanists. A few of them turned against the revolution. They became a little bit counterrevolutionary and went overboard and wanted to leave the country. But they were also ahead of their time."[71]

This ambivalence would become a defining feature of Charlie's political outlook as a Black American expatriate in Havana. He increasingly adopted the hegemonic Cuban prescription of dissent "from within the revolution," meaning constructive critique intended to clarify and improve the revolutionary process, as opposed to "crossing over" into critique that weakened or sought to undermine it. Of course, the devil was in the details. What some Cubans intended as principled critique to strengthen the revolution or rectify errors might be deemed by another as "divisive" to the political project of national unity and the construction of socialism for all. Those who brought the issue of racism to the fore were especially vulnerable to this charge. Nevertheless, Charlie was suspicious of what he saw as the tendency of some dissenters to transform critiques about shortcomings in one area of society, such as racism, into a broader condemnation of the revolutionary process. As he would later explain:

> It was as if they didn't know how to go about raising racial consciousness or struggling against racism without opposing the revolutionary system. And I'm not trying to criticize anyone, but you can't solve problems within a revolution by going counterrevolutionary and embracing the opposition's politics. I just don't believe that. So while a lot of these people were not "real" counterrevolutionaries—you know, they didn't have ties to Miami and didn't want to overthrow the revolution or anything like that—the effect became similar: dividing and conquering. A lot of these people became influenced by the counterrevolutionary ideas and movements. For Michael and Antar and me, we understood their critiques but did not feel that embracing counterrevolutionary ideas was a good away to address it, and so we began to stay away from them. Racism was not institutionalized in exactly the same way as it was in

> America. There weren't separate schools, neighborhoods, jobs. There was no segregation. Everyone lived together; you saw Black and white Cubans in all the same schools, all the same apartments. That changes the entire foundation of relations. Interracial couples were common. And racism was against the law. Sexism was against the law, although there was a big difference between the law and what people actually did. You don't just get rid of five hundred years of racism and machismo in a few years; it's not possible. That's why socialism is a process.[72]

As the one-year anniversary of their arrival in Cuba approached in fall 1972, Charlie, Michael, and Antar were feeling optimistic. With a widening circle of friends and comrades, from both Cuba and the United States, they were feeling more comfortable in their exilic home and hopeful about the future. They had impressed their Cuban hosts, they believed, and had done their best to differentiate themselves from the hijackers who had no desire to acclimate to Cuba.

The hijacking saga itself was also changing. When the RNA comrades had arrived in Cuba, the government had still been credulous of the claims of some of the Americans who insisted that they were fleeing political repression. More than a few of the hijackings had been undertaken by perpetrators who described racial persecution as among the motivations for their actions. "Most of the young cats who came here," Michael would say later, "were just people who got caught up in the whirlwind of black revolution in the United States."[73] A high-profile hijacking initiated by three Michigan men would demonstrate the complexity of the crisis, testing the willingness of the Cuban government to provide sanctuary to hijackers.

Louis Moore had been involved in a lawsuit against the city of Detroit in the years after the urban rebellion of July 1967. The city's police, notorious for violence and corruption, had been at the center of a series of public scandals. Moore, who had no criminal record prior to the hijacking and had been supporting himself as a freelance detective, had filed a $4 million lawsuit against the Detroit Police Department in November 1971, accusing it of engaging in a pattern of brutality against Black residents. The city offered to settle with him for $25.[74] Moore had recently testified against the department in a grand jury case related to the police killings of fifteen people—all but one of the victims Black—by officers within a special plainclothes anticrime unit. Shortly after he testified, however, police summoned Moore to the station and accused him of rape. He denied the accusation and became convinced that he was being retaliated against for his testimony. His family, Moore said, had also been threatened by police.[75] When Moore and his companions eventually staged the hijacking on November 10, 1972, they claimed that the act was a desperate attempt to draw national attention to Moore's legal persecution and the larger context of police misconduct and racism in Detroit.

Demanding a $10 million ransom and the opportunity to speak by telephone with President Richard Nixon, the hijackers took the airplane's kidnapped passengers and crew on a two-day multicity trip, landing nine times at airports in the United States, Canada, and Cuba. As the saga escalated, the hijackers allegedly threatened to fly the airliner full of passengers into the nuclear reactor at Oak Ridge National Laboratory in Tennessee. When the hijackers finally arrived in Havana, however, they were denied entry by Cuban authorities, who were alarmed by the hijackers' threats to crash the plane. In a highly unusual move, Cuban officials ordered the hijacked plane to return to US territory. The plane landed in Orlando, Florida, where FBI agents shot out several of the plane's tires. The hijackers then shot the plane's copilot, wounding him. The plane, now with crippled landing gear and a bleeding crew member, took off and headed back to Cuba. Airport workers in Havana scrambled to lay down foam fire retardant and, some thirty hours after the hijacking began, Moore and his companions were taken into custody in Havana. The plane was returned to the United States. Unlike previous hijackers to Cuba, Moore and his companions were tried and sent to a Cuban prison to serve eight-year sentences.[76]

Alarmed by the spate of hijackings, which had harmed the security of both nations and become a political lability for the Cuban government, Washington and Havana now engaged in rare high-level diplomatic communications to negotiate a bilateral antihijacking agreement, which the two nations eventually signed on February 15, 1973. However, the agreement was not retroactive. Cuba refused to extradite hijackers already on the island, citing its sovereign right to offer political asylum to those it deemed to be fleeing political persecution, a right that had been enshrined by Article 14 of the UN Universal Declaration of Human Rights.

Washington, for its part, had not responded to Havana's extradition requests to return Cuban hijackers to the island to face trial since 1959. It had portrayed Cubans who commandeered aircraft and boats to US shores, including those who used violence, as political refugees from communism, paralleling Havana's characterization of some Americans, including hijackers, as refugees from American capitalism and racism.[77]

Indeed, by the summer of 1972, the State Department, acknowledging the double standard that had characterized its calls for Havana to return US hijackers, had grown pessimistic about the prospects of securing the return of Charlie, Michael and Antar to New Mexico. US officials noted that the Cuban government's "undeviating practice has been to refuse to return hijackers against their will."[78] Now, with the signing of the 1973 US-Cuba antihijacking pact, their extradition seemed more remote than ever. In New Mexico, Governor Bruce King reported that the State Department had advised him that the antihijacking agreement would not apply to Charlie, Michael, and Antar, and that Havana had not responded to a renewed request for their extradition.[79] They would be able to stay in Cuba, it now appeared, as long as they wished.

In the end, it was human tragedy, not geopolitics, that had the greatest effect on their lives in Havana. On the afternoon of March 4, 1973, Antar went to Playa Santa María, a popular beach area east of the Havana, with a Colombian couple. Spring is a typically windy season on Cuba's north coast, with choppy surf and strong currents that produce shifting sand bars and drop-offs. As Charlie later heard the story, they had been relaxing and drinking beer on the beach when a sudden commotion in the water caught Antar's attention. The Colombian woman had slipped under the surface and was beginning to drown, pulling her partner down with her. Antar yelled to the lifeguard and then waded into the churning waves.

Locating the woman underwater, Antar grabbed ahold of her as the lifeguard reached her partner. Then they struggled against the current toward shallow water. When they reached shore, however, Antar was not there. "You have to grab a person in a special way, so they don't pull you under," Charlie later said. "Antar may not have known how to do that. He was a good swimmer, but he was not a lifeguard."[80] The lifeguards found Antar unconscious underwater and began performing lifesaving procedures, but he had taken in too much seawater. Attempts to revive him failed. Antar had drowned.[81]

The news reached the Americans at the MININT house in Siboney that evening. Darkness hovered over Antar's friends like a cloud. The Cuban government notified the US State Department of the death, likely through the Swiss embassy in Havana, as the United States government maintained no embassy in Cuba.[82] In Tanzania, Luther and Joye Goodwin had been contending with other personal tragedies: Luther had suddenly gone blind, while one of their daughters had been diagnosed with a cancer that would eventually claim her life.[83] It was up to Hope Goodwin, Antar's sister, to travel to Cuba in time for the service.[84] The funeral parlor on Calzada Street in Vedado was crowded. Several representatives from the Cuban government, including the Cuban Institute of Friendship with the Peoples and the UJC, paid their respects.[85]

Hope Goodwin stayed less than a week in Havana. "His family was very supportive of Antar, and of his decision to come to Cuba," Charlie recalled. Decades later, the event is still very difficult for Charlie to talk about. "It was really hard for us. It was so heartbreaking. It was a tragedy."[86] Charlie and Michael grieved for their friend. Each day was like a sad dream from which they could not awake. Antar's death left an irreparable void.

Hill, age eighteen, poses for a family portrait in his United States Army dress uniform in 1967. Courtesy of Hill.

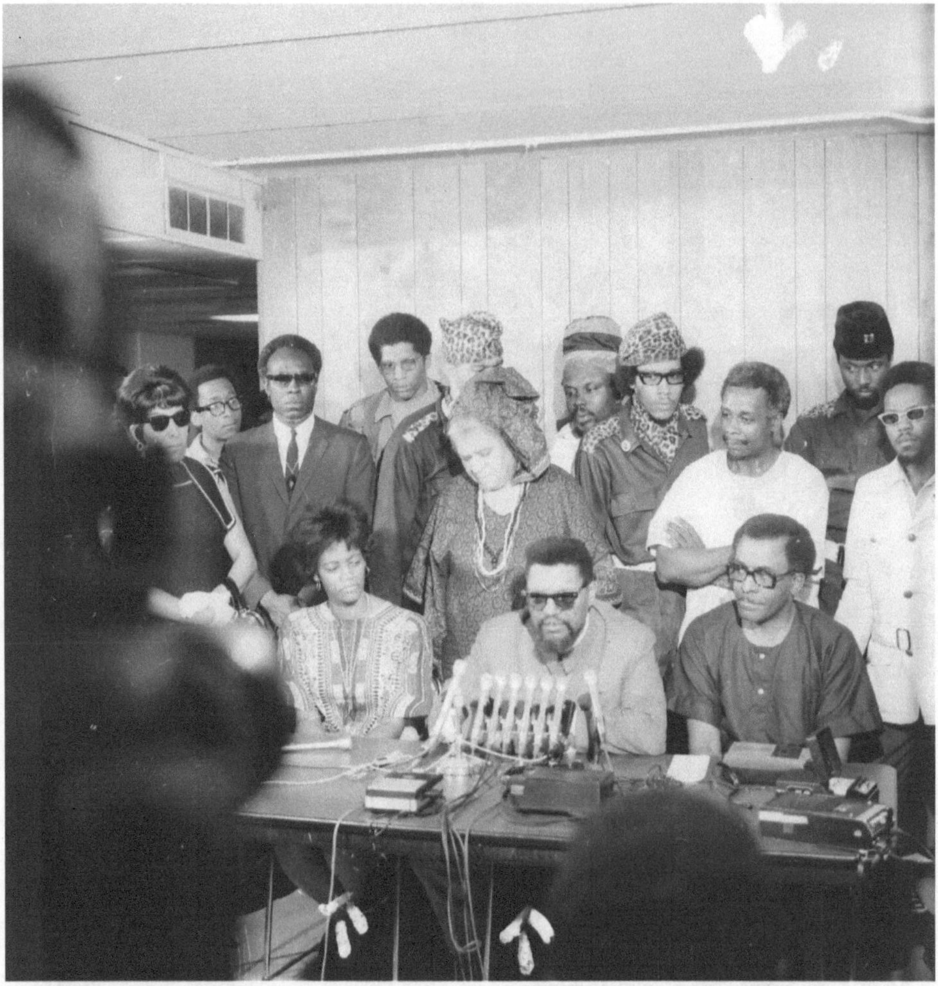

Members of the Republic of New Afrika hold a press conference in Detroit in 1969. Robert F. Williams is in front of the microphones, Mabel Williams sits to his right, and Audley "Queen Mother" Moore stands above them. To Robert Williams's left sits Milton Henry (Gaidi Obadele), with Richard B. Henry (Imari Obadele) directly above him. Courtesy of Walter P. Reuther Library, Archives of Labor and Urban Affairs, Wayne State University.

Eldridge Cleaver, at microphone, is guarded by William Lee Brent at a rally in California in 1968. Courtesy of Bob Fitch Photography Archive, Department of Special Collections, Stanford University Library.

A Republic of New Afrika leaflet demands the release of imprisoned members of the organization following the August 1971 joint FBI and police raid on its headquarters in Jackson, Mississippi. "Free the RNA-11" [broadside], Republic of New Africa Collection (T/027), box 2, folder 5, Archives and Records Services Division, Mississippi Department of Archives and History.

Hill in Havana between stints of volunteer labor in the countryside, circa 1974. Courtesy of Hill.

Geo López relaxes in Havana, circa 1974. Courtesy of Merriam Ansara.

Huey Newton and Gwen Fontaine greet reporters in Toronto, Canada, upon returning from exile in Cuba in 1975. Photo by Boris Spremo/Toronto Star via Getty Images.

Michael Finney near his apartment in Old Havana in 1980, with the capitol building behind him. Courtesy of Bruce Gilbert.

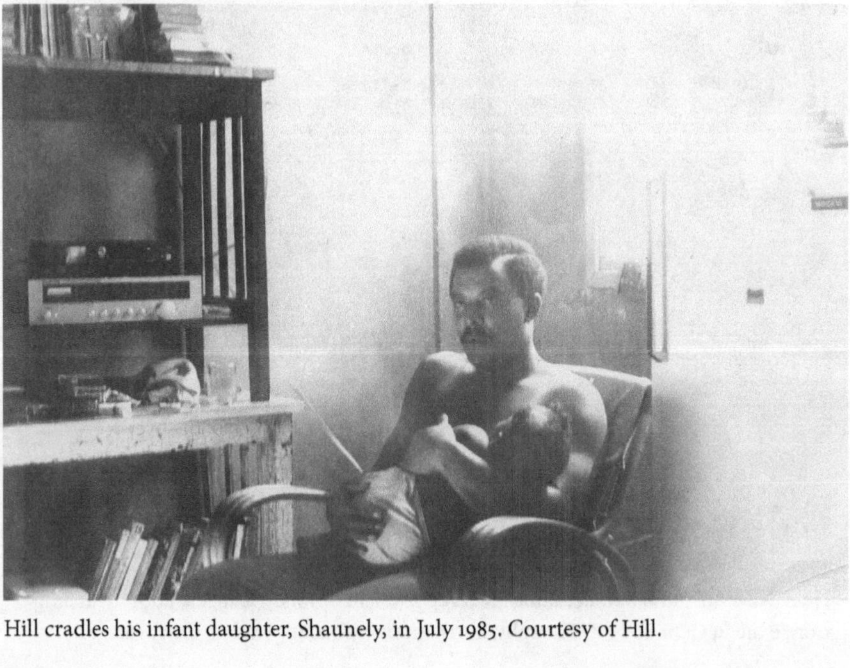

Hill cradles his infant daughter, Shaunely, in July 1985. Courtesy of Hill.

Assata Shakur, holding the manuscript of her autobiography, sits near El Castillo del Morro, with Old Havana and Central Havana in the background, circa 1987. Photo by Ozier Muhammad/Newsday RM via Getty Images.

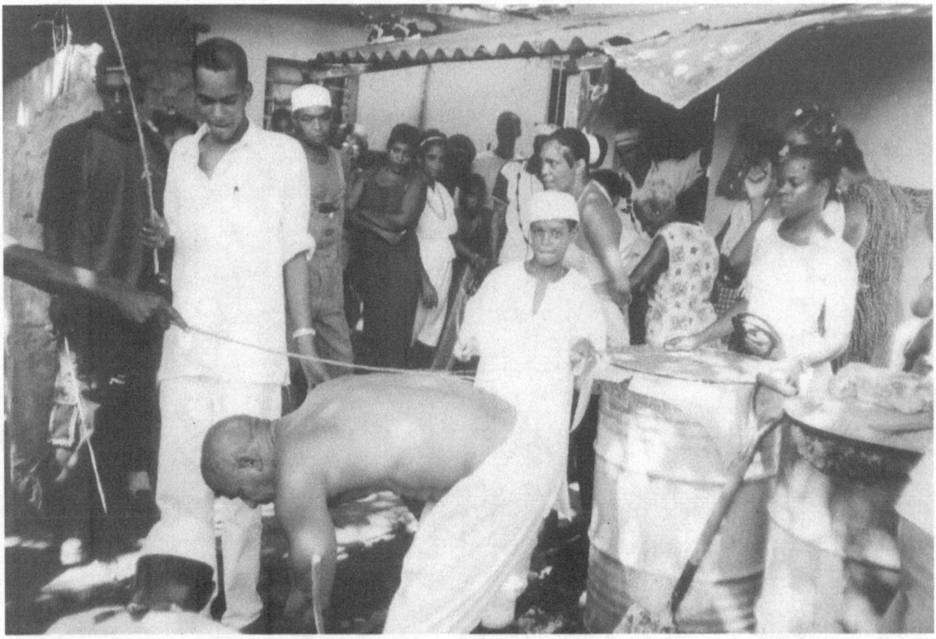

Hill undergoes his initiation ceremony into the Yoruba religion in Cuba, also known as Santería, July 2001. Courtesy of Hill.

Hill poses in front of the José Martí statue in Parque Central, circa 1999. Courtesy of Hill.

Hill and his daughter, Shaunely, in Santa Amalia, circa 2000. Courtesy of Dudley M. Brooks.

Patrick Critton in New York City in 2004, following his release from prison in Canada. Courtesy of Marco Williams.

Hill and Nehanda Abiodun share a drink and a laugh in Reparto Bahía, Havana, June 2013. Photo by author.

An FBI wanted poster that circulated in the United States in 2016 amid warming US-Cuba relations.

WANTED BY THE FBI

CHARLES LEE HILL

Unlawful Flight to Avoid Prosecution - Murder; Air Piracy; Kidnapping

Image obtained in 2015

Photograph taken in 1971

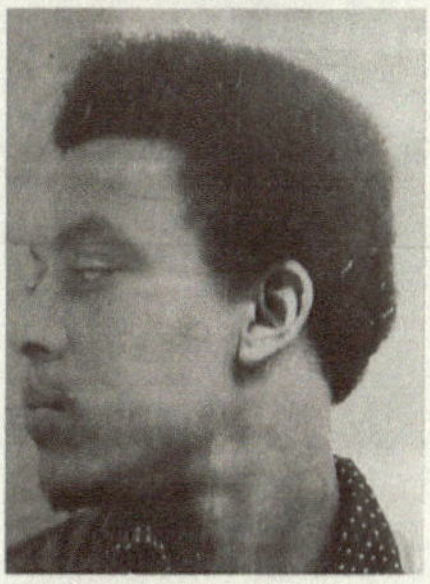

DESCRIPTION

Aliases: "Rashad", Fela Alatonsi, Charles Hill, Charlie Hill, Charlie Lee Hill, Fela Olatonsi, Fela Olatunji, Ronald Leon Thompson

Date(s) of Birth Used: December 15, 1949, October 4, 1950	**Place of Birth:** Olney, Illinois
Hair: Black	**Eyes:** Brown
Height: 5'9" to 5'11"	**Weight:** 165 to 170 pounds
Sex: Male	**Race:** Black
Nationality: American	**Scars and Marks:** Hill has a scar on his left cheek.
NCIC: W052050680	

CAUTION

Charles Lee Hill is wanted for his alleged involvement in a series of violent crimes that occurred in November of 1971.

On November 8, 1971, Hill was allegedly involved in the shooting death of a New Mexico State Police officer during a traffic stop approximately 15 miles west of Albuquerque, New Mexico. On November 27, 1971, Hill and two accomplices (believed to be deceased), allegedly also kidnapped a tow truck driver at gunpoint and forced him to drive the trio to the Albuquerque International Airport. The three men are alleged to have then hijacked a Trans World Airlines (TWA) flight, re-routing the plane to Tampa, Florida. After exchanging the hostages for fuel, Hill and his accomplices flew to Havana, Cuba.

On November 25, 1971, Hill was charged with murder by the Magistrate Court of Bernalillo District, State of New Mexico, and an arrest warrant was issued the same day for his arrest. On November 26, 1971, a federal arrest warrant was issued for Hill in the United States District Court for the District of New Mexico, Albuquerque, New Mexico, and he was charged with unlawful flight to avoid prosecution.

Additionally, on December 14, 1971, Hill was charged in the United States District Court for the District of New Mexico, Albuquerque, New Mexico, with six counts of possession of unregistered firearms, one count of air piracy, and one count of kidnapping.

SHOULD BE CONSIDERED ARMED AND DANGEROUS

If you have any information concerning this person, please contact your local FBI office or the nearest American Embassy or Consulate.

Field Office: Albuquerque

A 2016 FBI wanted poster featuring police mug shots of Hill taken in 1970 and 1971 in Fairbanks, Alaska. Hill has no middle name. "Lee" first appeared in Hill's military records and appears to have been a clerical error.

Nehanda Abiodun, photographed in her apartment in Reparto Bahía, 2017. Courtesy of Noah Friedman-Rudovsky.

Hill, flanked by his son, Antar, and his daughter, Shaunely, on Bélgica Avenue in Old Havana, January 2024. Photo by author.

Hill in Vedado, January 2023. Photo by author.

Chapter 9

Tricontinental City

In the summer of 1973, Charlie and Michael, together with members of the Revolutionary Collective and a few other Americans, moved out of the Ministry of the Interior (MININT) house in Siboney. With its hodgepodge of bunkmates who had been housed together after hijacking airplanes to the island, the residence had become a way station for the Americans who had little interest in participating in Cuba's revolutionary process and had resisted opportunities to work or study. "Some had gotten into trouble with the police, others had become counterrevolutionary," Charlie recalls. "We wanted to get away from them."[1]

Approving of their dedication to *microbrigadas* in San Agustín and Alamar and the Spanish-language courses that several of the Americans enrolled in at the University of Havana, MININT now provided some of them with a modest two-story collective house in the Miramar neighborhood of the Playa municipality of Havana. This was no halfway house for wayward hijackers. There would be no live-in Cuban officers. The Cuban Institute of Friendship with the Peoples (ICAP) would remain their political guardian, but they would be otherwise on their own.[2]

Now responsible for shopping and cooking for themselves, the Americans were given access to *la libreta de abastecimiento*, the system of socialist food distribution that provided monthly allotments of groceries, such as rice, beans, lentils, cooking oil, spaghetti, bread, pork, chicken, coffee, sugar, eggs, powdered milk and other staples, depending on availability, to all Cubans at dramatically subsidized prices. A whole family could eat for what amounted to pennies a day. Added allowances were provided for children and expectant mothers, the most calorically vulnerable members of society. Described in simplistic terms as "rationing" in the foreign press and presented as evidence of bureaucratic state control, *la libreta* was in reality a universal caloric safety net that made nutrition a social right. With food and other basic essentials provided, families could use their salaries to buy additional items in local markets.

La libreta ensured that everyone, from young workers to the elderly, had access to a guaranteed food basket and a baseline of sustenance. The capitalist market logic of supply and demand, in which demand measured only the ability of people in a society to pay for something, such as food, not their human need for it, had been eroded.[3] Adequate nutrition, like education, health care, access to the arts, child care, and housing, was now within the reach of all. *La libreta* also provided choices of finished goods such as shirts, shoes, undergarments, socks, pants, blouses, and dresses, and certain "luxury" items: cigarettes, coffee, mayonnaise, and rum. Soviet bloc industrial products, such as home appliances, were also distributed in this way. To ensure equal access, availability rotated. In a given month someone might choose between shoes or pants, for instance, or a dress or a blouse, but to get both through *la libreta* they would have to wait their turn. Bill Brent later recounted a popular Cuban joke that seemed to sum up Cubans' boundless capacity to recognize the humor in their unique reality. In it, Sherlock Holmes and Dr. Watson are strolling through Havana when they spot a man pull out a handkerchief and blow his nose:

> "That chap doesn't have on any underwear," Holmes whispers to Watson.
>
> "What a remarkable deduction, Holmes," Watson replies. "But how can you possibly know just by looking at the fellow?"
>
> "Elementary, my dear Watson. If he'd bought underwear, he wouldn't have a handkerchief."[4]

In addition to *la libreta*, Charlie and Michael received a base stipend of 40 pesos a month as wards of the immigration system, separate from the wages they earned from working. Cuba's economy was growing, owing to its incorporation into the Soviet bloc in 1972 as a member of the Council for Mutual Economic Assistance, which allowed the island to trade within a stable global economy on fair terms and to receive above-market value for exports, primarily sugar.[5] Between *la libreta* and state salaries, Cubans in the mid-1970s could expect to cover basic necessities and live well by the historical standards of the island, albeit without the bounty of consumer comforts that denizens of wealthy nations took for granted. A family in Havana might wait months or years for their turn to obtain a new refrigerator, an imported industrial product that was in chronically short supply but was distributed equitably. Even toys were rationed, including for the children of political exiles, to ensure access for all.[6]

As Cuban women increasingly entered the workforce in the 1960s and 1970s, household incomes rose, allowing families to take vacations and buy items such as televisions and appliances—if they were available. "On a basic material level," Patrick Critton would later write, "we learnt about the bare differences of food, clothing and shelter between the Third World and America." To Critton, scarcity did not feel like sacrifice. To live in Cuba in the early

1970s, he explained, was both "deprivation and liberation. We lived without the American Way of Life and survived."[7]

In the key population indices of life expectancy, infant mortality, education, and caloric intake, the material markers of human well-being were increasing in socialist Cuba.[8] The astonishing leveling of society also touched less obvious arenas. The tourist infrastructure that had once beckoned foreign tourists was now being used by everyday Cubans, in keeping with the socialist ideal that leisure should be a social right. Vacation packages were available at subsidized rates, and Charlie and Michael sometimes pooled their money to spend a few days at a hotel or resort with their girlfriends. The mass entrance of Afro-Cubans into the professional sector in the years after the revolution meant that vacationing families now stayed at establishments that their parents might only have entered as employees two decades earlier. Havana hotels such as the Inglaterra, the Capri, and the Nacional, once the domain of wealthy tourists, now catered to vacationing Cuban families together with a smattering of foreigners. When American tourists began to arrive in Cuba in the mid-1970s, after the administration of President Carter lifted the travel ban, they rubbed elbows with everyday people in Havana's iconic establishments. "I'm glad you Americans are back," a Cuban electrician told a writer for *Vogue* magazine, who was taking in the scene at the famous El Floridita bar in Old Havana, "though before the revolution you would have told a man like me to get the hell out of here."[9]

At night, La Rampa in Vedado, the epicenter of Havana youth culture, pulsed with activity. Charlie became a regular at nightclubs such as Karachi Club, which had begun featuring DJ nights in lieu of the former staple of live bands, affording the option of playing foreign music. State-run restaurants such as El Polinesio—an ornate tiki-styled prerevolutionary restaurant below the Habana Libre hotel, known for its woven-reed ceiling, polished bamboo decor, and hardwood statues—served a Cuban approximation of Polynesian fare, including fried rice and pork cooked over guava wood inside huge Chinese smokers. Posh prerevolutionary restaurants, now nationalized, served elegant meals at affordable prices to families of humble means enjoying a special night out.

Newer establishments were also on offer. Radical human rights attorney Michael Ratner, visiting Cuba with a delegation of the National Lawyers Guild in 1973, dined one night at Las Ruinas, a chic restaurant built on the remains of an old sugar mill in the newly inaugurated Parque Lenin, just steps from the park's white marble monument to the Russian revolutionary, food stands, and amusement parks for children. He marveled at seeing "such a fancy place . . . in the middle of a socialist revolution." One of the Cubans facilitating their trip explained that "there are no rich people in Cuba anymore. Working class people can come to this restaurant and afford it, at least a few times a year."[10]

Like Charlie and Michael, Patrick Critton was feeling right at home in Havana. The African lineages and cultural fusions of Caribbean culture were as obvious to his eyes in Cuba as they had been in New York, where African Americans and Latinos often shared the same neighborhoods. "I liked Havana very much and I got to appreciate the culture and rhythm and sounds of the Cubans. The women of Havana were very much like the women of New York physically. The black and Latino [*sic*] women in the Bronx and Harlem and East Harlem were beautiful. I knew them because my girlfriends were Spanish and African-American. . . . I was a good dancer and I knew how to dance to Latin music from my parties in the Paladium and other clubs in New York at the time. We, brothers and sisters in Harlem at that time danced to Tito Puente, Ray Barretto, and Eddie Palmieri as well as our soul music."[11]

Dorethea Hill sometimes managed to send her son money and clothing by entrusting it to a member of one of the left-wing political delegations that routinely traveled to Cuba. It was these organizations—including the National Lawyers Guild, the Center for Constitutional Rights, and the Venceremos Brigade—that Charlie and Michael relied on to maintain contact with friends and family. These trips also afforded them opportunities to maintain some contact with political movements stateside. Charlie and Michael sometimes acted as cross-cultural interpreters for visiting delegations. It was the start of what would become a regular political practice for Charlie: translating, distilling, and interpreting the complex realities of life in Cuba for visiting Americans and Europeans, both formal political activists and apolitical tourists.

Meetings with the Venceremos Brigade, whose participants hailed from across the spectrum of the multiracial American Left, were also opportunities to obtain movement news from back home. From a group of Chicano activists from New Mexico, for instance, Charlie learned that Albuquerque had recently witnessed a spate of repression against leftists. The police killings of Las Gorras Negras activists Antonio Córdova and Rito Canales outside Albuquerque on January 28, 1972, not long after Charlie, Michael, and Antar arrived in Cuba, had sent a chill through the Southwest. Córdova and Canales had apparently been investigating police brutality and mistreatment of prisoners. Decades later, intrigue would swirl when a police informant named Tim Chapa claimed to have infiltrated the organization and collaborated with the police to set up the two activists to be killed.[12]

Members of the Republic of New Afrika also visited Cuba. In spring 1973, Charlie, Michael, and Antar had been thrilled to learn that Chokwe Lumumba, an attorney and a key figure within the RNA's leadership, had traveled to the island with a National Lawyers Guild delegation organized in association with the University of Havana.[13] Lumumba invited them to the Hotel Nacional for a dinner hosted by ICAP. The RNA leader was full of questions about Cuba. Over mojitos and lobster thermidor, the exiled RNA activists related their experiences cutting sugarcane and working in the *microbrigadas* with Cuban workers and Latin American internationalists. Lumumba had brought a suitcase of things for them, including a coveted cache of books—the recently published volume by Guyanese historian and Marxist revolutionary Walter Rodney, *How Europe Underdeveloped Africa*, promptly become fodder for the Revolutionary Collective's study sessions—as well as letters from family and friends.[14]

Lumumba's visit was also an opportunity to glean news about the RNA. While the organization never achieved the visibility and influence of the Black Panther Party, it continued to grow even as the Panthers entered a period of decline in the 1970s. In March 1974, the *Los Angeles Times* published an article about the organization, titled "Dream of a Black Republic in US South Persists," that brought the RNA to a mainstream audience. "The heart of the program," the *Times* wrote, "is a series of New Communities to be built on virgin land all across Mississippi, a state heretofore known for violence and repression of Blacks." With a price tag of billions that could be paid, the RNA proposed, through reparations for slavery, the program would fundamentally remake the American South and "re-form the lives of at least ten million Black people."[15]

But the most high-profile member of the US Black freedom struggle to visit Cuba during this period did not come as a member of a political delegation. Huey P. Newton, the cofounder of the Black Panther Party, arrived as a formal political asylee in November 1974. Facing criminal charges in California for allegedly shooting a seventeen-year-old sex worker on a street corner and assaulting a man alleged to be his "tailor," Newton had fled the United States while a legal defense was being prepared.[16] Newton and his supporters maintained that the charges were fraudulent and were politically motivated. Advance approval for asylum was secured from the Cuban government. Arriving in Havana with his girlfriend and soon wife, Gwen Fontaine, and later joined by Fontaine's two children, Newton would spend almost three years on the island and gain a firsthand perspective of Cuban society.

Newton had acquired a keen sense of Cuban history prior to his arrival. Like legions of American teenagers in the 1950s, the Cuban insurgency against the dictatorship of Fulgencio Batista had fired Newton's imagination as a youngster. "I wanted to leave high school in 1958 and join the Cuban revolution," he later told a reporter from the *Richmond Afro-American*. "The only reason I did not come to join Castro was because my mother would not let me. I was only 16."[17] The socialist and internationalist Black Panther Party would become a strong supporter of the Cuban Revolution, and the organization's Oakland leadership maintained contact with New Left activists living in Havana during the late 1960s. One of them, Karen Lee Wald, a supporter of the Panthers who was also close to the Cuban revolutionary government, moved to Havana full-time in 1968 and maintained communication with the Panthers, including Newton.[18] When Wald traveled from Havana to California in 1970, she briefed Newton about Cuba, providing important context about the development of the revolution and opining on the mistakes that previous American émigrés and hijackers had made. Future American exiles, Wald suggested, would do well to respect Cuban sovereignty and laws, and should try to contribute something tangible to the ongoing revolution, "cutting cane or whatever was needed."[19]

By the time Charlie and Michael learned about Newton's presence in Havana, however, it was mid-1975 and the Panther leader had been in Cuba for almost a year. It is not clear whether Newton was even aware of their presence. The case of Charlie and Michael had never been well-known. While relations between the BPP and the RNA had been cordial, the two organizations, which had important differences in their political visions, had never been close allies. Unsure how to make contact, Michael eventually just telephoned the Habana Libre hotel, where Newton and Fontaine were rumored to be living. Newton invited them over, and the three talked for most of the night.

Newton told an engrossing story of his arrival on the island. The Panther leader did not hijack a plane to Cuba, yet his escape from a police dragnet in California with the help of a friend, Hollywood producer Bert Schneider, had been a drama fit for a movie.[20] After Newton jumped bail in California in August 1974, he and Fontaine traveled to Mexico on false identification, living first with friends on an island off the coast of Puerto Vallarta, then in Mexico City. After some three months in Mexico, Schneider secured passage to Cuba for them aboard a fifty-foot sailing yacht from the island of Cozumel. After six days at sea, they neared the Cuban coast on a blustery Thanksgiving Eve night. In the distance they could see the beacon light of the El Morro castle that guards the mouth of Havana harbor. Newton, concerned the yacht might be confiscated if it approached land, persuaded the captain to allow them to go in alone in the yacht's dinghy.

Convinced they would sink in the stormy conditions, the captain reluctantly helped Newton and Fontaine into a small Zodiac with a 9 hp outboard motor. "The captain dejectedly told us that he would go into Havana in a few days so that he could at least claim our bodies, so sure was he that we couldn't make it," Newton later wrote. "He gave Gwen a hug and a kiss and told me she was very brave and said goodbye."[21] In heavy seas, Newton and Fontaine motored toward the Cuban coastline for several hours in the darkness. "The waves were like 5 and 10 feet above our heads," Newton later said. "It was a terrifying experience."[22] Too late, they realized they had forgotten the life vests. As they neared the jagged shoreline, the tiny craft capsized. Washed onto the sharp rocks, they were picked up by alert members of the local Committee for the Defense of the Revolution. Among their waterlogged possessions was a letter in Spanish explaining who they were.[23]

The Cuban government requested that Newton maintain a low profile and refrain from using Cuba as a base of operations for the Panthers. Yet it appears to have placed no restrictions on his ability to give interviews or communicate with the BPP, and Newton was in regular communication with Elaine Brown, who led the organization during his absence and later visited Newton in Cuba.[24] After being given a monthslong tour of the island, visiting farms, hospitals, factories, and schools in the provinces of Pinar del Río, Havana, Matanzas, Las Villas, Camagüey, and Oriente, Newton and Fontaine were installed in a suite at the Hotel Capri in Havana. This was not to the liking of Newton, however, who was anxious to get a "proletarian experience" of everyday life in a socialist society.[25] "When I first arrived," Newton later said, "I had asked to work in the sugar cane fields, because I wanted to experience what many Cubans do—cutting cane."[26] The Cubans declined the request, suggesting instead that he could teach a course at the University of Havana. But Newton was determined. "I told them I'd rather work at a factory and live outside Havana in a more underdeveloped part of Cuba."[27]

Newton got his wish. Joined by Fontaine's two children, who were flown to Cuba, the family moved to Las Villas, as the province of Santa Clara was called at the time, where they were given an apartment in a residential neighborhood. Newton worked for six months in a garage helping to repair cement trucks with a crew of Cuban workers, logging ten-hour days to help the workplace maintain its merit prize for volunteer hours, a status that allowed workers to be first in line to receive scarce consumer items such as washing machines. At night, Newton, freed from leadership duties for the first time in years, had time to read, devouring Alex Haley's newly released epic *Roots*; Michael Harrington's *The Twilight of Capitalism*; and works by Marx, Lenin, Sartre, and Fanon.[28] Fontaine, meanwhile, taught English, while her kids "had a ball" attending a Cuban public school and learning Spanish, which they soon spoke fluently.[29] The Newton-Fontaine family also appears to have been included in *la libreta*. Driving out to Las Villas to visit one day, Bill Brent found, to his amusement, that Newton and Fontaine had been given a live chicken "as part of their monthly rations," but "neither of them had the slightest idea what to do with it," Brent later wrote. "I was surprised to find the leader of the Black Panther Party didn't know how to wring the neck of a chicken and cook it for dinner."[30]

The isolation of Las Villas made it difficult to maintain contact with the party stateside, however, and so Newton and Fontaine reluctantly moved back to Havana, living for a time in an apartment, which had been constructed by a volunteer microbrigade, in the neighborhood of Alamar, a place still teeming with Latin American political exiles, and then at hotels in Vedado. From the Habana Libre, Newton could call anywhere in the world, and as Brent described it, he received "a seemingly endless string of visitors from the States, including Party officials, lawyers, and Hollywood personalities."[31] Newton did ultimately teach, offering a semester-long seminar, titled History of Social Movements, at the University of Havana.[32] Meeting with Newton at his hotel several times during the coming months, Charlie and Michael pressed the exiled Panther leader for his perspectives on the Black freedom struggle and global politics. "You could see that the brother was very intelligent," Charlie recalled, "very sharp and quick-minded, well-read. I could see how he was a natural leader. He was very charismatic and talented."[33]

It is less clear what the Panther leader made of Charlie and Michael. Speaking with writer and counterculture activist Stewart Brand after his return to the United States, Newton opined that Bill Brent, with whom Newton attempted to keep in contact with after his departure, was "the only North American skyjacker who's really made an adjustment to the Cuban life. Just about all the other skyjackers—they have about 25—are in big trouble with the Cuban government for getting into black marketing and all sorts of things. They've gone to prison several times in fact, after they got out [of MININT detention] for invading the integrity of Cuban territory."[34] Indeed, given their legal fate less than a year later, Newton may well have been referring to Charlie and Michael. Their efforts to distinguish themselves from the other American hijackers during this period, including those who became entangled in Cuba's criminal justice system, may have been less successful than Charlie would later claim.

Whatever Newton thought of the RNA exiles, he had clearly developed a deep and abiding affection for Cuba. Yet he was also homesick. One of his lawyers, Paul Harris, would later recall the Panther leader's determination to return to Oakland. "I love Cuba," Newton had told him, "[but] I'd rather spend the rest of my life in prison in my home country than live in exile."[35] Charlie and Michael had chosen the opposite path. Yet like Newton, they too had been cautious about becoming too emotionally invested in Cuba, which they still hoped would be a way station on their route to Africa. Geo López had similarly tried to avoid becoming attached to Cuba. According to Harris, both Newton and López maintained an "exile mentality," intending their stay on the island to be only temporary. Therefore, despite his commitment to his university studies in Havana, Harris wrote, "[Geo] has . . . refused to take a permanent apartment or become totally involved in Cuban political life."[36]

In July 1977, Newton departed Cuba and returned to Oakland to face the legal charges against him. Interviewers asked him about his impressions of life in the Caribbean socialist republic. Cuba was different from the United States, Newton tried to explain, due to "the feeling that truly everybody is an extended family, and the concern for everybody else's welfare. . . . Here it's a feeling of alienation, and there it's a collective."[37] Cuba experienced chronic shortages, and neighborhoods experienced frequent electricity blackouts, he marveled, but with "no looting, no police."[38] Pressed repeatedly to discuss his perceptions of racism in Cuba, Newton denied witnessing any, although he had been alert for signs of it.[39] "I was most impressed by the full employment and lack of racism," Newton asserted to a reporter upon his return. "That was enough to make me fall in love with Cuba."[40]

At other times, however, the Panther leader was more circumspect. Speaking to the *Richmond Afro-American* while still in Cuba, Newton mused that his ability to perceive racism there might be limited by his outsider perspective and by his privileged status as a guest of the government. "I think it would take a black Cuban to really articulate this because I'm being treated in a very generous way. But I would like to say that racial attitude [*sic*] and prejudice are probably here."[41] Like Brent, Newton theorized that racist attitudes in Cuba had less opportunity to translate into institutional racist practices in arenas such as employment and grassroots political participation because of the government's integration of the entire population into the labor market and the civic life of the nation. "Discrimination is an act," Newton argued. "After you have the prejudices, the discriminations come out, if there is an institution for it[,] but the Cubans have attempted to create institutions free of discrimination."[42]

Newton's exuberance about Cuba notwithstanding, he was guarded with reporters from the mainstream press and protective of his Cuban hosts. "It's not perfect, but I don't feel free to talk of Cuban problems with an enemy of Cuba."[43] Instead, the Panther leader focused on the unexpected pleasures of exile. "Cuba was like an extended vacation, and you get sort of homesick. Cuba gave me the time to rethink many things, and I felt at peace there, comfortable for the first time in many years. It was like taking off your coat on a hot day. But I also started feeling guilty. Then I felt duty-bound to be back here, to struggle the way I know how to make change in the United States. I sort of asked myself, 'Can I really live here [in Cuba] for 20 years, like a hermit in some ways[?] Can I live in Shangri-la?' . . . 'No, I don't think so. I think I'll have to go back to hell.'"[44]

Many of the American hijackers were also mulling a return to the United States. For some of them, however, it was Cuba that was "hell." The Cuban government was more than happy to help them leave, and in 1974, MININT began placing American hijackers who wished to depart on flights to Jamaica. Others, less disillusioned with Cuba but ready to move on, also made their moves. "People were starting to go their own ways," Charlie recalls. "There were no hard feelings."[45]

One of those who decided to leave was Patrick Critton. Although he maintained his admiration of the Cuban Revolution—indeed, like Charlie and Michael, Critton appears to have fallen deeply in love with the island and its people—he had decided that it was time to realize his dream of traveling to Africa. Unlike most of the other hijackers, Critton had arrived with his American passport, giving him mobility that others lacked. Bidding his comrades in Havana good-bye in the late summer of 1974, Critton traveled to Cairo, Egypt, then on to Tanzania, making his way to the city of Dar es Salaam.[46]

Like Havana, Dar es Salaam in the 1970s was a hub of internationalism and anticolonial ferment, one that drew an eclectic assortment of political sojourners and radical exiles from Europe, the African continent, and the African diaspora, including the United States.[47] Critton was soon immersed in Dar es Salaam's cosmopolitan political scene. Cuba would continue to stamp his perspectives, however. "I set my standards by what I did and learnt in Cuba," he later wrote.[48] Indeed, Havana's support for African anticolonialism, augmented by the presence of Cuban doctors as the island's global medical missions grew, was already well-known throughout the continent. Tanzania was no exception. "That I had studied and worked in Cuba was my ticket of admission to many liberation movements[,] as was my Harlem birth."[49] Working as a teacher in Dar es Salaam for the next twenty years among a milieu of African and foreign activists, intellectuals, and revolutionaries, Critton eventually married, became a school headmaster, and started a family.

But Charlie had not seriously considered leaving. Not yet. He feared being detained abroad and extradited to the United States. And while he had sometimes pondered turning himself in to the FBI, he knew that would mean decades in prison. And so he concentrated on building a life for himself in

Cuba. The FBI visited his mother in New Mexico, trying to glean information about her son. "My mother told them that I had no plans to return. It was hard for her, but she was always very supportive of my decision to come to Cuba. She knew what was waiting for me if I came back."[50]

Charlie and Michael moved out of the collective house in Miramar in late 1974 and, with some of the remaining American hijackers and Latin American exiles, settled into new digs in a former hotel in Old Havana provided by MININT. Once luxurious, the Hotel Nueva Isla, located near Parque de la Fraternidad, had long since been nationalized and converted into basic housing for Cubans. Since the small apartments did not have full kitchens, Charlie and Michael were entitled to three free meals a day at the *cafetería* in the nearby Hotel New York. "The food wasn't good," Charlie recalls, "but it was a meal."[51]

Charlie had been accepted into the University of Havana, where he would study *historia universal*—world history—intermittently for the next two years. It was his second stint as a student in Cuba, having previously enrolled in an electrical engineering program while he had been working with the *microbrigada* in San Agustín. "They told me that with my twelfth-grade education, the program would be too easy—which was a joke. I could barely keep up. I had never studied physics and math, like Michael, and so he tutored me."[52] The limited residency program was designed for full-time workers. Nonetheless, studying and working proved too much, and he dropped out. Now, at the University in Havana, he was following his longtime intellectual calling to study history, which he had first pursued as a college student in Fairbanks.

To concentrate on his studies, Charlie quit his job at a steelworks in the distant Havana municipality of Cotorro. He found a new gig in the storeroom of a clothing store on Galiano Street in central Havana. Workplaces released workers who were studying at university for an allotted number of hours with full pay. But *historia universal* posed its own academic challenges. Charlie's writing ability in Spanish was nowhere near university proficiency. He loved the classes, however, and the professors received him warmly. One tutored him privately for the entire semester. "I learned a lot cutting sugarcane and working, but I really had to study Spanish hard when I went to the university. I had to take special courses in Spanish at the university, especially to help with writing. The professors went out of their way to help me."[53]

Charlie's primary scholastic endeavor, however, remained that of the organic intellectual. The remnants of the Revolutionary Collective, now based at the Hotel Nueva Isla, continued to function as a study group. In 1975, its members began examining gender as a category of political struggle. It wasn't a wholly new focus. According to Charlie, they had first tried to discuss themes related to gender at the collective house in Miramar at the insistence of their Cuban girlfriends. It didn't go well. Confronting patriarchy, Critton later admitted, was the last thing he had expected to do when he hijacked a plane to Cuba. "This issue of gender equality and women [*sic*] liberation," Critton later wrote, "was more complex, personal and sensitive for us than the issue of oppression, armed struggle and independence. We addressed this issue because the women in our society confronted us with a challenge."[54]

At the time, debates about gender seemed to be everywhere in Cuba. Indeed, the conversations that the Revolutionary Collective were attempting to have mirrored those occurring across the island, culminating in the adoption of the 1975 Family Code (Law 1289) by Cubans in a national referendum vote. As foreigners whose immigration status classified them as temporary residents, Charlie and Michael could not cast a vote. Nonetheless, they witnessed the vigorous public debates that preceded the referendum. Spearheaded by the Federation of Cuban Women, headed by chemical engineer and former guerrilla Vilma Espín, the adoption of the Family Code, which went into effect on March 8—International Women's Day—marked a milestone toward gender equality in Cuba. Defining marriage as "established with equal rights and duties for both partners," it defined the right of both partners to work or study outside the home, and it required both partners to share domestic responsibilities and child-rearing equally.[55]

Building on the socialization of child-rearing through the creation of free public nursery schools in Cuba in 1960, intended to free mothers to work outside the home, the Family Code codified important tenets of gender equality as a matter of law, with civil penalties for violations. Henceforward, husbands-to-be would have to affirm at their weddings, in writing, that they would share domestic responsibilities, and the relevant section of the Family Code was read aloud at marriage ceremonies.[56] In principle, a husband's failure to share home duties was now legal grounds for divorce. In practice, however, men often resisted sharing domestic labor, leaving intact the "triple duty" of women's housework, employment, and civic political engagement. It seemed patriarchy, like racism, could not be uprooted through juridical practices alone. Yet the Family Code, approved after months of public discussion in workplaces and neighborhood associations, set principles of gender equality into law as socialist ideals to be striven for. It was a radical achievement by the international standards of the day.[57]

For the hijackers, gender equality turned out to be the most contentious topic that they would address in their political study group. "In our criticism and self-criticism sessions we almost came to blows over discussion about our personal practice with our women and our desire to change," Critton later wrote. "We all had [to] unlearn our reactionary behavior because we were conditioned like all males in American society to accept the oppression and exploitation of women. . . . I can honestly say it was a liberating experience for all of us in the collective. This experience and education did not mean we would never again be guilty of such attitudes but it meant we would be able to recognize such feelings when they emerged in our relationships with women."[58]

The Revolutionary Collective had also attempted to examine sexual diversity. Beginning in 1965, the Cuban government had infamously sent gay men, together with a number of religious devotees and political dissidents, to rural Camagüey Province to participate in compulsory labor at agricultural camps, termed Military Units to Aid Production (UMAPs), a revelation that elicited heated debate within the US Left.[59] While the practice was officially ended in 1967, antigay discrimination continued throughout the 1970s. Cuba's national reckoning on homophobia—and eventual high-level support for LGTBQ rights within the government and the Communist Party itself—was still decades away.[60]

When the hijackers attempted to discuss the question of homosexuality at the original MININT house in Siboney, it was a brief dismissive affair. According to Charlie, it was only Antar who suggested that maybe there was nothing wrong with being gay. Antar had referenced Huey P. Newton's 1970 letter, published in the *Black Panther*, in which the Panther leader acknowledged that gay people constituted an oppressed class—possibly "the most oppressed people in the society"—that was denied freedom. "I do not remember our ever constituting any value," Newton had written, "that said that a revolutionary must say offensive things towards homosexuals, or that a revolutionary should make sure that women do not speak out about their own particular kind of oppression." A gay man, Newton had written, "should have the right to use his body in whatever way he wants to." On the contrary to being counterrevolutionaries, wrote Newton, "maybe a homosexual could be the most revolutionary."[61]

Charlie was also having doubts about whether homophobia and patriarchy made any sense within a "revolutionary value system."[62] His first Cuban girlfriend, Delia, had primarily dated women, even though she was a member of the Unión de Jóvenes Comunistas (UJC), the youth organization of the Communist Party of Cuba that had participated in the persecution of gay and lesbian youth in the 1960s.[63] Back at the MININT house in Siboney, Charlie had befriended Steven Pera, one of the Chicago teenagers who had allegedly tried to poison the city's water supply. "Steven was gay. The other hijackers picked on him. I'm a very social guy, and I have no prejudice because of sexual [orientation]—whatever people want to do, that's their business. Me and Steve became close. He was an obvious gay person, and some of the other hijackers criticized me for being friends with him. When the Cubans put us at the [Hotel] Nueva Isla, Michael and I shared a room, but they gave Steve his own room because they knew he was gay."[64]

By the mid-1970s, most of the American hijackers were in committed romantic relationships with Cuban partners. Charlie had fallen hard for a young woman named Mida. Worldly, educated, and revolutionary, she was a communist militant who had studied chemical engineering in the Soviet Union. A dedicated member of the UJC, she was now studying art history at the University of Havana. Charlie started spending most of his time at her house. Within a year they were married. Leaving the Hotel Nueva Isla, he moved in with Mida and her family. "They were wonderful to me," Charlie would later recall. And he admired them: Black Cubans, from humble backgrounds, who had seized Cuba's revolutionary transformation as their own and were working to build an egalitarian society. "The whole family was very revolutionary, totally committed."[65]

Politics was one thing; romance was another. Charlie and Mida had married on a youthful lark, but before long, they were having second thoughts. Still dreaming of Africa, Charlie was wary of putting down roots. Yet their relationship also became strained due to something unexpected. In Charlie's version of the story, it boiled down to cultural differences about gender norms. Despite the progressive Family Code, traditional values remained hegemonic. Men were expected to lead. "I would see a lot of Cuban couples," Charlie would later recall, bemused, "and the man would be holding tight to his girl's waist and guiding her as she walked around potholes and getting on the bus."[66] Charlie and Mida both led busy lives. She was now working as a Hungarian language translator while pursuing university studies in the evening, while Charlie continued to study world history and work at the clothing store. They maintained independent spheres, which suited Charlie just fine.

It did not, however, suit Mida, and her family also thought Charlie's attitude strange. At one point, his mother-in-law pulled him aside. He should be stricter with her daughter, she suggested. Don't allow her to stay out so late and require her to check in more. "You can't just allow her to do whatever she wants to do!" Sometimes her brothers or cousins would ask, Where is Mida? "They would give me perplexed looks. What do you mean you don't know where your wife is?" Charlie started going to pick her up after her evening classes and bringing her home. "But it was a drag. I would go all the way there after I had been working all day, even though she could easily have gotten home herself. The whole thing was illogical. It was depressing."[67]

The marriage lasted less than a year. Cuba's legal code made Charlie and Mida's divorce a simple process. In retrospect, it was clear that their lives were incompatible. Yet cultural ideas about gender, including the expectation of jealousy as proof of devotion, are what Charlie remembers most vividly. "I just couldn't adjust to the idea of surveilling someone. Her family was basically telling me to be more chauvinist with her. Wouldn't that be weird to you? . . . It was a chauvinist society, more than America, and it was hard to adjust to."[68] Influenced by the public debates in Cuban society that had proceeded the adoption of the Family Code in 1975 and the ratification of the Cuban Constitution in 1976, both of which contained important provisions for gender equality, Charlie had begun to see machismo as being in conflict with the ability of both men and women to fully realize themselves within a socialist society.

Charlie's ideas about himself and about the world, shaped by radical social and cultural transformations unfolding within Cuban society, were changing. But in 1976, this process was interrupted by events that would refocus the island's attention outward, especially on the rapidly growing Cuban diaspora—and on relations with the United States.

Chapter 10

Detention and Détente

The bombing of a Cuban civilian airliner in the skies over Barbados on October 6, 1976, shocked the world. Cubana de Aviación flight 455, crippled in midair by explosives planted by CIA-trained Cuban exiles, plunged into the ocean. All seventy-three people aboard perished, including twenty-four teenage members of Cuba's national junior fencing team, who had just won gold at a regional championship. In Havana, people cried in the streets. Mass rallies took place. The largest, held at dawn on October 15 in the Plaza de la Revolución, drew an enormous multitude estimated at well over one million people.[1] Charlie and Michael stood in the crowd, gazing at the vast sea of people and reading the pain that was written on their faces.[2]

Since its early days, the Cuban Revolution had faced a counterrevolutionary opposition.[3] Operation Mongoose, initiated by the CIA in 1962, facilitated a vast program of state-sponsored terrorism and sabotage inside the country whose singular purpose was to overthrow the Cuban government.[4] Other campaigns were led by Cuban exiles in Florida with direct or tacit support from Washington.[5] Machinery and crops were destroyed, fishing boats sunk, train tracks destroyed. Less common in recent years, the specter of political violence nevertheless generated an ambiance of foreboding. Only a month before Charlie, Antar, and Michael's arrival on the island in 1971, for instance, Cuban exiles, shooting a high-powered rifle from a speedboat at the seaside village of Boca de Samá in Oriente Province, had killed two and injured four, including two teenage girls.[6] The perpetrators escaped to Florida. "They killed innocent people, trying to destabilize the Cuban government and economic system," Charlie later recalled, still seething at the hypocrisy of Washington's complicity. "If people from the island had been doing this in the United States, they would have invaded Cuba."[7]

Charlie knew Cubans who had witnessed the bloody aftermath of the explosion aboard the French freighter *La Coubre* in Havana Harbor in 1960, feared to be an act of terrorism although no definitive proof had ever emerged. He had watched the testimonies of patriotic young Cubans who had mobilized by the thousands in popular militias to defend their country in 1961 during the battles of Playa Girón, known as the Bay of Pigs Invasion in the United States. Some of his neighbors had taken up rifles to join the militias that put down a CIA-backed counterrevolutionary insurgency in the Escambray

Mountains of central Cuba that lasted until 1965. By the mid-1970s, sabotage and political violence had become less frequent on the island. Instead, it spiked in Miami, where over one hundred bombings, most of them directed against moderate Cuban Americans who favored reconciliation with Havana, sent tremors through the city.[8] Cuban exile organizations carried out at least 279 violent actions around the world during this period, 144 on US soil.[9] Florida-based exiles in speedboats occasionally harassed the Cuban coast, shooting rifles and intimidating fishermen. Charlie and Michael became paranoid that they could be kidnapped. "ICAP [the Cuban Institute of Friendship with the Peoples] warned us to be careful meeting people, and to stay vigilant. The idea of counterrevolutionaries really scared us."[10]

Cubans on the island blamed Miami. Right-wing exiles in Florida, who used their emerging political power to lobby Washington for tougher policies against their homeland, were objects of ridicule and popular anger in Havana. Like his neighbors, Charlie heaped scorn on the counterrevolutionaries. "The leadership of the anti-Castro movement were all cowards," Charlie would later charge. "They paid mercenaries to do the dirty work, and some of them were completely incompetent. . . . The leaders of the anti-Castro movement never did the dangerous work themselves; they sent these low-paid clowns to do it and watched from afar."[11]

As Cubans sought to defend their young revolution in the early years, they had turned inward. Amid ongoing attacks and sabotage inside the country in 1960, Cuba created a national network of vigilance against counterrevolutionary activity that became the Committees for the Defense of the Revolution (CDRs). As a voluntary mass organization, each neighborhood democratically elected its leaders. With a presence on every block, the CDRs also implemented social welfare and health initiatives at the neighborhood level, including blood drives and the national campaign of vaccinations that began in 1962.[12] Yet guarding against counterrevolution meant watching. While most Cubans had a positive relationship with the CDRs, vigilance to some felt like surveillance to others.

Other battles were being waged in the arena of culture and ideology. Debates about national identity permeated all aspects of revolutionary society. One that Charlie remembers clearly concerned what people called *diversionismo ideológico*. Raúl Castro had invoked the idea of ideological diversionism in 1972 as a warning against what he saw as the appropriation of Marxism by those not actually committed to the construction of a socialist society but who nonetheless cloaked their opposition to socialism in leftist or Marxist language. According to the version of the critique later adopted by the Communist Party of Cuba (PCC), *diversionismo ideológico* was the practice of "criticizing Marxism from positions that are supposedly Marxist, with a false revolutionary or progressive disguise" and with "apparent impartiality or objectivity" but with the intention to "introduce ideas contrary to socialism within the revolutionary lines."[13]

But *which* vision of socialism and *which* interpretation of Marx? The ambiguities could be baffling. "It was so hard to distinguish who was who," Charlie later recalled. "We were guests. We tried not to get involved."[14] As Cubans debated the proper way to build socialism, those perceived as advancing ideas contrary to the prevailing vision of the leadership of the PCC or mid-level government bureaucrats could find themselves marginalized. Indeed, Charlie's arrival on the island coincided with a period of censorship of artistic and intellectual expression that came to be referred to as the *pavonato*, after Luis Pavón Tamayo, the key government official involved, or simply the *quinquenio gris*: a five-year gray period beginning in 1971.[15]

The desire of Cubans to resist the omnipresent cultural hegemony of the United States and the capitalist world—influences that were felt disproportionately in Havana—sometimes resulted in a reflexive rejection of music and art perceived as celebrating liberal individualism and materialism. Mass culture from the wealthy nations, some worried, could function like the "subtle weapon" of *diversionismo ideológico* to distract attention from the hard work of constructing a socialist egalitarian society in a small underdeveloped nation in the Global South.[16] Cuban cultural officials claimed that Western rock music, with its association with apolitical navel gazing, drug use, and idleness, might encourage Cuban youth to become "rebels without causes," as Charlie later put it, instead of rebels against imperialism and capitalism. The music of the Beatles had been withdrawn from Cuban state radio in 1964, the same year that the group became a sensation in the United States.[17]

Of course, Beatlemania also provoked a cultural backlash in America. While there were no public bonfires of Beatles paraphernalia by religious groups in Havana, the band's popularity among some youth stirred a social panic of a different sort. Many of the youth in Vedado who embraced American culture, preferred American to Cuban music, tried to approximate American fashions, and were fascinated by all things *estadounidense*, Charlie later insisted, *did* seem more likely to *also* be anticommunists. Many wanted to emigrate. "It was partly true. Some of these Cubans were reactionaries. They identified with the values of American culture, not with those of the Cuban Revolution."[18]

Dogmatic suspicion of culture from the capitalist world would recede in the coming years. Even amid the radio prohibitions of the 1960s, Cubans had continued to listen to whatever they wanted at home, and by the late 1970s, the atmosphere had lifted: Clubs in Vedado were playing foreign rock again, including the Beatles and the Rolling Stones. But a deeper reckoning with the cultural stagnation of this era was still years away. When a lifelike bronze statue of John Lennon was inaugurated in a Vedado park in December 2000, with Fidel and government ministers present, the Cuban leaders' public apology for the marginalization of the group's music coincided with an outpouring of expressions of love for the Beatles in Havana.[19] But for Charlie, the errors of the previous era remained obvious. "There was a lot of talk about divide and conquer. They knew that imperialism would try to influence Cuban culture with anything they could throw at it, including the use of culture, clothing, and music. Cuba is a Western country. The only way that the Cuban government could fully maintain control against counterrevolutionary movements was to monitor culture. They had to take extreme measures. They went overboard."[20]

Charlie's views on the dynamics of Cuba's internal political climate would be shaped by the Latin American political exiles who increasingly made up his friends. And the cost of political dissent in Cuba, they pointed out emphatically, was fundamentally different from that in their home countries. State terror, extrajudicial killings, enforced disappearances, torture, and sexual violence had been implemented in those Latin American countries on a large scale, often with the direct support of Washington and the CIA.[21] Discussion of the anticommunist violence unfolding in the Americas was everywhere in Havana—on street corners and buses, in bodegas and bars—and was chronicled in ghastly detail by the media. Gregory Randall, the American expatriate who spent much of his youth in Cuba, later recalled the electric atmosphere following the September 1973 coup against Allende, whose election had convinced some that a democratic path to socialism in the Americas was possible. "So many hopes died in Chile! We wept. I was almost thirteen at the time. And there was Fidel, in the plaza once again, explaining the disaster, telling stories of terror and calling on us all to express our solidarity with the Chilean Resistance. The dark decade of the seventies had begun."[22]

As Havana swelled with Latin American political exiles, the Ministry of the Interior (MININT) dispersed them around the city—and eventually the entire island—as it tried to conserve resources and ensure housing and food for all. So many refugees arrived that the government put many in hotels.[23] In 1978, Charlie, Michael, and James Cherry were relocated to a new hotel, La Isla de Cuba, on Monte Street, across from Parque de la Fraternidad. The three-story building with graceful arches, terraces, and ornate cast-iron rails had seen better days. Three meals a day were provided for the occupants, although the menu was monotonous. Although the accommodations were spartan, the hotel's central location, set among the stores and dilapidated but iconic splendor of Old Havana, just a few blocks from Cuba's national capitol building, made it an ideal abode.

La Isla de Cuba hotel was filled with other young internationalists. The Cuban government had provided many foreigners the opportunity to settle down in Cuba permanently, provided they work or study. Some of the Latin Americans accepted.[24] Although the Revolutionary Collective had become defunct with the departure of most of the Americans, Charlie and Michael continued to study and debate with their political friends, composed now of Latin American exiles. Most were communists who had been members of armed Marxist-Leninist movements: Tomás, a Mexican revolutionary who had fled the nation's repression against leftists; Orlando, a radical from the Dominican Republic; and a Brazilian internationalist who had fled the anti-Left political violence of the military dictatorship in his country and later joined the Nicaraguan Revolution.[25] It was through these young Marxists and organic intellectuals that Charlie became fully immersed in radical theory. Hanging out in smoky bars near the hotel, Charlie and his friends spent hours reading and debating. "Cuba at that time was the ideal place in Latin America to become educated."[26]

Under the tutorship of this eclectic community of radical organic intellectuals, Charlie's political orientation gradually became as much Marxist as Pan-Africanist. Eschewing the dry Soviet textbooks that were used in Cuban universities, Charlie devoured other texts, rereading the copy of Walter Rodney's *How Europe Underdeveloped Africa* that Chokwe Lumumba had brought them and studying Marx and Lenin under the tutelage of the Latin Americans. He spent months dissecting and debating Isaac Deutscher's biographical trilogy about Leon Trotsky, especially *The Prophet Armed: Trotsky, 1879–1921*, and *The Prophet Outcast: Trotsky, 1929–1940*. These study sessions would be a clarifying period in Charlie's political life:

> The main principle of Marx, that socialism was going to triumph primarily in developed countries, never came to be. What happened was that socialism took root in the weakest links in the chain: feudalist societies like Russia and China. So Marx gave birth to a child with defects. Socialism wasn't born in Germany or France or Sweden. It was born in feudalism. . . . Lenin wanted to have a revolution and develop capitalism to the point where they could use it to build a socialist society. So I began to study these contradictions, and studied what socialism could be and what it couldn't be. . . . Michael and I were reading and reading with the

Mexicans and Brazilians, many of whom were older than us and had read much more than us. The world began to make sense the more we read.[27]

Marxism belonged to the world, Charlie decided, not to Europe alone. Claims that Marxism was Eurocentric made little sense in Havana. Many of the political movements and governments that identified themselves with Marxism during the long era of decolonization were in the third world. Algebra may have originated in ancient Babylonia, but no one claimed that it was relevant only to the Middle East. Indeed, some of the egalitarian principles of Marxism, broadly conceived, seemed not a world away from African communalism. These collectivist principles, which had guided social organization in some parts of the African continent for millennia, were reinterpreted by Pan-Africanist Marxists such as Amilcar Cabral, Walter Rodney, and Thomas Sankara during the era of decolonization.

African-centered socialism had also been embraced by the RNA. While not a formally Marxist organization in the manner of the Black Panther Party, the RNA had embraced Tanzanian president Julius Nyerere's concept of *Ujamaa*. According to Nyerere, each member of society would be expected to contribute their fair share to the creation of the nation's wealth, and in return, the society would provide for each citizen through the socialization of key institutions. An individual, Nyerere wrote, need not "worry about what will happen to him tomorrow if he does not hoard wealth today. Society itself should look after him, or his widow, or his orphans. This is exactly what traditional African society succeeded in doing. . . . That is socialism."[28]

Despite the hegemony of Marxist thought in Cuba, ICAP did not pressure the Americans to study it. "The Cubans, as long as you're struggling against capitalism and imperialism, they don't care what ideology you have," Charlie later opined. "They knew that each movement in each country had to arise out of local and indigenous manifestations."[29] The Latin American exiles had also reported that their state minders from MININT and their contacts in the PCC's Departamento Américas, headed by Manuel Piñeiro Losada, did not attempt to interfere in the internal politics of their organizations while they were on the island.[30] Indeed, their primary contact was usually ICAP, which acted as custodian of the foreign exiles and ensured that their everyday needs were met. Although their legal status on the island was governed by MININT, under whose purview matters of immigration fell, throughout their time in Cuba Charlie and Michael would remain under the guardianship of ICAP, which also provided letters of reference for jobs and now dispersed their living stipend, which they picked up monthly from its Vedado headquarters. "ICAP was like our big brother in Cuba," Charlie would later explain.[31] ICAP's guardianship of Charlie and Michael, and MININT's decision to house them with Latin American exiles, suggest that the Cuban government viewed them as legitimate political asylees, of comparable status to those from any other country.[32]

Nevertheless, being a political asylee in Cuba did not shield foreign exiles in quotidian legal matters. When some of the Americans at the MININT house in Siboney had begun getting into trouble in the early 1970s, Charlie and Michael had tried to keep their distance. But despite their desire to be good revolutionary citizens, they eventually run afoul of the Cuban legal system themselves. Michael was the first. In the summer of 1978, he and Charlie were taken to police headquarters on suspicion of using American dollars to purchase consumer goods to sell on the black market. They were not charged, but it was clear they were under suspicion.

The Cuban government had opened special "dollar stores" in the mid-1970s to capture the hard currency that US tourists and Cuban Americans began bringing to the island in 1977, when Washington lifted the travel ban during the brief détente in US-Cuba relations during the presidency of Jimmy Carter. An earlier version of these stores—dubbed *diplotiendas* or *tecnotiendas* because only diplomats and foreign technicians could shop in them, such as American writer Jane McManus, who worked for Cuba's Organization of Solidarity of the Peoples of Asia, Africa and Latin America—had existed for years.[33] The stores sold consumer items, from cosmetics to food to appliances, sometimes purchased on the global capitalist market, that were unavailable through *la libreta*. The stores created a mechanism for inequality among a small subset of the population which was widely perceived among Cubans as antithetical to socialist values. To show their solidarity with Cuba's revolution, a few of the foreign professionals refused to access these stores or accept a special *libreta* that included extra items.[34]

From the perspective of state economic planners, however, the *diplotiendas* were a necessary contradiction. Thousands of Cuban professionals had left the island during the brain drain that followed the 1959 revolution. The state needed foreign professionals, who were often unaccustomed to the material scarcities of a socialist society, to stay in Cuba. The stores not only offered a modicum of access to the consumer goods of the capitalist world but also allowed the state to obtain hard currency, which was necessary to make purchases on the global capitalist market to supplement the island's incorporation into the Council for Mutual Economic Assistance. As foreign residents, Charlie and Michael were legally permitted to shop in these stores. No one was permitted to resell the items for profit, however, and this is what they had been doing, sometimes to Cubans who had given them pesos to make purchases in dollars. Michael was eventually charged and convicted of reselling items procured from the *diplotiendas*, and in spring 1978, he was sent to prison to begin a two-year sentence.

Political asylees were also not shielded from political scrutiny. The Cuban state did not deploy mass violence against its citizens, but it had other ways of maintaining social control. In June 1978, shortly after Michael was sent to prison and amid preparations for the highly anticipated 11th World Festival of Youth and Students, to be held in Havana, Charlie got a firsthand taste of the Cuban security state. Awakened at four in the morning by MININT officers at his door at La Isla de Cuba, he was told to pack his things. Tomás, Orlando, and James Cherry were also told to pack. "We apologize, but we have to relocate you," the officers informed them. "For security."[35] No other explanation was provided.

World Youth Festivals, convened for the first time in Prague in 1947 to celebrate the end of World War II amid the devastation, despair, and hope of the immediate postwar period, began with the dream, as one young British communist put it, of the "world's youth meeting in comradeship with the common aim of working together for a fuller, happier future."[36] Continuing for decades, the World Youth Festivals were massive gatherings where left-wing young people from around the world met, as scholar Pia Koivunen notes, "to celebrate, enjoy arts, compete in cultural and sports competitions, debate about politics, and tour around socialist, and a few times non-socialist, cities."[37] In 1978, the eleventh iteration of the festival was coming to Cuba under the slogan For Anti-Imperialist Solidarity, Peace and Friendship (Por la solidaridad antimperialista, la paz y la amistad). It would be the first World Youth Festival to be held in the Global South.

While much of the funding came from the Soviet bloc, the 1978 youth festival would assume a distinctly Cuban character. Workplaces, schools, and mass organizations went into mobilization mode to raise donations, produce artisanal souvenirs for the international attendees, and choose members of Cuba's two-thousand-member delegation, selected largely from the Union of Young Communists but also incorporating youth who were not members of mass organizations. Indeed, one of the defining features of the 1978 festival in Cuba would be its relaxed and heterodox atmosphere, in contrast to the sectarian dynamics that had sometimes characterized the festivals in other countries. The event was expected to draw thousands of participants for a week of political discussion, anti-imperialist networking, cross-cultural encounter, and, of course, lots of all-night partying.[38]

Charlie would not be part of this jubilant gathering of internationalist left-wing youth. The coerced supervision that he would experience was, at least on its face, due to the heightened atmosphere of surveillance in Cuba during the late 1970s. Taking place two years after the tragedy of Cubana de Aviación flight 455 and amid an uptick in bombings, assassinations, and violent attacks on Cuban embassies and personnel throughout the world, the 1978 youth festival in Havana, slated to draw participants from all over the world—an enormous and eclectic group of people that could not be thoroughly vetted—occurred during a tense time in which the Cuban government was facing off with an emboldened international counterrevolution. Security measures that would have been considered draconian in other countries were justified in Cuba as precautions to ensure national security.

Temporary detentions of those whose loyalty to the revolutionary process was not beyond question or whose actions could not be predicted had occurred previously during high-profile international events in Cuba. Indeed, one of the first tasks of the CDRs in April 1961, in anticipation of the Bay of Pigs Invasion, was to detain thousands of potential collaborators; later security dragnets sometimes swept up foreign political exiles. During Soviet general secretary Leonid Brezhnev's visit to Havana in January and February 1974, for instance, the American hijackers—including Charlie, Michael, and Bill Brent—had been picked up by state security and taken to a location outside the city.

As Brent later described the incident, an official from MININT came to his apartment one evening to inform him that he would be picked up the next morning. "I wasn't under arrest or charged with anything, but if I didn't catch the bus, I would be picked up and put in jail." Brent's girlfriend—Jane McManus, a respected and well-connected American leftist writer living in Havana—attempted to intercede, to no avail. "There was nothing anyone could do. The Soviet general secretary was too important to take chances with. The Ministry of the Interior was rounding up everyone they thought might cause trouble and holding them in a safe place until the activities at Revolution Square were over. I obediently climbed on the nearly full bus the next morning."[39]

Charlie's experience played out the same way. He insists that he was not bothered by the overnight sojourn. "The food was great," he later enthused. "The rooms were nice. The drinks were strong. Michael and I understood why the Cubans were doing this."[40] Brent recalled the event more somberly, describing the resort as a "beachfront social club surrounded by armed guards." Other hijackers and foreigners were there, including "quite a few Latinos dressed in their militia uniforms or white doctor's or nurse's smocks. A few were silently crying."[41] The detainees were returned to their homes after the conclusions of the day's events in Plaza de la Revolución. "The incident was widely talked about and heavily criticized for a few days and then forgotten as we all fell back into the rhythm of our daily routines."[42]

In June 1978, however, when MININT officers picked Charlie up at La Isla de Cuba, he was not taken to a beachfront resort. And, he soon learned, it would not be a short sojourn. He was being sent away from Havana for an indeterminate amount of time. His first stop would be a village in the rural interior of Holguín Province on the northeastern end of the island, hundreds of kilometers from Havana. Tomás and Orlando were going with him. James Cherry was being sent to a different part of the island: Manzanillo, a seaside city in Granma Province, also far from Havana on the southern coast of the island. Some of the Latin American exiles, especially the hijackers, were also being relocated.[43]

This time, however, Bill Brent remained in Havana, a change of fate that was likely due to his increasingly respected status in the eyes of the state. Determined to make it in socialist Cuba, where he expected to remain for the rest of his life, Brent made a supreme effort to adapt. Working his way up through a series of steady jobs, including a stint at Radio Havana Cuba, Brent eventually graduated from the University of Havana with a degree in Hispanic languages and began a career as an English teacher. His first post was at the Escuela Primaria William Soler Ledea, a high school in the working-class Los Sitios district of Havana. Settling down and marrying Jane McManus, the love of his life, Brent's exile in Cuba—although afflicted by the same feelings of rootlessness and homesickness as all of the émigrés—was testament to his ability to survive, and even thrive, against the odds.[44]

Charlie's exilic life would increasingly look very different from Brent's. And that life, MININT apparently believed, should be lived outside Havana. The MININT officials made it clear that they wanted Charlie and other foreign exiles who were being sent to the provinces to settle down there permanently. They would be given housing and found employment.

Charlie's heart sank as they arrived at the tiny village in Holguín. Once the site of a women's prison farm, it was now home to a police academy and a MININT training facility. A lieutenant was in charge, and there was an older couple who did the cooking and grew much of the food on an adjacent plot of land. There was no security, however, and the exiles had not yet been assigned any work.

Charlie was indignant. He had no intention of settling down in this backwater of eastern Cuba. "I'm not living out here permanently," he informed the MININT lieutenant. "If I'm not under arrest, I can go anywhere I want to go."[45] The lieutenant assured him that he was not under arrest, and the relocation would not be permanent. Charlie was not being "detained," the official explained opaquely, just *retained*.[46] Whatever that was supposed to mean, it was pointless to argue. Political exiles, as guests in the country, were under the supervision of the state. And the state had dispersed hundreds of formal political exiles from Latin America—those who had been invited to seek refuge from political violence in the Southern Cone—throughout the island. Many were sent to rural areas. Partly this was for security reasons, and partly it was to conserve housing, which was in particularly short supply in urban areas. As wards of the state, foreign political exiles in Cuba were provided with housing, food, and opportunities to work or study, and were expected to fully integrate into Cuban society. But they often had no choice about where they would live, at least initially.[47]

Despite his misgivings, however, Charlie was soon enjoying the bucolic environs of rural Holguín. He had first experienced the beauty of the Cuban countryside in 1973 in Pinar del Río, the island's westernmost province, where he had lived in the rural municipality of Sandino for several weeks. To his surprise, the green farmland of Pinar del Río, world renowned for its tobacco and legendary cigars, had been teeming with youth from Havana who were participating in Cuba's vaunted La Escuela al Campo (School to the Countryside) program, which was guided by Marxist principles of combining intellectual study with work. Outdoor education in an agrarian setting, it was believed, would help break down the urban-rural divide that had so characterized the island's prerevolutionary history. In 1972, a similar rural work-study program for adults—the Destacamento Pedagógico—was launched to train thousands of new teachers.[48] Charlie, not much older than the students and from a rural background himself, was fascinated by the programs. "All schools from junior high through high school had to spend forty-five days in the countryside," he later marveled, "so they would gain an appreciation for what country life was like, why that sector was so important to sustain the cities, and how hard the work was, how tobacco was farmed."[49]

The peaceful environment and simple rural pleasures of Holguín reminded Charlie of childhood trips to Alabama. With nothing else to do, he passed the time assisting the elderly couple with farm chores and helping in the kitchen. The house had a cast-iron stove reminiscent of one that his grandmother Molly had used in Wadley. Suppers were feasts. The rustic cuisine, traditional Cuban country fare, was a delicious respite from the monotonous fare back at the hotel: free-grazed chickens roasted whole over charcoal; pork shoulder and ribs marinated in garlic and the juice of *naranja agria* (bitter orange) and then smoked over aromatic guava wood; or a whole pig roasted in a pit, its belly cavity sewn up with seasoned rice and beans. When it was time to eat, there would be boiled yuca topped with *chicharrónes* (crunchy nuggets of fried pig skin) and served with *mojo criollo*, a savory sauce of garlic, citrus, and herbs; and, of course, *moros y cristianos* (also called *arroz moro*), consisting of black beans and rice cooked together, or *arroz congrí*, the same dish made with red beans (*frijoles colorados*), and a simple tomato or cabbage salad.[50] The property next door belonged to a kindly old farmer. Charlie started working on the man's farm, learning to plow with oxen and tending the stands of banana trees.

James Cherry eventually settled down in Manzanillo and started a family. He would live in the coastal city for two decades before eventually returning to the United States in 1992. But Charlie had no intention of spending his life in a rural village. The Cuban countryside, while beautiful, was also incredibly boring. Charlie became restless. As the time of *carnaval* arrived in late July, Charlie, Tomás, and Orlando absconded from the MININT camp and hitched a ride aboard an oxcart to the city of Holguín to enjoy the exuberant street festivities. When they returned two days later, the lieutenant scolded them but made no effort to limit their movements.

As the festivities of the World Festival of Youth and Students got underway in Havana in late July, all Charlie could do was look wistfully at the photo spreads in *Granma*. The festival, lasting almost a week, would ultimately host eighteen thousand youth from 145 nations. The Global South and the Soviet Bloc was well-represented, but so were the United States, Canada, and Western Europe, whose delegations, like those from the third world and the state socialist countries, were personally welcomed at meetings hosted by Fidel and other high Cuban officials. At the festival's inauguration on July 28, delegates from around the world, many dressed in traditional clothing and carrying flags and political banners, marched in long processions to thunderous applause. In the coming days, El Malecón would be decorated and closed to traffic to make space for an international carnival. Music concerts and street parties drew huge crowds as youth from around the world mingled and partied under the banner of internationalism and global anti-imperialist solidarity.[51]

The festival came and went, and still Charlie was puttering around the MININT camp in Holguín. No permanent job or housing had been offered, although the lieutenant claimed that they were working on it. Eventually, Charlie had had enough. Deserting the camp, he hitched a ride west to Havana. No one tried to stop him. In retrospect, says Charlie, it appears that MININT had relocated the exiles living at the hotel La Isla de Cuba as a routine security precaution for the World Youth Festival, with the hope that he would want to stay—as James Cherry did in Manzanillo—but with no intention of enforcing a permanent relocation.[52]

Charlie's return to Havana proved emotionally and economically fraught. The abrupt relocation by MININT had come as a surprise, bruising his feelings and his confidence in his Cuban hosts. "I understood the need to take measures for security, considering what Cuba was up against. It wasn't that. It was that they never asked me what I wanted to do. We didn't appreciate being put in the same security category with everyone else. They just picked us up and sent us away. . . . They could have come to me and communicated. So when I got back to Havana, it was a lull for me politically and mentally. For a number of months, I tried to figure out what I was going to do."[53]

Charlie spent several months sleeping on the floor at friends' apartments around Havana. Lacking a job, he began doing business on the street, as Michael had done, buying goods out of the *diplotiendas* and illegally reselling them on the black market. "It was an error on my part," Charlie later admitted. "I should have approached [ICAP] and tried to work something out."[54] With the influx of US tourists and Cuban Americans into Cuba, the dollar stores proliferated. If foreign currency arrived in Cuba in the form of a wire transfer, it first had to be converted to a government-issued currency document at a bank or hotel in order to be used to shop in the hard-currency stores. Charlie, who had become an adept operator of Cuba's new underground economy, began falsifying currency documents to reflect a higher balance than he had.

One day in early July 1979, however, Charlie went to his usual *diplotienda* to make a purchase. The manager pulled him aside. Police detectives had come to the store looking for him, the manager told him. He had been instructed to tell Charlie to wait for them to return. Charlie knew the game was up. "Tell them to come," he replied resignedly. A police detective arrived and informed Charlie of the charges. He would be confined to jail while the investigation proceeded. A car would be sent for him. The detective told the store manager to give Charlie lunch. "So I sat there and waited for the car. There was no point in trying to run and hide or something. No one can be a fugitive in Cuba. But to me it was heavy, the fact that he just left me there to wait, like he knew I wasn't going to try to do anything. For some reason, they knew my mental outlook, that I wasn't going to do anything rash."[55]

Charlie's first encounter with the Cuban criminal justice system occurred just as the nation's new penal code was set to take effect following the period of state building and institutionalization after the adoption of the Cuban

Constitution by popular referendum in 1976.[56] The island's legal system, while structured on the continental European civil law tradition, now also incorporated elements of socialist legality influenced by the Soviet Union.[57] Cuba's Penal Code of 1979 (Law No. 21) deepened the Cuban system's commitment to socialist legal doctrine with regard to crime and punishment, emphasizing the rehabilitation of persons convicted of crimes and their reincorporation into their communities as full members of society as the ideal of the Cuban penal system. In lieu of conceptualizing acts harmful to people and society as arising solely from individual choices, socialist legal theory aspired to consider the underlying contributors to crime, deviance, and violence, including material want, social alienation, and the breakdown of the community fabric of mutuality.[58]

The Cuban justice system therefore placed a premium on crime prevention, especially for children and youth, who held an exalted position in Cuban society, and on finding community-based means of addressing the root causes of individual acts that were harmful to society. During the 1970s and 1980s, the Cuban legal system instituted various mechanisms of socialization and social control as remedies to crime. Implemented in collaboration with grassroots participatory structures such as the neighborhood CDRs and mass organizations, measures included community mediation, youth outreach, and restorative justice. Informed by socialist values such as solidarity and reciprocity, this approach attempted to differentiate between crimes of survival or negligence and purposeful acts against stability and social order. The primary bulwark against crime, Cubans believed, was an equitable society made up of communities with strong social bonds.[59]

None of this meant that police and prisons had ceased to exist in revolutionary Cuba. Far from it. While overall crime in Cuba, especially violent crime, was low by global standards, and while community and nonpenal solutions to crime had shown success, imprisonment continued for a variety of offenses. The continuing need for a formidable criminal justice apparatus in a revolutionary society suggested a troubling paradox. As scholar Max Azicri observed, "Properly speaking, there is no significant poverty, unemployment, or hunger working as a motivational factor behind criminal acts. And yet, crime is still a reality in socialist Cuba."[60]

Charlie was charged with forgery of a currency document and sent to El Combinado del Este, a maximum-security prison in the Havana municipality of Guanabacoa, while he waited for his case to go to trial. In lieu of the common law tradition of juries, trials in Cuba took place in front of panels composed of both professional judges, who were elected by legislative bodies, and lay judges, who were everyday citizens nominated by workplaces and civil organizations to serve part-time for limited terms while maintaining their regular employment. In 1970s Cuba, as in later decades, it was the office of the *fiscal general*, the equivalent of a district attorney, that adjudicated whether to prosecute criminal cases after charges were brought by police. In addition to a public trial, the accused had the right to hire a defense attorney from a regulated system of *bufetes colectivos*, or collective legal offices, and defense counsel was required in cases where the charges could result in a prison sentence of longer than nine months.[61] Criminal charges filed by police did not imply that a conviction was inevitable. According to the president of the Havana Provincial Court, interviewed in June 1979 by visiting legal scholars from Harvard University, 28 percent of the cases brought before the court, which saw the highest case volume in Cuba, resulted in acquittals.[62]

Nonetheless, the Cuban legal system imposed harsh sentences, especially for repeat offenders. According to the Washington, DC-based Institute for Policy Studies, which conducted on-site evaluations of six Cuban prisons in 1988 with the permission of the Cuban government and interviewed approximately fifty prisoners serving time for politically motivated crimes, these prisoners had been convicted of offenses such as "illegal exit from the country, burning cane fields, conspiracy to assassinate Cuban leaders, participation in armed rebellion in the Escambray mountains, espionage, possession of counterrevolutionary literature, draft resisting, and desertion."[63]

There was also the matter of crimes deemed more ambiguously to be acts against the social order, or those conceptualized as "socially dangerous." As the Harvard scholars observed, "The provision of the new Penal Code on 'enemy propaganda' defines as a criminal act circulation in oral or written form, or indeed the mere possession, of 'false propaganda' as a means of 'incitement against the social order [or] the international solidarity of the socialist State.' . . . Although the notorious Law on Vagrancy has been superseded, there remains in force a provision for confinement of persons on state farms for purposes of re-education, even if they have committed no crime (so-called 'pre-delinquents') or after they have served a criminal sentence (so-called 'post-delinquents')." Cuban law, the American scholars observed, "is the law of a mobilized society, and is subordinate to the Revolution," a tension that seemed to trouble the conscience of some of the Cuban jurists they interviewed.[64] As one Cuban law professor told the visitors, "Weighing the interest of the individual against the social interest—that is the great problem of socialism."[65]

The capacity of the Cuban legal system to sacrifice the rights of the individual, however, also occurred in the quotidian ways of penal systems the world over. The accused in Cuba were supposed to be charged expeditiously, for instance, but in practice, an investigation could drag on for months while the accused languished in jail pending formal charges or awaiting trial, much like in the United States. Defendants in Cuba could legally be required to remain in confinement awaiting charges or trial for a time equaling the minimum sentence of the crime they were accused of.[66]

Charlie would taste the bitter fruit of this policy firsthand, waiting fourteen months in prison for his trail. He hired a defense lawyer from a *bufete colectivo*. When Charlie's case finally went to trial, his attorney defended him by questioning the prosecution's evidence: Where was the currency document, the one that had allegedly been forged? The prosecution replied that it had been "lost" but that it had been vouched for by the police detective who had conducted the investigation, and the signature on the document was Charlie's. "That was bogus, because I had never signed it," Charlie would later maintain. "A defense attorney can only defend you up to a certain point."[67] Charlie made a statement to the court. "I said that I did not falsify the document and was innocent of that, but I admitted that I had been doing illegal business, and I was guilty of that."[68]

The trial took less than an hour. Charlie was sentenced to six years in prison—a harsh sentence considering the nonviolent, petty nature of the crime—and sent back to El Combinado del Este. Outraged, Charlie protested, refusing to go into his cell until a prison official came to speak with him. A warden cajoled him into going inside his cell. The prison's population was currently in flux. Many sentences were being commuted. Rumors were circulating about a general amnesty for the Americans. The warden counseled Charlie to wait and be patient.

Charlie knew something about prison in Cuba from the experiences of Michael, with whom he had kept in touch through letters. Now the two of them would be housed in the same section of El Combinado del Este, reserved for male foreign prisoners. Although prison anywhere could be expected to be unpleasant, the conditions turned out to be far less squalid than Charlie anticipated. Prisoners, who were tasked with cleaning the prison, had an incentive to keep things tidy. Violence was uncommon, both in the foreigners' unit and in the general population, which was fortunate: Charlie's cell door lock, he soon discovered, was broken and could be opened from the outside with a fork. "Most of those guys were just trying to go home, so the last thing they wanted to do was make trouble."[69]

Charlie resigned himself to a boring and frustrating stint behind bars. Prison food, while bland, was at least varied. Lunch and dinner consisted mostly of rice and beans accompanied by sweet potato, or cucumber and shredded cabbage, and sometimes pork or chicken. Once a week there would be fried fish or Cuban-style spaghetti with a thin sauce of tomato paste. Breakfast consisted of bread and sweetened coffee. Prisoners with health conditions, including Charlie, who had been suffering from gastritis, received special diets. Foreigners in Cuban prisons usually lacked family on the island who could bring them food during prison visits, and so they received extra rations. Cuban prisoners were permitted to have family visits every two weeks, and they could bring bags of food, limited by weight, to their incarcerated loved ones.

Prisoners were also eligible for conjugal visits. A separate area, inside prison grounds but away from the main block, served as the prison's love motel. Inmates who were completing the last phase of their sentences in prison farms located outside the prison's walls, where inmates lived in barracks and worked for wages under minimal security, received regular passes to leave the prison and visit their family. Others worked on the outside unsupervised.[70] Despite the lack of formidable security on the prison farms, prisoners had little choice but to stay. Prison escapes were rare, since the nature of neighborhood security, overseen by the CDRs, and the socially close-knit nature of neighborhoods made it impossible for anyone to remain a fugitive for long. Nonetheless, most of the Cuban prisoners were not violent. "Most were not hardcore criminals. Just normal people who had committed petty crimes."[71]

Beyond the prison's walls, however, tensions were building in Cuba. The island experienced an economic recession in 1979–80 after disease claimed a third of the sugar crop—a key source of foreign exchange—and nearly all the tobacco harvest. The adoption of international limits on the range of fishing vessels restricted the Cuban fleet from its traditional waters, leading to declining catches after years of growth.[72] An epidemic of African swine fever, which had devastated the Cuban pig population after it suddenly appeared on the island in 1971, possibly after being introduced by CIA-backed Cuban exile saboteurs, struck again in the winter of 1980, leading to a national scarcity of pork.[73] The shortages of consumer items coincided fatefully with a surge in visits to the island by Cuban Americans—over one hundred thousand in 1979 alone—the result of historic negotiations between Cuban exiles, Fidel Castro, and Washington.

The influx of Cuban American visitors amid an economic downturn would reverberate through Cuban society in unexpected ways.[74] Arriving with suitcases stuffed with gifts for loved ones in Cuba—clothing, home appliances, shoes, cosmetics—the family visits highlighted the vast gulf in consumer living standards. Twenty years after the triumph of the revolution, those who had left for the United States seemed to have prospered. "That made a big influence on the Cubans who wanted a better life," Charlie later recalled of the late 1970s period in Cuba. "People started thinking, you know, 'Would life be better if I was in Miami?'"[75]

It mattered little to some Cubans that comparing consumer living standards against those in the "first world" was unrealistic; in the Cuban popular imagination, the United States, not the island's Caribbean and Latin American neighbors, had long been the point of reference.[76] Yet the proximity of the United States and the policies of Washington, which incentivized irregular migration under the 1966 Cuban Adjustment Act, which granted Cubans entitlements extended to no other immigrant group arriving in the United States, encouraged Cubans to make precisely that comparison—and to risk their lives to reach US soil. As the community of Cubans in the United States grew, so did the network of familial and institutional support for newcomers, and the gravitational pull of Florida's shores increased.[77]

The results were explosive. As consumer shortages appeared in 1979, the island witnessed an uptick in boat hijackings from Cuba to the United States. The perpetrators were not prosecuted in the United States, even when they resorted to violence, and the stolen craft were not returned to Cuba. Many were greeted in Florida as heroes. Cuban officials protested to Washington through diplomatic channels, but to no avail.[78] In a few cases, people used violence to enter Latin American embassies in Havana, which, in a parallel to the policies of Washington, would not accept Cubans attempting to emigrate through regular channels but granted asylum to those who forced their way onto embassy grounds.[79]

These dynamics came to a head on April 1, 1980, when six Cubans hijacked a bus and crashed it through the gates of the Peruvian embassy in Havana. Cuban guards opened fire, killing one of their own in the cross fire. Fidel, furious, ordered all guards withdrawn from the embassy, leaving it unprotected. Within three days, ten thousand people were on its grounds seeking asylum. The Cuban government, caught by surprise and facing a humanitarian crisis, was forced to backtrack. It directed Cubans wishing to emigrate to the port of Mariel west of Havana, where they could be picked up by private boats from Florida. The American immigration system was soon overwhelmed. "Now they will begin to harvest the fruit of their policy of encouraging illegal departures from Cuba," read a front-page editorial in *Granma* on April 21, "including the hijacking of boats."[80] But the political fallout for the Cuban government, which had underestimated the scale of popular disenchantment on the island—and the number of people who wished to leave the country—was immense.

Inside El Combinado del Este, rumors circulated of a prisoner amnesty for Cubans who wanted out—not just from prison but from the island itself. Sure enough, as the crisis ground on, the Cuban government granted many inmates the choice to either go to the United States or stay in prison. Many chose to leave. Then, the Americans were also freed. And so on October 27, 1980,

Charlie and Michael were among the thirty-three American prisoners granted amnesty by the Cuban government. Charlie had served fifteen months of a six-year sentence.[81]

Of the other Americans, all but three elected to return to the United States. They were flown to Miami on an airline chartered by the US Justice Department. One of them was Anthony Bryant, a man who had once joined the Black Panther Party. Hijacking a plane out of New York in March 1969, Bryant had allegedly proclaimed, "I would rather be in prison in Cuba than here." Now, he was overjoyed to be returning. "The United States," Bryant told reporters as he prepared to depart Cuba, "is the greatest country in the world."[82] Louis Moore of Detroit, one of the hijackers behind the Southern Airways hijacking of 1972, in which the hijackers had threatened to fly the plane into a nuclear reactor in Tennessee, also had a changed perspective. Speaking to a reporter, Moore reiterated that the hijacking had been an act of desperation. As for his perceptions of Cuba, which he had experienced only from the inside of a prison cell, Moore was somber. "The black man in the United States has been looking for a place to turn. I can best tell you where not to go."[83]

Charlie and Michael declined to be transported back to the United States, where they would face certain imprisonment, not only for hijacking but for the killing of officer Robert Rosenbloom. Nonetheless, speaking with a *New York Times* reporter, Charlie seemed to hint that he might be open to a plea deal. And then he did something inexplicable: He named Rosenbloom's killer. Antar, he told journalist Jo Thomas, had shot Rosenbloom in 1971.[84] Charlie would later backtrack, admitting that he had lied.[85] Charlie's statement to the journalist appears to have been impulsive, and he would soon regret it. Yet the damage to his credibility was done. Word of Charlie's willingness to pin the killing on an esteemed and deceased friend—not discreetly in a legal filing but publicly to the *New York Times*—tarnished his personal and political reputation, including among some in Havana who had known Antar.[86]

Yet the saga of airplane hijacking between the United States and Cuba was not quite over. While Charlie and Michael had dreamed of returning to the United States, some Cuban émigrés in the United States dreamed of Cuba. A few expedited their dreams by hijacking airplanes. One was Elvis Rafael Fonseca Machado. In the summer of 1980, Fonseca Machado, a Cuban citizen, came to the United States involuntarily as a passenger aboard a boat that had been hijacked from Cuba. A month later, Fonseca Machado, learning that his mother in Cuba was ill, boarded a Puerto Rico–bound flight in Miami on August 14, 1980, and hijacked it to Havana. He was tried and imprisoned in Cuba on air piracy charges. Released in 1985, he attempted to rebuild his life in Cuba.[87] Then in June 1993, at the height of the economic crisis in Cuba that followed the dissolution of the Soviet Union, Fonseca Machado left the island again—this time voluntarily—in a raft. Picked up by the US Coast Guard after being spotted near Key West by the Cuban exile group Brothers to the Rescue, he was imprisoned in the United States on charges related to the 1980 hijacking.[88]

Charlie and Michael had no intention of getting into a raft. And they had nowhere to go. Unlike most of the other released Americans, who could expect to spend several years in a US prison on hijacking charges, the RNA comrades faced murder charges. Remarkably, however, prison in Cuba had done little to dim their support of the island's revolutionary process. "Cuba had treated us well, all things considered," Charlie would later say. "There was no reason to leave what we had here, just to be in prison [in the United States]. We were really homesick, though. It gnawed at us."[89]

Back in Havana after their release from El Combinado del Este, Charlie and Michael discovered that many of their friends were gone. Most of the Latin American exiles had returned home. Marília Guimarães, who had arrived in Havana in 1970 after fleeing imprisonment (or worse) at the hands of the Brazilian military and had fallen deeply in love with Cuba, now prepared to return to Brazil after nearly a decade in exile. Throughout all of it, Guimarães would later write, "nostalgia for homeland" troubled the serene sanctuary of her life in Havana with her children. "The nostalgia for the smell of this blessed homeland is the same as on the first day. The Cubans cover us with joys, but they know that our moon, our sky, the earth we walked when we did not even know what life reserved for us, will never be the same."[90]

Chapter 11

Internationalism and Dreams Deferred

Charlie and Michael tried to rebuild their lives following their release from prison in fall 1980. The Ministry of the Interior (MININT) provided them with spartan hotel apartments at their old abode, La Isla de Cuba. Yet the place did not feel the same. All their Latin American friends had gone home. Havana, which once seemed to pulse with internationalist energy, now felt emptier.

Even as the Latin American political exiles departed in the late 1970s, however, Cuba would increasingly host visitors from Africa, paralleling the island's expanding engagement with the continent. In contrast to the Latin Americans, the Africans were primarily students, not *militantes* or political exiles. Africans were heavily represented among the foreign students at Cuban universities, where they studied engineering, agronomy, education, medicine and health sciences, and agriculture, joining students from across the third world, and in Cuban military academies.

Thousands of Africans also studied at facilities on the Isle of Pines, the large island and special municipality off Cuba's southwestern coast. In 1978, it was renamed Isla de la Juventud (Isle of Youth) in honor of the island's transformation into a center of education for international students in both secondary and higher education. By the mid-1980s, some twenty-two thousand students from more than eighty nations, many from the African continent, were studying there on scholarships provided by the Cuban government.[1] The symbolic reenvisioning of the island, once known for its prerevolutionary panopticon prison—the feared if architecturally striking Presidio Modelo—into a giant school, Charlie would come to realize, prefigured Cuba's later shift toward international medical education.

Cuba's involvement in humanitarian aid, unparalleled for a small nation in the Global South, would be increasingly propelled by both the idealism of proletarian socialist internationalism and the pragmatism of global economic realities. Already by the early 1980s, a wide variety of Cuban civilian global missions had become important sources of hard currency for the state.[2] Nonetheless, the humanitarian nature of many missions, in which the host nation paid nothing or provided compensation at well below market value, continued. In medical care, Cuba's global footprint would eventually become truly massive. "You could see Cuba's international solidarity in the third world everywhere you went," Charlie later marveled, "because those Africans and

Latin Americans and Asians were in Havana, receiving education or medical treatment. Cuba was helping the 'wretched of the earth,' that was part of the revolutionary mission."[3]

The conspicuous presence of so many Africans in Cuba only heightened Charlie's and Michael's desire to fulfill their dream of traveling there. They read constantly about events on the continent. The unfolding anticolonial struggles in Guinea Bissau, Zimbabwe, and Namibia, chronicled in the Cuban press, electrified their imaginations. And Cuba's role as a supporter of these movements was wholly unique. "No other Third World country projected its military power beyond its immediate neighborhood," historian Piero Gleijeses would later write of Cuba's legendary foreign policy. "Extracontinental military interventions during the Cold War were the preserve of the two superpowers, a few western European countries, and Cuba."[4] Cuba's revolutionaries framed these military engagements in explicitly anticolonial and antiracist terms. The most famous was Operación Carlota, a massive Cuban military incursion into Angola in 1975 in support of the socialist People's Movement for the Liberation of Angola, led by Agostinho Neto, against an Angolan opposition backed by apartheid South Africa and the United States. The operation was named for Carlota Lucumí, an African-born woman enslaved in Cuba, who led the largest slave uprising in the island's history: the 1843 rebellion at the Triunvirato plantation in Matanzas. The Cuban-backed side won in Angola.[5]

Operación Carlota, which pitted Cuban internationalist volunteers against South Africa's army of apartheid, mesmerized Charlie and Michael and captured the imagination of the global African diaspora. More than three hundred thousand Cubans served in Angola, and at least two thousand died.[6] The symbolism was not lost on South Africa. "In Angola, Black troops—Cubans and Angolans—have defeated White troops in military exchanges," wrote a South African military analyst in 1976. "Whether the bulk of the offensive was by Cubans or Angolans is immaterial in the color-conscious context of this war's battlefield, for the reality is that they won, are winning, and are not White; and that psychological edge, that advantage the White man has enjoyed and exploited over 300 years of colonialism and empire, is slipping away."[7]

Havana's military incursions into southern Africa would become legend. Cuban leaders characterized the island's armed internationalism in Africa as a fight to atone for the crimes of slavery. Fidel repeatedly emphasized that Cuba and its people were part of the African diaspora, owing not only to the nation's mixed racial composition and its history as a Spanish colony but also to its determination to fight to right past wrongs. "Those who once enslaved man and sent him to *América* perhaps never imagined that one of those peoples who received slaves would one day send their fighters to struggle for freedom in Africa," the Cuban leader declared at an April 1976 event marking the fifteenth anniversary of the CIA-backed invasion at Playa Girón. "We are a Latin-African people."[8]

Cuban internationalism was not simplistically altruistic; it was also premised, Cuban leaders acknowledged, on the revolutionary self-defense of Cuba. Since Washington had "globalized" its war against the island to "suffocate the revolution," Fidel explained, "we also globalized the revolutionary struggle against the United States."[9] This included supporting revolutionary movements inside nations allied with Washington.[10] Nonetheless, Cuba's missions, which hastened the fall of apartheid in South Africa, offered a glimpse of a different kind of international relations. Embodied in the slogan *patria es humanidad* (homeland is humanity), from a line written by José Martí in 1895, Cuban internationalism proposed that global solidarity, and the belief that the freedom and self-determination of all people were intertwined, was the highest aspiration of a nation. It was their duty, Cuba's internationalists believed, to serve the world and, if necessary, to fight and die on these principles. "Cubans came to our region as doctors, teachers, soldiers, agricultural experts, but never as colonizers," Nelson Mandela would later declare five years after his release from prison. "They have shared the same trenches with us in the struggle against colonialism, underdevelopment, and apartheid. Hundreds of Cubans have given their lives, literally, in a struggle that was, first and foremost, not theirs but ours. As Southern Africans we salute them."[11]

Charlie and Michael dreamed of joining the internationalist struggle against the forces of white supremacy and colonialism, even if it meant facing death. Charlie insists that he would have dropped everything and joined the Revolutionary Armed Forces of Cuba if given the opportunity. This was no quixotic impulse. A combat veteran, he certainly understood what he was volunteering for. And his ambitions were hardly unique. Havana in the 1970s teemed with young people with revolutionary dreams. Many of them had looked to Latin America, where revolutionary leftist movements—many with Cuban backing—were taking up arms against repressive US-backed right-wing dictatorships. Gregory Randall would later write of the scores of young people, some Cuban, some foreign-born, like him, who were profoundly inspired by the insurgencies of the Global South. "I, like many of my friends, dreamed of one day becoming an internationalist combatant who would participate in this epic. . . . For many young people of my generation in Cuba there was no question about any of this. Everything we did was part of our secret preparation for a future journey that would take us to our combat post."[12]

Most of these innumerable clandestine histories of the 1970s have never been publicly revealed by their participants. A few fleeting glimpses are provided in scholarship. As historian Tanya Harmer has documented, Uruguayan leftists in

Cuba joined military missions in Central America, including forty-nine members of the Marxist-Leninist Movimiento de Liberación Nacional-Tupamaros and three members of the Communist Party of Uruguay who fought with the Sandinista National Liberation Front in Nicaragua.[13] Exiled Chilean socialists, Harmer shows, who had been trained by Cuba's Revolutionary Armed Forces, also served in Nicaragua, often in the specialized irregular warfare battalions that fought against the US-backed counterrevolutionary Contra forces, under an agreement with Chile's Communist Party.[14]

Cuba's revolutionary history had itself been shaped by foreign-born protagonists. Charlie had been amazed to learn the story of Hatuey, a Taíno nobleman born in Hispaniola, who would later be honored in Cuba's eastern city of Baracoa as "the first rebel of the Americas." Traveling to Cuba to warn of the barbarism of the gold-worshipping European invaders, Hatuey waged a guerrilla campaign against the genocidal pogroms of the Spanish during the age of Columbus. Hatuey's pan-Indigenous internationalism prefigured the campaign of the Dominican-born Máximo Gómez, who served as the brilliant and ruthless commander of Cuba's independence forces during the Ten Years' War (1868–78) against the Spanish and again during Cuba's war of independence at the end of the century.[15]

As Charlie and Michael soon learned, US Americans had also played roles in Cuba's nineteenth-century struggle against Spanish colonialism. The most famous was a white man from Brooklyn, New York, named Henry Reeve, who fought in Cuba's Ten Years' War under Gómez. Fighting in hundreds of military engagements and decorated for his bravery, Reeve died in battle in 1876 in Matanzas. Long honored in Cuba, which later named its renowned global emergency medical response brigade after him—La Brigada Henry Reeve, inaugurated in September 2005 specifically to offer Cuban medical assistance to New Orleans, Louisiana, following Hurricane Katrina—Reeve's contribution to the island's struggle for independence exemplified the long arc of revolutionary internationalism, in which young volunteers dedicated their lives to the cause of freedom in foreign lands.[16]

Cuba's modern epic had also been shaped by foreign internationalists. The best known, of course, was the martyred Argentine doctor-turned-guerrilla Ernesto "Che" Guevara, an apostle of modern Cuban internationalism and third world liberation. Yet there were others, Charlie and Michael discovered, some of them US citizens, like them. William Morgan, a janitor from Toledo, Ohio, traveled to Cuba in 1958 to join the Cuban rebel army, eventually rising to the rank of a commander.[17] Bob Baldock, from Dayton, Ohio, became a soldier in Fidel Castro's own unit.[18] And Cuba's revolutionaries were often internationalists themselves. Cuban university students in the 1950s, for instance, Fidel among them, had once joined volunteers from across the Caribbean in an attempt to launch a military invasion, spearheaded by Dominican exiles, against the dictatorship of Rafael Trujillo in the Dominican Republic.[19]

Less known is the story of the only African to participate in the Cuban Revolution. It was not until decades later that Charlie first heard his name: Ronald Herboldt. A South African sailor, Herboldt had been aboard his ship, the *Constantia*, in the tiny Cuban port of Guayabal in December 1958 when it was boarded by *fidelista* fighters. The Cuban rebels explained their cause to the South African sailors, comparing the Cuban fight against the Batista dictatorship to the Mau Mau's struggle against British colonialism in Kenya. Herboldt, a man of mixed African and European descent, began paying attention. One of the Cuban rebels cheekily promised to take him to Kenya to meet the Mau Mau.

Herboldt abandoned his ship and joined the rebel insurgency against Batista. Settling down in Cuba after the triumph of the revolution, Herboldt married and raised a family, living in Havana for the next four decades. The Cuban fighter's extravagant promise aboard the *Constantia* never came to be. Yet Herboldt did go to Africa with Cuban revolutionaries: not to Kenya but to Angola. Traveling across the ocean in the company of an army of Cuban internationalist volunteers, Herboldt twice participated in the military campaigns in Angola that would lead to the weakening of the South African state and the eventual downfall of apartheid.[20] Herboldt, whose fluency in Afrikaans was a valuable asset to his Cuban unit, would participate in numerous battles against the South African army.[21]

Herboldt would later recount his impulsive decision to abandon his ship in the 2007 documentary *Brothers in Arms*. Sitting by the rustic seashore in the sleepy Cuban village of Guayabal, a row of simple wood-frame homes behind him, Herboldt describes the parallels between the Cuban Revolution, which the *fidelistas* often described in anticolonial terms, and the struggle against apartheid in his native South Africa. "You can see this is not a place that calls anybody's attention to stay," Herboldt explains in the documentary. "I went to the States, I went to Belgium, I went to a lot of places, fancy places, it never called my attention to stay. . . . But it's the struggle, that looks similar to ours. We have the northern part, like Kenya, we had the Mau Maus, and here the rebels were also called Mau Maus. . . . It has something like more or less comparable to each other. And I wanted to live that part."[22]

Charlie and Michael yearned to participate in a similar internationalist saga. They still held out hope that the Cuban government would accept them as volunteers. And so they waited. To make ends meet, Charlie had started working with a friend who made leather sandals with soles made from recycled car tires for a state enterprise. A government ministry provided the materials, setting a monthly production quota and paying them for what they produced. Once the quota was met, they were free to use the remaining material to make shoes to sell themselves at the Saturday market at Plaza de la Catedral in Old Havana. Michael, meanwhile, had enrolled in a journalism program at the University of Havana.

Between Charlie's wages and Michael's student stipend, supplemented by the modest monthly disbursement from the Cuban Institute of Friendship with the Peoples (ICAP), they could get by. The 1980s were comparatively prosperous years in Cuba. Availing themselves of the domestic tourist infrastructure, priced affordably for Cubans, they traveled widely. In July, Charlie visited the eastern city of Santiago, a renowned center of Afro-Cuban culture, for the expositions and street performances of the newly inaugurated Fiesta del Fuego (Festival of Fire), launched in 1981 by Casa del Caribe as an annual academic and cultural event celebrating Afro-Caribbean culture. Throughout the 1980s, Charlie made annual trips to attend, often staying for the colorful street parties of Santiago's legendary *carnaval* later in the month.[23]

Still, they were restless. "Africa had always been our dream," Charlie later recalled. "We knew we had to try."[24] While life in Cuba had been good, all things considered, something was missing. Despite the warmth of Cuban society, they still felt like outsiders, and they yearned for new experiences. "It was just anxiety. It was nothing that the Cubans had done," Charlie later explained. "We just felt that our lives weren't going anywhere, and we wanted to move on while we were still young. See new horizons."[25]

Their youthful wanderlust was interrupted in the fall of 1982, however, when MININT abruptly sent them away from Havana for the second time. Awakened at 5:00 a.m. by state security officers at their door, Charlie and Michael were informed that a car was waiting to relocate them for reasons of "security." This time, the officers assured them, the relocation would be brief. "Pack your bags," the officer told them. "Your apartment will be here for you when you return." Asked where they were going, the officer replied: Isla de la Juventud.

Annoyed but with no choice but to comply, Charlie and Michael allowed themselves to be driven by a MININT officer to the port village of Surgidero de Batabanó on the southern coast of Cuba to meet the ferry. As the launch left the turbid coastal waters, the sea turned a brilliant turquoise blue as the ferry skirted the shallows of the huge coral reefs. They were taken to the town of Santa Fe, known locally as La Fe. "They probably sent us all the way out there because I had escaped from Holguín," Charlie joked. "Now we'll have to swim!"[26]

They were installed in a small furnished apartment in a brand-new development that had been constructed by a *microbrigada*. They were given access to a local restaurant called El Ranchón for their meals. "The menu was dynamite," Charlie would later rave. "Sea turtle is traditional there. We had broiled sea turtle, and sea turtle cooked in a sauce. There was also grilled grouper [and] fried fish, and the menu also had smoked pork ribs, rice with black or red beans, and flan or ice cream for dessert."[27]

Other than eat, however, there was little to do in La Fe. In comparison to the cosmopolitan Havana, Isla de la Juventud—once nicknamed Isla del Tesoro (Treasure Island), in reference to its reputed eighteenth-century status as a pirates' haunt—was a backwater.[28] No employment had been arranged for them. And while evidence of the island's vaunted status as a hub for global education was apparent everywhere, most of the African students that they saw were youngsters: part of the thousands-strong cohort of Angolans, Mozambicans, and others studying at the newly built junior and senior high schools for foreign students from impoverished backgrounds.[29]

To stave off boredom, Charlie and Michael spent their time working out, practicing tae kwon do, and flirting with local women. The MININT officer had forbidden them from going into town, explaining that he had not been authorized to allow it. "Don't make trouble for me by running off somewhere," the officer told them grumpily. He had left his family on the mainland to watch over the two *americanos*. "Don't you think I want to go home too?"[30] Charlie and Michael went into town anyway, hanging out at bars and going to the beach. "Our attitude was that we'd go along with the relocations up to a certain point. We understood the reasons for the security measures. But we had no intention of being confined. If they wanted to stop us, that was their problem."[31] If the MININT officer knew of their excursions, he never said anything.

After a month, Charlie and Michael were taken back to Havana. They never learned the reason for the relocation. Charlie had mixed feelings about the compulsory sojourn. He understood the need for security measures, including those that violated what most North Americans, he later noted wryly, would consider to be their "individual liberties."[32] Charlie and Michael, after all, were foreigners and hijackers. They had recently been in prison, and not just any prison but one that also held high-profile counterrevolutionaries. "We were not just some regular guys. We had a history. They were taking no chances with us."[33] Still, the enforced relocation to a remote island caused hurt feelings and bruised egos. "It bothered us that the government had not asked us what we wanted to do. They just made a plan for us and picked us up."[34]

Charlie and Michael now refocused on traveling to Africa. The best route, they surmised, was via Jamaica. When Salvador Allende had been overthrown in 1973, Michael Manley's democratic socialist government in Jamaica became, for a time, Cuba's sole ideological counterpart in the hemisphere. In the late 1970s, a delegation of Manley officials had traveled to Havana during the tense period preceding the 1980 Jamaican elections. Some of the Jamaicans joined a volunteer *microbrigada* that was constructing houses in Alamar. Other members of the delegation, however, were receiving training outside Havana that they would not discuss. Manley's party, the People's National Party, was engaged in a bitter rivalry with the opposing Jamaica Labour Party, and political violence had become widespread. Manley's delegation in Cuba may well have been receiving intelligence or paramilitary training. Indeed, the Manley government needed all the help it could get, one of the delegates informed Charlie and Michael, and it would accept foreign volunteers. From Kingston, the delegate told them, they could travel to Africa once they were ready.[35]

But they were wary of Jamaica. Manley had lost the 1980 election. In Kingston, they feared, they might be vulnerable to apprehension by Interpol. But it wasn't just that. Richard Dixon and Ali Shanna (James Brewton) had traveled there together in 1974, although whether to work with supporters of the Manley government or to find a surreptitious route back into the United States, it was not clear. In any case, Dixon and Brewton had bidden good-bye to their friends in Havana and flown to Kingston.

And then came the terrible news.

Like their friends in Havana, Dixon and Brewton had grown restless in Cuba. "Even though the Cubans were good to us," Dixon later told a reporter, "it was not our home. You just get homesick."[36] Not long after they left, however, news reached Havana that Brewton had been killed in Kingston. He had allegedly been shot to death, apparently by Jamaican police, on December 15, 1975, Charlie's birthday.[37] According to a credible witness who was with him at the time, Brewton had tried to rob a bank in Kingston.[38] The news devastated Charlie. "He was my close friend, and I could not imagine him dying like that."[39]

It is not clear when Dixon learned the fate of his friend. Leaving Jamaica for Canada sometime in the fall of 1975, Dixon entered the United States, living quietly in a cabin outside South Haven, Michigan. Shortly thereafter, however, Dixon was charged with killing a police officer. Dixon later testified that he had walked into town to obtain firewood for his cabin and because he was "very lonely."[40] He had purchased a gun for protection. Dixon claimed that he was unaware that a car that had pulled up behind him in the dark was a police cruiser. "A large man jumped out and grabbed me by the front of my coat. . . . It startled me," Dixon testified. "My first reaction was to pull away. And as I pulled away he hit me in the face . . . maybe twice. He then grabbed me by the back of the coat and threw me toward the car. I then turned and fired."[41]

Details from Dixon's 1971 airplane hijacking to Havana were not admitted into the trial. Nonetheless, it did not take long for the specter of socialist Cuba to appear. County sheriff Robert Whitcomb went as far as to opine that Dixon, who police said had admitted to being a "communist," might be an agent working on behalf of the Cuban government. If true, that meant that Dixon needed protection—from Cuba! "We feel that since he is no longer of use to the Communist Party he may be a detriment to them," Whitcomb explained to the *Holland City News* after increasing security around Allegan County Jail. "If he suddenly starts talking about what he was doing up here they may want to silence him."[42]

Dixon was defended by the People's Law Office (PLO), the same radical legal collective that had defended Brewton in Illinois and fought for justice for Fred Hampton and Mark Clark after their 1969 assassination by police in Chicago. Dixon entered a not-guilty plea, but to no avail. This was a different kind of case. "The whole thing was tragic," PLO attorney Jeffrey Haas later said. "It was a Black police officer. And it was clear that Dixon had been trying to avoid apprehension. There was little [the lawyers] could do. It was an open and shut case."[43] Dixon was sentenced to life in prison in September 1976.[44] The news reached Charlie in Havana. "Richard was a very revolutionary guy, very strong-hearted, hardworking. Very conscious of racism. I had great affection for that dude. He was a great person."[45]

But Jamaica was their only option if they wished to leave Cuba. In October 1983, Charlie and Michael finally made their move. They informed MININT of their decision. MININT provided airline tickets to Jamaica. They sold their meager possessions, keeping just a few prized books, and they bid their friends good-bye. Unlike Cubans, Charlie and Michael needed no exit visa. A MININT officer drove them to José Martí International Airport. There was no exit interview. They were on their own now.[46]

The Cubana de Aviación airliner landed in Kingston. As they started down the jet stairs, Charlie was watchful. "Don't stare," he said to Michael, "but just take a little glance at those three dudes." Standing off to the right were several men. It was a hot October day in the tropics, but they were wearing heavy clothes, although not heavy enough to conceal the bulge of pistols. Or so Charlie imagined. "All three of them are packing," he muttered to Michael. Plainclothes security, perhaps?[47]

They got into the line for Jamaican customs. Now Charlie saw through the plate-glass window that a car had pulled up outside the terminal. Out stepped a tall, blond, American-looking white man carrying a briefcase. He looked conspicuously out of place. Was he from the United States embassy? Or was this Interpol, come to arrest them at last? They held their breath. Nothing happened. But they were now thoroughly spooked.

Leaving the customs queue, they walked over to the Cubana de Aviación booth to confer with the Cuban airline agent. They were political exiles wanted for crimes in the United States, they explained discreetly. Was Interpol known to apprehend people in this airport? The agent just looked at them, then said, "You should get back on that plane." They had known full well that the trip carried risks. Now, alone in Kingston's airport, they felt vulnerable and apprehensive. Taking the agent's hint, they got back on the airliner and returned to Cuba.

In spite of themselves, they were happy to be back in Havana. The excursion to Jamaica had finally clarified to them that Cuba was their only sanctuary. When they had first arrived in Cuba in 1971, following a massive manhunt in New Mexico and convinced that police would shoot them on sight if they found them, Michael had felt a flood of relief. "I had felt dead," Michael told a reporter in 1987, recalling the television images they had seen in Albuquerque of police putting young Black and Brown men down on the pavement at gunpoint as they searched for the Republic of New Afrika (RNA) fugitives. "That plane taking off was the first assurance I'd had in a month that I was not going to die."[48]

Nonetheless, they could not shake the psychic sensation of feeling stuck in Cuba. As Michael later explained, "We weren't sure exactly where we were heading—not from a real heavy sense of frustration but from a clear kind of unemotional sense that there was nowhere to go, there was no room to move here. We didn't see ourselves as capable of living normal lives here."[49]

There was no escape from exile, however. As Patrick Critton settled into life in Dar es Salaam among a community of expatriates in the Tanzanian capital, he, too, reflected on the costs of exile. "I think no one among the Latinos and Africans I met really knew or understood the consequences and repercussions of what leaving Mexico or South Africa really meant, materially, emotionally, or spiritually," he would later write. Like his former comrades in Havana, Critton was struggling with the psychic dislocation that exile produced. "I fell victim to these experiences and emotions. The negativity is normal, the depression is normal and the homesickness is normal. I passed through this exile phenomenon and I saw others in Havana and Dar struggle to understand this new experience of being a stranger in a foreign land."[50]

Back in Havana following their abortive escape to Jamaica, Charlie and Michael moved back into their old apartments at La Isla de Cuba. They had been gone less than a day. Having sold all of their belongings, they would have to start over. Charlie went back to hanging out with his political friends, reading and studying, and working at the state enterprise making shoes in Old Havana, although he continued to dabble in black market street business.

Michael now resolved to integrate fully into Cuban society. Completing the journalism program at the University of Havana, he took a coveted job as an

English-language announcer and translator at Radio Havana Cuba. There he would work for the next two decades, becoming an integral part of the station's multilingual team. "Michael had a great radio voice," one of his coworkers would later enthuse, and the station often relied on him for English-language programming and translation.[51] Hosting a show on Radio Taíno called *The Jazz Corner*, Michael used the deejay handle "Langston Wright"—a homage to his two favorite writers—to lace the airwaves with the latest American jazz, funk, and soul music. Cubans have always loved American music, and Michael's show gained a following.

Classified as a *técnico extranjero* (foreign technician) by the Cuban government due to his employment at Radio Havana Cuba, Michael received a comparatively higher salary and had access to a special store in the FOCSA building in Vedado that was stocked with imported goods purchased on the global capitalist market.[52] It was this access to consumer items, which the Cuban government had ensured in order to incentivize foreign professionals from the developed world to live and work amid the material scarcities of Cuba, that allowed Michael to purchase a luxury: a car from the Eastern bloc. The white two-cylinder Fiat Polski, not much bigger than a refrigerator, became Michael's pride and joy.

In 1984, changes to the Cuban housing code would remake the living conditions of Cubans and foreigners alike. That year, the Cuban government approved the first General Housing Law, which expanded the status of private property. Accordingly, all citizens—and, apparently, some temporary residents such as Charlie and Michael—were now entitled to ownership rights to the houses in which they lived. Rates of homeownership in Cuba were already high. The 1960 Urban Reform Law had nationalized land and structures, nullifying most forms of private property and land speculation, rendering landlords illegal. Urban properties were conveyed to the tenants and other occupants through lease-to-buy programs that amortized the cost of the dwelling through rents—capped at 10 percent of household income—paid to the government, which acted as the mortgagee. Now, the 1984 General Housing Law expanded homeownership by allowing those who remained in the state-owned properties to purchase them at fixed prices. Homeownership in Cuba rose to approximately 87 percent by 1988.[53]

Charlie and Michael jumped at the opportunity to become property owners. Michael, preferring the convenience of the central city, moved into an apartment on Neptuno Street in Central Havana, not far from Radio Havana Cuba. But Charlie was ready for a change. Still a country boy at heart, Charlie was weary of the treeless narrow streets and urban din of Old Havana. He visited an apartment block in Alamar that had been constructed by a *microbrigada* but decided that he didn't want to live so far away. The neighborhoods of Habana del Este in the eastern part of the city on the way to Alamar were also an option, but although Charlie thought the apartments were very nice, the problem was the same. "I'm not living all the way out here," Charlie told the MININT officer who took him house hunting.

The next day they drove in the pouring rain to the neighborhood of La Víbora in the Havana municipality of Diez de Octubre. The buildings were run-down and unappealing. Not particularly liking the look of the place, Charlie said, "OK, you can turn around now and take me back." The officer cajoled him. "We haven't even looked at this apartment," he said. "We should at least see it." When they opened the door to the apartment, Charlie was taken aback. "The rain had stopped, but it was still raining inside the apartment!"[54]

Finally, they pulled up to a house near Parque Santa Amalia in the Havana municipality of Arroyo Naranjo. It was small—just two rooms and a kitchen—but it would suffice. The nearby park had concrete benches and a jungle gym and swing sets for children. At the park's center a huge tree towered, its spreading branches reaching up to the sky. There was also an outdoor gym. The tranquil location was ideal. It was away from the bustling city yet just a few blocks from buses that went straight to Vedado and Old Havana, and *colectivos*, or collective taxis running on fixed routes—usually 1950s-era American Chevrolets and Fords, called *almendrones*—could have him downtown in thirty minutes. The house would cost him 3,000 Cuban pesos—a dramatically subsidized price—payable in installments over ten years in a manner similar to a mortgage.[55]

Charlie took enormous pride in his achievement of homeownership, one that had remained elusive to his parents in the United States. All of Charlie's neighbors in Santa Amalia also owned their houses. Charlie settled into the neighborhood, became active in the CDR, participated in volunteer night patrols to deter crime as well as nighttime guard duty outside the market. Participating in community events in the tight-knit neighborhood, he felt a newfound sense of rootedness in Cuba.

Throughout the 1980s, Charlie and Michael did their best to stay in contact with left-wing and Black political movements stateside. And while they had received fewer visitors over the years, they had not been forgotten. In 1984, Republic of New Afrika founder Imari Obadele, who would soon earn his PhD in political science from Temple University in his hometown of Philadelphia, published his account of the previous decade, titled *Free the Land!*, which chronicled the movement's long legal battles following the armed confrontation in Mississippi. In a short passage, Obadele described the RNA comrades that Alajo Adegbalola had sent on the fateful mission in November 1971 as "three brothers who had started into Mississippi from Oakland, California, just before Thanksgiving: the scholarly Antar Ra, Ralph Goodwin; Maceo Sundiata, Michael Finney; and Fela Olatunji, Charles Hill. Antar Ra was Oakland Consul. They would have made a superb team in Mississippi, but something had happened on a New Mexico highway. A state trooper had ended up dead, and the brothers had had to skyjack a plane to Cuba. Everyone was glad they were safe and still in the struggle: they were fine revolutionaries."[56]

The arc of Black radicalism in the United States would intersect with Cuba in other ways that year. The arrival in 1984 of Assata Shakur—the American political exile whose presence in Cuba would exert the greatest impact on relations between Havana and the remnants of the US Black freedom struggle—was initially kept low-profile. Granted political sanctuary by the Cuban government after more than a decade as a fugitive in the United States, Shakur spent her first year in Havana learning Spanish and spending time with her daughter, Kakuya, who had been born in prison.[57] Although Shakur was best known for her involvement in the Black Panther Party and later the Black Liberation Army, she also formally affiliated with the Republic of New Afrika in the late 1970s.[58] While rumors of Shakur's presence in Cuba had circulated quietly, her presence was not publicly confirmed until 1987, when a *Newsday* reporter published an interview with her from Havana.[59]

Cuba's allyship with the US Black freedom struggle and its support for African decolonization occasionally led to the arrival of unexpected guests. One was William Potts, a Black New Yorker who admired Cuba's support for African anticolonialism. On March 27, 1984, Potts hijacked a Piedmont Airlines flight to Cuba with the hope of being given military training in order to participate in the anticolonial struggle in Africa.[60] Unlike Shakur, a well-known activist whose 1979 escape from a New Jersey prison had made her akin to a modern-day Black radical folk hero, Potts was an unknown grassroots activist. He said that he had been a member of a clandestine Black activist group in New York. During the hijacking, Potts told his captive audience of passengers and crew that he was "a soldier in the Black Liberation Army," according to news reports, and expressed support for the anti-apartheid struggle in South Africa and the Sandinista government of Nicaragua.[61]

In other respects, however, Potts's actions were less comprehensible. His hijacking was not a bid to escape criminal charges. While he could have entered Cuba legally by traveling as a tourist via a third country such as Mexico, Potts appeared to be under the impression that a hijacking would impress the Cuban government and demonstrate his credentials as a revolutionary.[62] The unfortunate Potts had no idea what he was getting himself into. He had not researched the situation in Cuba and was unaware that Washington and Havana had signed an anti-hijacking accord in 1973.

Although the agreement included a loophole that allowed for the provision of asylum in cases of political persecution, the Cuban government had stopped invoking it for most hijackers, who would now be sentenced to lengthy prison terms. Arrested upon his arrival, Potts would spend the next thirteen years in a Cuban prison. Released in the late 1990s, Potts settled down in Cuba, got married, and tried his hand at farming.[63]

There was also Ishmael LaBeet, a troubled Vietnam veteran from the US Virgin Islands who said that he had joined the Black Panther Party while living in New York. LaBeet, also known as Ishmael Muslim Ali, was the accused ringleader of a robbery that resulted in the murder of eight people in 1972. The crime had occurred at the Fountain Valley Golf Course, a resort catering to wealthy foreigners that had become "the symbol of racial and economic inequality on St. Croix."[64] The event became known as the Fountain Valley Massacre. Ali and four co-defendants were charged with the killings. They were defended at the trial by a team of renowned civil rights attorneys including William Kunstler, Chauncey Eskridge, and Margaret Ratner Kunstler, who argued that the men, all of whom were Black in a case in which seven of the eight dead were white, had been subjected to violence and gross prosecutorial misconduct amid a climate of acute racial animus in Saint Croix. As military helicopters conducted patrols and the Pentagon dispatched soldiers to enforce an island-wide curfew, local authorities in Saint Croix, under intense pressure to identify the killers, brutalized and intimidated suspects with abandon. The men's confessions, their lawyers demonstrated in court, had been extracted under torture. "There isn't a constitutional right that hasn't been broken in this case," Kunstler said in an interview.[65]

A jury nonetheless sentenced the Fountain Valley defendants to life in prison.[66] There they remained for a decade. But on December 31, 1984, as Ali was being transported under guard from the Virgin Islands to New York aboard an American Airlines flight, he commandeered the plane. Armed with a gun that someone had hidden in the lavatory, Ali forced the plane with 185 passengers aboard to fly to Cuba.[67] Landing at José Martí International Airport in Havana, Ali was tried for air piracy by a Cuban court and sentenced to prison.[68]

With Potts and Ali in prison, and Shakur maintaining a low profile, Charlie and Michael were initially unaware of the presence of these new exiles. But Charlie had other things on his mind. He had been dating a woman named Caridad, and in late 1984 she became pregnant. Charlie was about to become a father again.

For the first time in his life, Charlie was ready to embrace parenthood. His past attempts, he admitted, had been failures. Charlie had maintained communication with Kathy in Fairbanks and with their son, who had been born in June 1972. They had named him Fela in keeping with Charlie's New Afrikan name, given by the RNA. But apart from long-distance phone calls, Charlie had no relationship with his son, who grew up five thousand miles away. Neither Kathy nor Fela ever visited him in Cuba.[69]

Charlie had first become a biological father at fifteen years old, after conceiving a child with a woman in Albuquerque who was three years his senior but still a teenager herself. Her name was Regina, and she was from Detroit. Upon discovering the pregnancy, Regina moved back to Michigan to be under the care of her mother. The baby girl was born in June 1965, and Regina named her Caroline, after John F. Kennedy's daughter. Charlie had played a minimum role in her life. Regina and Caroline had come to live with him for a time in Oakland, but it was clear that the relationship was not working. Charlie joined the US Army soon after and was eventually sent to Vietnam. Then he hijacked a plane to Cuba, ending any possibility of being in his daughter's life. Although Charlie had sometimes attempted to communicate with her through his mother, who maintained contact with Regina in Michigan, Caroline rebuffed communication with him.[70]

Now, Charlie and Caridad were expecting a baby girl in Cuba, and he was over the moon with excitement. Shaunely de la Mercedes was born on July 6, 1985, and her arrival would change Charlie's life forever. "I've loved every minute of being a parent in Cuba," Charlie would later say, beaming. "For the first time in my life, all I wanted to do was be a father."[71] For a while, politics seemed a world away as he tried to create a stable life for his daughter. Shaunely's birth, a turning point in Charlie's life, was also a turning point in his Cuban exile. From that moment on, he would prioritize being a father, which meant staying in Cuba. His dreams of joining the African anticolonial struggle slowly faded.

Charlie now focused on working legitimate jobs instead of selling items "*por la izquierda*," as Cubans called economic dealings on the black market. In 1986, Charlie began working at a supermarket that employed six full-time workers, eventually becoming a manager. Lax regulation of state enterprises had resulted in an epidemic of theft by managers and employees alike. "In those days, if a store operated on a deficit, the government would just wipe the slate clean and move you to other employment. Now, you go to jail." Charlie would later relate a story about a construction brigade of Cubans that had been contracted by a foreign company at the port of Mariel, a new free trade zone that the Cuban government had set up to entice foreign investment. A hammer had gone missing. When it did not turn up, its cost was deducted from the pay of all the workers. "You just don't steal from the capitalists, man!"[72]

Charlie insists that he did not steal from the socialists. He kept the store's books clean. If there were extra items at the end of the month, Charlie says, he distributed them to the workers. Two of the women who lived nearby often brought Charlie lunch, since he lived too far away to go home at break time. "The workers there were really good people. We tried to look after each other." When one of the employees asked Charlie if the store could advance her five pounds of rice, Charlie told her just to take it, because the store had run a surplus that month. When the woman received her allotment of rice from *la libreta* the next month, the woman tried to repay the store, but Charlie refused to take the rice. This began to happen regularly, as Charlie continued distributing surplus items to the workers. Eventually management found out and demanded an explanation. Charlie told his supervisors that since there was a surplus, he felt justified in helping the workers. The supervisors told Charlie that he had to stop. "That's what *la libreta* is for," they told him.

Legal trouble eventually found Charlie through a careless slipup. As he was walking home late one night, a bag of laundry slung over his shoulder, a police car stopped in front of him. The officers demanded to search the bag. Not wanting to be searched on a dark street with no one around, an instinct he had inherited from years of caution around police in the United States, Charlie asked to be taken to the station for the search. The officers acquiesced. "In those days it was hard for me to get used to the idea that police have a job to do, and that the world would be chaotic without them. . . . There was definitely no comparison to how it had been for us in the United States. I had seen enough to know that Cuban police are not just going to shoot you and ask questions later."[73]

Charlie got into the back seat of the police car, unhandcuffed, and rode to the station. At first, the police found nothing illicit. But then an officer noticed something on the ground. It was a marijuana joint. "The fact is, the joint was mine," Charlie would later say. "I was high, and I had forgotten that I had it with me."[74] He had no intention of going to prison for a joint, however, so he denied that it was his. The officers did not believe him.

For the second time during his stay in Cuba, Charlie was sent to prison. This time it was to La Cabaña, an imposing colonial-era stone fortress that guards the entrance to the Bay of Havana and includes El Morro castle, part of the historic defenses of the old city, which had been designated a UNESCO World Heritage Site in 1982. Every night at nine o'clock the thunderous boom of the *cañonazo*, the ceremonial firing of a canon atop the fort, echoed dully through the prison. From the area just outside the prison, where he was assigned to sweep and pick up trash, Charlie could see Old Havana just across the bay.

Inside the maximum-security prison, however, the scene was less picturesque. Locked in his cell, Charlie fumed at the injustice of being caged, potentially for years, for a miniscule amount of marijuana. A neighbor of Charlie's had recently met a similar fate. "I don't think the Cuban policy is scientific or medical," Charlie later said. "It's been proven that alcohol causes much more harm than marijuana. The Cubans are eventually going to have to come to this [conclusion] and change, just like they did with gender, or homosexuality, or racism."[75]

Punishment in Cuba for marijuana possession was more punitive than in the United States. A range of other nonviolent offenses, especially for corruption or political crimes, could result in similarly long stints in confinement. So harsh were sentences for certain classes of crimes that Cuba had achieved the dubious distinction of having one of the world's largest per capita prison populations. Yet crime on the island was low. What explained the contradiction? The rate of incarceration circa 1988—roughly 320 per 100,000 persons, according to data provided by the Cuban government—was lower than that of the United States (roughly 380 per 100,000) but well above global averages. According to the Institute for Policy Studies (IPS), a Washington, DC-based progressive think tank, the paradox of a large prison population in a country with low crime was indicative of "extraordinarily long sentences."[76]

Charlie's second incarceration coincided with the fact-finding delegation to the island by the IPS, which had been granted permission by the Cuban government to study conditions in prisons and evaluate the treatment of prisoners. Visiting six facilities in different parts of the country, the IPS was granted full access to all areas of the prisons and conducted confidential interviews with more than 120 prisoners, the majority of them selected at random.[77] The IPS concluded that the Cuban prisons they visited contained various features that were "humane and constructive," especially those that emphasized rehabilitation, and some that were "harsh and cruel," whose primary purpose was punishment.[78] According to the IPS, the former included the high rate of paid employment among prisoners, who worked under conditions comparable to nonincarcerated workers and earned two-thirds of standard civilian wages, allowing them to support families on the outside or amass savings. The prisons visited were all "clean and hygienic," conjugal visits existed at all prisons they visited, and many prisoners acquired practical work skills and education up to the ninth grade. The IPS delegation "heard no complaints that prisoner-against-prisoner violence is commonplace," and the prisons had adequate medical facilities, although some prisoners held on political charges reported "failure or delays in access to medical care."[79]

Despite its generally complementary assessment of the Cuban prison system, the IPS did not mince words about its "harsh and cruel" aspects. While these included infrequent mail service and few opportunities to receive visits, the delegation noted with particular concern the use of cramped punishment cells for prisoners "who resist re-education or violate prison discipline."[80] At their worst, punishment cells measured approximately five by seven feet, or a total of thirty-five square feet of floor space, and housed two or three prisoners; some punishment cells lacked bedding.[81] Comparable in size to the notorious isolation units in US prisons for solitary confinement, the housing of prisoners in such conditions—in Cuba, the United States, or anywhere else—had been deemed a form of torture under the United Nations Convention Against Torture and Other Cruel, Inhuman or Degrading Treatment or Punishment, adopted in 1984.[82] Additionally, in two prisons visited by IPS, Boniato and El Combinado del Este, the delegation "encountered frequent complaints that prisoners who did not conform to the prison regime had been beaten with rubber hoses (*mangueras*), or with fists or sticks."[83]

Charlie's summation of incarceration in Cuba, based on his experience in two correctional institutions, is similarly ambivalent. "Prison anywhere is going to be unpleasant, and this was that, even though the Latin American guys, every single one of them, said that prison in Cuba was a picnic compared to their home countries."[84] Black and *mulato* Cubans appeared to be overrepresented among the prison population, confirming other reports of racial disparities.[85] In contrast to his experience in El Combinado del Este in 1979–80, violence among the prisoners in La Cabaña seemed to be more common: "I don't know how to measure it, or what to compare it to. There were no gangs in Cuban prison. But it seemed like you heard of people getting stabbed with homemade knives, stuff like that." But the food was satisfactory, and there was enough of it. "You would get fish, chicken, pork, and your rice and beans." And the prison was clean. "It was spotless, man, just like El Combinado, one step from being impeccable."[86]

Charlie again hired a defense attorney from a local *bufete colectivo*. After five months in the general population in La Cabaña, Charlie was sent back to the foreigners' section of El Combinado del Este. When the trial began, Charlie's lawyer argued that the joint had been found on the ground, not on Charlie's person, and so there was no proof that it was his. The panel of professional and lay judges charged with adjudicating the case was unconvinced. Charlie was convicted of marijuana possession. However, since Charlie had already been confined for eight months awaiting trial, the sentence was reduced to time served, and he was released a week later.

Back home in Santa Amalia, Charlie vowed never to return to prison. As an exile in Cuba who was legally classified as a temporary foreign resident, he would now have to strengthen his relationship with ICAP, which was still functioning as the political guardian of the foreign exiles. Working with ICAP, he hoped, might also allow him to maintain some contact with US left-wing movements. However, he was leery of showing his face at the institute's offices in Vedado. Would they judge him for his stints in prison? But if his incarceration had prejudiced ICAP against him, the *compañeros* and *compañeras* did not show it. Charlie's commitment to Cuba's revolutionary project was not in question. His crimes had been petty, nonviolent, and nonpolitical offenses. In keeping with the Cuban legal system's emphasis on the incorporation of the formerly incarcerated back into their communities as full members of society, all criminal convictions were eventually expunged from Charlie's official record.[87]

Michael's postcarceral experience in Cuba also supports the premise that incarceration was not a permanent mark against revolutionary citizenship. Within a few years of his release from prison, Michael had graduated from a university professional program and obtained a position at Radio Havana Cuba, a prestigious post within the network of state media outlets, which came with stringent security protocols and a clear expectation of revolutionary ideals. Like Charlie, he had been convicted of a petty, nonpolitical offense. Michael's tenure at the station signaled that he was perceived as a trustworthy and responsible member of Cuban revolutionary society.

Of course, none of this meant that Michael never daydreamed about returning home to the United States. And his feelings about the US Black freedom struggle had not changed. "I still believe in the same things," Michael had told an American reporter in May 1985. "We did something important. Maybe not the way it should have been done, but it was done."[88] Although he had made a way for himself in Cuba against the odds, there was no denying the visceral ache of homesickness. "I have contemplated the possibility of going back and perhaps going to prison for what we did. I would be willing to do five years just for the purpose of going back to the United States."[89] Michael knew the prison sentence would not be five years.

Charlie insists that no one ever discriminated against him in Cuba because he had been incarcerated. The staff at ICAP continued to be as warm and professional as ever. "They didn't seem to treat me any different or judge me. They just said, you know, 'Try not to go back to jail, man!'"[90] When a reporter had inquired about Charlie in June 1987 during his stint at La Cabaña, Michael refused to discuss his friend's imprisonment, saying only that Charlie had experienced "difficulties adapting, which has been the rule for most of the exiles here. Not just Americans, but the Latin Americans, too. It's not a political thing. It's culture shock. Exile."[91]

Chapter 12
Resolviendo

In 1989, Charlie could sense that Cuba was entering a crossroads. The storm clouds of the crisis that would eventually lead to the dissolution of the Soviet Union—and with it, the disappearance of Cuba's primary trading partner and source of economic aid—had darkened considerably. Mikhail Gorbachev's visit to the island in April, which sought to reaffirm flagging Moscow-Havana ties, nevertheless put on display the tensions between Fidel's vision of "rectification," with its renewed commitment to socialism and central economic planning, with the liberal market reforms of Gorbachev's perestroika. Most alarming for Cubans, the Council for Mutual Economic Assistance (Comecon), the Soviet trade bloc that provided loans and preferential trade agreements to member socialist countries, had repeatedly downgraded its commitments to Havana. The stage was set for a major economic shock in Cuba.[1]

Charlie tried to shrug off the turmoil in the Soviet bloc. Embracing fatherhood and becoming a homeowner had given him a newfound sense of purpose in Cuba. He had thrown himself into the joys of parenthood and became more involved in his neighborhood's Committee for the Defense of the Revolution. But as rumors of economic hard times swirled, Charlie was again doubting whether the island could be his permanent home. Although he still had no serious complaints about life in Cuba, it was hard to shake the sinking sensation that exile was a dead end.

Charlie and Michael had maintained a low public profile in recent years. Foreign journalists wrote about them occasionally, often in response to anticipated shifts in US-Cuba relations. Interviewed by a *Boston Globe* reporter in February 1989, Charlie acknowledged his sense of frustration and uncertainty. "What am I going to do with my life? Where the hell am I going to go?"[2] He would even consider the Soviet Union as a destination, he joked, if Gorbachev would just extend an invitation. "I've thought about the Soviet Union. I'd like to go to Russia."[3] On his worst days, Charlie had even mulled turning himself in to the FBI. "I'm looking for a deal. . . . I'd talk to these people," he told the *Globe* reporter. "If I could do maybe five or 10 years, I'd go back, you dig. But the State Department says no deal. They want me 100 years in prison, man."[4]

American society had also changed during the Reagan and Bush years. Inequality had widened, and the prison population had more than doubled.

Charlie and Michael followed the news from the United States closely. They tried to stay attuned to the social movements stateside that animated the era—the subterranean radicalism that historian Bradford Martin calls "the other eighties."[5] But the 1960s era of radical hope had clearly come to an end. "I don't see progress having occurred in the States, except to a very small part of a black middle class that didn't exist 30 years ago," Michael told reporter Anne Marie O'Connor in 1991. "The great majority seem worse off. In fact, the Eighties generation was the first since slavery that cannot hope for a better future for their children. Social programs are being defunded. It is consumer society at its most monstrous. Alienation at its most frightening. Blacks have become an expendable class."[6]

As the afterglow of the idealism of the sixties faded, the world slowly forgot about the exiled American radicals in Cuba. "At first, a lot of groups in the United States wanted to help us, testify on our behalf," Charlie had told the *Globe*. "Now nobody knows what we're doing. Even here, nobody is much interested in our story anymore."[7] Charlie now viewed his past in a different light, owing partly to the passage of time and partly to the fact that he had now seen enough to grow disillusioned. In hindsight, the RNA's clarion call for the creation of a territorial Black nation inside the United States seemed hopelessly naive. "I don't regret what I believed in. But the way we went about it was wrong. I was young. I wasn't clear in my thinking. We misjudged armed struggle in the United States, and we didn't understand clearly the historical process of black liberation."[8]

Michael had come to similar conclusions. "As human beings, we are very much products of our times," Michael told O'Connor. "And those were times of sweeping rebellion among black Americans that affected millions of people. Many were killed, incarcerated. Many became frustrated or joined the mainstream. Others probably became drug addicts. But it was the most widespread, deep-seated black rebellion in the history of America."[9] Like Charlie, however, Michael sensed the futility of evaluating his past radicalism through the lens of the present. "It's not the same moment in history. There is not an anticolonialist revolution going on in Africa. There is no Black Panther Party. Conditions are different. The Nineties are not the Sixties."[10]

In Tanzania, Patrick Critton was also mulling his past. He had built a life for himself in Dar es Salaam and Arusha, gotten married, and enjoyed a successful teaching career and a wide circle of friends. But he, too, was succumbing to the gnawing sensation that he was stateless. He was homesick. Eventually he applied for a US passport at the American embassy in Tanzania using his Social Security number and his real name. The passport was granted.[11] In 1994, Critton decided that it was time to face the past. "I was tired of exile and willing to face captivity in a prisoner of war cell," he later wrote.[12]

Bidding what he hoped would be a temporary good-bye to his wife and children at the airport in Tanzania, he boarded a New York–bound flight and landed at John F. Kennedy airport, more than half expecting to see the FBI waiting for him.

But nothing happened. No one was there to arrest him. Although Critton had traveled under his real name, his movements had somehow gone unnoticed. His involvement in the botched 1971 Harlem bank robbery had passed the statute of limitations. The Thunder Bay airline hijacking had unfolded outside US jurisdiction.[13] Critton now hoped to rebuild his life in the United States. He found work at a pre-college education program in Brooklyn during the summer of 1994. Critton eventually settled in Mount Vernon, New York, where he was joined by his two sons. Building a career as a teacher and a mentor for youth, he lived quietly, seemingly forgotten.[14]

Charlie had little hope of slipping unnoticed into the United States. As the first signs of economic malaise began to grip Cuba, his daily routine became consumed with trying to meet his basic needs. As Charlie recalls it, the crisis that would become known as El Período Especial en Tiempos de Paz (the Special Period in Times of Peace) seemed to hit the streets of Havana with full force after the 1991 Pan American games in Havana. Soviet bloc oil imports had already slowed; then, with the disintegration of Comecon in 1991, they plummeted. Without access to Soviet credit, Cuba suddenly had to purchase imports on the international capitalist market with hard currency. Imports declined dramatically. Almost overnight, Cuba was plunged into its most serious economic depression since the 1930s. As the Soviet Union came apart, Cuba's leaders grappled with the enormity of ensuring the revolution's survival in a world that would soon be reshaped by free trade globalization, neoliberalism, and the triumph of market ideology.[15] "Ours is the only socialist country in the West," Fidel noted somberly in 1991. "We are alone—all alone—here, in this ocean of capitalism that surrounds us."[16]

The Special Period would wreak havoc on the lives of ordinary Cubans. As the nation entered a war footing, the relationship between citizens and the state changed as the government became unable to guarantee earlier levels of socialist distribution of resources to the population, regardless of need.[17] Education and health were protected—indeed, they were invested in heavily—but the contents of *la libreta* were cut by a third as a paucity of imports and low domestic production created widespread consumer shortages.

At the nadir of the austerity between 1993 and 1995, demoralizing blackouts, or *apagones*, became routine, and electricity service was so sporadic that the lights sometimes only came on during *alumbrones*: brief "light ups" of electricity when service was restored for a few hours. Food spoiled in refrigerators. Without fans, people spent sleepless nights in the summer heat. Some camped out on El Malecón to catch the ocean breeze. "It wasn't a matter of when the lights would be off but when they would be on," Charlie later recalled.[18] Without fuel or spare parts, public transportation came almost to a standstill. The streets filled with people riding Chinese Flying Pigeon and Phoenix bicycles—perhaps a quarter of a million in Havana alone—which the government imported. Without electricity, workplaces closed for weeks at a time. Without spare parts, manufacturing slowed. GDP cratered at a rate normally witnessed in nations at war. Cuba inched closer to a precipice.[19]

In 1960, Lester D. Mallory, the US deputy assistant secretary of state, had expressed the objective of the US sanctions in plain terms: "Every possible means should be undertaken promptly to weaken the economic life of Cuba . . . denying money and supplies to Cuba, to decrease monetary and real wages, to bring about hunger, desperation, and overthrow of government."[20] For thirty years this avowed program of economic warfare had failed to produce its stated objectives. Yet such was the havoc wrought by the Special Period that doubt began to seep into the minds of even stalwart revolutionaries. "The economic blockade meant that Cuba couldn't turn to anyone else for its trade," Charlie later recalled. "I was scared, man. I wasn't sure that the government was going to make it. Cuba was alone for those years."[21]

Tensions in Havana reached a boiling point in the summer of 1994 as hundreds of Cubans, then thousands, risked their lives to leave the island in makeshift rafts. US immigration policies, which limited legal visas but granted a ready path to citizenship to any Cuban who reached land in the United States, incentivized people to take their chances in rafts or resort to violence. Some people tried to hijack boats, leading to deadly confrontations with police, including the July 13 sinking of a hijacked tugboat at sea in which thirty-seven people drowned.[22]

Then, on August 5, two Cuban police officers were killed during the attempted hijacking of a ferry in Havana harbor, touching off the first mass political protest in the history of the postrevolutionary nation.[23] In what came to be known as the Maleconazo, several thousand Cubans marched amid the tenement *solares* of central Havana. Shops were looted and police arrested dozens, at one point firing into the air to disperse a crowd. The rebellion only subsided after Fidel himself arrived. In a scene that would become a Cuban legend, the Cuban president, accompanied only by a few officers, waded into the angry, seething crowd, speaking animatedly with anguished citizens and eventually giving an address. "That's what I appreciated about Fidel. He was never in some back room. He was ready to die," Charlie would later remember.

"I saw it on TV, and I knew people who were there. Fidel has never been a coward. You have to respect those things."[24]

Three days later, however, a nineteen-year-old hijacked a Cuban navy vessel, killing the ship's lieutenant, Roberto Aguilar Reyes, and made for Florida. The Cuban government called for the return of the hijacker and the vessel, but to no avail. The accused killer was eventually granted political asylum in the United States.[25] In New Mexico, the *Albuquerque Journal* drew parallels to a hijacking that had occurred more than twenty years earlier in New Mexico: the airliner that Charlie, Michael, and Antar had hijacked to Havana. "Cuba's demands that the United States hand over the ship hijackers," the *Journal* editors wrote, "might be more favorably received were it not for Cuba's past history where the situation was reversed."[26] Of course, the "past history" of US-Cuba relations with regard to hijacking began before 1971. As the *New York Times* acknowledged, Washington had repeatedly failed to respond to Havana's requests to return Cuban hijackers who reached the United States under identical circumstances in the early 1960s, contributing to a dynamic in which Havana had little incentive to extradite hijackers to the United States until there was diplomatic reciprocity and respect for Cuban sovereignty.[27]

In a bid to avert catastrophe as the economy continued to founder, the Cuban government legalized foreign currency, including US dollars, in July 1993 with Decree Law No. 140. It also began to build tourism infrastructure, an investment that would make possible the tourist boom of the next decade. In 1994, the Cuban government introduced a new currency, the *peso convertible* (abbreviated as CUC), whose value was pegged to the US dollar. Now forced to purchase consumer goods on the global capitalist market with hard currency, economic ministers made the CUC the domestic currency for most imported finished goods. Many essentials, from laundry detergent to cooking oil to powdered milk, could now be purchased only with CUC, which also became the official currency of hotels and the expanding tourist sector. A small range of private enterprises were also legalized, including *paladares*—privately owned restaurants that Cubans opened in their living rooms and patios. For the first time since 1978, small businesses began to gain a toehold in the hitherto planned economy. And as private economic activity increased, so did inequality.[28]

Fidel had warned that the island's compulsory dance with capitalism would create a gap in the classes. The 1970s and 1980s had witnessed a period of astonishing equality by historical standards. Cuba's efforts to eliminate the stark inequities of the prerevolutionary period had been extraordinarily effective.[29] Now, some of that socialist equality was being eroded. The new self-employed, called *cuentapropistas*, became a class unto themselves. A taxi driver working in the private sector could now easily net ten times the state salary of a doctor. With the legalization of US dollars in 1993 came an infusion of money, initiating the process that would eventually make remittances one of the state's primary means of capturing hard currency. "Money started to flow into Cuba, and bigger black markets were created," Charlie recalls. "The Cuban government wasn't ready for it. Materialism rose. Before, everyone more or less wore the same clothes."[30]

The government also established an updated iteration of the *diplotienda* dollar stores to capture foreign currency and redirect it to national economic priorities. This included the importation of consumer items, which—without Soviet trade agreements or credit—now had to be purchased at global market prices. This created a dynamic in which Cubans with access to hard currency remittances from family living abroad could live far better. It also produced racial inequality. Cubans living abroad were overwhelmingly white. When Afro-Cubans did live abroad, they occupied lower sectors of the labor market and had less income to remit to family on the island.[31]

The legalization of foreign currency and the rise of tourism in an era of scarcity contributed to the conspicuous return of freelance prostitution and *jineterismo*, a Cuban term denoting a range of street hustling practices targeting tourists. Although transactional sex had existed locally on a small scale in Havana for decades, the visible rise of sex workers around hotels and tourist zones in the 1990s shocked many Cubans. It brought back uncomfortable memories of the pre-1959 era, when Havana was the abode of the American mafia. Sex tourism in the Caribbean, at times predicated on the fantasy of sexual access to an eroticized racial "other," meant that for some, Cuba's appeal as a tourist destination hinged on its exoticized sex appeal.[32] These dynamics led to an increase in social surveillance of young women, especially Afro-Cubans who were already marginalized in newly dollarized sectors of the economy. "Neighbors and co-workers might see a girl with new clothes and wonder how she had gotten them," Charlie remembers. "Was she a prostitute? Someone might get an expensive television set from a dollar store, and the neighbors would wonder."[33]

The economic crisis also energized the counterrevolutionary movement. The 1990s witnessed an uptick of counterrevolutionary sabotage and terrorism from Florida-based paramilitary groups targeting the emerging tourist infrastructure, culminating in a spate of hotel bombings in Havana in 1997.[34] One of the most obvious symbols of Cuba's vulnerability was the penetration of its airspace by Cessna airplanes piloted by a Florida-based Cuban exile group called Brothers to the Rescue (BTTR). Led by José Basulto, a former Central Intelligence Agency (CIA) operative who had once fired a 20 mm cannon from a speedboat at a Havana hotel, the purpose of the flights was to harass authorities, drop political leaflets exhorting Cubans to rebel, and demonstrate the inability of the Cuban government to stop them.[35]

For months, Cuban officials protested the violations of its airspace to Washington through every available diplomatic channel, but BTTR pilots ignored the warnings.[36] The incursions continued, and on January 13, the group's planes dropped half a million political leaflets over Havana in full view of the Cuban air force. "People watched from Malecon as MiGs made warning passes against their planes," Fidel later told *Time* magazine. "People were criticizing the Cuban air force."[37] Walking through the Cayo Hueso neighborhood in Central Havana the next day, Charlie saw the black-and-white antigovernment flyers still lying in the gutter. People in the street were furious.[38] Cuban diplomats warned the Clinton administration that further incursions into Cuban airspace would not be tolerated and that the planes could be shot down.[39] Predictably, on February 24, 1996, Cuban Air Force MiG fighters finally did. Four BTTR pilots died as Basulto escaped to Florida. International condemnation of Cuba was swift. The planes, after all, had been unarmed civilian aircraft and posed no military threat to the island.[40]

Like his Cuban friends, however, Charlie raged against the hypocrisy and imperial hubris of it all. Would the United States have allowed aircraft from Cuba to do the same, flying low over Washington and dropping political flyers? The BTTR flights brought back old memories of sabotage flights from Florida that had dropped incendiary bombs on farms and sugarcane fields during the CIA's Operation Mongoose. Speaking before the UN General Assembly on March 6, 1996, Cuban foreign minister Roberto Robaina González framed the issue through the polestar of sovereignty. "Today we are asking this Assembly if the sovereign right to defend the borders and national security of countries is only a prerogative of the powerful and not of poor and small countries."[41]

For decades, Cuba had been subjected to incursions into its airspace by aircraft from the United States. In the 1970s, the thunderous sonic booms generated by SR-71 "Blackbird" reconnaissance planes sent by the Nixon and Carter administrations had broken windows and rattled nerves in Havana. Unlike the earlier U-2 spy flights, which had also violated Cuban airspace, the SR-71 missions lacked intelligence-gathering value. Instead, their purpose was to intimidate.[42] Now, as BTTR buzzed Havana and dropped leaflets, popular pressure mounted for the Cuban military to do something. "It was so humiliating," Fidel told *Time*. "The US would not have tolerated it if Washington's airspace had been violated by small airplanes."[43]

The Cuban president was voicing broadly felt sentiments. Charlie remembers his neighbors in Santa Amalia being furious at the disregard for Cuba's basic territorial integrity. In the United States, of course, most people blamed the Cuban government. The indignation of stateside critics, Charlie later fumed, reflected the casual arrogance of so many Americans, who had become so psychologically accustomed to superpower dominance that the reciprocity of a small nation came as a surprise. Like many people in Havana, Charlie remembered vividly the sonic booms of the 1970s and the fear and anger in the streets. "Imagine if planes from Cuba flew over Washington, dropping leaflets telling Americans to overthrow the government? What do you think would happen?"[44]

But there was no time to dwell on this unfolding geopolitical drama. Like most Cubans, Charlie spent the majority of his waking hours trying to find food—not only for himself but for his daughter, Shaunely. Prices of consumer goods had risen dramatically in Havana despite government price controls. In the countryside, however, food was more plentiful—if you could get there. Fuel shortages had greatly reduced public transportation. Charlie had a mountain bike that had been given to him by Pastors for Peace, a newly-formed progressive Christian organization from the United States that organized humanitarian brigades to Cuba, in the tradition of the Venceremos Brigades, to challenge the US travel ban and bring badly needed medical supplies and other donations to the island. Pedaling the bike out to Autopista A4, the main highway connecting Havana to the western province of Pinar del Río, Charlie would leave the bike with a friend and hitchhike on A4 out into the countryside. There he would buy food—jars of homemade tomato paste, bags of dry beans, and fresh malanga and yucca—and lug it back to Havana to use and sell. The population of Havana, a city whose composition had long been shaped by migration from the provinces, was again in flux. "During that time," Charlie recalls, "people wanted to move back out to the countryside, just to have reliable access to food."[45]

Buying and selling goods without a license was illegal. Cuban police sometimes searched vehicles. But the island's fledging private-sector businesses could not function without a black market. *Paladares* relied on runners to bring fish, meat, and produce, a practice that operated in a gray area of the law as people adapted to the opportunities and inequities of Cuba's compulsory but often chaotic experiments economic liberalization. Like his Cuban neighbors, Charlie became an adept operator in this subterranean economy as he tried to make ends meet, traveling deep into the countryside several times per month. On one occasion, he traded three mosquito nets and some soap—gifts from an English tourist friend—for a live pig in the picturesque village of Soroa. At a roadside *cafetería*, Charlie bought the hungry animal five orders of *congrí*—all that was available on the menu that day—and gave it some water. Dosing off on the ride to Havana in the back of a truck, Charlie awoke to shouts from the other passengers and a warm sensation on his legs: The pig had pissed all over him. As if on cue, the truck's wooden railing gave way as they went around a bend, taking the pig with it. It ran into the forest with Charlie in pursuit, but the unlucky animal's escape ended when its leash became caught in the brush. Back home in Santa Amalia, Charlie slaughtered the pig and sold the meat.[46]

Charlie was walking down Infanta Street in Central Havana one afternoon in early 1991 when he was startled out of his thoughts by a woman's voice calling his name in American-accented English: "Free the land, brotha!" Charlie froze. Looking up, he saw a tall, medium-complexioned Black woman with fine dreadlocks framed by a balcony. "Free the land, sista!" he replied. "But who are you?" She introduced herself as Nehanda.

Nehanda Isoke Abiodun, a member of the Republic of New Afrika and a member of the Black Liberation Army, had spent years living underground in the United States to evade capture by the FBI. Sought for her alleged role in aiding Assata Shakur's 1979 prison escape and for allegedly driving a getaway vehicle during a botched 1981 robbery of a Brink's armored truck in which a security guard and two police officers were shot to death, Nehanda had avoided apprehension even as the FBI closed in on one of her accused coconspirators, the beloved acupuncturist and revolutionary Mutulu Shakur, who was captured in 1986.[47] Nehanda spirited herself into Cuba in 1990—"I didn't fly, and I didn't swim!" was all she would later say about the precise manner of her arrival—with the help of a national network of comrades. She was granted political asylum by the Cuban government.[48]

For Charlie and Michael, Nehanda's arrival in Havana was a breath of fresh air. Although the three of them had not met in the United States, they saw themselves as members of the same Black revolutionary struggle. Indeed, they were members of the same revolutionary organization, since Nehanda, too, had been a member of the RNA. "It was so good to have someone to talk to," Charlie later recalled. "We had our Cuban friends, but Nehanda, she understood us."[49]

One of the things Nehanda understood was the pain of exile. Over the next two and a half decades, their lives would intersect continually as each struggled to navigate homesickness and the loneliness of separation from loved ones. Michael had recently confronted these feelings firsthand when Njeri—now his ex-wife—had visited Cuba in 1988 with their daughter, Malaika. When they arrived, feelings of joy and terror had mingled in Michael's mind. "It was both exhilarating and painful," he later told a reporter of the meeting. Malaika was now twenty-years old. "I went to the airport to meet a person whose diapers I had changed, who I'd loved, held, and fed. I wanted to see a little girl run up to me, throw her arms around me, and say, 'Daddy.' Instead I saw a very mature, somewhat standoffish lady who was sizing me up, trying to figure out who I was. She was coming to see someone she didn't know, with a certain amount of resentment at me for not having been there."[50]

In addition to Nehanda, the inchoate community of American political exiles and voluntary expatriates in Havana in the early 1990s included two recent additions. Longtime peace activist Ron Ridenour immigrated to Cuba in 1988 and began writing about the island. In January 1991, his book about Cuban intelligence agents who infiltrated the CIA was published in English by a Cuban publishing house.[51] Days later, as American bombs began falling on Baghdad as the Gulf War commenced, Ridenour burned his passport in front of the American Interests Section on El Malecón in Vedado and renounced his US citizenship in protest of the war.[52]

The same year that Ridenour immigrated to the island as a voluntary expatriate, Puerto Rican nationalist William Morales arrived as a clandestine political exile. A bomb maker for the Fuerzas Armadas de Liberación Nacional (FALN), which used armed struggle in its campaign to liberate an American colony—Puerto Rico—from eight decades of foreign control, activists like Morales occupied the militant edge of a multifaceted political movement that advocated full independence for the island nation.[53] The FBI and the CIA responded with repression.

The most radical Puerto Rican *independentistas* deployed terrorism and the classic tactics of anticolonial insurgency inside the United States. The FALN claimed credit for dozens of political bombings, including a January 1975 lunchtime blast at the Fraunces Tavern in Manhattan, which killed four people. The FALN said the attack was retribution for a bombing in Puerto Rico two weeks prior at a restaurant in Mayagüez that was frequented by nationalists. The blast "murdered Angel Luis Chavonnier and Eddie Ramos, two innocent young workers who supported Puerto Rican Independence and the conscienceless maiming of ten innocent persons and one beautiful Puerto Rican child six years old," the FALN said in a note found near the Fraunces Tavern. "You have unleashed a storm from which you comfortable Yankies [*sic*] cannot escape."[54]

In July 1978, Morales was allegedly constructing a bomb at an apartment in Queens, New York, when it exploded, destroying one of his hands and most of another and blinding him in one eye. Sentenced to prison, Morales was confined to Bellevue Hospital's high-security prison ward. But on May 21, 1979, Morales—handless and still bandaged—escaped through the third-floor window of the prison ward. Using a makeshift rope, Morales somehow managed to lower himself down, where he was met by co-conspirators from the Black Liberation Army and the former Weather Underground.[55]

Morales traveled surreptitiously to Mexico, where he was eventually captured in Puebla in 1983. Yet the Mexican government refused to extradite him. Instead, to the great anger of the Reagan administration, it allowed Morales, whose arrest had resulted in a shoot-out in which a Mexican police officer died, to travel to Cuba to seek political asylum.[56] As hemispheric anger over Washington's support for death squads in Central America swirled, Mexican diplomats, under pressure from leftist politicians in the government, reminded Washington of the terms of the 1978 Mexico–United States extradition treaty, which stipulated that "extradition shall not be granted when the offense for which it is requested is political or of a political character."[57] It was politically impossible, one Mexican official explained, for Mexico "to turn a Puerto Rican David over to the Yankee Goliath."[58]

Yet most of the American leftists who traveled to Cuba in the 1990s did so not as revolutionaries and political exiles but as international solidarity activists. As the magnitude of the island's economic crisis became apparent, US-based progressive organizations stepped up their efforts to provide humanitarian aid. The Venceremos Brigade, which had continued to send delegations of volunteers to Cuba to participate in construction and agricultural projects, now also brought donations as well as volunteers.

Yet it was Pastors for Peace, founded in 1988 as a project of the New York–based Interreligious Foundation for Community Organization (IFCO), that organized the largest grassroots shipments of material aid from the United States to Cuba during this period. Led by the Reverend Lucius Walker, who founded the organization after he and fellow IFCO activists survived a deadly terrorist attack on a civilian ferryboat in Nicaragua by right-wing antigovernment guerrillas, Pastors for Peace dedicated itself to the mission of providing humanitarian aid to the victims of US-sponsored violence in the Americas. Cuba, which had provided significant military and civilian aid to the socialist Sandinista government, was an ideal collaborator in these humanitarian efforts. By 1983, over twenty thousand Cuban teachers were serving in Nicaragua, even as Washington provided massive military aid to the anticommunist Contra guerrillas, who used terrorism and asymmetrical warfare in a bid to unseat the Sandinista government.[59] The attack on the civilian ferryboat, Reverend Walker told the *Washington Post*, had forced them to come "face to face with the terrorism of our own government."[60] Pastors for Peace began traveling to Cuba in a humanitarian capacity in 1992.[61]

Charlie started attending Pastors for Peace events held at the Centro Memorial Dr. Martin Luther King, Jr., the organization's institutional partner in Cuba. A project of a Baptist church in the Havana municipality of Marianao, the MLK Center was founded by Raúl Suárez, a minister whose ambitious community education programs fused Cuban interpretations of

Christian liberation theology with Brazilian philosopher Paulo Freire's ideas about popular education and Italian Marxist theorist Antonio Gramsci's ideas about civil society and social change.[62]

Charlie loved meeting the intrepid solidarity activists from Pastors for Peace. Students, teachers, retirees, progressive Christians, elderly peaceniks, and wizened civil rights activists—all risked steep fines from the US government's Office of Foreign Assets Control (OFAC) for violating Washington's ban on travel to Cuba by US citizens. On one occasion, Charlie joined Nehanda and Assata Shakur on a panel discussion about life in Cuba and the effects of the US sanctions. The next day, a few members of the delegation used their day off to meet up with Charlie. He spent the afternoon giving them a tour of historical sites in Old Havana and took them to a *paladar*. Although Charlie had worked as a paid guide for travelers in the past, these solidarity activists were not tourists. "I could not ask them for money. These people had to be dedicated because the police were after them. Not everyone is willing to commit themselves to that."[63]

The Pastors for Peace events were often attended by well-known figures. At one of these events in 1997, Charlie met Stokely Carmichael—now Kwame Ture—who was ecstatic to be back in Cuba after a long absence. Traveling with his mother and a few comrades, Ture had been invited by the Cuban government to attend the thirtieth anniversary of the Latin American Solidarity Organization conference. Underneath his joy at returning to Cuba, however, Ture was unwell: He had been diagnosed with cancer. Ture decided to seek a second medical opinion while on the island, spending fourteen days at the Clínica Central Cira García, an international medical facility in Havana's Miramar neighborhood, where he was visited daily by Assata. With the approval of his Cuban doctor and with Assata acting as his translator, Ture sought holistic treatment from a Cuban herbalist in the countryside as an adjunct to the cancer drugs, and he sought "treatment of the spirit" from a Santería *babalawo*.[64]

Despite his illness, Ture seemed strangely radiant. "Stokely had a nice face, and you could see the intelligence in his eyes," Charlie would later recall. "He was a listener. He wanted to know what you thought."[65] Ture wanted to know what Charlie thought about life in Cuba as a Black American émigré. Charlie obliged, relishing the interest that the legendary activist took in the quotidian details of his humble life in Santa Amalia. They also talked of Africa, where Ture had been living in self-imposed exile in Guinea, although he had continued to traverse the globe as an emissary of Pan-African revolution.[66]

But of the liberation of the African continent itself, Ture was somber. The anticolonial struggles of the previous decades had ended, giving way to complex realities. Everywhere now, capitalism was triumphant. The domestic profiteers of the continent's postcolonial exploitation were the Black "national bourgeoisie" that Frantz Fanon had hauntingly warned would become the indigenous accomplices of the foreign "cartels and monopolies" of global capitalism and neocolonialism.[67] "He said there were a lot of African leaders that were now in power, who were not necessarily doing things that were beneficial for the people," Charlie recalled of the conversation. "Corruption was real, and this was the 'counterrevolution.' Other leaders, such as Nelson Mandela, had political power, but not economic power. There were a lot of places in Africa that had natural resources but were still poor, because there was no socialism or redistribution of the wealth."[68]

Ture died on November 15, 1998. "He didn't say much about his medical treatment, but he said he had been under treatment for some time. I kind of got the sense that Cuba was his last hope. He was a good brother. We lost one of our best leaders."[69]

The Black radical icon whose visit to Cuba meant the most to Charlie during this period, however, was Imari Obadele. Around 1995, Charlie and Michael had received unexpected news that the RNA cofounder was in Havana—and wanted to meet them. The news churned up a sea of old emotions. Charlie, for his part, remained proud of his past association with the RNA. It was less clear to him whether the feeling was mutual. The RNA had provided virtually no support for Charlie and Michael during their exile in Cuba. In fact, they had not received a single visitor from the organization since Chokwe Lumumba's 1973 stay in Havana, much less a care package or money. Charlie and Michael had felt abandoned by the RNA. Charlie later ruefully summed up the feeling: "It's like being loved, or not being loved."[70] Now, Obadele was waiting for them at his hotel in Old Havana. Swallowing his hurt feelings, Charlie reluctantly went to see the leader of his former organization.

Obadele embraced him. Charlie tried to put on an amiable face, then gradually relaxed as the RNA elder's genuineness and warmth put him at ease. Charlie spent the next few days with Obadele and his wife. He showed them around Old Havana and Vedado and answered their questions about Cuba. They were sometimes joined by Fulani Sunni-Ali, a world-traveling RNA activist who had served as a national cochair of the Venceremos Brigade. Fulani was also the daughter of Alajo Adegbalola, the RNA leader who had sent Charlie, Michael, and Antar on their fateful mission to Mississippi in 1971.[71]

Obadele's mind was on the present, however, and he was full of curiosity about Cuba—and about Charlie's life as an émigré. Did he regret their decision to seek exile in Cuba, Obadele asked, instead of another country? "No, man, if you gotta be in exile, this is the place to be," Charlie enthused. "You don't want to go to China or North Korea in the 1970s. We knew, even before coming here, that the best place for us to be was in Cuba. It was a multiracial society, you have all shades of Black here. Cuba has its problems, but they've also come a long way."[72] Cuban culture was easy for Black Americans to adapt to, Charlie opined, because it was part of the African diaspora, owing first to its history of slavery and second to the extensive political, humanitarian, and medical ties that the revolutionary state had forged with the continent. "Can you imagine three Black guys like us trying to assimilate into Chinese culture? I know two brothers here, the sons of a diplomat in Uganda. Before, they were studying in China. After the first year, they said they didn't want to go back. They said they had no social life. China was a very tight-knit society, and culturally they just could not adapt. Cuba was more Western and open."[73]

Obadele believed that Cuba continued to play an important role in the global Pan-African struggle. Over Chinese food at a state-run restaurant in Havana's historic Barrio Chino, Obadele proposed that Charlie become an "at large" minister of foreign affairs for the RNA in Havana. The role would be honorific; nonetheless, Charlie was moved by the gesture. He was, in fact, well-positioned to serve as an informal ambassador for the RNA in Havana. In recent years, his interactions with visiting foreign activists, political delegations, and apolitical tourists alike had provided valuable opportunities to translate—both literally and figuratively—the Cuban experience for visitors. This inchoate political practice, of interpreting the complex realities of Cuban life and politics for foreigners, would increasingly become part of Charlie's repertoire of political engagement as an exile in Cuba.

But Michael did not even go to meet Obadele. Part of it was his hurt feelings over what he viewed as the RNA's abandonment of them in Cuba. But it was also political. Michael had stopped believing in the organization's core philosophy of Black nationalism, according to Charlie, because the ideology was at odds with Michael's increasingly Marxist and internationalist worldview. During his years in Havana, Michael had become a socialist who believed in Black liberation in the context of struggling to create an egalitarian, classless, multiracial society.[74] Michael was now critical of the RNA's political platform of creating a territorial Black ethnostate in the American South, which he believed was theoretically flawed and politically impractical. It was "insane" to keep up the old ideology, Michael had insisted to Charlie. The RNA had clearly failed to achieve its stated objectives.[75]

Charlie was offended at his friend's refusal to see Obadele. While he conceded many of Michael's critiques of the RNA's political program, his snub of Obadele seemed disrespectful. The two friends argued. "Well, that was what we believed at the time," Charlie recalls retorting to Michael. "What is the brother Imari supposed to do," he continued, "say it was all a big mistake? I don't personally believe it was all a mistake. Did I think our platform was feasible back then? Yes, I did. Do I think it is feasible now? No. You get smarter, and times change. When I look back on it, it's obvious that our plan was not going to work. The US government would eliminate us physically before they would ever let it happen."[76]

It was a watershed in Charlie and Michael's friendship. The two comrades had weathered their fraternal ups and downs, but this felt different. Their differences now seemed as much political as brotherly. The differences also reflected different paths taken in Cuba. While Charlie had largely eschewed formal employment and supplemented his monthly stipend from ICAP with odd jobs and a portfolio of income-generating activities in the informal economy, Michael had gone to university and dedicated himself to Radio Havana Cuba. His circle of friends increasingly included Cuban and foreign professionals in Havana's sprawling network of media outlets, cultural centers, political institutes, and think tanks.

Michael had also fully embraced Cuba's Marxist-Leninist project of developing state socialism, although as someone legally classified as a foreign resident, he could not join the Communist Party of Cuba (PCC). Michael was genuine in his political convictions and continued to be "completely a revolutionary," Charlie believed, yet he had also become "completely a communist." It was a dismissive barb, one that, in the Cuban context, could be used to denote someone who is deemed excessively and uncritically supportive of every aspect of the Cuban political project as articulated by the Central Committee of the PCC. Charlie also believed in the state socialist project and supported the PCC, yet he maintained vigorous critiques that he was not willing to suppress. As Charlie later put it hyperbolically, Michael had "embraced the whole Cuban political system. There was [*sic*] no errors, everything was perfect."[77] The two friends were drifting apart.

Members of the RNA continued to visit Havana throughout the 1990s to attend conferences sponsored by Cuban mass organizations, such as the Federation of Cuban Women, and to strengthen bonds with two prominent members of the movement who were exiled in Cuba: Nehanda and Assata. In 1997, Fulani Sunni-Ali returned to Cuba with her two teenage daughters, spending several weeks in Havana, some of it sleeping on the floor in Charlie's tiny living room in Santa Amalia.[78]

Fulani and Charlie developed a bond. As one of her daughters later recalled, referring to Charlie by his RNA "free" name: "Alajo had told my mother, 'Make sure not to forget the people in Cuba.' That included Uncle Fela. That's what he was to us: a member of our extended family. And that's how Fela treated us. He embraced my sister and I [*sic*] as family, and he looked out for all of us in Cuba. He made sure we were taken care of. 'I'm your uncle,' he would say.

My mother had a huge soft spot for Fela. She held him in high regard. Having been underground, she could empathize with what Fela must have been going through as an exile in Cuba."[79]

Nehanda and Assata played important roles as bridges between the Cuban government and the broader milieu of Black radical movements stateside. Both women were also involved in the island's nascent hip-hop scene. Nehanda became an important intermediary between Cuban *raperos* and the Cuban government. She also mentored Cuban youth and held ad hoc political education classes in the cramped living room of her third-floor apartment in Reparto Bahía.[80] Although she remained critical of mainstream American hip-hop, which she considered to be mired in misogyny, materialism, and capitalist individualism, she recognized the art form's cultural power and political potential. In Cuba, the *raperos*' penetrating critiques of the socialist project, she believed, which had occasioned historic advances in racial equality but had fallen short of eliminating racism, could help the Cuban Revolution more fully live up to its egalitarian ideals. The boisterous young *raperos*, Nehanda argued, are "revolutionary because they are willing to point out the contradictions that exist. And in pointing them out they are saying that they want things to be better, they are not satisfied with it being the way that it is, and that's a revolutionary stand."[81] In pointing out the contradictions of revolutionary Cuba in the late Special Period, Cuban hip-hop challenged fundamental assumptions of "raceless" national identity, suggesting that antiracism was part of Cuba's "unfinished revolution."[82]

Charlie's principle cultural pursuit in the 1990s, however, was Afro-Cuban religion, which was referred to on the island by a variety of names, including Religión Yoruba, Regla de Ocha-Ifá, Regla de Lukumí, and, less commonly in modern times, Santería. Charlie had never been religious, and his parents had not been devoted churchgoers. As he grew older, he had come to view the church as a stumbling block that impeded Black people from liberating themselves from the spiritual shackles white supremacy. "Christianity has been pushed upon Africans and Native Americans, and that turned me off to it. That and the idea of a white Jesus. It's been five hundred years of religious racism. Religion should be to bring peace of the mind, love in the heart, not exploitation or self-hate or economic gain."[83]

Charlie had been drawn to African religion since his time in Oakland. Now, this calling was finding fertile ground in Havana. The enslaved in Cuba, in contrast to the United States, had maintained important elements of their religious practices. "Enslaved people in many Caribbean nations," Charlie learned, "were not stripped of their culture in the same way."[84] African religions survived enslavement in the Antilles in a multitude of forms, and nowhere was this truer than in Cuba. Charlie had started reading about the history of Afro-Cuban religion in the 1970s as he became fluent in Spanish. "The more that I studied, the more I began to personally see the sixteen principles of Ifá as revolutionary."[85] Charlie's first readings with *babalawos*, intended to shed light on the past, the present, and the possible futures, had been profound spiritual experiences. "They hit me right on target, as if they were seeing right into me," Charlie would later say. "Things that there is no way they could have known."[86] In the late 1990s, Charlie began working intermittently at the Asociación Cultural Yoruba de Cuba in Old Havana, serving as an English translator in the museum for foreigners and tourists who took drumming and dance lessons.

But despite his newfound spiritual awakening during the social upheaval of the Special Period, Charlie had begun to experience bouts of depression, which led him to succumb to the siren comfort of alcohol. Although rarely a heavy drinker previously, Charlie now began to regularly drink to excess for the first time in his life. "The causes of drinking are always internal," he would later reflect. "Sadness. Lack of focus, lack of concentration."[87] All of this was augmented by economic hard times. Prior to the 1990s, Charlie rarely hung out in Parque Santa Amalia near his house, preferring to spend nearly all his time in Old Havana or Vedado. As public transportation became more unreliable amid the fuel shortages of the Special Period, he hung out more in the park, where a group of men who drank could always be found.

Charlie and Michael had received little media attention from US journalists during the 1990s, but that would begin to change as the decade came to a close. In November 1999, Charlie and Michael were interviewed by a KOAT-TV reporter from Albuquerque for a story that was later picked up by the Associated Press. Questioned about the shooting twenty-five years earlier in New Mexico, Michael was defiant: "Officer Rosenbloom was not murdered," he had insisted. "He was killed in self-defense in a confrontation between two armed adversaries who were determined to pursue their goals: his, the defense of the status quo; ours, the defense of a people who have suffered unmentionable abuse."[88]

That same year, President Bill Clinton granted clemency to eleven imprisoned Puerto Rican anticolonial nationalists—members of the FALN, William Morales's organization—who had been serving sentences of up to ninety years in federal prison. None had been convicted of crimes that resulted in bodily injuries or deaths, and clemency was granted on the condition that the prisoners renounce violence. "The prisoners were serving extremely lengthy sentences . . . which were out of proportion to their crimes," Clinton explained in a letter. "Our society believes . . . that a punishment should fit the crime."[89]

But to some, the FALN commutations also held a symbolic subtext. They were an implicit acknowledgment of the existence of oppressed national communities fighting for self-determination, including through armed struggle, inside the United States. As the effervescence of the 1960s era of radical dreams receded further into history and became increasingly incomprehensible to newer generations, US political exiles residing in Cuba were a reminder of the unresolved status of America's internal Black nation—the "national question" that had brought the RNA into existence three decades earlier.

Chapter 13

New Millennium

The new millennium brought George W. Bush to the White House, but in Havana, the most consequential election of the era was undoubtedly the 1998 democratic victory of Hugo Chávez in Venezuela. In the years to come, Cuba's sagging economy would be buoyed by its beneficial trade relationship with the oil-rich South American nation. Foreign exchange from the growth of Cuba's innovative biotechnology sector would also play an increasingly large role, as would contracts to hire Cuban medical professionals in the Global South. Yet it was the government's strategic pivot toward tourism as a means of capturing foreign currency that would most noticeably shape the social landscape of Havana, creating new opportunities and confounding paradoxes. As Cuba's economy began to lurch out of the malaise of the Special Period, this shifting terrain would have a profound effect on Charlie's experience of exile.

The trickle of tourism in previous decades had always included a small cohort of discreet US visitors. Arriving in effective violation of Washington's ban on travel to Cuba, first imposed in 1963, intrepid American tourists had to travel via third countries, often Mexico or Canada, the only two countries in the hemisphere to maintain diplomatic relations with Cuba following the 1959 revolution. If they arrived aboard the national airline, Cubana de Aviación, the flight crew sometimes took to the intercom as they entered Cuban airspace and welcomed passengers with a revolutionary greeting: "Welcome to Cuba, free territory of *América*!"[1]

To assist US Americans in avoiding detection by US customs upon their return home, Cuban customs agents continued their long-standing practice of not stamping the passports of American travelers. In 1989, when Jane McManus—the US expatriate writer and Cuba solidarity activist who later married Bill Brent—published one of the first English-language Cuba travel guides, which was aimed at Canadian travelers, who were not prohibited from travel to Cuba by their government, she included a wink to those "other" North Americans considering a trip to the forbidden island: "Find out how you can travel to Cuba."[2]

Encountering the rare American tourist in Havana in decades past, Charlie had sometimes offered his services as a guide and translator. Brett Skakun, a reporter for Atlantic City's *The Press*, met Charlie on La Rampa in Vedado in 1981. "The visitors were discussing Cuba's educational system when a muscular man speaking clear English emerged from the sidewalk. [He said,] 'Excuse me, but maybe I can explain a little more about education here. I don't get too many chances to talk to Americans.'"[3] Charlie offered to be their guide at the Museo de la Revolución, the museum of the 1959 Cuban Revolution, which had opened in 1974 in the old prerevolutionary presidential palace. "After the tour," Skakun wrote, "Hill offered to buy the beer. In a steamy, darkened bar, huddled over beer bottles, Hill told of his commitment to the Cuban government and its ideology and his new life in Havana."[4] The occasional journalist notwithstanding, however, the great majority of Americans for whom Charlie had served as an informal guide during the 1980s and 1990s were members of political solidarity delegations, whose connection to Cuba was primarily political and humanitarian.

That was about to change. When the Clinton administration relaxed restrictions on travel to Cuba for US citizens in 1999, opening a loophole for legal tourism and authorizing direct charter flights, it led to a marked increase in visitors from the United States.[5] Enterprising Cubans, navigating a sea of regulations on entrepreneurial activity, tried to figure out how to cater to them. Although Cuban state travel agencies existed, they charged more and steered travelers toward conventional tourist locales. American travelers, less likely than Europeans to speak Spanish, were more limited in their options. As few travel guidebooks were available in English, many American travelers were grateful for the services of a bilingual chaperone. Charlie was soon in high demand:

> I could offer things as a guide that most Cubans cannot. I speak both languages fluently, I know Cuba, but I'm also an American, and I know how Americans think. A lot of Americans that I found in the tourist areas wanted to get out of that. So, I'd take them out to regular places where Cubans go, see the real Cuba. Sometimes we go to the countryside, and we don't travel as tourists. I take them to the houses of friends, I let them meet and hang out with everyday regular people, Cubans that have nothing to do with tourism. I would take them to a *bodega* and explain the ration book. That's what many Americans want to see. A lot of the Europeans are like this too. I've taken people as far away as Guantánamo and Santiago. Some people also had specific things they were trying to find that were off the beaten path, like underground tattoo places, camping or hiking, see a cockfight or go to a baseball game, or wildlife. I did all that with them.[6]

Operating out of his "office" of Parque Central, an ideal place to meet tourists, Charlie became a fixture in Old Havana's newly renovated historic zone. *Washington Post* journalist and future Pulitzer Prize winner Eugene Robinson described Charlie as akin to "a full-service tourist agency" to legions of travelers who needed a trustworthy guide. "For any English-speaking foreigner in Havana, especially any American, it was hard *not* to run into Charlie. For me, meeting him was an especially lucky break. He seemed to know everybody in town, seemed to know how everything worked, and the people and places he introduced me to over the years were simply invaluable."[7] But Charlie had his rules. "I did not want to help people find drugs, or women. If people find a woman or man on their own, I'll translate, but I'm not a matchmaker or a pimp." He also refused to associate with "counterrevolutionary activities" or to help anyone trying to undermine the Cuban system.

Many US travelers found Charlie to be a fascinating character in his own right. Meeting him, some said, was like stepping into a time warp. Charlie's speech, peppered with dated slang and old-fashioned idioms, made it sound like he had been plucked off Telegraph Avenue in Berkeley in 1970. Michael often made a similar impression on travelers. "Finney's Spanish has grown perfect, but his English remains in a time capsule," a reporter once wrote. "Friends from the states have told him that talking to him is like going back to the '60s. He laughs about it."[8]

Although there was seldom a formal monetary agreement between Charlie and the travelers whom he guided, many insisted on compensating him. Journalists depended on his knowledge and contacts to research their stories, like those from the Minneapolis *Star Tribune* who enlisted him in January 2000 on the recommendation of another foreign reporter. "At the time," they recounted, "we did not know the full extent of the crimes Hill allegedly had committed."[9]

Tourists, too, depended on Charlie. As a guide and translator, however, he was more than a linguistic intermediary. Intentionally or not, he shaped the impressions of Cuba that travelers took home with them. If the foreigners that Charlie had occasionally guided in decades past had been leftwing solidarity activists, now his interlocutors were usually regular people. Charlie offered an interpretation of Cuba—one premised on support for the revolutionary process, although not uncritically—that was new to many tourists. His ability to convey the quotidian nuances and political complexities of socialist Cuba in plain but vivid language made him a kind of popular educator. As a partisan cross-cultural interpreter, Charlie did not hide his support for the island's socialist and anti-imperialist project, yet as an independent guide, he also remained conspicuously beyond state control.

Journalists and tourists alike probed his perceptions of Cuba. When the topic turned to the government, he sometimes found himself defending it against what he perceived as bad faith critiques. As the *Star Tribune* put it: "Like many in Cuba, Hill is capable of sarcastic comments about government inefficiencies. But mostly, he appears to be a true believer in Castro and, at times, angrily denounces Cubans who express dissatisfaction with conditions in the country. 'Fools compare us to the United States, not to other Third-World countries,' he fumes of those who complain. 'I believe that this government does try to act in the best interest of the people.'"[10]

Many foreigners believed that Cuba should adopt a market economy. But capitalism, Charlie tried to point out, had not lifted Jamaica, the Dominican Republic, or Haiti out of poverty and underdevelopment. Cuba's accomplishments and failures, he argued, must be compared to nations that had emerged from similar histories of colonization. Nonetheless, he eventually decided that there was something to be learned from otherwise facile comparisons between Cuba and the United States. Indeed, even after the debilitating effects of the Special Period, Cuba could offer startling contrasts with its northern neighbor. American tourists often noticed this. How, they marveled to Charlie, could a low-income nation like Cuba offer universal health care to its citizens, but the United States could not? Visiting the island encouraged Americans to gaze back at a reflection of their own society through the looking glass of Cuban socialism.

Expatriate American writer Margaret Randall would later reflect on what her years living in Cuba in the 1970s had taught her about national priorities. "It's impossible to describe what living in that aura of fairness felt like, how simple the solutions to the social inequities seemed if the will to change was there," she wrote in her memoirs. "All the fabricated reasons why such solutions weren't possible in the other countries where I'd lived suddenly seemed coverups for obscene corruption and greed."[11] Cuba's ability to enshrine education, health, housing, nutrition, and culture as social rights exposed the pernicious consequences of free markets, in which access to life's necessities was allocated not according to human need but by one's ability to pay.

Charlie knew Cubans who had immigrated to the United States, only to return with changed perceptions of the capitalist society they had once romanticized. In Santa Amalia, for instance, one of Charlie's neighbors sold his house to pay for his passage to Florida. Cuba was the dregs, the man raged, and "communism" was to blame. But two years later the man was back in Havana. The Miami neighborhood he had lived in was plagued by something rare in Cuba: violent crime. Jobs in Miami paid far more than they did in Havana, it was true, but the high cost of living consumed much of the difference. His neighbors, both immigrant and native-born, seemed always to owe money. Basic necessities such as rent, food, and medical care were shockingly expensive, turning people into debtors to credit card companies and hospitals, an unheard-of condition in Cuba. "He didn't turn into a revolutionary," Charlie would later say of his neighbor after he returned, "but he had a different attitude about life in Cuba when he got back. He had a broader perspective."[12]

Like Charlie, Nehanda Abiodun sometimes noted the tendency of her Cuban friends to compare living standards on the island to those in the United States, a place they had never been. She marveled that the socialist gains of the revolution had become so normalized that they could be taken for granted. To Abiodun, this was a positive sign of how far Cuba had come. "It should be *normal* to have food and medicine and education!"[13] At other times, though, she fretted about the youngsters that she had taken under her wing in Havana. "This younger generation doesn't know what it took to get to this point," she told a journalist in 2000, "where you don't have to worry about a drive-by [shooting], where you don't have to worry about getting your teeth fixed, where you don't have to worry about paying for college."[14]

Abiodun often related a story about a former boyfriend that she found both instructive and amusing. Dispirited with the daily grind of life in Cuba's planned economy, he had immigrated to New York to pursue the American dream. Living with his American girlfriend, he washed dishes and bused tables in Manhattan. He even saved some money to send home. But he also witnessed the economic precarity of his coworkers, most of whom were Black Americans or immigrants, who worked long hours but had no health insurance, who could not afford to go to the doctor, and who were often a paycheck away from eviction. He struggled to fit in with his girlfriend's family and friends, who had none of these problems. Two years later he was back in Havana and, Abiodun joked, "more socialist than Fidel!"[15]

American political exiles, born into capitalism, were in a unique position to offer a critical insider's view to would-be Cuban émigrés. Charlie's access to lifesaving medical care, from his first moments of life in rural Illinois, was owed not to a public health system but to the private charity of the good doctors at the Olney Sanitarium, who recognized that free markets could not guarantee medical care to poor people. "No person was turned from its doors," the *Herald and Review* newspaper wrote in 1983 of the Olney hospital where Charlie had been born.[16] Founded in 1898 by a physician named George Weber in a former hotel and staffed by his sons, the hospital was run in an unorthodox manner. "Profits meant nothing to the eight Weber doctors. Each year they pooled what money they did make to offset the deficit sustained because of people who could not afford to pay for their services."[17]

Most US neighborhoods were not fortunate enough to have an Olney Sanitarium. Yet its basic economic model, in which revenue from those who could afford to pay was used to subsidize the treatment of those who could not, resembled the one that Cuba employed in its international medical missions. Revenue from wealthier Global South nations that could pay for

Cuban doctors, such as Brazil or South Africa, subsidized Cuban internationalist medical brigades in countries that could not, such as Haiti or the Gambia.[18] When Charlie had been hospitalized in Fairbanks in 1970 with hepatitis, he was cared for, free of charge, at a much larger American health institution than the one that had brought him into the world in Olney: the US Veterans Administration (VA).[19]

The socialist logic of universal health care in Cuba, Charlie perceived, was not a world away from the socialized medicine of the VA, yet Cubans did not have to fight in a war to see a doctor. They did not even have to leave their neighborhood. With the massive investment in the island's health system that occurred in the 1960s and 1970s, community-based medicine became the norm. By 1975, Cuba had one doctor for every 1,000 people, roughly the same ratio as Japan or the United Kingdom for that year. By 1985, Cuba had one doctor for every 500 people, and by 2005, the ratio was one physician for every 167 people, the lowest doctor-to-patient ratio in the world.[20] Cuba's family practice doctors usually lived in the same neighborhoods as their patients. In Santa Amalia, Charlie's *policlínico*, as second-level local clinics offering outpatient care are called in Cuba, was two blocks from his house. If a patient was not well enough to leave home, a doctor would make a house call. "Some of my family in the States have debt from medical bills, and they are amazed," says Charlie, "because I don't pay anything when I go to the doctor in Cuba."[21]

Plying the streets of Old Havana as a guide, however, Charlie began to witness another side of Cuba's tourism boom: racial profiling. For decades, prior to the 1959 revolution and after its triumph, popular prejudices and cultural ideas had linked Blackness and criminality. "Tenía que ser un negro" (It was probably a Black), someone might say if a theft was reported. During the Special Period, these ideas assumed new power. Those stopped at the entrance to a hotel—at least until the staff realized their mistake—or ticketed by police for "bothering tourists" or asked by officers for their Carné de Identidad (identification card) while their white companions were ignored could be Black Cubans or Black foreigners mistaken for being Cuban.[22]

Reports of racial profiling in the tourist zones began to receive media coverage.[23] Even foreign graduate students and scholars conducting fieldwork on the dynamics of race in Cuba reported experiences.[24] Cubans had been prohibited from staying at tourist hotels during the Special Period, a practice that authorities justified as necessary to discourage prostitution and theft targeting foreigners. To protect the tourism sector, a special police unit was created.

However, enforcement was sometimes racialized: Afro-Cubans were more likely to be profiled as sex workers and thieves. Prior to the 1990s, the vast majority of foreign tourists in Cuba had been white, reinforcing popular associations between wealth, leisure travel, and whiteness. Any person of African descent might therefore be presumed Cuban by the hotel staff and police. "The Cubans have to solve this," Charlie remembers thinking. "It's a serious problem."[25]

Public attention to racism during the Special Period led to rare admissions of the problem by Cuban officials. Many Cubans had believed that the early gains of the revolutionary process meant that prejudice and discrimination were no longer urgent concerns. Fidel himself had declared that racial and gender discrimination had been "suppressed" and "solved" in the 1960s.[26] As inequality increased during the Special Period, however, that confidence suddenly seemed spectacularly premature. Speaking at a Cuba solidarity rally in Harlem, New York, in September 2000, the Cuban president acknowledged the incompleteness of the nation's structural approach to eradicating inequality. "I am not claiming that our country is a perfect model of equality and justice," he told a largely Black audience at Riverside Church. "We believed at the beginning that when we established the fullest equality before the law and complete intolerance for any demonstration of sexual discrimination in the case of women, or racial discrimination in the case of ethnic minorities, these phenomena would vanish from our society. It was some time before we discovered that marginality and racial discrimination with it are not something that one gets rid of with a law or even with ten laws, and we have not managed to eliminate them completely, even in forty years."[27] Nonetheless, concrete government action on *la problemática racial* (the race question) in Cuba would remain elusive and the subject, largely taboo.[28]

Charlie had experienced the minor inconvenience of police stops in the tourist zones, but on one memorable occasion in the early 2000s, a check of his identification card led to an argument and a rough arrest. Leaving the Hotel Vedado, where he had been hanging out with some Norwegian friends after a beach trip to Varadero, he approached a Lada tourist taxi, which had to be paid for in US dollars. A white police officer from the tourism unit, assuming that Charlie was Cuban, approached and requested his identification card. In those days, the Carné de Indentidad Para Extranjeros—the identification card for foreigners, which included those legally classified as foreign residents, such as Charlie—was an unlaminated booklet bearing a photograph and official stamps indicating when it had been renewed. An underground market existed for this document, which some people purchased or stole from foreign students in order to falsify it under a different identity. Police had been cracking down. The officer accused Charlie of having a counterfeit card. Charlie argued with the officer, urging him to call the station to verify his identity. The officer handcuffed him over his protests. When Charlie argued some more, the officer hit him in the legs with his baton.[29]

Taken to the police station, Charlie demanded to speak with the lieutenant, but to no avail. He spent the night in jail. In the morning, the charges were dropped. Indignant, Charlie demanded an investigation. "I asked at the desk, 'Who wrote up this report, why was I brought in?' And nobody gave me an explanation."[30] Charlie decided to just go home. As time went by, Charlie saw less profiling around the tourist hotels, particularly after 2008, when the Cuban government lifted the restriction on Cubans staying in them.[31] "Partly I think this was Cubans finally learning that, you know, not all tourists are white! Also, they started to get trained better."[32]

In later years, though, Charlie's thoughts sometimes strayed back to his arrest. It wasn't that he had been in real danger. Few Cubans seemed to fear the police. Indeed, the dynamic between citizens and the police felt different from anything he had experienced in the United States because the two societies themselves were so different. Cuba was remarkably tranquil. Crime, especially violent crime, was low. Private gun ownership was heavily restricted. The streets were safe not only because the nation had achieved a high degree of social equality and embraced ideals of solidarity and common purpose but because entire neighborhoods helped prevent crime through active deterrence, community engagement, and surveillance. In many cases, the police were not even involved. Neighborhood associations—the ubiquitous Committees for the Defense of the Revolution (CDRs)—maintained a registry of every person living in the neighborhood, addressed youth delinquency with early intervention and social programs, and organized community night patrols and guard duty. In those days, every neighborhood also had a civilian law officer (*el jefe de sector*, masculine form), who lived on the block they were responsible for policing.[33]

To be sure, Cuba had a strong police force, and no one wanted trouble with the law. A Santería-inflected popular idiom referencing the white patrol cars and blue beacon lights of the National Revolutionary Police summed it up: "Cuidado con la 'yabó de la felpa azúl"—roughly, "be careful of the one dressed all in white with the blue button." Some officers were boorish or racially profiled—as Charlie had discovered. While there was no comparison to the United States, where deadly police violence was commonplace, problems clearly existed. For Charlie, these contradictions needed to be addressed within the revolutionary process through public debate and reform. Cuba had not reached communism, a society so harmonious that the state withers away and the police are obsolete. Instead, Cuba was a *socialist* society, one that still aspired to see itself, at least officially, as building the foundation upon which something like communism might be able to emerge in some indeterminant future. In the meantime, though, the state had a responsibility to ensure the safety and security of the society that actually existed. Surprising some of his American friends, who had never lived in a socialist society and whose ideals about the role of police were shaped by the harsh realities of a very different context, Charlie had become a passionate advocate of the premise, commonsense among his Cuban friends and neighbors, that the police were a necessary—indeed, vital—institution of Cuba's actually existing socialism.[34]

None of this had made him feel any better during his night in jail. The experience was a violation of the rights that socialism was supposed to guarantee. "I wasn't bitter, and I wasn't angry at the revolution. People are humans, they make mistakes."[35] But there had been no accountability. "It hurt me that I knew it was useless [to pursue an investigation] and that the Cuban hierarchy had not recognized that there was racism in Cuba. That hurt me. It's always bothered me, from the beginning. . . . It hurt me emotionally and from the political point of view, in the sense that these people are supposed to be a lot more politically advanced and smarter . . . but they kept negating that [racism] existed.[36]

Charlie had other things on his mind in the early aughts besides Cuba's long struggle for racial equality. The events of September 11, 2001, were reverberating around the world. Within minutes of the attacks, Fidel had communicated Cuba's "heartfelt sympathies to the American people" and offered to send blood plasma and Cuban medical personnel to the United States.[37] However, Washington's rush to war against Afghanistan and Iraq soon tempered Havana's overture. When Havana accused Washington of using the attacks "as a pretext to impose on the planet a policy of terror and force" and condemned the use of the US naval base at Guantánamo Bay to confine prisoners "kidnapped for years, overriding any legal procedure," US-Cuba relations sank even lower.[38]

With the world's attention fixed on the World Trade Center and the Pentagon on the morning of September 11, however, few people probably paid much attention to newspaper headlines reporting the arrest of an airplane hijacker in a New York suburb a few days earlier. The hijacker, an American citizen, had commandeered a commercial jet from Thunder Bay, Ontario, to Havana in 1971. A Canadian detective, investigating cold cases, had decided to try a simple internet search of the suspect's name. A few seconds later, the detective was looking at a news story about a man with the same name who had been mentoring Black youth in Mount Vernon, New York. His name was Patrick Critton.

After slipping back into the United States in 1994, Critton had lived quietly. Cultivating a wide circle of friends and colleagues, the charismatic and talented former urban guerrilla rededicated himself to his old passion: teaching and mentoring youth. Hired by the New York Board of Education, Critton led SAT preparation courses at public high schools in Brooklyn, taught Black studies at a Mount Vernon middle school, counseled youth at a juvenile correctional detention center, and directed a United Way program for at-risk teenagers. In 1997, his two sons from Tanzania arrived to live with him.[39] Eventually, history caught up with him again. Opening his front door on September 8, 2001, to find FBI agents and Canadian detectives standing outside, Critton reportedly flashed a smile. "What took you so long? I've been waiting for that knock on the door for seven years."[40]

Critton's arrest was announced two days later. Briefly a national news item the next morning—September 11—the coverage was promptly buried after the first hijacked jetliner hit the North Tower of the World Trade Center at 8:46 a.m. Critton was eventually sentenced to three years in prison for his 1971 hijacking from Thunder Bay, which, his attorney emphasized, had resulted in no injuries.[41] Among those who had mixed emotions about Critton's arrest were his former colleagues and students in Mount Vernon. "We really loved this man," the principal of A. B. Davis Middle School told the *New York Times*. "A lot of kids cried when he left, but I told them, 'That was his former life. We can still honor him for the work he did in our building and not abandon all the trust and honor he brought here.'"[42]

In Cuba, however, the dawning of the 9/11 era and the war on terror refocused attention on the US political exiles, especially Assata Shakur. The FBI had previously classified the Black Liberation Army as a terrorist organization. Now, the presence of American political exiles in Havana allowed the Bush administration to use the discourse of antiterrorism to amplify hostility toward Cuba. The State Department had first designated Cuba as a state sponsor of terror in 1982, citing Havana's support for armed left-wing movements fighting against violent dictatorships—US allies—in Central America, and for Cuba's military involvement in Africa during the era of decolonization. The 9/11 terrorist attacks provided Washington with a fresh pretext for the continuation of economic sanctions and diplomatic hostility against Cuba.[43]

The increased scrutiny of the American exiles in Havana drew them closer together. Nehanda had begun working in an unofficial capacity to support some of the US medical students who were studying at the Latin American School of Medicine (ELAM) in Havana on scholarships provided by the Cuban government. The program, the fruit of a collaboration between members of the US Congressional Black Caucus and Fidel Castro, allowed Americans from working-class backgrounds, primarily Black and Latino, to study medicine for free in Cuba with the expectation that they practice in medically underserved communities in the United States upon becoming doctors. It was during those years that Nehanda began to host what she mischievously called "anti-imperialist thanksgiving" dinners on the fourth Thursday of November for some of the US medical students who were unable to be with their families.[44] She sometimes invited Charlie, who was particularly vulnerable to melancholy around Thanksgiving.

Charlie's isolation from his family in the United States had been a source of continual heartache. His mother died in July 1982, but he only learned about it weeks later. The news had left him numb. His father passed less than a year later, in March 1983.[45] Neither of Charlie's parents ever traveled to Cuba. While Michael had received visits from both of his parents, as well as from his former wife, Njeri, and their daughter, Malaika, Charlie would not receive a visit from a member of his US family until 2024.[46] When he did get news about his family stateside, it was often because someone had died. But it was a letter in February 2003 from his former girlfriend in Alaska, Kathy, that would stir the most painful memories. Their thirty-year-old son, she told him in the letter, had been shot dead on January 27, 2003, in Fairbanks. He had been the victim of a homicide. The case was never solved.[47] It was a singularly painful event for Charlie.[48]

Michael, meanwhile, had tried to overcome the pain of separation by building a new family in Cuba. Unable to maintain a partnership with Njeri in California, the two had long since gone their separate ways. In the mid-1980s, Michael began dating a woman named Esther, a doctor by profession, with whom he eventually had a daughter, Antara, named in memory of his dearly departed friend.[49] Around that time, Michael also saw his father for the first time in almost two decades. Michael's mother had already visited, but this was his father's first trip to Cuba. "It was very heart warming, very moving for both of us," Michael later said. "My old man has always, in his own way, cheered for me. When I began to get into radical politics, he said, 'Look, I know you're a good kid and I know you know the difference between right and wrong. I just don't want to have to identify your bullet-riddled body in some morgue.'"[50]

In 2004, Michael began to feel ill. Tests revealed that he had throat cancer. He began undergoing radiation treatment, but the condition did not improve. One afternoon Charlie went to visit him at his apartment on Neptuno Street. "I'm sorry," Michael told him. "For what?" Charlie replied. "I'm just sorry," Michael said. Charlie understood. "Man, I am too."[51] The two men had drifted apart in recent years. Michael's diagnosis had finally forced them to confront the loss of the brotherhood they once shared. "We hugged each other," Charlie would later recall, and then they apologized for the past. "Sorry for each other's mistakes. . . . We both made errors, but we still loved each other as brothers and friends."[52] The two men went out and had a couple of beers and laughs, reminiscing about the old days. Then Charlie went home. In the coming months Charlie visited Michael regularly while he was undergoing radiation treatment. On one of the last occasions, Michael would not open the door, and so the two talked through the grate. "He didn't want me to see him like that. He had lost his hair, and he was really sick."[53]

Michael died in January 2005. Although burials and cremations in Cuba usually take place within a day or two, the funeral was delayed in order to allow a member of Michael's family to travel to Cuba. A service was held at the home of a Canadian friend on Línea Street in Vedado, with Michael's Cuban family, friends, and coworkers in attendance. Assata, Nehanda, and Charlie made statements honoring his life. Afterward, they walked down to El Malecón and scattered his ashes in the ocean waves.[54] Michael Robert Finney, Charlie's friend and confidant throughout the years of exile, was gone. Charlie was now the last of the three friends who had come to Cuba more than three decades before. He struggled to shake off the feeling of isolation and loneliness that enveloped him.

Charlie was still grieving for Michael when the US political exiles in Cuba abruptly reentered the news cycle. The focus was Assata Shakur. Police officials had long refused to refer to her by her chosen name. In May 2005, the State of New Jersey announced that it was raising the reward for "information leading to the capture of Joanne Chesimard and her safe return to New Jersey to continue her prison sentence" to $1 million. The reward had previously stood at $50,000.[55] In an unprecedented development, the US government classified her as a domestic terrorist. Earlier that year, Rick Fuentes, superintendent of the New Jersey State Police, traveled to the Dominican Republic to brief officials from the Caribbean and Latin America. "Joanne Chesimard," the press release from New Jersey's Office of the Attorney General read, "will be looking over her shoulder a lot more in Cuba now."[56]

Assata now moved out of her home in the Havana municipality of Playa. From then on, she would live a semi-underground existence in Cuba, protected directly by Cuban state security. Living at a location undisclosed to even her friends, she now lived as an exile in exile.[57] Nonetheless, she found ways to maintain contact. One night, during one of the "anti-imperialist Thanksgiving" dinners, Charlie was sitting in Nehanda's living room with a group of US ELAM students. There was a knock on the door. To the surprise and delight of everyone, it was Assata, who had come unannounced for security reasons. To Charlie, the scene had a beautifully surreal quality. "I saw her sitting on Nehanda's sofa, talking to the students, and I thought, 'This is like a dream.' This was my life. I was in Cuba as a political exile, with other exiles. American students were studying in Cuba to be doctors, and here we all were together, at Nehanda's house, and Assata was telling the students that 'the Black woman's place is in the struggle.'"[58]

Within weeks of the May 2005 announcement of the $1 million reward, rumors of bounty hunters surfaced in Havana. In a city that had, in living memory, witnessed attacks by Florida-based Cuban counterrevolutionaries arriving in speedboats, the threat posed by foreign bounty hunters felt real. Not long after, Charlie's contact from state security, a Ministry of the Interior officer who routinely checked in on him in Santa Amalia, knocked on his door unexpectedly. "He told me that the Cuban government would continue to protect me," Charlie says. "But he also asked me to keep a low profile."[59]

The security concerns of the American exiles were heightened by tense US-Cuba relations during the presidency of George W. Bush. The American invasion of Iraq in fall 2003 had triggered international condemnation and the largest antiwar protests since the Vietnam era. But Washington would be bound by neither global opinion nor international law. Cubans viewed the American war against Iraq, one of whose stated objectives was regime change, with trepidation: If Washington could use a flimsy pretense to justify a "pre-emptive" war of aggression against a sovereign nation half a world away, what could it do to Cuba?[60]

With US exiles back in the media spotlight, internal developments in Cuba fueled more speculation about the American political exiles. In July 2006, the Cuban news media announced that Fidel Castro was ill—so ill that he was temporarily delegating power to his younger brother, Raúl, who was currently vice president of the governing Council of State. Fidel, the historical leader of the Cuban Revolution, was no longer in power, although he continued to exert political influence. Fidel never fully regained his strength. In February 2008, Raúl was elected head of state by the National Assembly of People's Power. Some speculated about what this historic transfer of power might mean for the US émigrés. Would Raúl uphold their status as protected asylees, or would he pursue a different policy?

A few months after Fidel was hospitalized, Bill Brent fell ill with bronchial pneumonia. He did not recover, and on November 4, 2006, Brent passed away in a hospital in Havana. He was seventy-five. Charlie and Bill had never been particularly close, and the two had seen each other infrequently in recent years. Nonetheless, his death, coming little more than a year after Michael's, affected him. More and more, Charlie was thinking about his own life, legacy—and mortality.

Somehow, history seemed to be speeding up. In November 2008, the same year that Raúl became president, the United States experienced its own historic political transition. The election of Barack Obama surprised as many Cubans as US Americans. "I thought for sure that a Black man could not become president," Charlie later admitted.[61]

Yet Obama had already pleasantly surprised Cubans with campaign trail promises of engagement with the island instead of confrontation. While his administration's later move toward full normalization of diplomatic relations was not yet public knowledge, Obama kept his promises, signing Executive Order 13492, which called for the closure of the US naval base at Guantánamo Bay. Three months later, his administration lifted restrictions on travel to Cuba and family remittances.[62] Conservative hard-liners and law enforcement leaders, however, insisted that the extradition of the American exiles, especially Shakur, must be a precondition of détente. In June 2009, New Jersey state lawmakers introduced a resolution urging the United States "to delay normalizing relations with Cuba until Joanne Chesimard is extradited."[63]

The State of New Jersey's 2009 resolution resulted in a flurry of media attention on the American exiles in Cuba. Interviewed by journalist Tracey Eaton, Charlie offered a candid portrayal of his experiences of exile: "I'm not a bitter old revolutionary," he insisted. "I'm not angry at anyone. I just keep on living. I don't feel anybody owes me anything."[64] Asked about the socialist system in Cuba, Charlie replied that Cuba is "not a perfect society. . . . They've made some mistakes just like all governments have. But I've always felt they're constantly trying to work for the people. See, this is the basic difference. I don't think the United States government works for the American people. I believe the American government works for US dollars." Charlie acknowledged that racism continued to exist in Cuba. "They're doing it in their own way. Who am I to say how to do things? I don't want to be an arrogant American and say, 'Well, they should do it this way, or that way.' I'm an uninvited guest."[65]

In other interviews, Charlie discussed the events leading up to his arrival in Cuba. In a October 2009 article in *USA Today*, reporter DeWayne Wickham wondered whether better US-Cuba relations would result in the extradition of the US political exiles. Interviewed for the story, Charlie tried to contextualize the events that had unfolded on the highway in New Mexico in 1971. "I need someone to write a book about my life. I need someone to tell my story who understands what could happen back then when a cop stopped a car with three black men wearing Afros," Charlie told Wickham. "I regret that a life was lost, but it had to be that way. He drew his gun and he was going to kill us."[66] Prison, Charlie maintained, was not the only kind of sentence one could endure. "I paid my price for that. I paid for that with the 38 (years) that I've been here in exile."[67]

Following the *USA Today* article, however, Wickham says he received an unexpected voicemail. The message was from Elizabeth Walthall, one of the flight attendants on the TWA flight that Charlie, Michael, and Antar had hijacked. Walthall wanted Wickham to know that she did not believe that Charlie had been the killer of Officer Rosenbloom. Walthall insisted that it had been Michael. "I think I know enough that he didn't commit that murder that it would be criminal of me not to say so," she later told Wickham over the phone. "I'm in favor of capital punishment . . . but I don't believe in punishing someone for a murder they didn't commit."[68] According to Walthall, who had positively identified each of the hijackers for the FBI and saved evidence to allow investigators to collect the fingerprints of each, Michael had exclaimed during the flight, "[I] already killed somebody. . . . I didn't like it, but I could do it again." Walthall also claimed that Antar had confirmed Michael as having been the shooter.[69]

But these details were trivial. Charlie had never denied playing a role in Rosenbloom's killing, even if he had not been the shooter. Sensing that he would never again set foot in the United States, Charlie had decided that he wanted his Cuban children to have the option of US passports, which, as the children of a US citizen, they might be entitled to. In the fall of 2013, Charlie and Shaunely, now a grown woman, went to the US Interests Section in Vedado. Established in 1977 during the Carter-era diplomatic thaw and located in the old 1953 US embassy building on El Malecón, the almost comically stern-looking building—seven stories of brutalist architecture and tinted windows—juts out imposingly in Vedado. Its "dark frame, glass walls, and 20-foot-high metal fences become the embodiment," one American urban planner wrote, "of how the socialist government wants its citizens to see America: big, dominating, impersonal, ugly, and uncaring."[70]

As they approached the building, the Cuban guard looked at his identification card and said, "Oh, you're Charlie Hill," although the card listed his name as "Charles."[71] Entering the waiting area, Charlie noticed a wanted poster for Nehanda on the wall. Over by the entrance, visible to all who entered the building, was a much larger poster proclaiming the reward of $2 million—a fortune in Cuba—for information leading to the apprehension of Assata Shakur.

As they prepared to leave, a guard stopped them. An American official wanted a word with Charlie. Shaunely burst into tears. "Don't worry," Charlie reassured her. "Nothing is going to happen." A tall, gruff-looking, baldheaded white man strode out and introduced himself as something like the chief of security. He looked every bit the part. "He was perfect. Just like you'd picture a US marshal or FBI agent to look."[72] The bald man invited Charlie into a private room. The Interests Section, Charlie knew, did not have diplomatic inviolability, despite being under the authority of the Swiss embassy. He was still under Cuban jurisdiction. The officer made his best pitch. Relations between the countries might be about to improve, he said, eyeing Charlie pointedly. "You should consider turning yourself in. Who knows what could happen if the United States and Cuba normalize relations?" Charlie said that he would consider it "if Shaunely was granted US citizenship." He gave the officer his cell phone number and asked him to call if he wanted to talk about it.[73] For Shaunely, the experience was traumatic. "[It was] the worst day of my life. I was terrified. And I felt like the worst person in the world, thinking that my papa would be trapped inside the embassy. He would be deported and extradited because he tried to get papers for me."[74]

Reflecting later on the visit to the US Interests Section, however, Charlie wondered whether the security official knew something. By that point, Cuba and the United States were deep into secret talks to negotiate a historic opening in diplomatic relations.[75] "It was weird. I'm glad we visited then, not the next year, 2014, when everything changed."[76]

Chapter 14

Possible Futures

Charlie was visiting his *compadre* in Cárdenas, a small port city in Matanzas Province, on December 17, 2014, when the television program they were watching cut to a special noon broadcast: a scheduled address to the nation from President Raúl Castro. Cuba, Raúl said, remained willing to engage in "respectful dialogue with the United States" on the basis of mutual respect and "sovereign equality." This was nothing new, Charlie thought: It had been Cuba's official position for decades. But Raúl was not finished. Havana and Washington, he said, had been engaged in high-level dialogue, including "a phone conversation I had yesterday with President Obama."[1]

This was unprecedented. Everyone crowded around the television. The Cuban president continued. The Cuban Five—undercover Cuban intelligence agents who had been imprisoned in the United States since 1998 for infiltrating Cuban American terrorist and paramilitary organizations in Florida—had been released and were now on Cuban soil. The room broke into applause at the surprise announcement. For years, protests in Havana had demanded the release of the prisoners, who had become Cuba's revolutionary causes célèbres. Charlie had been part of more than one raucous demonstration in front of the US Interests Section on their behalf.[2]

But as Raúl continued to speak, it became clear that he was arriving at something else. "We have also agreed to renew diplomatic relations," he finally said, almost as an aside. The room fell silent. "This in no way means that the heart of the matter has been solved," Raúl continued. "The economic, commercial, and financial blockade, which causes enormous human and economic damages to our country, must cease." The Cuban president called on Obama to use his executive power to undo the regime of sanctions and other obstacles to normal relations. "While acknowledging our profound differences, particularly on issues related to national sovereignty, democracy, human rights and foreign policy, I reaffirm our willingness to dialogue on all these issues."[3] At the White House, Barack Obama was making a simultaneous televised announcement. A new era in US-Cuba relations was about to begin.

The historic thaw created a flurry of pent-up interest in Cuba as a travel destination. "What we hear from the American public," Dagoberto Rodríguez Barrera, the head of Cuba's Interests Section in Washington, had stated more than a decade earlier, "is that there is a great desire to have normal and civilized relations. . . . [But] what we hear from [US] government officials is that there are no great possibilities that it could ever happen."[4] Cubans on the island had long referred to the US economic sanctions on Cuba as "el bloqueo" (the blockade) because, contrary to misconceptions, it impeded normal commercial relations not only between the United States and Cuba, as an "embargo" would do, but also between Cuba and the rest of the world due to their extraterritorial provisions.[5] Although the blockade was supported by a complex web of legislation that could not be undone by presidential order alone, one of the immediate effects of the Obama-era US-Cuba détente was the effective decriminalization of travel to Cuba by US citizens. The opening to Americans also prompted a noticeable uptick in European tourism. As pundits predicted that Cuba would soon be inundated by McDonald's and Starbucks, travelers from around the world rushed to see the island—presumably now a relic of the socialist past, a country notable for its almost total absence of any commercial advertising or foreign chain stores—before it changed.

Amid the tourism boom, however, Charlie suddenly found himself the object of unwelcome attention. The historic détente amid the US-Cuba cold war led to media speculation about the fate of the American political exiles. Cuba had provided sanctuary to a diverse cast of American dissidents for over five decades. Was this chapter of history now drawing to a close?

Havana responded to the speculation by declaring that extradition was off the table. "Every nation has sovereign and legitimate rights to grant political asylum to people it considers to have been persecuted," Josephina Vidal, Cuba's top diplomat in charge of relations with the United States told the Associated Press. "We've explained to the US government in the past that there are some people living in Cuba to whom Cuba has legitimately granted political asylum."[6] In New Jersey, Governor Chris Christie, who had just penned a letter to Obama demanding the return of that state's most wanted fugitive—Assata Shakur—immediately lashed back. In a televised interview, Christie argued that Shakur's presence in Cuba justified Washington's designation of Cuba as a state sponsor of terrorism. He insisted that Shakur, who had faced an all-white jury in her 1977 trial for the killing of a NJ state trooper, had been "convicted by a jury of her peers in what is without question the fairest and most just criminal justice system in the world. . . . These thugs in Cuba have given her political asylum. . . . It's unacceptable."[7]

The Cuban government, for its part, now tried to reassure Charlie personally. A few weeks after returning home from Cárdenas, Charlie had been visited again by the officer from the Ministry of the Interior (MININT). "He said he was there to reassure me that my asylum in Cuba was safe. Cuba was still my home."[8] Nonetheless, with virtually every new development came fresh foreign media speculation about the fate of the American political exiles. When Democratic New Mexico Senator Tom Udall prepared to travel to Cuba in May 2015 with a congressional delegation to discuss trade and tourism, he expressed hope that Cuba would hand Charlie over to US authorities, maintaining that "the extradition of criminals is an important part of any normal relations between countries."[9]

In early 2015, a New Mexico–based attorney named Jason Flores-Williams contacted Charlie to offer his legal services, pro bono. "When I went to meet him in Havana," Charlie remembers, "it was a hot day. I see this Latino cat in a full suit! I said to myself, that's got to be him."[10] Flores-Williams advised Charlie on his options for returning to the United States. Charlie was skeptical. "I knew it was a long shot but I wanted to hear him out."[11] Flores-Williams filed a motion seeking the dismissal of some charges, contending that New Mexico Governor Susana Martinez had "politicized" the case by referring to the RNA as "a terrorist group" in a letter to the Obama administration, which was preparing to remove Cuba from its list of nations that sponsor terrorism.[12]

Press coverage of Flores-Williams's legal advocacy resulted in more media requests. In April 2015, Charlie was contacted by CNN's correspondent in Havana, Patrick Oppmann. Despite his misgivings, Charlie agreed to be interviewed on camera in Parque John Lennon in Vedado. "I miss my country," Charlie told Oppmann in the segment that aired. "I miss my family. I would like to go back and see where my grandparents were born, where I was born, where I went to junior high. Eat some blackberry pie. Even go to McDonald's. That's only natural."[13] Unable to resist the cliche, Oppmann wrote that although Charlie was "still a revolutionary," he "craves the kind of French fries that only capitalism can make."[14]

Oppmann, however, had come to the park to play hardball. Charlie sat on a bench near the bronze statue of the Beatles icon. The cameras rolled. Oppmann asked about the murder charges in New Mexico. "I want to accomplish [*sic*]," Charlie began, "that people understand that I'm not a criminal, that I'm not a terrorist."[15] Oppmann asked Charlie directly if he was a "cop killer." Charlie responded emphatically: "No, I've never killed cops. I've never been guilty of that. I'm a Vietnam veteran, [and] people don't ask me, did I kill Vietnamese."[16]

When Oppmann contacted Elizabeth Walthall, the flight attendant who had spoken with journalist DeWayne Wickham in 2009, she confirmed her earlier account. Charlie, she said, had put the blade of a knife to her throat. "He told me to do what he said because 'this is no butter knife.' I told him, 'Well, I am no piece of bread.'" Charlie had laughed, Walthall said, and lowered the knife. She reiterated her belief that Michael had been the shooter. "Finney said he would shoot us and that he had already killed a man."[17]

CNN also interviewed attorney Flores-Williams in the park. "If I knew that he was going to get the same kind of trial as a wealthy person, or a person of white skin in America, and this man would be given his rights," the lawyer explained, "then I would say, Mr. Hill, I believe you have an opportunity here to fight for justice."[18] But Flores-Williams was not optimistic. Speaking with journalist Alexander Zaitchik several months later, the lawyer suggested that Charlie's legal prospects had been doomed the moment he was stopped on a dark highway in New Mexico. "This is 1971. Everyone knows why they were pulled over: driving while black. They had convicted him before he was even arrested."[19]

Following the CNN interview, Charlie became more cautious about speaking with foreign journalists. His new reticence was partly the result of pressure from MININT. A few weeks after the CNN newscast, the usual officer visited Charlie at home. He made it clear that MININT was not happy about the public attention that the newscast had drawn to Charlie—and, by implication, to the other American political asylees, such as Assata Shakur. The Cuban government, while prepared to maintain its commitments to provide political sanctuary, nonetheless wished to avoid unwarranted publicity or the perception that it was flaunting their presence to Washington. Cuba's refusal to extradite them had been a diplomatic stumbling block in US-Cuba relations. Throughout the decades, Cuban officials had publicly addressed the matter of the American asylees only when pressed to do so by foreign media coverage or diplomatic pressure.

MININT did not expressly prohibit Charlie from speaking with journalists, however, and Charlie was soon giving interviews again. In them, he often returned to the murder charges. "I don't feel guilty," he told Cuban writer Carlos Álvarez Rodríguez. "I was a revolutionary. The death of Rosenbloom is unfortunate, but there are many unfortunate deaths, many black men hanged, many black men lynched."[20] Álvarez Rodríguez pointed out that Rosenbloom's widow considers him a murderer. "That's her right," Charlie replied.[21]

As cultural fascination with all things Cuba continued in the United States, other figures stepped out of the shadows of history. In 2014, the *National Geographic* documentary series *I Am a Rebel* featured an episode about Louis Moore, the Detroit man who had hijacked a plane to Cuba in 1972. The documentary chronicles Moore's 1971 legal case against the Detroit police department prior to the hijacking.[22] Two years later, *The Skyjacker's Tale*, a documentary about the case of Ishmael Muslim Ali—formerly known as Ishmael LaBeet, the man accused of orchestrating the Fountain Valley

Massacre in the US Virgin Islands—was released.[23] Canadian filmmaker Jamie Kastner had traveled to Cuba in 2013 to meet Ali, "figuring at that point that I was on my way to meet a mass murderer."[24]

Ali turned out to be a more complex protagonist. "I started off looking into one crime and I discovered another crime," Kastner said of his research for the documentary. "And I don't know who committed the first crime, the Fountain Valley killings. But I have a pretty good idea who committed the second crime, and that was the torture of these young black men who had been rounded up as part of a wide scale sweep of young black men who were also rounded up and tortured, on whom Guantanamo-like techniques were used on American soil. And then in spite of overwhelming evidence presented by the best lawyers in America of the day, an unbelievably corrupt system threw the book at these guys."[25]

With access to the internet in Cuba expanding, Charlie sometimes now encountered people who had read about him online. One of them was the woman he was dating. Charlie and Yeskenia had met in his neighborhood several years earlier. On their first date, Charlie took her to his favorite restaurant, Tien-Tan—a venerable Chinese eatery in Havana's old Barrio Chino—for bowls of seafood soup and plates of fried rice. Within a few months, she was expecting a child. Their son, who they named Antar Charles, was born in August 2006.[26]

Now, a decade later, Yeskenia was learning things about her son's father. So were her friends. Foreign media coverage of the FBI and New Jersey rewards for Assata Shakur's apprehension often contained photos of the other US fugitives in Havana, including Charlie. "People saw his photo," Yeskenia later recalled, laughing, "and thought that the reward was also for Charlie." At the time, however, it was not so funny. "I was scared; I didn't want to leave the house with him!"[27] Some people began avoiding him. Charlie once had to explain the situation to some frightened neighbors. "Look, you idiots," he sputtered, jabbing his finger at an image of the wanted poster on his phone. "The article says $1 million for Assata. *Assata*. Not for me!"[28]

Nonetheless, his neighbors seldom had trouble comprehending his predicament. Cubans were accustomed to horror stories about the US criminal justice system. The Cuban media had long covered police killings of citizens in the United States, something that was exceedingly rare in Cuba. Robust legal defense under American-style capitalism cost a fortune. The justice system in the world's premier democracy, Cuban journalists noted, was stacked against poor people and people of color. Estonian filmmaker Kadri Koop's short 2016 film, *Charlie*, shows the titular protagonist watching television coverage of his case with some of his neighbors, who counsel him against returning to the United States to face trial. "You are a Black man in a trial in

America," one points out, "in a court where you have been accused of killing a white police officer." Another neighbor chimes in off-camera: "You can see that every time they show you on television. Who is more likely to win? You are Black and poor."[29]

Upon arriving in Cuba in 1971, as they were still learning Spanish, Charlie, Michael, and Antar began introducing themselves using some helpful phrases that Cubans had taught them—"Soy estadounidense, pero no soy Yankee: Soy un negro revolucionario y un socialista" (I'm an American, but I'm not a Yankee: I'm a Black revolutionary and a socialist)—in order to make their intentions and political commitments clear. It worked. Any Cuban reading newspapers and periodicals in the late 1960s and early 1970s would have been familiar with figures such as Black communist intellectual Angela Davis and civil rights activist Stokely Carmichael, or the socialist Black Panther Party. For this generation of Cubans, the icons of the Black freedom struggle in the United States were embraced as kindred spirits in a global battle against capitalist exploitation, racism, and imperialism. Now, in 2016, as Charlie tried to explain himself in Santa Amalia, he was aided by the collective memory of that era. Cuban television regularly aired documentaries and historical dramas about the social movements of the epoch. Indeed, an American tourist in Havana during this period might well have turned on the television in their hotel or Airbnb and been greeted by US productions such as *The Black Power Mixtape, 1967–1975*; *The Black Panthers: Vanguard of the Revolution*; or the biopic *Nina*, all of which aired on Cubavisión in 2016 and 2017.[30]

Yet despite his professed confidence that the Cuban government would protect him from extradition, Charlie knew that his fate could change. Pressed by CNN's Patrick Oppmann in Parque John Lennon, for instance, Charlie had explained that although he trusted the government's word, he would also accept a change of policy if it was for the good of the Cuban people. "If the Cuban government feels that me going back is for the benefit of twelve million people," he told Oppmann, "that's my sacrifice. I don't worry about that."[31]

Shaunely did not share her father's equanimity. Fear of a shift in US-Cuba relations had long been a shadow in the back of her mind. "I usually think that the government has a good opinion of him, because if not they would not have given him asylum," she explained in 2018. "The government welcomed him, gave him the opportunity to make a life. In those times when he came here, there was Fidel's struggle, which resembled the struggle of the Republic of New Afrika. They fought for almost the same thing, but in different countries," Shaunely argued. "However, I've always been afraid that Cuba will renew relations with the United States and maybe something will happen to him, he will go to prison. I have always been afraid of that. That's a fear that's always going to be there."[32]

Shaunely had a point. Even after decades on the island, Charlie had to admit that he understood little about his precise legal standing. For immigration purposes, MININT still classified him as a temporary resident, which should have legally disqualified him from outright property ownership. Yet he owned his house in Santa Amalia and had the papers to prove it. However, despite verbal assurances from MININT that his sanctuary was secure, the government had never given him any document attesting to his legal standing as a political asylee. This liminal status—of being verbally assured protection but without any paperwork to back it up—had always made Charlie uneasy. Perhaps, he speculated ruefully, the ambiguity left ajar a back door through which he could be summarily ejected if the need arose. When Charlie had attempted to apply for permanent residency status in the early 2000s, the request was twice denied without explanation.[33]

If there was ambiguity about Charlie's legal standing in Cuba, there were also other intangibles. One was his personal and political reputation—qualities that mattered in Cuba. In comparison to most of the other foreign exiles, who had taken regular jobs and remained active in political and civic life, Charlie had remained largely on the margins. Bill Brent, for instance, had become an English teacher at secondary schools in Havana, eventually taking a post at the Lenin school, or La Lenin, as people called Havana's prestigious Vladimir Ilich Lenin Vocational Pre-University Institute of Exact Sciences for high-achieving students. Ronald Herboldt, the South African expatriate, served for decades as an administrator at the Museum of the Revolution in Havana, an important state institution by any measure. Michael built a career at Radio Havana Cuba. Nehanda, although eschewing state employment like Charlie, found ways to maintain an engaged political praxis, from liaising with Black radical movements stateside as a member of the Malcolm X Grassroots Movement, an offshoot of the RNA, to mentoring Cuban youth, to befriending legions of visiting students and academics.[34]

There was also Assata, who in some respects occupied a category all her own among the American exiles. As a former Black Panther activist, she had been known in Cuba prior to her arrival. In 1978, as she waged a high-profile legal battle against false imprisonment in the United States, *Granma* had referred to her as a "poetess and historian . . . a courageous activist in the Black civil rights movement," and a "political prisoner." In 2005, when the State of New Jersey raised the reward for her apprehension to $1 million, Fidel himself had publicly defended Cuba's provision of asylum to her, referring to Assata as "a true political prisoner" who had been victimized by the "infamous lie" of the terrorism charges against her.[35] By that time, Assata was well-known within the intellectual and political communities of Havana, where she had forged relationships with a wide variety of entities and people, from Communist Party functionaries to cultural workers and hip-hop artists.

Fair or not, comparisons between the Cuban government's perception of Charlie and its perception of the other American political exiles, especially Assata, were not uncommon. As Cuban writer Carlos Álvarez Rodríguez had mused bluntly, while Assata had "even received public support from Fidel Castro," Charlie's presence seemed more "like an irritating burden, an uncomfortable remnant of another time."[36] Charlie had not held a steady job since his stint at the supermarket in the 1980s, choosing instead the ad hoc flexibility of guide work and a portfolio of entrepreneurial income-generating activities. His propensity for hustling—doing business *por la izquierda*, as it is colloquially known in Cuba—had once landed him in jail. While this kind of low-level transgression of the law had become a necessary survival strategy for innumerable Cubans during the Special Period and the precarious years that followed, Charlie had adopted these activities much earlier, in the 1970s and 1980s, when it was harder to justify them. The Cuban criminal justice system's professed emphasis on rehabilitation notwithstanding, and Charlie's own insistence that imprisonment had not stigmatized him by barring him from employment or housing, no one was prepared to argue that incarceration was a positive mark on one's reputation in Cuba.

Nehanda would later claim that Charlie's confinement in the 1980s for marijuana possession was symbolic of his "irresponsibility to the movement," which she accused him of having abandoned.[37] Although Nehanda readily acknowledged her own entrepreneurial hustles during her exile, such as selling cigars of questionable origin to foreigners—"I've done what I have to do to survive!"—substance use in Cuba, even marijuana, carried a social stigma. It also carried stiff prison sentences, harsher than those in the United States. Nehanda had been open about her struggles with alcoholism in Cuba and drugs in New York. "This is a different context. We are guests here," Nehanda would later say of Charlie. "Of course, there have been times in Cuba when I was tempted. But I could never allow myself to get high, because my comrades were counting on me. I could not let them down by doing something dumb and going to jail here."[38]

Nehanda's biting critique of what she viewed as Charlie's abandonment of political activity was not unique. As the years went by, Charlie maintained little contact with the RNA or any other political movement or organization. He became dependent on the financial generosity of friends and acquaintances during the many lulls when he had no tourists to guide. Perceptions of Charlie as in need of perpetual economic assistance had come to define his reputation. As one American acquaintance of his put it in 2019, "I hear from Charlie when he needs money."[39]

Despite their personal and political differences, however, the American exiles in Havana were bound together by the vagaries of US-Cuba relations. The US State Department had long included the extradition of US fugitives residing in Cuba as a precondition for the normalization of US-Cuba relations. Now, amid the historic rapprochement of the Obama era, diplomatic pressure was ratcheting up again. When California Congressman Jerry McNerney, who had been a passenger on the TWA flight that Charlie, Michael, and Antar hijacked in 1971, began a renewed push for Charlie's extradition in 2016, the State Department reassured him that the exiles remained a priority. "We consistently raise this issue with the Cuban government," McNerney said the State Department told him in a letter, "at every appropriate opportunity."[40]

Decades earlier, Eldridge Cleaver had worried about precisely this kind of diplomatic pressure. Ousted from Cuba in 1969, Cleaver had taken up residence in Algeria. Initially treated as an honored guest in Algiers and allowed to establish an international section of the Black Panther Party, the Algerian government's support eventually expired. "I heard that every time the US had private talks with the Algerians about relations, they would always bring us up as a condition for recognition," Cleaver would later say. "We were to be sacrificed because we were such an embarrassment to them. For a while the Algerians could play with us both. In the beginning it was more useful for them to be friendly to us because it evoked such a response from the US and of course it helped them with their Third World image. But as time went on they realized, like all emerging countries do, that the power all rests with the imperialists, then they change and start to betray their previous commitments."[41]

But Cuba was not Algeria. Since the 1959 revolution, national sovereignty had been the leitmotif of all Cuban foreign relations, the master trope of its very political identity. Decades passed, and still Havana maintained asylum for Americans, at significant cost to its relations with Washington and its efforts to be free of the crippling regime of unilateral economic sanctions. In 2014, as the Cuban government moved to normalize relations with its northern neighbor, Havana's insistence on its right to grant political sanctuary to foreigners, including Americans, was an outgrowth not only of revolutionary Cuba's genuine solidarity with left-wing social justice movements inside the United States but also of its determination to engage with the United States with what Raúl Castro had called "sovereign equality."[42]

Throngs of people lined the streets to catch a glimpse of the armored black presidential limousine that carried the Obama family from the airport into

Old Havana on the evening of March 20, 2016. In the United States, Obama's political opponents had worked hard to portray his historic diplomatic overture as a naive concession to a dictatorship. Then, a few days before Obama's state visit, Col. Rick Fuentes, superintendent of the New Jersey State Police, used the pages of the *Miami Herald* and the *New York Post* to issue a warning to would-be tourists: "Americans, beware. Unlike the president and his entourage, you aren't dignitaries with security teams, or part of a pampered and propagandized political delegation fattened and flattered by the type of cuisine and accommodations most Cubans can only dream about."[43]

As Obama's visit approached, Charlie stayed home. Remembering his compulsory sojourns to Holguín in 1978 and Isla de la Juventud in 1983 at the hands of state security, Charlie decided not to push his luck. Neither Charlie nor Nehanda received any specific directive from MININT ahead of the US president's visit. Nevertheless, Charlie decided to play it safe. As advance teams of US Secret Service personnel were glimpsed in Old Havana, accompanied by Cuban agents, and as Charlie's *socios* in Parque Central spotted "strange dudes with binoculars" on rooftops, Charlie decided to stay in Santa Amalia, foregoing his usual forays into Old Havana to look for tourists. He would have plenty of time to recoup his financial losses, he reasoned, as record numbers of American tourists continued to visit Cuba amid the historic diplomatic détente.

An abrupt shift in US-Cuba relations would soon upend all of it.

Chapter 15

La continuidad

Charlie was at home on a Friday night listening to his favorite program, a music show on Radio Taíno, when the broadcast was interrupted at midnight. Other stations also paused their programs. Then Raúl Castro's voice came over the airwaves. "People of Cuba. With profound pain, I come here to inform our people, our friends of *América* and the world, that today, the 25th of November 2016, at 10:29 p.m., died the chief commander of the Cuban Revolution, Fidel Castro Ruz."[1] Across Cuba, those who followed on television watched as Raúl, seated under portraits of Máximo Gómez, José Martí, and Antonio Maceo, icons of Cuba's long struggle for freedom and independence, read brief prepared words. Cuba's greatest revolutionary leader of the modern era, a legend of the Global South and a towering figure of the twentieth century, was no more.

The music did not return to Radio Taíno that night, nor the next. A nine-day period of mourning followed Fidel's death as the nation observed a syncretic *novena*, observed in both Catholicism and Santería, without alcohol sales or concerts.[2] For Charlie, it was a period of reflection. "Fidel died victoriously," he would later say. The Cuban leader had outlived six American presidents who had called for his ouster. He had weathered assassination plots and decades of destabilization. The Cuban Revolution's historical leader died of old age. "His legacy lives on, and his ideas live on. What he professed about Cuban sovereignty, the nation's independence, will still be here. I may criticize some of the things he did, like his economic policy, but I loved him. Fidel was one of the greatest leaders of all time. He did more for Africa, in my opinion, than any other non-African person."[3]

November had already been a gloomy month in Cuba. Two weeks before Fidel's passing, Donald Trump lost the popular vote but won the 2016 presidential election in the United States. Most Cubans recoiled in dismay. Barack Obama's historic efforts to normalize diplomatic relations and "cut loose the shackles of the past" had provoked an infectious optimism on the island.[4] As Josefina Vidal, Cuba's top diplomat in charge of relations with the United States, later observed, the historic change had been possible because, for the first time since 1959, "Cuba was treated as an equal" and negotiations were based on "respect and reciprocity."[5] In Havana, people had celebrated in the streets, cried, and hugged one another when Rául and Obama made their simultaneous announcements on December 2014. Now, the promise of an end to hostilities and a more normal relationship with the United States was being undone. The mood of shock and sadness in Havana was palpable.

Charlie was not entirely caught off guard by the business mogul's populist appeal to the American electorate. "When I saw him campaigning, I thought, Well, Trump is rich, he's racist, and ignorant. He can win!"[6] But if Trump's political rise appeared to many in Cuba less as an aberration than as the spilling over of deep currents coursing within the body politic of their northern neighbor, his presidency also symbolized old dynamics within the history of US-Cuba relations. Within months of coming to power in 2017, the Trump administration initiated a campaign of "maximum pressure" against Cuba. Abrogating Obama's policy of engagement, Washington now embraced coercion, tightening the economic sanctions and ratcheting up anticommunist rhetoric and talk of regime change.[7] Thus, even under the influence of the White House's most erratic and unconventional occupant in memory, Washington was reverting to time-worn patterns of chauvinism and imperial paternalism toward Cuba, in which it assumed the right to dictate the internal political affairs of its smaller Caribbean neighbor. Trump's policies on Cuba represented continuity, not rupture.

In April 2018, Cuba's National Assembly voted Miguel Díaz-Canel Bermúdez as president of the Council of State, a post that was renamed president of the republic with the ratifying of the nation's new constitution the following year. The Cuban Constitution, approved by Cuban voters in a popular referendum following months of discussion in public forums, reaffirmed the socialist character of the Cuban system, which would continue as a one-party revolutionary state, but also contained a number of updates. A new government slogan appeared: "*Somos continuidad*" (We are continuity). If the phrase was meant to communicate the Cuban government's resolve to stay the course of the revolutionary process in uncertain times and amid a historic shift in leadership, however, it was also an apt description of Washington's policies. More than a century after Martí and Maceo had fought to secure the island's independence from foreign domination, Cuba was still preoccupied with the question of its sovereignty as a small nation living in the shadow of a hostile superpower.[8]

Cuba was entering an epochal shift, a rupture between past and present, and a transition to an uncertain future. While many among a younger generation of Cubans, increasingly alienated from the political process that had been initiated by the revolutionary generation of the 1960s, had been increasingly vocal in their calls for reforms, pressure from the United States encouraged an environment that was uniquely unconducive to it. The stated purpose of Washington's more than half century of sanctions was the asphyxiation of the island's economy to bring about regime change. "A policy informed with malicious intent," historian Louis A. Pérez would later write, "designed purposely to foster deprivation and foment destitution, does not readily allow Cubans to envision the future in any form other than as an outlook of urgent immediacy."[9]

In this context of full-spectrum exterior pressure, in which the avowed purpose of Washington's policies was to encourage Cubans to rebel against their government, the response of the state to political dissent was predictable. As Pérez noted, "The state—any state—does not equivocate on matters of national security. One cannot be surprised that a policy designed to foment political protest as a means of subversion enables the Cuban government to proscribe political protest as an act of subversion."[10] The Cuban government's claims that individual dissidents were funded by US intelligence agencies were often difficult to prove, but their activities occurred in a context in which US intelligence had worked assiduously for decades to destabilize the Cuban political system by funding or training a vast array of political dissidents, nominally independent media, academic initiatives, and opposition figures who advocated the overthrow of the government. Regime change programs, many of them euphemistically termed "democracy promotion" campaigns, funded by US agencies such as the National Endowment for Democracy and the United States Agency for International Development, channeled tens of millions of dollars per year into civil society initiatives whose express purpose was to change Cuba's political and economic system.[11] The United States had never stopped trying to overthrow the Cuban Revolution.

These tensions between sovereignty and reform would define Cuba's political culture in the coming years. For some among the younger generation, Díaz-Canel's call for "continuity" had been a tone-deaf departure from the relative openness of Raúl, whose promise to "cambiar lo que debe ser cambiado" (change everything that ought to be changed), a homage to Fidel's affirmation of the Cuban Revolution's guiding principles in May 2000, had marked a period of optimism, suggesting that the nation would not repeat the mistakes of the past.[12]

Some Cubans also advocated fundamental democratic changes to Cuba's one-party political system, including the legalization of opposition parties and the direct election of the nation's president by the populace instead of by the National Assembly of People's Power. The National Assembly's members were chosen by universal secret ballot in direct elections characterized by very high national voter turnout in Cuba, and the candidates for this body were selected by a grassroots process of nomination by local popular assemblies. This political process created a high degree of grassroots participatory democracy but also insulated the national governing body from challenges. As people debated new drafts of the constitution in public forums across the island in preparation for a 2018 national referendum, a Cuban man in his mid-twenties who worked as a guide for tourists summed up this sentiment: "Trust us. Trust the next generation," he said, noting that the World Bank had recently lauded Cuba's education system as Latin America's finest. A self-described leftist and socialist, the young man explained that the Cuban government should have nothing to fear from an open political system. "Cuba is one of the best educated countries in the world. The revolution gave us the right to study, free university. Trust the people you educated to make the right choice."[13]

Charlie, now a consummate Leninist, regarded such arguments sympathetically but saw them as unworkable. An open political system, he believed, would simply allow the United States and its corporate interests to reassert control. Cuba could not have an open political field, he believed, if it wished to preserve its national sovereignty. That was the choice under the present conditions, as unpalatable as it was, and it would not change until Washington and Miami stopped trying to overthrow Cuba's socialist system. "The Cuban government does not allow a formal opposition, and should not," Charlie insisted flatly.[14] Charlie's position was a common one among the older generation of Cubans who remembered the prerevolutionary period of foreign domination and subservience to the United States.

For Charlie—and likely a large part of the 86.85 percent of Cuban voters who approved the 2019 overhaul of the constitution—the solution therefore lay in political and economic reforms leveraged "*within the revolution.*"[15] This political position held that the revolution was a fundamentally positive historical process, and that while adjustments would be necessary to continually improve it, the basic characteristics of that revolution—collectivist, egalitarian, sovereign, internationalist, and based on social justice—should remain intact.[16] For many Cubans, the most pressing issues were not lack of political freedom but the nation's weak and dysfunctional economy. While economic reforms would be necessary, as well as greater integration into the global economy, this had to be accomplished while minimizing inequality. No one seemed clear on how to accomplish that. Economic reforms had thus far been halting and noncommittal. Cuba, a small socialist nation drifting alone in a sea of globalization and unfettered markets, was truly in uncharted waters.

An economic downturn began to be felt in Cuba in a palpable way in 2019 in response to a raft of new punitive sanctions from the Trump administration. Sporadic shortages of food and fuel followed across the island. Superstitious observers might have pointed to two unusual recent events as bad omens: the deadly crash of a Cubana de Aviación flight in Havana in May 2018 that killed 112 people, and an exceedingly rare climatic event—a powerful tornado—that caused extensive damage in the city in January 2019. But the worst was yet to come.

The COVID-19 pandemic that upended the world in spring 2020 had severe consequences for Latin America. Cuba initially seemed to be weathering the storm. Infection rates remained low throughout the first year.[17] To help people quarantine, the government delivered food to homes. Neighbors organized mutual aid, distributing care parcels to the elderly, and applauded the teams of doctors and medical students who went door-to-door checking on residents. At home in Santa Amalia, Charlie received baskets of rice, dry beans, sugar, tomato paste, and handmade face masks sewed from African cloth from a community solidarity project that a mother and daughter, owners of Cuba's first Afro-Cuban clothing line, had organized in their living room with local donations.[18] The government fast-tracked the development of domestic COVID-19 vaccines, two of which, Abdala and Soberana, demonstrated world-class efficacy. "Cubans felt really proud of that," Charlie later marveled. "We had our own vaccine. It saved so many lives, and Cuba did it all on its own."[19]

But frustration and anger bubbled under the surface. Supplies of food and medicine, already affected by the Trump-era sanctions, dwindled as the Cuban economy experienced a dramatic COVID-induced contraction. Tourism plummeted almost overnight in the spring of 2020, and Cuban civil society came to a virtual halt. To slow the spread of the virus, social gatherings were banned, strict sanitary curfews were imposed for months on end, and the nation's beaches closed for over a year. *Apagones* (blackouts) became more common, causing sleepless nights without fans and spoiled food in refrigerators. In November 2020, Western Union halted money transfers to Cuba citing new US sanctions, cutting off one of the last electronic routes through which Cubans could receive remittances from relatives in the United States. In January 2021, the Cuban government implemented a long-delayed monetary restructuring to end the two-currency system, in which the Cuban convertible peso (CUC) had existed alongside the Cuban peso. A necessary reform, it was implemented with the worst imaginable timing. Inflation ensued. Like many other Cubans, Charlie spent his days standing in lines, waking up at 4:00 a.m. to secure his spot in a queue to enter a store to buy rationed allotments of subsidized food that sometimes ran out before his turn came.

Then, in the spring of 2021, before the Abdala and Soberana vaccines were deployed, infection rates on the island suddenly surged. As the Delta variant of the virus became globally dominant over the summer, the Cuban city of Matanzas experienced a full-blown medical crisis as patients overwhelmed hospitals and deaths mounted. Cuba had gone from being a symbol of an effective public health response to COVID-19 to an epicenter of the virus. Cuba was a society on the edge. Havana began to feel like a tinderbox.

The protests that occurred on the island on July 11, 2021, have been analyzed in various accounts, many of them conflicting.[20] What is clear is that the unrest, which began south of Havana in the town of San Antonio de los Baños amid an extended power outage and then spread across the island, was both a manifestation of seething popular frustration about deteriorating living conditions as a result of the pandemic and the result of organized activity by political dissidents, including the anonymous antigovernment activists behind the Facebook group that organized the initial street protest in San Antonio de los Baños.[21] What followed were the largest popular protests, some of them violent, in the island's post-1959 history. It was a moment of national reckoning in Cuba. As the economic crisis deepened in the following months, record numbers of people left the island, contributing to the largest wave of outmigration in the modern era.[22] The Special Period of the 1990s was a severe economic downturn, but this was something even more profound.

Popular frustration over the erosion of Cuba's egalitarian socialist dream, and anger at the perception that the government had broken its promises, predated the COVID-19 pandemic. In a bid to stimulate the economy and conserve scarce resources, the government had decreased social spending in 2009 but opened new opportunities for self-employment, initiating a dynamic that would deepen in the coming years as the state tried to figure out how to create a tax base while preserving social equality. Even prior to reductions in its contents in 2009, *la libreta* had provided only 36 percent of each person's caloric intake.[23] Many Cubans continued to rely on it, however, and recoiled in fear at proposals to cut or eliminate it. As the state sector continued to shrink, even the celebrated health-care system evinced concerning signs of strain.

Charlie had heard these criticisms for years in Santa Amalia. Some people wanted capitalism to come to Cuba, but the great majority saw little prospect for a market economy to meaningfully improve their daily lives. Indeed, it was the perception that the state was embracing capitalism through liberal economic reforms and foreign investment—so visible in the construction of tourist hotels amid austerity—that provoked the sternest popular condemnation. "Most of the people in my neighborhood, they wanted socialism to work better. They did not want to get rid of it," Charlie would later reflect. "Cubans still believed in equality, the ideals of the revolution."[24]

One of those who might have agreed was Ronald Herboldt. For years the South African expatriate had lived just blocks from Charlie, although the two never met. In 2007, Herboldt repatriated to South Africa to reunite with his long-lost family in Cape Town. He had been away almost half a century. After spending most of his life in Cuba, Herboldt's support for the ideals of the revolution had remained firm, even as his feelings about the state had become ambivalent. In *Brothers in Arms*, a documentary about his life, Herboldt expresses love for the Cuban people and admiration for the nation's internationalist project, especially its role in the liberation of South Africa from apartheid, but also anger at the government, whose bureaucracy encumbered his efforts to repatriate to his homeland.

In *Brothers in Arms*, Herboldt explains that his "loyalty is to the people of Cuba" but not to the state.[25] Yet he leaves little doubt about his deeper political convictions. At a family reunion in Cape Town, one of Herboldt's uncles takes the stage and tearfully expresses his jubilation at being reunited with his long-lost nephew. He speaks of Herboldt's "suffering" under Cuba's socialist distribution system of *la libreta*. The family in South Africa, the uncle recounts, once sent Herboldt a parcel of clothing during a period of shortages. "They are limited to a pair of shoes for the year, two trousers, a jacket or something, that's all the clothes you are entitled to, being a communist country."[26] Herboldt embraces his uncle, then takes the microphone:

> I want to clarify something. . . . A communist country is a country where everybody has got the same right. Because we have two trousers, to share or whatever, is because everyone has got to have the same right. Here in South Africa we've got a free South Africa, we've got everything we want, but there are millions of people in this country that hasn't got a plate of food to eat. He hasn't got two trousers, he hasn't got one pair of shoes. And I want to clarify, my brother, because I love him also, because I told him once about how we used to live [in Cuba]. We were living like that with honor, because we shared what we had. And today we still share. We share with the world. We share with even people in America. People in Africa. We share our doctors. We share our teachers. We share our blood; when there is a catastrophe anywhere in the world we donate our blood in the Cuban banks that will go over to those places. It's the people we fight for! We don't fight for governments, we fight for people! . . . That is a communist country. And I'm proud of living in a communist country with the little few things that we had, but we all shared the same things. . . . I'm not trying to get you to be communist, I'm just trying to get you [to] open your eyes and see what's going on around you. Everything that happens in the world happens to us.[27]

These are the final words that Herboldt speaks in the film. In August 2007, three months after repatriating to South Africa, Herboldt died of a heart attack in Cape Town. The only African to take part in the 1959 Cuban Revolution, he had been away from his homeland for almost five decades.[28]

Charlie had nowhere to repatriate to, though, and he remained deeply committed to the ideals of the Cuban Revolution even as he had witnessed concerning signs of the deterioration of living standards. He was also not ready to give up on the state as the arbiter of the revolutionary process. While there was plenty to criticize, reform would have to happen within the revolutionary process, Charlie believed, through its incremental improvement, not its destruction.

The presidency of Raúl Castro had presided over notable reforms. It also made public admissions of past errors, including on social issues. The government's support for gay rights had been institutionalized through the Centro Nacional de Educación Sexual (National Center for Sex Education), directed by Mariela Castro Espín, the daughter of Cuban revolutionary Vilma Espín and Raúl Castro. In a 2010 interview, Fidel had taken personal responsibility for the persecution of gay Cubans during the 1960s. "If anyone is responsible, it's me," he told Mexico's *La Jornada* newspaper. "I'm not going to place the blame on others."[29] As Charlie was quick to point out, Raúl had publicly acknowledged the persistence of racial and gendered discrimination in Cuba. "Personally, I consider the insufficient advance on this matter in fifty years of Revolution to be an embarrassment," the Cuban president explained at the closing session of the National Assembly of People's Power in December 2009. "Despite the fact that 65 percent of the workforce is composed of women and that the citizenry form a beautiful racial rainbow without any formal privileges, they persist in practice."[30]

For Charlie, these were welcome signs. While some of Cuba's leaders were inept and unpopular, the majority were genuinely committed to the well-being of the nation, Charlie insisted, but were constrained by an impossible structural situation for which there were no simple solutions. This was socialism in a real nation of the twenty-first century, with all its contradictions and challenges, not some armchair theory of how the Cuban economy and society should be run. "I know, from my experience, that the Cuban government is not operating on behalf of the 1 percent of the population, as happens in many countries," Charlie maintained. "Cuba is not perfect, but the leaders are more humble. They don't live in mansions, and they are not being lobbied."[31] He scoffed at claims, especially from the United States, that Cubans were disenfranchised because there were no direct presidential elections. "People criticize the Cuban system for electing the president through the National Assembly, but in the US it's the Electoral College that selects the president, not the people who vote, and the Electoral College is not even elected by the population. Is that democratic?"[32]

But change in Cuba, unfolding in the shadow of past errors, had been erratic and painfully slow. This was especially apparent in the arena of racial equality. In 1986, Fidel had promoted a new initiative, amounting to a policy of affirmative action, to ensure that the Central Committee of the Communist

Party reflected the true diversity of the nation. "We can't leave it to chance to correct historical injustices," the Cuban president had declared to the third congress. "To really establish total equality takes more than simply declaring it in law. . . . We can't leave the promotion of women, blacks, and mestizos to chance. It has to be the work of the party; we have to straighten out what history has twisted."[33]

Proclaiming racism solved, as the government and much of the populace had done in the early 1960s, had been "an error of idealism and wishful thinking," Cuban scholar Esteban Morales Domínguez would later write. "As a direct result, the subject of race has become the most avoided and ignored topic in our social reality."[34] Educational attainment, for instance, could not explain low Afro-Cuban representation in the highest offices of the government during past decades because the socialist system had succeeded in eliminating precisely those educational disparities.[35] "The paradox," Cuban and British writers Pedro Pérez Sarduy and Jean Stubbs observed in 1993, "is not that such questions should have to be asked after 30 years of revolution. Thirty years is a relatively short period of time for deep-seated attitudes and values to change. It is rather that they cannot be adequately answered, and largely because of revolutionary policy."[36] Cuba's revolutionary ideology linked advancement to merit, hard work, and education on a playing field that was assumed to have been leveled but with no inquiry into the causes of extant racial disparities and racist attitudes that remained. The paradox was therefore that revolutionary policy had perpetuated a national silence on race even when faced with unmistakable evidence of racial inequality and in a society that was clearly animated by "an implicit, underlying language of racial (and other) codes, signs, and meanings."[37]

Now, Charlie believed, some noteworthy progress was occurring on *la problemática racial.* "They are taking huge steps" Charlie argued, referring to the creation in 2009 of the José Antonio Aponte Commission by the National Union of Writers and Artists of Cuba and the approval in 2019 of the National Program Against Racism and Racial Discrimination, chaired by President Díaz-Canel. "They are talking openly about these important details about life in Cuba."[38] The representation of Afro-Cubans in the upper reaches of the government had gradually increased in the 1990s and 2000s until it roughly matched the racial composition of the population.[39] With the National Assembly elections of April 2018, half of the six vice presidents in the Council of State—the nation's highest political body that governs with the president—were Black Cubans who had made careers in civil service, including the first vice president of Cuba, Salvador Valdés Mesa, an agricultural engineer from Las Tunas and a longtime member of the Communist Party. Two of the remaining vice presidents were Black women: Inés María Chapman

Waugh, a hydraulic engineer from Holguín, and Beatriz Johnson Urrutia, a chemical engineer from Santiago, both longtime leaders in professional and government associations and members of the Communist Party.[40]

Racial diversity had long been the rule in numerous professional sectors. Charlie took great pride in pointing out the predominance of Afro-Cubans in the medical and scientific spheres, especially women, whose large presence attested to the equalizing impact of the nation's massive investment in education.[41] "My dentist is a Black woman. She's a sharp-dressing lady with natural hair. A real smart lady. My ophthalmologist also is a stylish older Black woman. She explained to me about the condition of my eyes, and she was really funny, which helped me relax. After discussing my eyesight, she said, 'You know these things can happen when you get old, Charlie!' There's another Black emergency medicine doctor in my *policlínico* who is the same way. These Black professional Cubans always seem very comfortable with who they are, conscious about who they are, where they come from, and where they are going."[42]

But not all was well in Cuba. Like his neighbors in Santa Amalia, Charlie had watched with alarm as inequality widened in tandem with strategic economic liberalization and an increasingly dollarized economy. Some of this inequality was clearly racialized. Although income gaps had emerged during the Special Period, Cuba had managed to remain remarkably equal by hemispheric standards in the core social indictors of education, health, and nutrition.[43] The state maintained robust funding for public social programs in order to minimize inequality. Now, the emerging private sector, with its lucrative opportunities for those positioned to take advantage of them, was threatening equality in ways that were reminiscent of the dynamics of the Special Period of the 1990s. Waiters, taxi drivers, and renters of flats for tourists had long earned far more than engineers and dentists in the state sector.[44] Afro-Cubans, still far less likely to have family living abroad, had less access to remittances that could be used as capital to start businesses, buy or rent vehicles, and renovate properties. Afro-Cubans were more likely to be concentrated in dilapidated housing due to historical disadvantages, including the inability of state planning to entirely undo prerevolutionary racialized housing patterns, making them less able to participate in the new economy as owners.[45]

In the before times, Charlie had been critical of how Marxism-Leninism had been interpreted in Cuba. "The idea was that as long as socialism, an egalitarian society, was being built, racism would eventually all come out in the wash. We in the Revolutionary Collective didn't agree with that. We said, you have to talk about racism, you have to recognize it, and you have to address it as you build socialism. It's not automatic."[46] This view, long articulated by a small but vocal group of Afro-Cuban intellectuals and activists, had been gradually embraced by important sectors of the revolutionary state. It was less clear what this would mean for everyday people. Would greater Afro-Cuban representation within the high echelons of the government, as was now occurring, mean more racial equality in the society as a whole? In the past, it had been possible to argue that the state's structural approach to building socialism—by lifting all boats, the most marginalized would also be lifted—had taken the nation further toward class, gender, and racial equality than ever before. But now the state sector was shrinking. In its place were savage market forces that were very difficult to control. The government had proven unable to adapt to the crisis. More than ever before, Cubans sensed that the revolutionary process—perhaps the viability of the state and the revolution itself—was at a crossroads.

Charlie was feeling melancholic as November 27, 2021, approached, the day that would mark the fiftieth anniversary of his arrival in Cuba. Two days earlier, the American Thanksgiving holiday, a day that passes like any other in Cuba, had come and gone. Late November often found Charlie at home, depressed and alone. At least in late December, he could look forward to the festivities of *La Nochebuena* (Christmas Eve), when Cubans traditionally gather with family for food and merriment. As the days grew shorter and his seventy-second birthday (December 15) approached, Charlie's thoughts often drifted to his past. Sometimes he thought about those fleeting months that he had spent with the Republic of New Afrika (RNA) in California and about that fateful trip to Jackson, Mississippi, in 1971 that had rerouted his life.

The legacy of the RNA was still being felt in Jackson. Some of the organization's members—citizens of the Republic of New Afrika—eventually put down roots in the city. They began organizing, founding innovative grassroots institutions and launching political campaigns. In June 2013, Chokwe Lumumba, the RNA leader who Charlie had met in Havana in 1973, was elected mayor of Jackson. Lumumba died suddenly less than a year later. While the indefatigable Black nationalist activist and attorney left an indelible mark on Mississippi, not all were sorry to see him go. "I'm glad he's dead," one white Jackson resident told a reporter. "I don't know what the hell he thought he was doing. He was trying to turn this place into Cuba."[47] Charlie had to laugh when he heard. "In some ways that was probably true!"[48]

Yet Lumumba's vision of Black self-determination lived on. Less than three months after his death, political descendants of the RNA in Mississippi founded Cooperation Jackson on May 1, 2014—International Workers' Day. Cooperation Jackson's program of grassroots economic democracy, eventually outlined as the Jackson-Kush Plan, was nothing less than a blueprint for economic and environmental justice: a testament to the continuing relevance of the RNA's original vision of Black self-determination.[49] Charlie had no contact with Cooperation Jackson. Members of the organization traveled to Cuba in November 2019 to attend an international conference but did not communicate with him.[50] Charlie, who had maintained little contact with the original RNA, likewise had minimal contact with the organization's political descendants in later decades.

Cuba itself played only small roles in mainstream American politics during those years. Never a priority for the Trump administration, the specter of socialist Cuba surfaced most often as a conjured hobgoblin for far-right commentators. Occasionally, this ferment bubbled up to the White House. In June 2017—coincidentally the same month that Lumumba's son, Chokwe Antar Lumumba, following in his father's footsteps, was elected mayor of Jackson—GOP politicians began calling for the extradition of the US political exiles in Cuba. Eventually these calls emanated from Trump himself, who publicly demanded the return of Assata Shakur, who he referred to in one speech as "the cop-killer Joanne Chesimard."[51]

One of those who understood the plight of the US political exiles in Cuba was Fernando González Llort. One of the Cuban Five intelligence agents imprisoned in the United States for spying on right-wing Cuban exile paramilitary groups in Florida, Llort became the director of the Cuban Institute of Friendship with the Peoples in 2017. Charlie met him a few months later. Llort's experience of confinement in maximum-security facilities, he would later tell Charlie, confirmed for him the class-based nature of incarceration in the United States. It was the poor of all races, Llort later wrote, that he had encountered in America's prisons. The experience also taught him about political prisoners in Cuba's northern neighbor. Indeed, Llort spent four years sharing a cell with legendary Puerto Rican independence activist Oscar López Rivera. Antonio Guerrero Rodríguez, another of the imprisoned Cuban Five agents, formed a close friendship in prison with revolutionary activist and acupuncturist Mutulu Shakur, a former comrade of Assata and Nehanda and the alleged mastermind of Assata's legendary 1979 prison escape.[52]

The renewed scrutiny of the US exiles might explain the call from the FBI that Charlie's sister, Janet, received in Albuquerque. Charlie and his siblings had communicated only sporadically throughout the decades. Their relationship had been strained by Charlie's absence and by the events leading up to his exile in Cuba. The murder charges, the manhunt, and the hijacking had all come as a huge shock to his family. "They never understood," Charlie would later say. He would later recall a telephone conversation with his brother, Eddie. "That was a dumb thing that you did," his brother told him.[53]

Janet's life had taken a very different path from that of her older brother. While Charlie had been a fugitive in Cuba, Janet had embarked on a career as a corrections officer in Albuquerque's criminal justice system. As she neared retirement, however, she began communicating with her exiled brother more regularly. And then something unexpected happened. An FBI agent called Janet out of the blue on her cell phone. The agent asked Janet whether Charlie might be open to turning himself in. The FBI, he told her, had never stopped watching the Hill family.[54]

Charlie had now been separated from his US family for more than five decades. Perhaps for this reason, his Cuban family had become the very center of his world. As he approached his golden years, he derived his greatest satisfaction from the simple pleasures of parenthood. What is it like to be the child of an American exile in Cuba? For Shaunely, her dad's political past is a source of pride. While she does not consider herself to be an activist in Cuba, she credits her dad with instilling in her a deep sense of social justice. "I am 100 percent a feminist! I am struggling for the rights of women, for equality. We are all equal, no matter our social class, no matter race, or sex."[55] Shaunely has a degree in gastronomy, but her dream is to become a lawyer and to visit the United States and see the rural Illinois town where her father was born.

Antar, now in his late teens, also describes his dad in political terms. "He is a humble man who fought for the freedom of Blacks in the United States," Antar says. "He struggled against racism."[56] Privately, however, it has been difficult for Antar. When classmates in Santa Amalia saw a social media post from a right-wing Cuban American commentator lambasting the Cuban government for its protection of the US political exiles, they teased him for having a dad who is wanted for murder. Charlie obviously cares deeply about his son's perception of him. His children, he explains, are all that will remain after he is gone.

During the making of a short film about Charlie's life, Estonian filmmaker Kadri Koop tried to capture Charlie's sense of rootlessness and, at times, his uncertainty about his ultimate legacy. The online documentary *Charlie*, released in 2016, opens with the protagonist reading aloud a letter to his son. "My dear son Antar," the letter begins. "Today you are only nine years old. Someday, you may have questions. You may want to understand who I was and why I did what I did. To the US government, I'm a fugitive. To my sisters and brothers in the struggle, I'm a revolutionary. As your father, I hope you will see me as more than just a tragic story."[57]

Epilogue

Fugitive States

"I want to talk about the exile blues," Charlie says as we drink strong Cuban coffee on a muggy afternoon in Havana in July 2019. Sitting in my rented apartment a few blocks from the University of Havana, we have been talking about his life for the past three days.

Nehanda Abiodun is gone. She joined the ancestors in January, dying peacefully but unexpectedly in her sleep. We are sharing memories of the woman with the force-of-nature personality, the godmother of Cuban hip-hop, whose sharp intelligence and warm charisma touched scores of young Cubans and foreign visitors alike. Charlie last saw Nehanda at a low-key pool party at her neighborhood in Bahía. I saw her at a small Christmas Day dinner in Havana, her daughter from the United States in attendance, just weeks before her death.

In ill health in recent years, Nehanda had retained her indomitable spirit. The previous summer, at an academic panel I organized for the Caribbean Studies Association conference in Havana titled "Cuba, U.S. Black Radicalism, and Transnational Emancipatory Thought," Nehanda, not content to quietly observe, stood up after the presentations and lectured the standing-room-only audience about her experiences as an activist in New York and a political émigré in Havana. A week later, attending a Latin jazz concert at a popular Havana nightclub, Nehanda suddenly disappeared from our group, reappearing moments later onstage, where she danced with the surprised members of the band and, illuminated by spotlights, playfully conducted their performance. Scolded a few days later by her Cuban state security contacts, she laughingly brushed off their concern that an American fugitive, wanted by the FBI, had given a spontaneous public performance to an audience of several hundred people, including American tourists. Charlie and I laugh about it.

Nehanda's passing was hard on him. Although their friendship had been strained in recent years, Charlie appreciated knowing that she was there, that he could call her, someone who understood his loneliness and his homesickness, the interior life of a perpetual foreigner. Nehanda, in short, understood what it was like to be an exile.

"Exile," the Palestinian literary critic Edward Said once pointedly observed, "is strangely compelling to think about but terrible to experience. It is the unhealable rift forced between a human being and a native place, between the self and its true home: its essential sadness can never be surmounted."[1] For Charlie, this ensemble of emotions had been a defining feature of his life in Cuba. The figure that Charlie returns to again and again to explain the movement of history and the machinations of politics, perhaps surprisingly, is Vladimir Lenin. "Lenin compared exile with death. To me, there's one step before that: prison. Prison is worse than exile. But in exile, although you're walking the streets, it's not the same. A part of you is dead."[2]

Nehanda's time in Cuba was also inexorably shaped by the pain of separation. Cut off from family and the political community of comrades from which she had derived purpose, she struggled to avoid what Cuban cultural critic Roberto Zurbano, referring to another American political exile in Cuba, had called "political death."[3] When I asked Nehanda in 2018 how she would describe how it felt to experience exile, she fell uncharacteristically silent. "It is a feeling of emptiness," she finally replied, "that nothing can cure."[4]

Other American émigrés in Cuba have similarly reflected on the psychic condition of exile. In the closing lines of his autobiography, published in 1996, Bill Brent alluded to a sensation of perpetual motion and rootlessness: "I have been away from my people for a quarter of a century. Much has changed. The flight I commandeered all those years ago is still not over. It is a flight without end."[5] For Michael Finney, to be in exile was to be perpetually out of place. Exile, he once told a reporter, is "probably one of the most difficult human conditions that exists. . . . You're always homeless. You're always in a place that's not yours."[6]

American political exiles in Cuba sought solace in bonds of kinship and community. Nehanda found connection in a sprawling transnational network of cherished comrades and confidants. Separated from her daughter by geographic distance, she nonetheless mentored scores of Havana youth and proudly appointed herself "Cuban mother" to more than a few American students visiting Havana. Michael found sanctuary in the love of his Cuban family, purpose in his work at Radio Havana Cuba, and community in his neighborhood and within the radio station's network of revolutionary professionals. Charlie found solace and purpose in his love for his children, meaning through political study with comrades, and friendship in his neighborhood and in a diverse cast of foreign visitors to Cuba that included activists, academics, tourists, journalists, and sojourners of various stripes. All of them found inspiration in their abiding belief in the ideals of the Cuban revolutionary project, and gratitude in their love for the Cuban people who had embraced them.

But homesickness, a psychic state born of a material condition, is notoriously difficult to cure through individual force of will. And so Nehanda, Michael, and Charlie tried to cope with the dislocation of exile in Cuba through adaptation. They built lives for themselves. They developed and matured politically, had families, lived as fully as they could. Sometimes they thrived. At times they slipped into sadness. Sometimes they did both. They grew into old age. Yet the materiality of separation remained. "Exile is life led outside habitual order," Said concluded. "It is nomadic, decentered, contrapuntal; but no sooner does one get accustomed to it than its unsettling force erupts anew."[7]

Charlie and I sit in front of a rickety old fan drinking our *cafecitos*. We can hear a storm approaching. Thunder booms faintly in the distance. Next door, the neighbors are playing a raucous game of *dominó*. Charlie is trying to put these feelings of loss and separation, which he calls the "exile blues," into words.

"I want to talk about my own struggles with alcohol, about how I justified drinking, or drinking too much. I knew that I felt lonely, felt that nobody cared. And so, I would just go on a hell of a binge. But it would always make me feel bad. . . . Michael would drink in the 1980s, as a functional alcoholic. I think Michael drank for the same reasons. He had a girlfriend, but that doesn't necessarily take the loneliness away. The desire to see your mother, your father, your children, eat turkey with American stuffing on Thanksgiving, sweet potato pies, BBQ, you miss all those things."[8] Now the last surviving member of the three RNA comrades who arrived in Cuba in 1971, he misses his friends. "I still dream with Antar and Michael all the time," Charlie says, Spanish diction now evident in the construction of some of his English sentences.[9]

Charlie is forthright about his interior battles. As he once told a journalist, "Sometimes depression takes hold of me and I throw myself onto my bed, either to turn restlessly or [to] read a book. But I mustn't let the depression take over."[10] Material privation is also hard on Charlie. As Cuba's economy tightened in 2019 amid new US sanctions under the first Trump administration, Charlie wondered what the future would hold for Cuba. "I'm scared to death. I have enough food here to last for a while, but if it gets really bad, I don't know what will happen. I don't know how I will make it."[11]

Charlie's thoughts still stray to Vietnam. "Everyone processes combat a little bit differently. Some people snap. I often wondered what would have happened if I had not been in Cuba. . . . When you've seen certain things, and have certain things in your head afterward, if you're in a peaceful place your mind processes those things different. You begin to let it go and forget it. I think it really helped me being in a peaceful community." One of Charlie's Cuban friends in Santa Amalia is a veteran of a Cuban internationalist mission to Guinea-Bissau during the African nation's struggle against Portuguese colonialism. But the two never talk about war. "We always avoided the topic. It's too painful."[12]

In September 2019, Charlie saw an ESPN documentary, *The Return*, about football legend Rocky Bleier. Drafted by the Pittsburgh Steelers in 1968, he was then drafted again—by the US Army—and sent to Vietnam. The documentary chronicles Bleier's return to Vietnam at seventy-two years old to visit the area in the Hiep Duc Valley where four soldiers in his platoon died during a firefight that left him wounded. "You think about those guys that got killed," Bleier says, then breaks down, sobbing. Shortly afterward, Bleier collapses from heat stroke. "All of a sudden I had an overwhelming feeling of loss and sadness," he later explains. "Why did we fight this war? Why did we lose 58,000 soldiers, and in all honesty for what? Maybe for the first time I can understand on a slight basis the impact that our soldiers go through and maybe just a little what post-traumatic stress might be and how the body reacts to all the emotions."[13] The segment deeply affected Charlie when it screened on Cuban television.

The trauma of Vietnam is one reason Charlie feels fortunate to call Cuba home. "The only problems that I've encountered here in Cuba have been my own. Adjusting to life in Cuba, learning the Cuban cultural idiosyncrasies. Learning how to live everyday life. I've never been a big rice eater, so that's hard here." He laughs. "I like beans and soups and green beans. And collard greens," he says, invoking a staple of his childhood supper table. "But it's OK. In Cuba you eat your beans and rice and pork and keep on moving, man. I think about all of the hard times that I had, being in Vietnam, then underground, and so being in Cuba has been a relief. I don't have stress here."[14]

In 2018, when we began talking about this book, I asked Charlie if he sometimes daydreamed of returning to the United States. "Of course," he replied. "But Cuba is now my home."[15] Five years later, Charlie's petition to the Ministry of the Interior for permanent resident status was finally granted, giving him some peace of mind. With each passing year, Charlie's old life recedes further into the past. "Do I want to try to find my old friends and family? Of course I do. And I want to eat blackberry pie and sweet potato pie again. I would go if I could avoid prison, and if the Cubans would let me come back to the island. I have no other home but Cuba now. After a while, you just learn to accept your life. They'll bury me here at the Cementerio de Colón I guess."[16]

The storm has now moved out to sea, but the electricity goes out anyway. Neighbors let out a collective groan followed by jokes and laughter. The old fan falls silent. Luckily, it has cooled off and there is a breeze from the window. The game of *dominó* goes on. Charlie finishes his *cafecito* and stands up. He is smiling. He is going to see his daughter in Old Havana.

Acknowledgments

This book would have been impossible to complete without the support of numerous people and institutions. At the University of North Carolina Press, I had the good fortune to begin this journey with Brandon Proia and to complete it with Dawn Durante. Without Brandon's early belief in the feasibility of an unorthodox biography of this kind, it probably never would have been written. Dawn's expert shepherding of the manuscript through the revision process made publication possible. Thanks, as well, to Kerinna Good and to the editorial and production staff. Two external reviewers contracted by the press provided useful critiques of the manuscript; their early confidence in the project helped more than they know. In Cuba, Esther Pérez and Ed Augustin generously read a draft of the manuscript and offered detailed comments. For their critiques of chapters or excerpts, I am also grateful to Raúl Fernandez, Sara Kozameh, Edward Onaci, Tanalís Padilla, Margaret Randall, and Henry Louis Taylor. Of course, responsibility for the book's shortcomings is mine alone.

A legion of colleagues and interlocutors, on and off the island, enriched this book project with their perspectives or assisted me in obtaining research material, including Jesús Arboleya, Ed Augustin, Dan Berger, Joshua Bloom, Chris Cloonan, David Correia, Robert Fikes Jr., Aisha Finch, Justin Gifford, Eva Golinger, Conner Gorry, Reynier Guerra, Winston James, Hal Klepak, Sara Kozameh, Walter Lippman, Jorge Luis Casas Batista, Geo Maher, Rolando Manfugás, Yurena Manfugás Terry, Aaron Coy Moulton, Edward Onaci, Frank Padrón Rojas, Esther Pérez, Tomás Robaina, Zuleica Romay, Louis Segal, Karin L. Stanford, Asantewa Sunni Ali, Henry Louis Taylor, Deyni Terry, Eliomar Terry, Akinyele Umoja, Ernesto Vigil, Mark Villegas, Gayle Wald, Marco Williams, and Roberto Zurbano. Eli Kirshner provided invaluable genealogy research services. Others consented to be interviewed or were willing to communicate with me regarding the project, and for that I gratefully acknowledge Nehanda Abiodun, Merriam Ansara, Orlaida Cabrera, Shaunely de la Mercedes Hill, Antara Finney, Hope Goodwin, Jeffrey Haas, Paul Harris, Tania Hernández Castellanos, Antar Charles Hill Cardona, Janet Hill King, Asantewa Sunni Ali, Ayana Sunni-Ali, Flint Taylor, Karen Lee Wald, Roberto Zurbano, and others whom I have granted anonymity. Special thanks also to Merriam Ansara, Dudley M. Brooks, Bruce Gilbert, Noah Friedman-Rudovsky, and Marco Williams for agreeing to license images.

This project benefited from the support of various institutions. At Thomas Jefferson University, a Faculty Project Completion Grant from the Office of Applied Research allowed me to conduct key archival research in California and Maryland and to pay for indexing and image licensing. Jefferson's College of Humanities and Sciences covered a last-minute research expense. In Havana, special thanks to Orlaida Cabrera, Leima Martínez Freire, and Sandra Yisel Ramírez Rodríguez at the Instituto Cubano de Amistad con los Pueblos. As the manuscript took form, I benefited from opportunities to share the work in progress at academic venues and receive critical feedback. Special thanks to Par Kumaraswami for the invitation to present an early iteration of this work for the University of Nottingham's Cuba Research Forum, and to Jorge Marturano for the invitation to present it at the International Institute at the University of California, Los Angeles.

It would have been impossible to conduct the research for this book without the expertise and assistance of librarians and archivists. In Havana, thanks especially to the wonderful periodicals staff at the Biblioteca Nacional de Cuba José Martí in Havana. In the United States, thanks to Tim Noakes at the Department of Special Collections and University Archives at Stanford University; Keith Rice at the Tom & Ethel Bradley Center at California State University, Northridge; and Jeremy Brett at the Cushing Memorial Library and Archives at Texas A&M University. Thanks also goes to the archivists at the Mississippi Department of Archives and History; the Walter P. Reuther Library, Archives of Labor and Urban Affairs, Wayne State University; the Bancroft Library at the University of California, Berkeley; the Center for Southwest Research and Special Collections at the University of New Mexico; the Schomburg Center for Research in Black Culture; and the National Archives at College Park, Maryland; as well as to John Vance at Thomas Jefferson University's Gutman Library.

Charlie Hill's suggestion that I write this book initially fell on skeptical ears. So when it unexpectedly blossomed into an all-consuming fascination spanning seven years, he was as taken aback as I was. What an adventure this was! Thank you, Charlie. Last but definitely not least, Yurena, granddaughter of Cuban revolutionaries, lived with this project almost from the beginning, on the island and beyond, and provided a sounding board, occasional logistical assistance from Havana, and unflagging encouragement. Thank you, Yurena, for sharing this journey with me!

Notes

Preface

1. A legal analysis of political asylum, political violence, and terrorism falls outside the purview of this biography. For discussions of Posada Carriles, see Peter Kornbluh, "A Safe Harbor for Luis Posada Carriles," *NACLA Report on the Americas* 39, no. 4 (2006): 16–17; "Posada Carriles, Child of Scorn: Yet Another Example of the White House's Denigration of Its War on Terrorism, Which Woefully Lacks Integrity, Coherence or Consistency," Council on Hemispheric Affairs, May 16, 2007, https://coha.org/posada-carriles-child-of-scorn-yet-another-example-of-the-white-house%E2%80%99s-denigration-of-its-war-on-terrorism-which-woefully-lacks-integrity-coherence-or-consistency/.

2. For the State Sponsor of Terrorism designation, see Robert L. Muse, "Taking Cuba Off the Terrorist List: A Question of National Interest," remarks at National Press Club, Washington, DC, March 7, 2013.

3. For the influence of US-Cuba hijacking on diplomatic relations through the early 1970s, see Dan Porat, "Plane Hijackings Between Cuba and the United States and the Opportunity for Diplomacy (1958–1973)," *Historical Journal* 67, no. 2 (2024): 1–22; Teishan A. Latner, "Take Me to Havana! Airline Hijacking, U.S.-Cuba Relations, and Political Protest in Late Sixties' America," *Diplomatic History* 39, no. 1 (2015): 16–44.

Introduction

1. Lee Lockwood, *Conversation with Eldridge Cleaver: Algiers* (New York: McGraw-Hill, 1970), 11.

2. Piero Gleijeses, *Conflicting Missions: Havana, Washington, and Africa, 1959–1976* (Chapel Hill: University of North Carolina Press, 2003); Anne Garland Mahler, *From the Tricontinental to the Global South: Race, Radicalism, and Transnational Solidarity* (Durham, NC: Duke University Press Books, 2018); Thomas C. Wright, *Latin America in the Era of the Cuban Revolution and Beyond*, 3rd ed. (Westport, CT: Praeger, 2018); Tanya Harmer and Alberto Martín Alvarez, eds., *Toward a Global History of Latin America's Revolutionary Left* (Gainesville: University of Florida Press, 2021); Aldo Marchesi, *Latin America's Radical Left: Rebellion and Cold War in the Global 1960s* (Cambridge: Cambridge University Press, 2017). Despite its limitations, "Global South" is employed in this text in the modern sense of the term to denote the nations of Africa, Asia, and Latin America that were subjected to European colonialism, including in ways that acknowledge histories of underdevelopment under capitalist globalization, and as a post–Cold War equivalent to "Third World."

3. For Burdsall, see her memoir, Lorna Burdsall, *More Than Just a Footnote: Dancing from Connecticut to Revolutionary Cuba* (published by the author, 2001); Jane Rubinsky, "Lorna

Burdsall: Dancing from Connecticut to Cuba," *Juilliard Journal*, March 2009. For Piñeiro Losada, see Luis Suárez Salazar, *Barbarroja: Selección de testimonios y discursos del Comandante Manuel Piñeiro Losada* (Havana: Ediciones Tricontinental/SIMAR S.A., 1999).

4. For Veltfort, see Anna Veltfort, *Goodbye, My Havana: The Life and Times of a Gringa in Revolutionary Cuba* (Stanford: Redwood Press, 2019). For the Havana-based North American Friends of Cuba organization, see "Americans in Cuba Celebrate July 4," *Militant* (July 10 and 17, 1961): 25–28; "Small Band of U.S. Expatriates Giving Vocal Support to Castro," *New York Times*, June 3, 1962.

5. See EcuRed, "Pablo Menéndez," last modified December 29, 2022, 18:29, www.ecured.cu/Pablo_ Menéndez; Barbara Dane, *This Bell Still Rings: My Life of Defiance and Song* (Berkeley: Heyday, 2022), 313–14.

6. See Margaret Randall, *To Change the World: My Years in Cuba* (New Brunswick, NJ: Rutgers University Press, 2009); Margaret Randall, *I Never Left Home: Poet, Feminist, Revolutionary* (Durham, NC: Duke University Press, 2020).

7. For McManus, see Olga R. Rodríguez, "True Believers," in *Capitalism, God, and a Good Cigar: Cuba Enters the Twenty-First Century*, ed. Lydia Chavez (Durham, NC: Duke University Press, 2005), 131–46.

8. See Philip Agee, *Inside the Company: CIA Diary* (New York: Farrar, Straus and Giroux, 1975); Kaeten Mistry, "A Transnational Protest Against the National Security State: Whistle-Blowing, Philip Agee, and Networks of Dissent," *Journal of American History* 106, no. 3 (2019): 362–89.

9. For Abiodun and Shakur, see Teishan A. Latner, "Assata Shakur Is Welcome Here: Havana, Black Freedom Struggle, and U.S.-Cuba Relations," *Souls: A Critical Journal of Black Politics, Culture, and Society* 19, no. 4 (2018): 455–77.

10. There is a deep literature on American political expatriation. See, for instance, Kevin K. Gaines, *American Africans in Ghana: Black Expatriates and the Civil Rights Era* (Chapel Hill: University of North Carolina Press, 2008); Diana Anhalt, *A Gathering of Fugitives: American Political Expatriates in Mexico, 1948–1965* (Santa Maria, CA: Archer Books, 2001); Tyler Stovall, *Paris Noir: African Americans in the City of Light* (Boston: Houghton Mifflin, 1996); Donald W. Maxwell, *Unguarded Border: American Émigrés in Canada During the Vietnam War* (New Brunswick, NJ: Rutgers University Press, 2023); Joy Gleason Carew, *Blacks, Reds, and Russians: Sojourners in Search of the Soviet Promise* (New Brunswick, NJ: Rutgers University Press, 2010); Seth M. Markle, *A Motorcycle on Hell Run: Tanzania, Black Power, and the Uncertain Future of Pan-Africanism, 1964–1974* (East Lansing: Michigan State University Press, 2017).

11. Karl Marx, "The Eighteenth Brumaire of Louis Bonaparte," in *The Marx-Engels Reader*, ed. Robert C. Tucker, 2nd ed. (New York: W. W. Norton, 1978), 595. Originally published in 1852 in *Die Revolution*.

12. For broad discussion of these themes, see Alejandro de la Fuente, *A Nation for All: Race, Inequality, and Politics in Twentieth-Century Cuba* (Chapel Hill: University of North Carolina Press, 2001); Esteban Morales Domínguez, *Race in Cuba: Essays on the Revolution and Racial Inequality*, ed. and trans. under direction of Gary Prevost and August Nimtz (New York: Monthly Review Press, 2013); Zuleica Romay Guerra, *Elogio de la altea o las paradojas de la racialidad* (Havana: Casa de las Américas, 2014).

13. For detailed treatments of these dynamics, see Devyn Spence Benson, *Antiracism in Cuba: The Unfinished Revolution* (Chapel Hill: University of North Carolina Press, 2016),

153–97; Cynthia A. Young, *Soul Power: Culture, Radicalism, and the Making of a U.S. Third World Left* (Durham, NC: Duke University Press, 2006), 18–53.

14. "A New Kind of Crowd," *New York Citizen-Call*, September 24, 1960, quoted in Rosemari Mealy, *Fidel and Malcolm: Memories of a Meeting* (Baltimore: Black Classic Press, 2013), 48, 49; for Castro in Harlem, see Simon Hall, *Ten Days in Harlem: Fidel Castro and the Making of the 1960s* (London: Faber and Faber, 2020), 50–53, 57–62.

15. For "U.S. Third World Left," scholar Cynthia A. Young's term, see Young, *Soul Power*. For "Black Power generation," historian Donna Jean Murch's term, see Murch, *Living for the City: Migration, Education, and the Rise of the Black Panther Party in Oakland, California* (Chapel Hill: University of North Carolina Press, 2010), 4–5.

16. Timothy B. Tyson, *Radio Free Dixie: Robert F. Williams and the Roots of Black Power*, 2nd ed. (Chapel Hill: University of North Carolina Press, 2020), 292–94; Robeson Taj Frazier, *The East Is Black: Cold War China in the Black Radical Imagination* (Durham, NC: Duke University Press, 2014), 141–43, 262–65.

17. Stokely Carmichael, *Ready for Revolution: The Life and Struggles of Stokely Carmichael (Kwame Ture)*, with Michael Ekwueme Thelwell (New York: Simon and Schuster, 2003), 582–94. See also Sarah Seidman, "Tricontinental Routes of Solidarity: Stokely Carmichael in Cuba," *Journal of Transnational American Studies* 4, no. 2 (2012): 1–25.

18. For Cleaver, see Lockwood, *Conversation with Eldridge Cleaver*; Henry Louis Gates Jr. and Eldridge Cleaver, "Cuban Experience: Eldridge Cleaver on Ice," *Transition*, no. 49 (1975).

19. See, for instance, Keisha N. Blain, *Until I Am Free: Fannie Lou Hamer's Enduring Message to America* (Boston: Beacon Press, 2021); Diane C. Fujino, *Heartbeat of Struggle: The Revolutionary Life of Yuri Kochiyama* (Minneapolis: University of Minnesota Press, 2005); Justin Gifford, *Revolution or Death: The Life of Eldridge Cleaver* (Chicago: Lawrence Hill Books, 2020); Peniel E. Joseph, *Stokely: A Life* (New York: Basic *Civitas*, 2014); Lorena Oropeza, *The King of Adobe: Reies López Tijerina; Lost Prophet of the Chicano Movement* (Chapel Hill: University of North Carolina Press, 2019); Barbara Ransby, *Ella Baker and the Black Freedom Movement: A Radical Democratic Vision* (Chapel Hill: University of North Carolina Press, 2005).

20. James N. Green, *Exile Within Exiles: Herbert Daniel, Gay Brazilian Revolutionary* (Durham, NC: Duke University Press, 2018).

21. Carole Boyce Davies, *Left of Karl Marx: The Political Life of Black Communist Claudia Jones* (Durham, NC: Duke University Press, 2008), 1.

22. See especially Dan Berger, *Stayed on Freedom: The Long History of Black Power Through One Family's Journey* (New York: Basic Books, 2023); David Correia, *An Enemy Such as This: Larry Casuse and the Fight for Native Liberation in One Family on Two Continents over Three Centuries* (Chicago: Haymarket Books, 2022); George Lipsitz, *A Life in the Struggle: Ivory Perry and the Culture of Opposition*, rev. ed. (Philadelphia: Temple University Press, 1995).

23. See Terry Bisson, *On a Move: The Story of Mumia Abu-Jamal* (New York: Litmus Books, 2001); Paul J. Magnarella, *Black Panther in Exile: The Pete O'Neal Story* (Gainesville: University Press of Florida, 2020).

24. For this usage of "common sense," see Antonio Gramsci, *Prison Notebooks*, ed. and trans. Joseph A. Buttigieg, vol. 2 (New York: Columbia University Press, 1996), 347.

25. Patrick Oppmann, "Admitted Hijacker Dreams of Home After 43 Years Hiding Out in Cuba," CNN, April 9, 2015, www.cnn.com/2015/04/09/americas/us-cuba-fugitive-charlie-hill.

26. Howard Zinn, *A People's History of the United States* (New York: HarperCollins, 2003), 9–10. For social biography, see Jan Willem Stutje, "The Social Biography: Pitfalls and Temptations," *International Review of Social History* 68, no. 1 (2023): 163–71.

27. This framing owes to Joy James, who suggests that Cuba "shares an 'outlaw' status with the black female fugitive it harbors." James, "Framing the Panther: Assata Shakur and Black Female Agency," in *Want to Start a Revolution? Radical Women in the Black Freedom Struggle*, ed. Jeanne Theoharis, Komozi Woodard, and Dayo F. Gore (New York: New York University Press, 2009), 141.

28. Despite the full meaning of "Americans" to denote people of all nations and territories of the Western Hemisphere, for ease of use the word is often used in this book more narrowly to denote citizens or residents of the United States and is used interchangeably with "US Americans" and "North Americans," depending on the context.

29. The concept of "within the revolution," indicating ideological tolerance within the strict parameters of the Cuban revolutionary project, is often associated with Fidel Castro's June 1961 speech to intellectuals and artists. See Antoni Kapcia, *Cuba in Revolution: A History Since the Fifties* (London: Reaktion Books, 2008), 84–88; Par Kumaraswami, "Cultural Policy and Cultural Politics in Revolutionary Cuba: Re-Reading the *Palabras a Los Intelectuales* (Words to the Intellectuals)," *Bulletin of Latin American Research* 28, no. 4 (2009): 527–41.

30. Ada Ferrer, *Cuba: An American History* (New York: Scribner, 2021), 3.

Chapter 1

1. James A. Hill, Certificate of Death, State of Alabama, Department of Health and US Public Health Service Cooperating, January 23, 1954, No. 3914.

2. For central Alabama's Indigenous history, see John A. Walthall, *Prehistoric Indians of the Southeast: Archaeology of Alabama and the Middle South* (Tuscaloosa: University of Alabama Press, 1990). For the Creeks and white settlers, see J. Mills Thornton, *Politics and Power in a Slave Society: Alabama, 1800–1860* (Baton Rouge: Louisiana State University Press, 1978), 28–30.

3. An autosomal DNA test performed by the author at Charlie Hill's request in January 2022 confirms this account.

4. 1910 US Census, Randolph County, Alabama, population schedule, Precinct 9 (Louina Beat), enumeration district 150, sheet 17B (penned), family 265, dwelling 268. The town of Wadley was incorporated in 1906.

5. Charlie Hill, Certificate of Birth, State of Illinois, Division of Vital Statistics and Records, December 15, 1949, Primary Distribution No. 3593.

6. Charlie Hill, interview by author, Havana, June 2018.

7. Charlie Hill, Certificate of Birth.

8. Despite later appearances of his name in military and police records as Charles, his legal birth name is Charlie.

9. Charlie Hill, Certificate of Birth; Scott Simons, "Weber Family Supplied Medical Care for All," *Herald and Review* (Decatur, IL), October 30, 1983.

10. Charlie's birth certificate records James Hill's profession as "Brick Layer" and Dorethea Mooring's as "Housekeeper."

11. Charlie Hill, interview by author, WhatsApp, April 3, 2020.

12. Charlie Hill, interview by author, WhatsApp, February 18, 2020.

13. Hill, interview, February 18, 2020.

14. Charlie Hill, interview by author, WhatsApp, February 19, 2020.

15. Hill, interview, February 18, 2020.

16. Hill, interview, February 18, 2020.

17. Hill, interview, February 18, 2020.

18. Charlie Hill, interview by author, WhatsApp, April 5, 2020.

19. One foundational treatise is Emma Tenayuca and Homer Brooks, "The Mexican Question in the Southwest," *Communist* 18, no. 3 (March 1939): 257–58.

20. For Tijerina and the land grant movement, see Lorena Oropeza, *The King of Adobe: Reies López Tijerina, Lost Prophet of the Chicano Movement* (Chapel Hill: University of North Carolina Press, 2019); Reies López Tijerina, *They Called Me "King Tiger": My Struggle for the Land and Our Rights* (Houston: Arte Público Press, 2001).

21. Martin Waldron, "Guardsmen Defended by Chief over Stabbings in New Mexico," *New York Times*, June 7, 1970; Oropeza, *King of Adobe*, 183–89. See also David Correia, "'Rousers of the Rabble' in the New Mexico Land Grant War: La Alianza Federal de Mercedes and the Violence of the State," *Antipode* 40, no. 4 (2008): 561–83.

22. Charlie Hill, interview by author, WhatsApp, April 3, 2020.

23. Joaquin Lujan, interview by Federico Reade (director), *American Blowback: New Mexico's Black Berets*, work in progress.

24. For a history of the health clinic, see Betita Martínez, "Health Is a Human Right," *El Grito del Norte* 6, no. 4 (May 1973).

25. *Venceremos: Papel del Barrio* 1, no. 2 (June 1971), Tomas Atencio papers and Academia de la Nueva Raza/Rio Grande Institute records, 1923–2013, Center for Southwest Research and Special Collections, University of New Mexico Libraries.

26. Quoted in Correia, "'Rousers of the Rabble,'" 574.

27. Tomas O. Martinez, "Speakers at Meeting Blame Police for Riot," *Albuquerque Journal*, June 17, 1971.

28. "Sceresse Asks Check on Death in Police Case," *Albuquerque Journal*, August 16, 1968.

29. "Duke City Board to Talk Demands of Brown Berets," *Las Cruces Sun-News*, August 21, 1968.

30. See David Correia, *Properties of Violence: Law and Land Grant Struggle in Northern New Mexico* (Athens: University of Georgia Press, 2013); Sam Klug, "'What, Then, of the Land?' Territoriality, International Law, and the Republic of New Afrika," *Journal of the History of International Law* 23, no. 1 (2020): 184–205.

Chapter 2

1. Donna Jean Murch, *Living for the City: Migration, Education, and the Rise of the Black Panther Party in Oakland, California* (Chapel Hill: University of North Carolina Press, 2010), 4–5.

2. For postwar Oakland, see Robert O. Self, *American Babylon: Race and the Struggle for Postwar Oakland* (Princeton, NJ: Princeton University Press, 2003).

3. Charlie Hill, interview by author, Havana, June 6, 2018.

4. Charlie's cousin, Aubrey Clayton Mooring, was known within the Republic of New Afrika as Amia Olatunji.

5. Hill, interview, June 6, 2018.

6. Marjorie Heins, "Los Siete de la Raza," *Ramparts*, March 21, 1971, 21.

7. James Baldwin, quoted in *Take This Hammer*, directed by Richard O. Moore (National Educational Television, 1964).

8. "Hotline . . . Beautiful News from Hunters Point," *Black Panther* 1, no. 6 (1967): 1–12, 18.

9. "White House Will Tackle Job Problem," *San Francisco Examiner*, September 29, 1966.

10. "The Spark: Young Girl Stunned by Billy Club," *Flatlands*, October 22, 1966, 3, http://revolution.berkeley.edu/spark-young-girl-stunned-billy-club/#menu-main-nav.

11. Agnes Woods, "Free at Last: The Important News About the Boycott," *Flatlands*, November 5, 1966, 1, 3, http://revolution.berkeley.edu/agnes-woods-free-last-important-news-boycott/#menu-main-nav.

12. The Castlemont Riots, as the incidents came to be known, became national news. See, for instance, "250 Negroes Riot and Beat Teachers; Oakland School Shut," *New York Times*, October 20, 1966.

13. Charlie Hill, interview by author, WhatsApp, April 5, 2020.

14. Charlie Hill, interview by author, WhatsApp, February 20, 2020.

15. Charlie Hill, interview by author, WhatsApp, May 2, 2020.

16. Hill, interview, May 2, 2020. Hill's military records state that one of his brothers suffered from insanity.

17. Charles Hill, Service No. RA 15 783 326, Armed Forces of the United States, Record of Medical History, DD Form 214, Report of Transfer or Discharge, National Personnel Records Center, National Archives, St. Louis, MO, 4.

18. Charles Lee Hill, Record of Assignments, United States Army, National Personnel Records Center, National Archives, St. Louis, MO, FOIA by author, January 2020. The use of "Lee" in this record appears to have been a clerical error.

19. Hill, Record of Medical History, 2.

20. James E. Westheider, *Fighting on Two Fronts: African Americans and the Vietnam War* (New York: New York University Press, 1999), 2.

21. Kimberley L. Phillips, *War! What Is It Good For? Black Freedom Struggles and the U.S. Military from World War II to Iraq* (Chapel Hill: University of North Carolina Press, 2014), 188–200.

22. Thomas A. Johnson, "G.I.'s in Germany: Black Is Bitter," *New York Times*, November 23, 1970; Maria Höhn, "The Black Panther Solidarity Committees and the Voice of the Lumpen," *German Studies Review* 31, no. 1 (2008): 138.

23. Johnson, "G.I.'s in Germany."

24. "100 Black GIs Battle Police in Stuttgart," *Los Angeles Times*, August 14, 1972.

25. David Cortwright, "Black GI Resistance During the Vietnam War," *Vietnam Generation* 2, no. 1 (1990): 55.

26. Westheider, *Fighting on Two Fronts*, 131–68.

27. "War Crime Trial," *Gazette and Daily*, August 15, 1967; Convicted Ex-Nazi Freed at Stuttgart," *New York Times*, September 16, 1967, 1.

28. Westheider, *Fighting on Two Fronts*, 70–72.

29. Hill, interview, April 5, 2020.

30. "Westmoreland Requests 206,000 More Men, Stirring Debate in Administration; Force Now 510,000," *New York Times*, March 10, 1968.

31. Martin Luther King Jr., "Beyond Vietnam," Riverside Church, New York, April 4, 1967.
32. Charlie Hill, interview by author, WhatsApp, April 6, 2020.

Chapter 3

1. Geronimo Ji-Jaga Pratt, interview, *Bars and Stripes*, episode 5, "Prisoners of War: Political Prisoners in the US," directed by DeeDee Halleck (1997, Deep Dish/Free Speech TV). Pratt was echoing a foundational essay by Huey P. Newton, who had compared the occupation of Vietnam by US forces to the "occupation of our communities by the racist police." Huey P. Newton, "The Functional Definition of Politics," *Black Panther*, May 15, 1967, 4. This perception was common among Black GIs. Herman Graham, *The Brothers' Vietnam War: Black Power, Manhood, and the Military Experience* (Gainesville: University Press of Florida, 2003), 112–19.

2. For Pratt's experience in Vietnam, see Jack Olsen, *Last Man Standing: The Tragedy and Triumph of Geronimo Pratt* (New York: Doubleday), 29–35.

3. Charlie Hill, interview by author, WhatsApp, April 5, 2020.

4. Charles Lee Hill, Record of Assignments, United States Army, National Personnel Records Center, National Archives, St. Louis, MO, FOIA by author, January 2020.

5. Charles Hill, Appointments and Reductions, Service No. RA 15 783 326, Armed Forces of the United States.

6. Charlie was assigned to the Fifth Transportation Battalion, an organic unit of the 101st Airborne Division.

7. Charles Hill, Service No. RA 15 783 326, Armed Forces of the United States, Record of Medical History, DD Form 214, Report of Transfer or Discharge, National Personnel Records Center, National Archives, St. Louis, MO. For the history of E Company, see National Records and Archives Administration, Records of US Forces in Southeast Asia: 1965–1970, RG 472, Infantry Units, 2nd Battalion, 502nd Infantry Organizational History, 1965–1970, especially Infantry box 1079, folder Org. Hist, 1965–66/68.

8. The movements and activities of Hill's reconnaissance platoon within E Company, although usually without personnel identifiers, are cataloged in After Action Reports and Daily Staff Journals, National Records and Archives Administration, Records of US Forces in Southeast Asia: 1965–1970, RG 472, 2nd Battalion, 502nd Infantry, Assistant Chief of Staff for Operations (S-3), Situation Reports, 1 January–31 December, Infantry box 1084, folder 5-3, Situation Reports, Jan–June 1969; Infantry box 1092, folder S-2/3, Daily Journal Jan–March 69.

9. Charlie Hill, interview by author, Havana, May 30, 2018.

10. Body-count activities and examination of graves and corpses in the field is widely documented in the After Action Reports and Daily Staff Journals consulted here. See, for instance, National Records and Archives Administration, Records of US Forces in Southeast Asia: 1965–1970, RG 472, 2nd Battalion, 502nd Infantry, Assistant Chief of Staff for Operations (S-3), Situation Reports, 1 January–31 December, Infantry, box 1084, folder 5-3, Situation Reports, Jan–June 1969, "Messages and Spot Reports for the Journal of 6 April 1969."

11. Charlie Hill, interview by author, Havana, May 22, 2024.

12. Hill, interview by author, Havana, May 22, 2024.

13. Charlie Hill, interview by author, Havana, May 31, 2018.

14. Hill, interview, May 22, 2024.

15. Olsen, *Last Man Standing*, 34.

16. Hill, interview, May 31, 2018.

17. The original injury is recorded in Hill's military records.

18. The accuracy and chronology of these events, recounted by Hill to the author more than fifty years after they occurred, is uncertain. Hill's military records indicate two separate AWOL incidents after 1967: on March 23, 1969, lasting eight days, and on May 3, 1969, lasting five days. The records include only one narrative of a disciplinary violation, on February 2, 1969, while serving as a specialist fifth class in the Fifth Transportation Battalion, in which Hill "abandoned himself from the company area" of Camp Eagle.

19. Charlie Hill, interview by author, Havana, June 3, 2018.

20. Charlie Hill, interview by author, Havana, June 2, 2018.

21. Hill, interview, June 2, 2018.

22. Hill, interview, June 2, 2018.

23. The court-martial is not reflected in Hill's military records.

24. "South Viet Nam: Soul Alley," *Time*, December 14, 1970; *Soul Alley*, directed by Ted A. Irving (BeingUS.tv, 2018), 62 min.

25. Charles Hill, Service No. RA 15 783 326, Armed Forces of the United States, DA Form 20, National Personnel Records Center, National Archives, St. Louis, MO, 4.

26. Kimberley L. Phillips, *War! What Is It Good For? Black Freedom Struggles and the U.S. Military from World War II to Iraq* (Chapel Hill: University of North Carolina Press, 2014), 226.

27. James E. Westheider, *Fighting on Two Fronts: African Americans and the Vietnam War* (New York: New York University Press, 1999), 103.

28. "Long Binh Jail: 'The Black House,'" *Black Panther*, December 25, 1971, 9; Cecil Barr Currey, *Long Binh Jail: An Oral History of Vietnam's Notorious U.S. Military Prison* (Washington, DC: Brassey's, 1999).

29. Hill, interview, May 31, 2018; Charles Hill, Service No. RA 15 783 326, Armed Forces of the United States, Report of Medical Examination, June 8, 1969, National Personnel Records Center, National Archives, St. Louis, MO.

30. Charlie Hill, interview by author, Havana, May 29, 2018.

31. Hill, Record of Medical History.

32. Hill, interview, May 30, 2018.

33. Hill, Record of Assignments.

34. Hill, interview, May 30, 2018.

35. Hill, interview, May 30, 2018.

Chapter 4

1. Edward Onaci, *Free the Land: The Republic of New Afrika and the Pursuit of a Black Nation-State* (Chapel Hill: University of North Carolina Press, 2020), 16–31. For more on Detroit, see Dan Georgakas and Marvin Surkin, *Detroit: I Do Mind Dying: A Study in Urban Revolution* (Chicago: Haymarket Books, 3rd ed., 2012); Stephen M. Ward, *In Love and Struggle: The Revolutionary Lives of James and Grace Lee Boggs* (Chapel Hill: University of North Carolina Press, 2020), 37–59.

2. Imari Abubakar Obadele, *War in America: The Malcolm X Doctrine*, rev. ed. (Detroit: Malcolm X Society, 1968), 4.

3. For the conceptualization of citizenship, see Onaci, *Free the Land*, 59–65. See also Dan Berger, *Captive Nation: Black Prison Organizing in the Civil Rights Era* (Chapel Hill: University of North Carolina Press, 2016), 230–35.

4. Republic of New Africa [*sic*], "New African Ujamaa," Declaration of Economic Intent, Milwaukee, December 13, 1970, FBI, file no. 157-2274-685; Onaci, *Free the Land*, 54–55.

5. Republic of New Africa, "RNA Confirms Drive for New Communities and Beautiful Life for All," news release, December 20, 1970, 10, FBI, Miami, FL, file no. 157-2691, February 25, 1971.

6. Charlie Hill, interview by author, WhatsApp, June 23, 2020.

7. Hill, interview, June 23, 2020.

8. Charlie Hill, interview by author, WhatsApp, May 29, 2020.

9. James Monroe Willard was killed in combat in Vietnam on September 16, 1969, US Military Fatal Casualties of the Vietnam War for Home-State-of-Record: New Mexico, Vietnam Conflict Extract Data File, as of April 29, 2008, Defense Casualty Analysis System (DCAS) files, RG 330: Records of the Office of the Secretary of Defense, National Archives, National Archives and Records Administration, College Park, MD.

10. Report of Casualty, James Monroe Willard, No. A 8692, RVN 24589, Department of the Army, Washington, DC, Office of the Adjutant General, September 23, 1969.

11. Charlie Hill, interview by author, WhatsApp, June 24, 2020.

12. Charlie Hill, interview by author, WhatsApp, January 22, 2022.

13. *Black Panther* 3, no. 22 (1969).

14. Charlie Hill, interview by author, WhatsApp, May 8, 2020.

15. Charlie Hill, interview by author, WhatsApp, May 21, 2020.

16. Hill, interview, May 21, 2020.

17. Transcript, Charlie Hill, fall semester 1970, Office of Admission and the Registrar, University of Alaska Fairbanks.

18. "Two Held After Burglary, Wrecks," *Fairbanks Daily News-Miner*, November 2, 1970; "D.A.'s Office Runs Short of Attorneys," *Fairbanks Daily News-Miner*, June 2, 1971.

19. "Marijuana Seized," *Fairbanks Daily News-Miner*, February 6, 1971. The Fairbanks Police Department retains no records older than twenty-five years. Author's correspondence with City Clerk of Fairbanks, email, August 13, 2020.

20. "Jim Nabors Rapping," *Berkeley Barb* 8, no. 10 (1969): 4.

21. Berkeley Police Department, Hall of Justice, Michael R. Finney. File appears to have been compiled in response to a request from the Albuquerque Police Department, November 1971.

22. Charlie Hill, interview by author, WhatsApp, July 6, 2020.

23. Charlie Hill, interview by author, Havana, May 31, 2018.

24. Charlie Hill, interview by author, WhatsApp, July 5, 2020.

25. Quoted in Onaci, *Free the Land*, 76.

26. See Daniel Widener, *Third Worlds Within: Multiethnic Movements and Transnational Solidarity* (Durham, NC: Duke University Press, 2024), 14–15; Edward Onaci, "The Captive New Afrikan Nation, the Politics of Solidarity, and the Ongoing Struggle for Liberation," *Lateral: Journal of the Cultural Studies Association* 12, no. 2 (2023).

27. See, for instance, Eve Tuck and K. Wayne Yang, "Decolonization Is Not a Metaphor," *Decolonization: Indigeneity, Education and Society* 1, no. 1 (2012): 1–40; Kyle T. Mays, *An Afro-Indigenous History of the United States* (Boston: Beacon Press, 2022), 114–18. Wording is borrowed, of course, from KRS-One, "Sound of da Police" (Jive Records: 1993).

28. Document reproduction by FBI. Republic of New Africa, "New African Ujamaa," Declaration of Economic Intent, Milwaukee, December 13, 1970, FBI, file no. 157-2274-685.

29. Onaci, *Free the Land*, 44, 77.

30. Charlie Hill, interview by author, WhatsApp, July 21, 2020.

31. Onaci, "Captive New Afrikan Nation."

32. Onaci, *Free the Land*, 79–80.

33. Charlie Hill, interview by author, Havana, July 21, 2019.

34. Imari Abubakar Obadele, *War in America: The Malcolm X Doctrine*, rev. ed. (Detroit: Malcolm X Society, 1968), 2 (italics in original).

35. Leaflet, Republic of New Africa, undated, box 1, folder 6, 96.04: Republic of New Africa, 1968–1976, Brown-Tougaloo Exchange, Tougaloo College Archives, http://cds.library.brown.edu/projects/FreedomNow/collect.php.

36. Charlie Hill, interview by author, WhatsApp, June 6, 2020.

37. Hill, interview, June 6, 2020.

38. Michael would later recount this story to a reporter in Havana. Ellen Hampton, "For Former Black Militant, Island Is End of the Road," *Miami News*, June 16, 1987.

39. "Tac Squad Called in Lincoln Melee," *San Francisco Examiner*, February 26, 1969.

40. "Blacks, Whites Unite for Peace," *San Francisco Chronicle*, March 1, 1969.

41. Michael later recounted this story to a reporter. Hampton, "For Former Black Militant, Island Is End of the Road."

42. Undergraduate transcript, Michael Robert Finney, Office of the Registrar, University of California, Berkeley.

43. "3 Picket Groups Circle U.C. Gate," *Oakland Tribune*, February 14, 1969.

44. Anne Marie O'Connor, "Michael Finney's Last Flight," *Miami New Times*, May 8, 1991.

45. O'Connor, "Michael Finney's Last Flight."

46. Finney, who abandoned his free name in the 1980s after growing disillusioned with the RNA, is referred to in this book by his birth name.

47. Antar used his free name until his death, and so he is referred to by this name throughout the book. The spelling of his middle name is from his Berkeley transcript. For more on the designation of Oakland consul, see Imari Abubakari Obadele, *Free the Land! The True Story of the Trials of the RNA-11 in Mississippi and the Continuing Struggle to Establish an Independent Black Nation in Five States of the Deep South* (Washington, DC: House of Songhay, 1984), 168.

48. Robert Fikes Jr., "Pioneers, Warriors, Advocates: A History of San Diego's Black Legal Community, 1890–2010," *Journal of San Diego History* 60, nos. 1 & 2 (2014).

49. Blanca Gonzalez, "Joye Speights Goodwin; Addressed Civil Rights, Teen-Pregnancy Issues," *San Diego Union-Tribune*, April 23, 2009.

50. David J. Thompson, "As a UCLA Student George Brown Jr. Shared His Room with History," *Cooperative Housing Bulletin*, Winter 2014.

51. "110 Jailed at Auto Showroom," *San Francisco Examiner*, March 15, 1964; Fikes, "Pioneers, Warriors, Advocates."

52. People of the State of California v. Samuel Jordan and Fania Jordan, 19 Cal.App.3d 362, 97 Cal.Rptr. 570 (Cal. App. 1971).

53. Undergraduate and graduate transcripts, Ralph Laurence Goodwin, Office of the Registrar, University of California, Berkeley.

54. BSU flyer, "To All Black People," May 11, 1970, BANC Film 2757, series 2, CTN 5:3, reel 16, folder 14, Social Protest Collection, 1943–1982, Bancroft Library, UC Berkeley.

55. BSU flyer, "Free Bobby, Off ROTC," April 23, 1970; BSU flyer, "Community Films," July 1970, BANC Film 2757, series 2, CTN 5:3, reel 16, folder 14, Social Protest Collection, 1943–1982, Bancroft Library, UC Berkeley.

56. Charlie Hill, interview by author, WhatsApp, June 28, 2020.

57. Onaci, *Free the Land*, 58.

58. For this history of Black armed defense, see especially Charles E. Cobb Jr., *This Nonviolent Stuff'll Get You Killed: How Guns Made the Civil Rights Movement Possible* (Durham, NC: Duke University Press, 2015); Akinyele Omowale Umoja, *We Will Shoot Back: Armed Resistance in the Mississippi Freedom Movement* (New York: New York University Press, 2013).

59. Imari Abubakar Obadele, *War in America: The Malcolm X Doctrine*, rev. ed. (Detroit: Malcolm X Society, 1968), 7.

60. Hill, interview, June 28, 2020.

61. Hill, interview, May 31, 2018.

62. Edward J. Littlejohn and Peter J. Hammer, *No Equal Justice: The Legacy of Civil Rights Icon George W. Crockett Jr.* (Detroit: Wayne State University Press, 2022), 244–45.

63. Littlejohn and Hammer, *No Equal Justice*, 244–45.

64. "Statement by Judge Crockett," *South End* 27, no. 102 (1969): 3; Littlejohn and Hammer, *No Equal Justice*, 243–46.

65. The author's August 2020 FOIA to the FBI for files pertaining to the RNA in the narrowed search area of California, New York, and New Mexico, 1966–76, yielded over three thousand pages of released documents.

66. Hampton, "For Former Black Militant, Island Is End of the Road."

67. Ericka Huggins, interview in *Bastards of the Party*, directed by Cle Sloan (2005), 95 min.

68. Nancy K. Bristow, *Steeped in the Blood of Racism: Black Power, Law and Order, and the 1970 Shootings at Jackson State College* (Oxford: Oxford University Press, 2020).

69. Chokwe Lumumba, "Short History of the U.S. War on the R.N.A.," *Black Scholar* 12, no. 1 (1981): 73.

70. Paul Delaney, "Black Separatists Raided in Jackson, Miss," *New York Times*, August 19, 1971.

71. Charlie Hill, interview by author, WhatsApp, August 4, 2020.

72. Hill, interview, August 4, 2020.

73. "State Vehicles at 'War Camp,'" *Oakland Tribune*, October 28, 1971.

74. O'Connor, "Michael Finney's Last Flight."

75. O'Connor, "Michael Finney's Last Flight"; "'Warfare Training' Denied," *Oakland Tribune*, October 30, 1971.

76. "State Vehicles at 'War Camp,'" *Oakland Tribune*, October 28, 1971.

77. "State Vehicles at 'War Camp.'"

78. For more on Adegbalola, see Imari Obadele, "Our Brothers Were in Custody . . . Again!," *Southern Exposure* 3, no. 1 (1975).

79. Charlie Hill, interview by author, WhatsApp, July 30, 2020.

80. Charlie Hill, interview by author, WhatsApp, May 18, 2025.

81. While unconfirmed, this theory has been persistent. See Onaci, *Free the Land*, 152. A bag belonging to Michael, located near the car by the FBI in Albuquerque, included "one manila folder containing literature on Hinds County Jail" in Jackson, Mississippi, where Obadele was imprisoned. SAC Albuquerque to FBI director, memorandum, "Killing of New Mexico State Police Officer Bob Rosenbloom," November 10, 1971, 2.

82. *Oakland Tribune*, October 31, 1971.

83. FBI, field office file no. AQ 184–2, title redacted, December 10, 1971, 66.

84. Hill, interview, July 6, 2020.

Chapter 5

1. Albuquerque Police Department, Violent Crimes (Against Person) Report, Offense no. 208325, Robert Rosenbloom (Victim), November 9, 1971.

2. New Mexico Police Department, Inter-Departmental Correspondence, Subject: Murder of Officer Robert Rosenbloom, November 22, 1971. Name of operator redacted. FBI, field office file no. AQ 184–2, title redacted, December 10, 1971, 8, FOIA by author, November 2021; Chuck Anthony, "Californian Sought in Policeman's Slaying," *Albuquerque Journal*, November 10, 1971.

3. See "Journey to Cuba Began with New Mexico Killing," *Albuquerque Journal*, May 14, 1985; Tomás Martínez, "A Routine Check Ended in Death," *Albuquerque Journal*, October 9, 1979; Chuck Anthony, "Suspects' Guns, Clothing Found," *Albuquerque Journal*, November 11, 1971. On November 17, the *Albuquerque Journal* reported that Rosenbloom had issued a citation to the car's driver, but the nature of the citation was "unknown since the officer's citation book was stolen," according to the state police. See Chuck Anthony, "Police Awaiting FBI Reports on Second Suspect's Identity," *Albuquerque Journal*, November 17, 1971.

4. Charlie Hill, interview by author, Havana, June 5, 2018. This account is consistent with what Hill related to journalists. See, for instance, Eugene Robinson, *Last Dance in Havana: The Final Days of Fidel and the Start of the New Cuban Revolution* (New York: Free Press, 2004), 198.

5. See, for instance, Doug Grow, "'Thug' or Revolutionary, He's a Fugitive in Havana," *Star Tribune*, February 6, 2000, 17A; Serge F. Kovaleski, "Havana Is Haven for Fugitive '70s Hijacker," *Washington Post*, August 31, 1999.

6. Supplementary Offense Report, Homicide, Officer R. Rosenbloom, Albuquerque Police Department, Case No. 208325, November 9, 1971.

7. Charlie Hill, interview by author, WhatsApp, March 14, 2022.

8. Hill provided virtually identical versions of this account to the author between March 2021 and February 2024.

9. According to the *Albuquerque Journal*, Vine's signed statement says that he picked up Charlie, Michael, and Antar at Charlie's mother's home on November 9.

10. FBI, field office file no. AQ 184-2, title redacted, December 10, 1971, 61.

11. Albuquerque Police Department, Supplementary Offense Report, Homicide, Robert Rosenbloom, Case No. 208325, November 9, 1971.

12. FBI, field office file no. AQ 184-2, title redacted, December 10, 1971, 43; Chuck Anthony, "Suspects' Guns, Clothing Found," *Albuquerque Journal*, November 11, 1971.

13. SAC Albuquerque to FBI director, memorandum, "Killing of New Mexico State Police Officer Bob Rosenbloom," November 10, 1971, 2–3.

14. SAC Albuquerque to FBI director, memorandum, "Killing of New Mexico State Police Officer Bob Rosenbloom," November 10, 1971, 3–4.

15. SAC Albuquerque to FBI director, memorandum, "Killing of New Mexico State Police Officer Bob Rosenbloom," November 10, 1971, 2.

16. It's not clear why Michael brought his passport on the trip, or if he had previously traveled internationally. Anthony, "Suspects' Guns, Clothing Found."

17. Chuck Anthony, "Police Awaiting FBI Reports on Second Suspects Identity," *Albuquerque Journal*, November 17, 1971; Finney charge: APB Nationwide, November 16, 1971, in Albuquerque Police Department, Violent Crimes (Against Person) Report, Offense no. 208325, Robert Rosenbloom (Victim), November 9, 1971.

18. Anthony, "Police Awaiting FBI Reports." With Michael implicated, news of the highway shooting in New Mexico was now reported in Oakland. See "Oaklander Sought in Cop Death," *Oakland Tribune*, November 17, 1971.

19. FBI, field office file no. AQ 184-2, title redacted, December 10, 1971, 65.

20. Anthony, "Police Awaiting FBI Reports."

21. "Second Suspect Is Charged in Death of State Policeman," *Albuquerque Journal*, November 20, 1971.

22. "Wilson Asks FBI for Full Probe of Garcia Death," *Albuquerque Journal*, December 17, 1970.

23. David Correia, "The Return of the Albuquerque Death Squads," *CounterPunch*, November 23, 2011.

24. Martin Waldron, "Albuquerque Divided over Cause of First Major Riot," *New York Times*, June 20, 1971.

25. Waldron, "Albuquerque Divided"; Richard Moore, interview in *American Blowback: New Mexico's Black Berets*, directed by Federico Reade (forthcoming).

26. Tomás Martínez and Mike Padget, "Nine Shot as Polce Battle Mob," *Albuquerque Journal*, June 14, 1971; Robert V. Beier, "FOP Bldg. Is Damaged by Firebomb," *Albuquerque Journal*, June 18, 1971.

27. Tomas O. Martinez, "Speakers at Meeting Blame Police for Riot," *Albuquerque Journal*, June 17, 1971.

28. "Alianza Says 'Oppression' to Blame for Disturbance," *Albuquerque Journal*, June 15, 1971.

29. *Venceremos: Papel del Barrio* 1, no. 2 (1971).

30. "The Rebellion," *El Grito del Norte* 4, no. 6 (1971): 1.

31. Martin Waldron, "Guardsmen Defended by Chief over Stabbings in New Mexico," *New York Times*, June 7, 1970.

32. Charlie Hill, interview by author, WhatsApp, June 28, 2020.

33. "Journal Offers Reward," *Albuquerque Journal*, November 11, 1971; "Police Get First Lead on Suspect," *Albuquerque Journal*, November 16, 1971.

34. Criminal Complaint and Affidavits, State of New Mexico v. Charles Hill, D. A. File No. 71-1019, November 25, 1971.

35. Hill, interview, June 28, 2020. In 1969, the ratio of Black versus white men killed as a result of "legal intervention" reached 10 to 1 in the United States. See Nancy Krieger, Mathew V. Kiang, Jarvis T. Chen, and Pamela D. Waterman, "Trends in US Deaths Due to Legal Intervention Among Black and White Men, Age 15–34 Years, by County Income Level: 1960–2010," *Harvard Public Health Review* 3 (January 2015).

36. Hill will not reveal the identity or occupation of the employee.

37. Criminal Arrest Warrant and Affidavit, Charles Hill, Criminal Docket No. A091006, Magistrate Court of Bernalillo County, November 25, 1971.

38. Charlie Hill, interview by author, WhatsApp, August 5, 2020.

39. Eldridge Cleaver, *Soul on Fire* (Waco, TX: Word Books, 1978), 138.

40. Juanita Diaz-Cotto, *Gender, Ethnicity, and the State: Latina and Latino Prison Politics* (Albany: State University of New York Press, 1996), 78; Orisanmi Burton, *Tip of the Spear: Black Radicalism, Prison Repression, and the Long Attica Revolt* (Berkeley: University of California Press, 2023), 110–12.

41. Charlie Hill, interview by author, WhatsApp, August 4, 2020.

42. John Ira Petty, "Suspect Seized in Harboring of Fugitives," *Albuquerque Journal*, December 1, 1971.

43. Charlie Hill, interview by author, Havana, July 23, 2019.

44. FBI, field office file no. AQ 184-2, title redacted, December 10, 1971, 86.

45. FBI, field office file no. AQ 184-2, 86.

46. FBI, field office file no. AQ 184-2, 86.

47. Ellen Hampton, "For Former Black Militant, Island Is End of the Road," *Miami News*, June 16, 1987.

48. As related to Estonian filmmaker Kadri Koop in *Charlie*, directed by Kadri Koop (2016), 13 min.

49. An unnamed airport employee who was aboard the plane related a similar story to the FBI. FBI, field office file no. AQ 184-2, 89.

50. Hill, interview, July 23, 2019.

51. FBI, field office file no. AQ 184-2, 93.

52. Quoted in Robert Siegel, "Calif. Congressman Pushes Cuba to Extradite Man Who Hijacked Plane in 1971," NPR, March 18, 2016.

53. FBI, "D. B. Cooper Hijacking," accessed August 11, 2025, www.fbi.gov/history/famous-cases/db-cooper-hijacking.

54. "3 Slaying Suspects Hijack Airliner and Crew to Cuba," *New York Times*, November 28, 1971.

55. FBI, field office file no. AQ 184-2, 106.

56. Anne Marie O'Connor, "Michael Finney's Last Flight," *Miami New Times*, May 8, 1991.

57. "3 Slaying Suspects Hijack Airliner"; FBI, field office file no. 164-550, title redacted, January 13, 1972, 9, 10.

58. "Jet Flies Back from Cuba After Hijacking by 3," *New York Times*, November 29, 1971. This account of the shooting closely resembles one that was provided to the FBI by a flight attendant. See FBI, field office file no. 164-550, 6.

59. FAA air traffic control transcript, FBI, field office file no. AQ 184-2, 93, 105.

60. Robert V. Beier, "Good Case Noted for Extraditions," *Albuquerque Journal*, November 30, 1971.

61. FBI, field office file no. 164-550, title redacted, January 13, 1972, 6.

62. Hospitality to the hijacked was extended to US Americans and Latin Americans alike. See, for instance, Massimo Di Ricco, *Los condenados del aire: El viaje a la utopía de los aeropiratas del Caribe* (Bogotá: Icono Editorial, 2020), 18; John Greif Sr., "Hijacked to Cuba," *Brukdownn: The Magazine of Belize*, no. 4 (1977): 23.

63. FBI, field office file no. 164-550, 10.

64. Charlie Hill, interview by author, Havana, July 23, 2019.

65. O'Connor, "Michael Finney's Last Flight."

66. Belden's *China Shakes the World* (New York: Harper and Brothers, 1949) was republished by Monthly Review Press in 1970. "Gold Flower's Story" was also published separately as *Goldflower's Story: A Peasant Woman in the Chinese Revolution* in 1979 by New England Free Press.

67. Hill, interview, July 23, 2019.

68. Beier, "Good Case Noted for Extraditions."

69. "Jet Flies Back from Cuba."

70. "Cuba Plans to Probe Hijack, Charges Under Its Own Law," *Albuquerque Journal*, December 1, 1971.

Chapter 6

1. Jason M. Ferreira, "With the Soul of a Human Rainbow: Los Siete, Black Panthers, and Third Worldism in San Francisco," in *Ten Years That Shook the City: San Francisco, 1968–1978*, ed. Chris Carlsson and Lisa Ruth Elliott (San Francisco: City Lights Books, 2011), 32.

2. Marjorie Heins, "Los Siete de la Raza," *Ramparts*, March 21, 1971, 20, 25.

3. The most detailed account of the Los Siete case and the social movement it spawned remains Marjorie Heins, *Strictly Ghetto Property: The Story of Los Siete de la Raza* (Berkeley: Ramparts Press, 1972). See also Ferreira, "With the Soul of a Human Rainbow."

4. Flyer, "Who Are Los Siete," event for November 21, 1970, BANC Film 2757, series 2, CTN 7:3, reel 23, folder 16, Social Protest Collection, 1943–1982, Bancroft Library, UC Berkeley.

5. For "defense organization," see flyer, "Who Are Los Siete." See also Heins, "Los Siete de la Raza," 22.

6. Ferreira, "With the Soul of a Human Rainbow," 36–38, 46; Earl Caldwell, "Coast Radicals Rally Behind 6 Latin Youths on Trial in Slaying of Policeman," *New York Times*, October 11, 1970; see also *Black Panther*, June 28, 1969.

7. "S. F. Pigs Attempt to Arrest Entire Brown Community," *Black Panther*, May 19, 1969, 14. Police raids continued after the acquittal. See "Rally" flyer, protest event for Folsom Playground, San Francisco, January 23, 1971, BANC Film 2757, series 2, CTN 7:3, reel 23, folder 16, Social Protest Collection, 1943–1982, Bancroft Library, UC Berkeley.

8. "Free Los Siete de la Raza!" *Black Panther*, August 15, 1970, 21.

9. Ernesto B. Vigil, *The Crusade for Justice: Chicano Militancy and the Government's War on Dissent* (Madison: University of Wisconsin Press, 1999), 102. Some commentators, including Vigil and attorney Paul Harris, spell López's first name as Gío; the reasons for this spelling are unclear.

10. Ferreira, "With the Soul of a Human Rainbow," 46.

11. It is unclear how Cherry reached Cuba. Court records state that Cherry traveled to Cuba sometime between October and December 1970, with no reference made to a hijacking. See United States v. Cherry, 10 F.3d 1003 (3rd Cir. 1993).

12. Carl C. Claiborne, "Breakfast Program Short on Supplies," *Atlantic City Press*, March 6, 1970.

13. "Trial of Barry Farmer, James Cherry and Clyde Burton," *Black Panther*, March 15, 1970, 18; Claiborne, "Breakfast Program Short on Supplies."

14. "Atlantic City Black Police Charge Own Department with Racism, Bias, and Brutality," *Philadelphia Tribune*, August 15, 1970, 1, 3, quoted in Omari L. Dyson, *The Black Panther Party and Transformative Pedagogy: Place-Based Education in Philadelphia* (Lanham, MD: Lexington Books, 2013), 146.

15. Samuel H. Schwartz and Alex Stern, "K-9 Officer Slain, 1 Suspect Caught," *Atlantic City Press*, October 1, 1970.

16. Cherry's legal case merited no mention in the *Black Panther* in 1970–71, and the party does not appear to have supported Cherry publicly. The October 10, 1970, issue of the *Black Panther*, little more than a week after the shooting, featured only a story on water contamination affecting Atlantic City's Black community. Court documents would later contend that Cherry had become "disenchanted with the movement" prior to the shooting. It is feasible that the national Panther organization, bogged down by mounting legal battles, believed that Cherry was guilty of a crime that had no obvious political import and was thus a liability for the organization. See State of New Jersey v. Cherry, 289 N.J. Super. 503, 674 A.2d 589 (1995). Letters sent by the author to Cherry at New Jersey State Prison in 2020 and 2021 were not answered.

17. Michael Newton, *The Encyclopedia of Kidnappings* (New York: Facts on File, 2002), 167. Little information about Won exists. See Jeffrey O. G. Ogbar, *Black Power: Radical Politics and African American Identity* (Baltimore: Johns Hopkins University Press, 2005), 172. Won is alleged to have committed suicide in Cuba, either by jumping off the roof of a Havana hotel or by "falling on his machete" at a Cuban prison farm. *U.S. and Foreign Registered Aircraft Hijackings*, Department of Transportation, Federal Aviation Administration, Office of Civil Aviation Security, January 1, 1981, 20; John Greif Sr., "Hijacked to Cuba," *Brukdownn: The Magazine of Belize*, no. 4 (1977): 23.

18. Greif, "Hijacked to Cuba," 21–23.

19. "Hijacker Spotted by EAL's System Before Boarding," *Miami News*, October 11, 1971; "Aviation: Gift for Castro," *Time*, August 4, 1961.

20. "Hijacker Dislikes U.S. Life," *Kansas City Star*, October 9, 1971.

21. Lawrence Mahoney and Jay Maeder, "Ex-Convict Hijacks Airliner, Expounds on Leftist Causes," *Miami Herald*, October 10, 1971.

22. "Hijacker Dislikes U.S. Life."

23. Orlaida Cabrera, interview by author, Havana, June 21, 2023.

24. Orlaida Cabrera, interview by author, Havana, June 15, 2023.

25. Charlie Hill, interview by author, WhatsApp, August 2, 2023.

26. See Teishan A. Latner, *Cuban Revolution in America: Havana and the Making of a United States Left, 1968–1992* (Chapel Hill: University of North Carolina Press, 2018).

27. Lars Schoultz, *That Infernal Little Cuban Republic: The United States and the Cuban Revolution* (Chapel Hill: University of North Carolina Press, 2011), 351–52, 675.

28. *Granma* and *Juventud Rebelde* alone featured near-daily coverage of the volunteer brigades throughout January, February, and March 1972.

29. Charlie Hill, interview by author, Havana, June 6, 2018.

30. Marília Guimarães, *Nuestros años en Cuba: Un exilio entre sinsontes y el sabiá* (Havana: Casa Editora, 2008), 125 (author's translation). See also Margaret Randall, *I Never Left Home: Poet, Feminist, Revolutionary* (Durham, NC: Duke University Press, 2020), 198–209.

31. See also Massimo Di Ricco, *Los condenados del aire: Crónica del secuestro aéreo más largo de la historia* (Madrid: Libros del K.O., 2024) (author's translation).

32. Guimarães, *Nuestros años en Cuba*, 23.

33. For an account of Latin American asylees in Cuba, see Tanya Harmer, "Refuge in Revolution: Chilean and Uruguayan Exiles in Cuba, 1973–1990," *Cold War History*, July 8, 2024, www.tandfonline.com/doi/epdf/10.1080/14682745.2024.2329281?needAccess=true, 19.

34. Darío Croc Ures, *La colonia tupamara en Cuba: Un testimonio* (Montevideo: Argumento, 2019), 81.

35. Di Ricco, *Los condenados del aire*, 16.

36. Di Ricco, *Los condenados del aire*, 185–91.

37. "George Mason Murray BFP #11 vcb His Experiences in Cuba August 1968," National Archives online, collection RR-GUBAUD: Ronald Reagan's Gubernatorial Sound Recordings Collection, Gubernatorial Sound Recordings, https://catalog.archives.gov/id/169489499.

38. Charlie Hill, interview by author, Havana, July 5, 2018.

39. According to Charlie, all the Latin American exiles he met participated in ideological study in Cuba. See also, for instance, Croc Ures, *La colonia tupamara*, 91; Harmer, "Refuge in Revolution," 9.

40. For a description of the study sessions, see Patrick Critton, *Lion in the Foliage, Full Moon in the Sky: The Autobiography of Patrick Critton* (pub. by author, 2009), 116–18.

41. For Brent's account of the union, see William Lee Brent, *Long Time Gone: A Black Panther's True-Life Story of His Hijacking and Twenty-Five Years in Cuba* (New York: Times Books, 1996), 218–24.

42. Critton, *Lion in the Foliage*, 67.

43. Critton, *Lion in the Foliage*, 62.

44. Critton, *Lion in the Foliage*, 27.

45. "South African Office Here Bombed," *New York Times*, April 13, 1971.

46. Critton, *Lion in the Foliage*, 64.

47. R. v. Critton (P.D.), [2002] O.T.C. 451 (SC), 7.

48. "Kidnapping Charge May Be Sought Against Hijacker," *Star-Phoenix*, December 28, 1971.

49. R. v. Critton (P.D.), [2002] O.T.C. 451 (SC), 9, 13.

50. Critton, *Lion in the Foliage*, 89.

51. "Kidnapping Charge May Be Sought Against Hijacker"; R. v. Critton (P.D.), [2002] O.T.C. 451 (SC), 9.

52. *Liberation News Service*, no. 375, September 15, 1971, 1; Pat Holmes, "Change Comes to Northeast," *Southern Illinoisan*, September 6, 1970.

53. Holmes, "Change Comes to Northeast."

54. Reggie Brown, *A View from the Inside: On the Front Line of Afro-American Liberation* (Carbondale, IL: Saluki, 2017), 17.

55. Brown, *View from the Inside*, 22.

56. For the assassination of Clark and Hampton, see Jeffrey Haas, *The Assassination of Fred Hampton: How the FBI and the Chicago Police Murdered a Black Panther* (Chicago: Lawrence Hill Books, 2011); Joshua Bloom and Waldo E. Martin, *Black Against Empire: The History and Politics of the Black Panther Party* (Berkeley: University of California Press, 2016), 237–46.

57. Jeffrey Haas, interview by author, Zoom, October 12, 2022.

58. Paul Good, "Cairo, Illinois: Racism at Floodtide," US Commission on Civil Rights, Clearinghouse Publication no. 44, October 1973, 4. See also Rich Limacher, "Cairo, Illinois: A Steel-Plated Nightmare," *Vidette* 83, no. 30 (1970).

59. "On the Battlefield in Cairo, Illinois," *Black Panther*, July 4, 1970, 5.

60. Haas, *Assassination of Fred Hampton*, 138.

61. Interviews with neighbors are contained in the documentary *778 Bullets*, directed by Angela Aguayo (2010), 18 min.

62. "Peoples Law Office—20 Years," November 18, 1989, event program, http://freedomarchives.org/Documents/Finder/DOC510_scans/NLG/510.NLG.Peoples.Law.Office.20.Years.pdf.

63. Flint Taylor, interview by author, telephone, November 10, 2022.

64. Flint Taylor, "Uncovering the Truth About a Raid on the Black Panthers," *Literary Hub*, February 25, 2019. See also Flint Taylor, *The Torture Machine: Racism and Police Violence in Chicago* (Chicago: Haymarket Books, 2019); Haas, *Assassination of Fred Hampton*, 135–41.

65. "Two Shot in Miami Hijacking," *St. Petersburg Times*, March 8, 1972; Edna Buchanan, "Militant Named in Hijack Here," *Miami Herald*, March 14, 1972.

66. Bloom and Martin, *Black Against Empire*, 139–60.

67. Brent, *Long Time Gone*, 119–20.

68. The BPP's leadership would later back away from its claim that Brent was an agent. "Being Honest with the People Concerning Bill Brent," *Black Panther*, April 20, 1969, 7.

69. Brent, *Long Time Gone*, 137–43.

70. Karen Lee Wald, interview by author, Fort Lauderdale, July 30, 2018. Cleaver assisted the Cuban government in evaluating American hijackers coming into the country. Henry Louis Gates Jr. and Eldridge Cleaver, "Cuban Experience: Eldridge Cleaver on Ice," *Transition*, no. 49 (1975): 35.

71. "Black Scholar Interviews: A Black Expatriate in Cuba," *Black Scholar* 4, no. 5 (1973): 49. While the *Black Scholar* does not disclose the identity of the interviewee, it is undoubtedly Brent. Brent would later describe his Cuban detention in less charitable terms. See Brent, *Long Time Gone*, 147–70.

72. Brent, *Long Time Gone*, 170–71. Although Brent arrived in Cuba two years before Charlie, Michael, and Antar, he had been away cutting sugarcane and working at a pig farm when the RNA comrades were released to the MININT house.

Chapter 7

1. The *Black Panther*, for instance, regularly ran features and news updates about African anticolonial movements, sometimes with arresting photographs of fighters. See, for instance, "Mozambique Guerrillas Determined to Carry Armed Struggle Through to End," *Black Panther*, April 6, 1969, 19. For revolutionaries in Havana, see "Napalmed Guineans on Cuban TV," *Black Panther*, November 16, 1968, 9.

2. Charlie Hill, interview by author, Havana, July 6, 2018. *Granma* featured continual coverage of Castro's trip during May 1972.

3. Hill, interview, July 6, 2018.

4. William Lee Brent, *Long Time Gone: A Black Panther's True-Life Story of His Hijacking and Twenty-Five Years in Cuba* (New York: Times Books, 1996), 178.

5. Teishan A. Latner, *Cuban Revolution in America: Havana and the Making of a United States Left, 1968–1992* (Chapel Hill: University of North Carolina Press, 2018), 94–115.

6. Marília Guimarães, *Nuestros años en Cuba: Un exilio entre sinsontes y el sabiá* (Havana: Casa Editora, 2008), 191 (author's translation).

7. William M. LeoGrande, "Foreign Policy: The Limits of Success," in *Cuba: Internal and International Affairs*, ed. Jorge I. Domínguez (Beverly Hills: Sage, 1982), 169–85; Tanya Harmer, "Refuge in Revolution: Chilean and Uruguayan Exiles in Cuba, 1973–1990," *Cold War History*, July 8, 2024, www.tandfonline.com/doi/epdf/10.1080/14682745.2024.2329281?needAccess=true, 19; Massimo Di Ricco, *Los condenados del aire: El viaje a la utopía de los aeropiratas del Caribe* (Bogotá: Icono Editorial, 2020), 152–55.

8. For Cuba's support for the remnants of the Allende government, see Tanya Harmer, "The View from Havana: Chilean Exiles in Cuba and Early Resistance to Chile's Dictatorship, 1973–1977," *Hispanic American Historical Review* 96, no. 1 (2016): 109–46. For military support, see Harmer, "Refuge in Revolution," 21–22.

9. Luis Cubas, interview by Tanya Harmer, in Harmer, "Refuge in Revolution," 16.

10. Brent, *Long Time Gone*, 179.

11. Brent, *Long Time Gone*, 179.

12. Martin Schram and John Wallach, "Unhappy Landings," *Penthouse*, April 1973, 54.

13. Schram and Wallach, "Unhappy Landings," 54.

14. Paul Harris, "Los Siete Exile Talks About Life in Cuba," *El Tecolote*, August 1977.

15. Seventeen successful hijackings involving US-registered aircraft terminated in locations other than Cuba during this period. Federal Aviation Administration, Civil Aviation Security Service, "Hijacking Statistics: U.S.-Registered Aircraft (1961–present)," April 1, 1975, www.ojp.gov/pdffiles1/Digitization/28885NCJRS.pdf.

16. Critton, *Lion in the Foliage*, 89.

17. Critton, *Lion in the Foliage*, 89–90.

18. Indeed, Cuban intelligence would famously use precisely this tactic—an airplane hijacking ostensibly committed for the purpose of political defection from Cuba—to sneak one of its agents, René González, into the United States in 1990 to infiltrate right-wing Cuban American terrorist groups in Florida.

19. Quoted by the Swiss ambassador, who had spoken with Castro. Henry Kissinger to the president, memorandum, "Aircraft Hijacking," February 7, 1969, 3, declassified June 2004. US Department of State online archive.

20. See Latner, *Cuban Revolution in America*, 137–42; Lee Lockwood, *Conversation with Eldridge Cleaver, Algeria* (New York: Dell, 1970), 19.

21. Brent, *Long Time Gone*, 187.

22. Ministry of Foreign Affairs, *Hijacking of Aircraft: A Boomerang Hurled at Cuba by the Imperialist Government of the United States of America* (Havana: Abel Santamaria Printing Office, 1970).

23. Ministry of Foreign Affairs, *Hijacking of Aircraft*. Cuba's perception of many of the American hijackers as common criminals often extended to Latin American hijackers. See Di Ricco, *Los condenados del aire*, 154–55.

24. Teishan A. Latner, "Take Me to Havana! Airline Hijacking, U.S.-Cuba Relations, and Political Protest in Late 1960s America," *Diplomatic History* 39, no. 1 (2015); Lars Schoultz, *That Infernal Little Cuban Republic: The United States and the Cuban Revolution* (Chapel Hill: University of North Carolina Press, 2011), 256–59.

25. Henry Louis Gates Jr. and Eldridge Cleaver, "Cuban Experience: Eldridge Cleaver on Ice," *Transition*, no. 49 (1975): 34–35.

26. Schram and Wallach, "Unhappy Landings," 122–23.

27. James Reed and Beverly Reed, "Hijackers Find Life in Cuba Unpleasant," *Albuquerque Journal*, November 29, 1971.

28. Reed and Reed, "Hijackers Find Life in Cuba Unpleasant."

29. W. Seth Carus, "R.I.S.E.," in *Toxic Terror: Assessing Terrorist Use of Chemical and Biological Weapons*, ed. Steven E. Miller (Cambridge: MIT Press, 2000), 58–59.

30. US newspapers later reported that Schwander died in a Cuban prison in 1974. Art Petaque and William Braden, "Chicagoan Killed in Cuba Jail?," *Chicago Sun Times*, March 29, 1978; Carus, R.I.S.E.," 69; W. Seth Carus, "Bioterrorism and Biocrimes: The Illicit Use of Biological Agents Since 1900 (working paper, Center for Counterproliferation Research, National Defense University, Washington, DC, August 1998, rev. February 2001), https://irp.fas.org/threat/cbw/carus.pdf, 103.

31. Schram and Wallach, "Unhappy Landings," 124. See also John Fenton Wheeler, *Last Man Out: Memoirs of the Last U.S. Reporter Castro Kicked Out of Cuba During the Cold War* (Spokane, WA: Demers Books, 2008), 129–34.

32. Gregory Randall, *To Have Been There Then: Memories of Cuba: 1969–1983*, trans. Margaret Randall (Brooklyn: Operating System, 2016), 42.

33. Charlie Hill, interview by author, WhatsApp, September 20, 2020.

34. Quoted in Ellen Hampton, "For Former Black Militant, Island Is End of the Road," *Miami News*, June 16, 1987.

35. Schram and Wallach, "Unhappy Landings," 54.

36. Lockwood, *Conversation with Eldridge Cleaver*, 17.

37. Voice of Vietnam (announcing the fall of Saigon): April 30, 1975, reception location: Plymouth, Minnesota: https://archive.org/details/sraa-voice-of-vietnam-announcing-the-fall-of-saigon-april-30-1975.

38. Gates and Cleaver, "Cuban Experience," 32; Eldridge Cleaver, *Soul on Fire* (Waco, TX: Word Books, 1978), 107.

39. Latner, *Cuban Revolution in America*, 107–15.

40. Latner, *Cuban Revolution in America*, 94–115.

41. Eldridge Cleaver, interview by Henry Louis Gates, *Frontline*, PBS, spring 1997, www.pbs.org/wgbh/pages/frontline/shows/race/interviews/ecleaver.html; Justin Gifford, *Revolution or Death: The Life of Eldridge Cleaver* (Chicago: Lawrence Hill Books, 2020), 157–60.

42. Joshua Bloom and Waldo E. Martin, *Black Against Empire: The History and Politics of the Black Panther Party* (Berkeley: University of California Press, 2016), 119, 425.

43. Lockwood, *Conversation with Eldridge Cleaver*, 18. Karen Lee Wald, who traveled to Cuba aboard the same ship from Canada and worked closely with the Cuban government

during this period, believes that Cleaver's seclusion was intentional: "The Cubans were not terribly impressed with Eldridge." Wald, interview by author, Fort Lauderdale, July 30, 2018.

44. Gates and Cleaver, "Cuban Experience."

45. Lillian Guerra, "Poder Negro in Revolutionary Cuba: Black Consciousness, Communism, and the Challenge of Solidarity," *Hispanic American Historical Review* 99, no. 4 (2019): 681–718.

46. Lockwood, *Conversation with Eldridge Cleaver*, 19–21.

47. Byron Booth, interview by Keith Rice and Karin Stanford, October 3, 2016, African American Life in Los Angeles Oral History Project, California State University Northridge.

48. Latner, *Cuban Revolution in America*, 58.

49. Quoted in *¡Salud!*, directed by Connie Field (MEDICC, 2006), 93 min.

50. Booth, interview.

51. Booth, interview.

52. Booth, interview.

53. Booth, interview.

54. Booth, interview.

55. See James Pringle, "Cleaver Is Found in Havana Working on a Book," *New York Times*, May 25, 1969.

56. Paul Magnarella, *Black Panther in Exile: The Pete O'Neal Story* (Gainesville: University Press of Florida, 2020); Lockwood, *Conversation with Eldridge Cleaver*, 23.

57. Fenton Wheeler, "Life Worse in Cuba, Unhappy Black Panthers Wail," *Miami Herald*, June 26, 1969.

58. Schram and Wallach, "Unhappy Landings," 123.

59. Wheeler, "Life Worse in Cuba."

60. Wheeler, "Life Worse in Cuba."

61. Wheeler, "Life Worse in Cuba."

62. "Bobby Seale on National Airlines Hijacking," KPIX-TV, June 26, 1969, https://diva.sfsu.edu/collections/sfbatv/bundles/206989.

63. For Williams in Havana, see Timothy Tyson, *Radio Free Dixie: Robert F. Williams and the Roots of Black Power*, 2nd ed. (Chapel Hill: University of North Carolina Press, 2020), 220–43.

64. Tyson, *Radio Free Dixie*, 285–89.

65. Quoted in Tyson, *Radio Free Dixie*, 292–93.

66. Robert F. Williams, "Views and Opinions: Blacks Told Not to Hijack," *Chicago Defender*, January 25, 1969.

67. Charlie Hill, interview by author, WhatsApp, July 8, 2020.

68. Alberto Ulloa Bornemann, *Surviving Mexico's Dirty War: A Political Prisoner's Memoir*, ed. and trans. Arthur Schmidt (Philadelphia: Temple University Press, 2007), 105, 114.

69. Harmer, "Refuge in Revolution," 13.

70. Hill, interview, July 8, 2020.

71. "Black Scholar Interviews: A Black Expatriate in Cuba," *Black Scholar* 4, no. 5 (1973): 54.

72. Charlie Hill, interview by author, Havana, July 26, 2019.

73. Critton, *Lion in the Foliage*, 103.

74. Elizabeth (Betita) Sutherland Martinez, "Neither Black nor White in a Black-White World," in *Hands on the Freedom Plow: Personal Accounts by Women in SNCC*, ed. Faith S. Holsaert, Martha Prescod Norman Noonan, Judy Richardson, Betty Garman Robinson, Jean Smith Young, and Dorothy M. Zellner (Urbana: University of Illinois Press, 2010), 533. See also Elizabeth Sutherland, *The Youngest Revolution: A Personal Report on Cuba* (New York: Dial Press, 1969).

75. Martinez, "Neither Black nor White," 532.

76. Critton, *Lion in the Foliage*, 99.

77. Critton, *Lion in the Foliage*, 105–6.

78. Paul Harris, interview by author, telephone, March 13, 2023.

79. Paul Harris, "Los Siete Exile Talks About Life in Cuba," *El Tecolote*, August 1977.

80. Harris, "Los Siete Exile Talks."

81. Harris, interview.

82. Brent, *Long Time Gone*, 175.

83. Police likely placed Dorethea's house under surveillance before the hijacking, after deducing that Charlie had been at the scene of Rosenbloom's killing. Albuquerque Police Department, Wanted or Missing Persons Report, Offense no. 208325, Charles Hill, November 25, 1971.

84. Barbara Lawless, "Fugitive Harboring Charges Dropped Against Mrs. Hill," *Albuquerque Journal*, January 28, 1972.

85. Supplementary Offense Report, Homicide, Robert Rosenbloom, Albuquerque Police Department, Case No. 208325, December 2, 1971.

86. "Vines Gets 5 Years on Harboring Charge," *Albuquerque Journal*, January 29, 1972; "State's 'Harboring' Charges Dismissed," *Albuquerque Journal*, February 3, 1972.

87. Charlie Hill, interview by author, WhatsApp, November 2, 2020.

88. Hill, interview, November 2, 2020.

89. Hill, interview, November 2, 2020.

90. Janet Hill King, interview by author, WhatsApp, August 1, 2022.

91. Don Canter and Robert Hollis, "Wife Was Visiting Son in Cuba," *San Francisco Examiner*, May 26, 1976.

92. Charlie Hill, interview by author, WhatsApp, February 25, 2021.

93. King, interview.

94. This account is provided by Merriam Ansara, who was Antar's girlfriend in Cuba, and by Robert Fikes, who interviewed Hope Goodwin, Antar's sister. See Robert Fikes Jr., "Remarkable Healers on the Pacific Coast: A History of San Diego's Black Medical Community," *Journal of San Diego History* 57 (Summer 2011): 45–64.

95. For Tanzania during this period, see Seth M. Markle, *A Motorcycle on Hell Run: Tanzania, Black Power, and the Uncertain Future of Pan-Africanism, 1964–1974* (East Lansing: Michigan State University Press, 2017). For African American political exiles in Tanzania, including Pete O'Neal and Geronimo Pratt, see Magnarella, *Black Panther in Exile*.

96. Charlie Hill, interview by author, Havana, July 24, 2019.

97. Hill, interview, July 24, 2019.

98. Charlie Hill, interview by author, Havana, June 6, 2018.

99. Hill, interview, July 24, 2019.

Chapter 8

1. "Todos a la Plaza Con Fidel. ¡Viva el Primero de Mayo!" *Granma*, May 1, 1972, front page.

2. Charlie Hill, interview by author, Havana, June 2019. Photos published in *Granma* the next day show a massive crowd before the José Martí Memorial.

3. Patrick Critton, *Lion in the Foliage, Full Moon in the Sky: The Autobiography of Patrick Critton* (pub. by author, 2009), 98.

4. Critton, *Lion in the Foliage*, 97–98.

5. "Inside Latin America—Cuba," *Black Panther*, May 14, 1977, 22.

6. Howard Glazer, "Housing in Cuba," in *Cuba: A Different America*, ed. Wilber A. Chaffee and Gary Prevost (Totowa, NJ: Rowman and Littlefield, 1989), 80.

7. See, for instance, "De la noche a la mañana, o si no que lo diga Cirico," *Granma*, February 7, 1972, 4.

8. Critton, *Lion in the Foliage*, 98.

9. The first Chilean exile to arrive was Beatriz Allende, Salvador Allende's daughter. Tanya Harmer, "The View from Havana: Chilean Exiles in Cuba and Early Resistance to Chile's Dictatorship, 1973–1977," *Hispanic American Historical Review* 96, no. 1 (2016): 109.

10. Marília Guimarães, *Nuestros años en Cuba: Un exilio entre sinsontes y el sabiá* (Havana: Casa Editora, 2008), 121 (author's translation).

11. The "project homes" for Chilean children are the subject of *El edificio de los Chilenos*, directed by Macarena Aguiló (Magic Lantern Films, 2010). See also Gregory Randall, *To Have Been There Then: Memories of Cuba: 1969–1983*, trans. Margaret Randall (Brooklyn: Operating System, 2016), 161–62.

12. Charlie Hill, interview by author, WhatsApp, July 10, 2020.

13. Photograph of 1972 rally reproduced in *Cuban Studies Newsletter* 3, nos. 4–5 (1976): 12.

14. Randall, *To Have Been There Then*, 100.

15. For one example in the spring of 1972, see Mirta Rodríguez Calderón, "Partió hacía la República Democrática de Vietnam la Brigada Médica Cubana, *Granma*, May 4, 1972, 2; Roberto Salas, "Médicos Cubanos en Hanoi," *Granma*, May 29, 1972, 15.

16. For an overview of Cuban civilian aid in the 1970s, see Susan Eckstein, "Why Cuban Internationalism?," in *Cuban Political Economy: Controversies in Cubanology*, ed. Andrew Zimbalist (Boulder, CO: Westview Press, 1988), 157–60.

17. Tanya Harmer, "Refuge in Revolution: Chilean and Uruguayan Exiles in Cuba, 1973–1990," *Cold War History*, July 8, 2024, www.tandfonline.com/doi/epdf/10.1080/14682745.2024.2329281?needAccess=true, 23.

18. Paul Harris, "Los Siete Exile Talks About Life in Cuba," *El Tecolote*, August 1977.

19. Harmer, "Refuge in Revolution," 23.

20. Charlie Hill, interview by author, WhatsApp, July 20, 2020.

21. Critton, *Lion in the Foliage*, 111, 113.

22. William Lee Brent, *Long Time Gone: A Black Panther's True-Life Story of His Hijacking and Twenty-Five Years in Cuba* (New York: Times Books, 1996), 202.

23. Reinaldo Funes-Monzote and Steven Palmer, "Challenging Climate and Geopolitics: Cuba, Canada, and Intensive Livestock Exchange in a Cold War Context, from the 1960s

to the 1980s," in *Itineraries of Expertise: Science, Technology, and the Environment in Latin America*, ed. Andra B. Chastain and Timothy W. Lorek (Pittsburgh: University of Pittsburgh Press, 2020), 138.

24. For Ángel Castro's state, see Jonathan M. Hansen, *Young Castro: The Making of a Revolutionary* (New York: Simon and Schuster, 2020), 24, 35–37, 42–44.

25. Charlie Hill, interview by author, WhatsApp, July 19, 2020.

26. Charlie Hill, interview by author, WhatsApp, July 18, 2020.

27. Critton, *Lion in the Foliage*, 98.

28. Critton, *Lion in the Foliage*, 108–9.

29. Dozens of articles in *Granma* covered this theme. See, for instance, "Despliegue de tropas en el ghetto negro de Baton Rouge vaticinal nuevos enfrentamientos," *Granma*, January 12, 1972.

30. These terms—*comunista afronorteamericana* and *joven revolucionaria negra*—were often used interchangeably in descriptions of Davis. See, for instance, "Inician juicio contra Angela Davis y arrestan a 18 personas que protestaban frente al tribunal de San José," *Granma*, February 2, 1972. See also "La causa contra Angela Davis," *Verde Olivo* 14, no. 5 (1972): 55.

31. Charlie Hill, interview by author, WhatsApp, July 9, 2020.

32. René Trujillo, interview by author, Havana, 2015.

33. Hill, interview, July 19, 2020.

34. Isabel Story, *Soviet Influence on Cuban Culture, 1961–1987: When the Soviets Came to Stay* (Lanham, MD: Lexington Books, 2020), 77–79, 25.

35. Hill, interview, July 19, 2020.

36. Hill, interview, July 19, 2020.

37. Alina Pérez, "La Unión de Jóvenes Comunistas," in *Apuntes para la historia del movimiento juvenil comunista y pioneril cubano*, ed. Carmen Ferrer, Zenaida Gómez, Alina Pérez, and Lilian Vizcaíno (Havana: Editoria Política, 1987), 75–76; Anne Luke, *Youth and the Cuban Revolution: Youth Culture and Politics in 1960s Cuba* (Lanham, MD: Lexington Books, 2018), 82–88.

38. Hill, interview, July 19, 2020.

39. Greater racial integration in Cuba also predated the 1959 revolution. For assessments of racial inequality between 1959 and the 1980s, see, especially, Devyn Spence Benson, *Antiracism in Cuba: The Unfinished Revolution* (Chapel Hill: University of North Carolina Press, 2016); Alejandro de la Fuente, "Race and Inequality in Cuba, 1899–1981," *Journal of Contemporary History* 30, no. 1 (1995): 131–68; Alejandro de la Fuente and Stanley R. Bailey, "The Puzzle of Racial Inequality in Cuba, 1980s–2010s," *Du Bois Review* 18, no. 1 (2021): 73–96.

40. De la Fuente, "Race and Inequality in Cuba," 153, 160–61.

41. For more on Brazil, see de la Fuente, "Race and Inequality in Cuba," 309–11.

42. Esteban Morales Domínguez, *Race in Cuba: Essays on the Revolution and Racial Inequality*, ed. and trans. Gary Prevost and August Nimtz (New York: Monthly Review Press, 2013), 71–72.

43. Morales Domínguez, *Race in Cuba*, 97.

44. Socialist systems outperformed capitalist ones in thirty of thirty-six country comparisons. Shirley Cereseto and Howard Waitzkin, "Capitalism, Socialism, and the Physical Quality of Life," *International Journal of Health Services* 16, no. 4 (1986): 643–58. See also Hugh F. Lena and Bruce London, "The Political and Economic Determinants of Health

Outcomes: A Cross-national Analysis," *International Journal of Health Services* 23, no. 3 (1993): 585–602; Vicente Navarro, "Has Socialism Failed? An Analysis of Health Indicators Under Capitalism and Socialism," *Science and Society* 57, no. 1 (1993): 6–30.

45. De la Fuente, "Race and Inequality in Cuba," 161.

46. Elizabeth Sutherland, *The Youngest Revolution: A Personal Report on Cuba* (New York: Dial Press, 1969), 140.

47. Sutherland, *Youngest Revolution*, 141.

48. Hill interview, July 18, 2020.

49. Quoted in Fenton Wheeler, "Life Worse in Cuba, Unhappy Black Panthers Wail," *Miami Herald*, June 26, 1969.

50. Quoted in Wheeler, "Life Worse in Cuba."

51. De la Fuente, "Race and Inequality in Cuba," 160–61.

52. "Black Scholar Interviews: A Black Expatriate in Cuba," *Black Scholar* 4, no. 5 (1973): 51–52. For more on racial diversity in leadership positions in Cuba, see Alejandro de la Fuente, *A Nation for All: Race, Inequality, and Politics in Twentieth-Century Cuba* (Chapel Hill: University of North Carolina Press, 2001), 310–12.

53. Teishan A. Latner, "Assata Shakur: The Political Life of Political Exile," in *Black Power Afterlives: The Enduring Significance of the Black Panther Party*, ed. Diane C. Fujino and Matef Harmachis (Chicago: Haymarket Books); Teishan A. Latner, "Assata Shakur Is Welcome Here: Havana, Black Freedom Struggle, and U.S.-Cuba Relations," *Souls: A Critical Journal of Black Politics, Culture, and Society* 19, no. 4 (2018): 455–77.

54. Assata Shakur, *Assata: An Autobiography* (Chicago: Lawrence Hill Books, 1987), 269 (lowercase "I" in original).

55. Teishan A. Latner, *Cuban Revolution in America: Havana and the Making of a United States Left, 1968–1992* (Chapel Hill: University of North Carolina Press, 2018).

56. Fidel Castro, speech to the third congress of the CCP, February 7, 1986, published in the *Black Scholar* 20, no. 5/6 (1989): 9.

57. "Black Scholar Interviews," 52–53.

58. Charlie Hill, interview by author, WhatsApp, July 14, 2020.

59. Hill, interview, July 14, 2020.

60. Charlie Hill, interview by author, WhatsApp, September 21, 2020.

61. Henry Louis Gates Jr. and Eldridge Cleaver, "Cuban Experience: Eldridge Cleaver on Ice," *Transition*, no. 49 (1975): 39.

62. Danielle Pilar Clealand, *The Power of Race in Cuba: Racial Ideology and Black Consciousness During the Revolution* (Oxford: Oxford University Press, 2017), 36–38.

63. Hill, interview, July 9, 2020.

64. For Carmichael's description of the OLAS visit, see Stokely Carmichael, *Ready for Revolution: The Life and Struggles of Stokely Carmichael (Kwame Ture)*, with Michael Ekwueme Thelwell (New York: Simon and Schuster, 2003), 583–94.

65. See Sarah J. Seidman, "Angela Davis in Cuba as Symbol and Subject," *Radical History Review*, no. 136 (January 2020): 11–35.

66. For the early period of the 1960s, see Benson, *Antiracism in Cuba*. See also Seidman, "Angela Davis in Cuba."

67. Hill, interview, July 9, 2020.

68. Hill, interview, July 9, 2020.

69. Morales Domínguez, *Race in Cuba*, 119.

70. Danielle Pilar Clealand, "Who Are the Black Revolutionaries? Resistance in Cuba and the State Boundaries That Endure," *Souls: A Critical Journal of Black Politics, Culture, and Society* 21, no. 4 (2020): 323.

71. Hill, interview, July 9, 2020.

72. Charlie Hill, interview by author, Havana, June 5, 2018.

73. Ellen Hampton, "For Former Black Militant, Island Is End of the Road," *Miami News*, June 16, 1987.

74. Jo Thomas, "Havana Releases 33 Americans, and All but Three Return to U.S.," *New York Times*, October 28, 1980.

75. See also Robert Allen, "Ex-Detroiter Behind Infamous 1972 Skyjacking Tells His Story," *Detroit Free Press*, June 6, 2016.

76. Allen, "Ex-Detroiter."

77. Latner, *Cuban Revolution in America*, 146–48.

78. "U.S. Note on Hijackers Pessimistic," *Albuquerque Journal*, August 29, 1972.

79. "Pact Won't Apply to N. M. Suspects," *Albuquerque Journal*, March 15, 1973.

80. Charlie Hill, interview by author, Havana, June 10, 2018.

81. "Skyjacker Drowns in Cuba," *Oakland Tribune*, March 15, 1973. Date of death also listed in Michael Newton, ed., *The Encyclopedia of Kidnappings* (New York: Facts on File, 2002), 109; *Aircraft Hijackings and Other Criminal Acts Against Civil Aviation Statistical and Narrative Reports* (Washington, DC: Federal Aviation Administration, Office of Aviation Security, May 1983), 23.

82. "Skyjacker Drowns in Cuba," *Oakland Tribune*, March 15, 1973.

83. Robert Fikes Jr., "Pioneers, Warriors, Advocates: A History of San Diego's Black Legal Community, 1890–2010," undated paper. A revised version of this text was published by the *Journal of San Diego History* in 2014 but without key information about Goodwin.

84. Hope Rebecca Goodwin was known to her friends as Becky.

85. Hope R. Goodwin, telephone conversation with author, July 19, 2022.

86. Hill, interview, June 10, 2018. According to Charlie, Antar was laid to rest in a Havana cemetery.

Chapter 9

1. Charlie Hill, interview by author, Havana, June 5, 2018.

2. Bill Brent describes MININT's provision of this house in his memoir, suggesting that there was more tension between its occupants and the Cuban government than Charlie acknowledges. William Lee Brent, *Long Time Gone: A Black Panther's True-Life Story of His Hijacking and Twenty-Five Years in Cuba* (New York: Times Books, 1996), 239.

3. This critique of supply and demand appears more elegantly in Aviva Chomsky, *A History of the Cuban Revolution* (Hoboken, NJ: Wiley-Blackwell, 2010), 9.

4. Brent, *Long Time Gone*, 204.

5. Helen Yaffe, *We Are Cuba! How a Revolutionary People Have Survived in a Post-Soviet World* (New Haven, CT: Yale University Press, 2020), 23–25. See also Andrew Zimbalist, ed., *Cuban Political Economy: Controversies in Cubanology* (Boulder, CO: Westview Press, 1988).

6. Gregory Randall, *To Have Been There Then: Memories of Cuba: 1969–1983*, trans. Margaret Randall (Brooklyn: Operating System, 2016), 32.

7. Patrick Critton, *Lion in the Foliage, Full Moon in the Sky: The Autobiography of Patrick Critton* (pub. by author, 2009), 120–21.

8. For a rebuttal of commonplace misrepresentations of Cuba's social progress during this period, see José Luis Rodríguez, "Cubanology and the Provision of Basic Need in the Cuban Revolution," in *Cuban Political Economy: Controversies in Cubanology*, ed. Andrew Zimbalist (Boulder, CO: Westview Press, 1988), 83–106.

9. Kathleen Tynan, "Jazzing into Cuba," *Vogue*, September 1977, 384.

10. Michael Ratner, *Moving the Bar: My Life as a Radical Lawyer* (New York: OR Books, 2021), 158.

11. Critton, *Lion in the Foliage*, 93–94.

12. Chapa's story has not been verified. See *Tim Chapa Interview: By David Correia, Lauro Silva, John Redhouse*, videotaped by Brian Lucero, Zimmerman Library, Albuquerque, NM, July 27, 2007.

13. Ratner, *Moving the Bar*, 156.

14. Charlie Hill, interview by author, Havana, July 22, 2019. With the imprisonment of Imari Obadele following the August 18, 1971, shoot-out in Jackson, Lumumba became the most visible spokesperson for the New Afrikan Independence Movement during the 1970s. Akinyele Umoja, "The People Must Decide: Chokwe Lumumba, New Black Power, and the Potential for Participatory Democracy in Mississippi," *Black Scholar: Journal of Black Studies and Research* 48, no. 2 (2018): 7–19.

15. Francis B. Kent, "Dream of a Black Republic in U.S. South Persists," *Los Angeles Times*, March 17, 1974.

16. Joshua Bloom and Waldo E. Martin, *Black Against Empire: The History and Politics of the Black Panther Party* (Berkeley: University of California Press, 2016), 382–83.

17. Raymond H. Boone, "Huey P. Newton Ready to Come Home," *Richmond Afro-American*, April 24, 1976. For more on American youth and the Cuban Revolution, see Van Gosse, *Where the Boys Are: Cuba, Cold War and the Making of a New Left* (New York: Verso Books, 1993).

18. See also letters, box 2, folder 12: Karen Wald 1971, Subseries 1: Personal, Series 1: Huey P. Newton Papers, Dr. Huey P. Newton Foundation Inc. collection, 1968–1994, M0864, Dept. of Special Collections, Stanford University Libraries.

19. Karen Wald, email correspondence with author, May 23, 2022.

20. Newton wrote at least two narratives of the escape, which he hoped to commercialize to pay for the Panther's political work. The versions portray some key events in slightly different ways. See Newton, untitled manuscripts, undated, box 47, folder 13: H. P. N. Cuba, Subseries 5: Manuscripts, Series 1: Huey P. Newton Papers, Dr. Huey P. Newton Foundation Inc. collection, 1968–1994, M0864, Dept. of Special Collections, Stanford University Libraries. Newton's escape from California and arrival in Cuba was dramatized in 2024 in *The Big Cigar*, season 1, episodes 1–6, developed by Jim Hecht, directed by Don Cheadle et al., premiered May 17, 2024, on Apple TV+.

21. Newton, untitled manuscript 1, undated, box 47, folder 13: H. P. N. Cuba.

22. Jack Slater, "Huey Newton Speaks Out," *Los Angeles Times*, August 25, 1977.

23. Newton, untitled manuscript 1, undated, box 47, folder 13: H. P. N. Cuba.

24. Newton, "Sanctuary in Cuba," interview by Stewart Brand, *CoEvolution Quarterly*, Fall 1977, 27–28.

25. Les Ledbetter, "Newton Doubts U.S. Needs Socialism," *New York Times*, July 16, 1977.

26. Slater, "Huey Newton Speaks Out."

27. Slater, "Huey Newton Speaks Out."

28. Newton, "Sanctuary in Cuba," 27.

29. Brent, *Long Time Gone*, 236; Newton, "Sanctuary in Cuba," 25–29; Robert Trumbull, "Newton Plans to Resume Control of Black Panthers," *New York Times*, June 28, 1977.

30. Brent, *Long Time Gone*, 236.

31. Brent, *Long Time Gone*, 236.

32. Newton, "Sanctuary in Cuba," 28.

33. Charlie Hill, interview by author, Havana, May 31, 2018.

34. Newton, "Sanctuary in Cuba," 28.

35. Paul Harris, interview by author, telephone, March 13, 2023.

36. Paul Harris, "Los Siete Exile Talks About Life in Cuba," *El Tecolote*, August 1977.

37. Newton, "Sanctuary in Cuba," 28.

38. Ledbetter, "Newton Doubts U.S. Needs Socialism."

39. Slater, "Huey Newton Speaks Out."

40. Trumbull, "Newton Plans to Resume Control."

41. Boone, "Huey P. Newton Ready to Come Home."

42. Boone, "Huey P. Newton Ready to Come Home."

43. Slater, "Huey Newton Speaks Out."

44. Slater, "Huey Newton Speaks Out."

45. Charlie Hill, interview by author, WhatsApp, July 1, 2022.

46. Although Critton had a passport, it is not clear how he was able to enter Egypt. Critton's exit from Cuba was likely facilitated by the Cuban government. Critton, *Lion in the Foliage*, 131.

47. See Andrew Ivaska, "Movement Youth in a Global Sixties Hub: The Everyday Lives of Transnational Activists in Postcolonial Dar es Salaam," in *A Global Age: Transnational Histories of Youth in the Twentieth Century*, ed. Richard Jobs and David Pomfret (New York: Palgrave Macmillan, 2015); George Roberts, *Revolutionary State-Making in Dar es Salaam: African Liberation and the Global Cold War, 1961–1974* (Cambridge: Cambridge University Press, 2021).

48. Critton, *Lion in the Foliage*, 104.

49. Critton, *Lion in the Foliage*, 151.

50. Charlie Hill, interview by author, WhatsApp, June 8, 2020.

51. Charlie Hill, interview by author, WhatsApp, June 23, 2020.

52. Charlie Hill, interview by author, WhatsApp, June 24, 2020.

53. Hill, interview, June 24, 2020.

54. Critton, *Lion in the Foliage*, 125.

55. Cuban Family Code, February 14, 1975, sec. 1, art. 24; sec. 2, arts. 26–28; official Cuban English translation published in *Center for Cuban Studies Newsletter* 2, no. 4 (1975).

56. For one such account, see Randall, *To Have Been There Then*, 124.

57. Hope Bastian Martínez, "Cuban Women and the State: Women's Lives in the 1970s and the New Reproductive Bargain," in *Cuba's Forgotten Decade: How the 1970s Shaped the Revolution*, ed. Emily J. Kirk, Anna Clayfield, and Isabel Story (Lanham, MD: Lexington Books, 2018), 123–24; Carrie Hamilton, *Sexual Revolutions in Cuba: Passion, Politics, and Memory* (Chapel Hill: University of North Carolina Press, 2014), 33–34; Max Azicri, "The Cuban Family Code: Some Observations on Its Innovations and Continuities," *Review of*

Socialist Law 6, no. 1 (1980): 183–91; Julie Marie Bunck, "Women's Rights and the Cuban Revolution," in *Cuban Communism, 1959–1995*, ed. Irving Louis Horowitz (New Brunswick, NJ: Transaction, 1995), 427–48.

58. Critton, *Lion in the Foliage*, 123–25.

59. Lourdes Arguelles and B. Ruby Rich, "Homosexuality, Homophobia, and Revolution: Notes Toward an Understanding of the Cuban Lesbian and Gay Male Experience," pt. 1, *Signs* 9, no. 4 (1984): 683–99; Ian Lekus, "Queer Harvests: Homosexuality, the U.S. New Left During This Period, and the Venceremos Brigades to Cuba," *Radical History Review*, no. 89 (Spring 2004): 57–91.

60. "Sexual diversity" (*la diversidad sexual*), as opposed to "LGBTQ," is the more commonly used term in modern Cuba. For more on UMAPs and the broader context of antigay repression, see Emilio Bejel, *Gay Cuban Nation* (Chicago: University of Chicago Press, 2001), 95–112; Hamilton, *Sexual Revolutions in Cuba*, 39–41, 121–22. For the evolution of the government's position, see Emily J. Kirk, *Cuba's Gay Revolution: Normalizing Sexual Diversity Through a Health-Based Approach* (Lanham, MD: Lexington Books, 2017), 7–28; Lois M. Smith and Alfred Padula, *Sex and Revolution: Women in Socialist Cuba* (Oxford: Oxford University Press, 1996), 173.

61. Huey P. Newton, "A Letter from Huey to the Revolutionary Brothers and Sisters About the Women's Liberation and Gay Liberation Movements," *Black Panther*, August 21, 1970, 5.

62. Charlie Hill, interview by author, WhatsApp, November 26, 2023.

63. Anne Luke, *Youth and the Cuban Revolution: Youth Culture and Politics in 1960s Cuba* (Lanham, MD: Lexington Books, 2018), 87–88; Lillian Guerra, *Visions of Power in Cuba: Revolution, Redemption, and Resistance, 1959–1971* (Chapel Hill: University of North Carolina Press, 2012), 24–28.

64. Hill, interview, November 26, 2023.

65. Charlie Hill, interview by author, WhatsApp, March 1, 2025.

66. Charlie Hill, interview by author, Havana, June 4, 2018.

67. Hill, interview, June 4, 2018.

68. Hill, interview, June 4, 2018.

Chapter 10

1. Numerous Cuban publications commemorate and analyze the bombing and the popular response. See, for instance, *El Mismo Pueblo: Contra el Terrorismo y Contra la Guerra* (Havana: Editorial Politica, 2001); *Cuba, la Historia No Contada* (Havana: Editorial Capitán San Luis, 2003).

2. Charlie Hill, interview by author, WhatsApp, December 3, 2023. Among the best compendiums of sources in English on Cubana de Aviación flight 455 is Peter Kornbluh and Yvette White, eds., "Bombing of Cuban Jetliner 30 Years Later," October 5, 2006 (updated October 6, 2016), National Security Archive, George Washington University, https://nsarchive2.gwu.edu/NSAEBB/NSAEBB202/index.htm.

3. For an overview of these dynamics, see Jesús Arboleya, *The Cuban Counterrevolution*, trans. Rafael Betancourt (Athens: Ohio University Press, 2000); Fabián Escalante Font, *The Secret War: CIA Covert Operations Against Cuba 1959–62*, trans. Maxine Shaw (Melbourne: Ocean Press, 1995).

4. Lars Schoultz, *That Infernal Little Cuban Republic: The United States and the Cuban Revolution* (Chapel Hill: University of North Carolina Press, 2011), 175–88; "Kennedy and Cuba: Operation Mongoose," October 3, 2019, National Security Archive, George Washington University, https://nsarchive.gwu.edu/briefing-book/cuba/2019-10-03/kennedy-cuba-operation-mongoose.

5. See Arboleya, *Cuban Counterrevolution*; Warren Hinckle and William W. Turner, *The Fish Is Red: The Story of the Secret War Against Castro* (New York: HarperCollins, 1981); Peter Kornbluh, ed., *Bay of Pigs Declassified: The Secret CIA Report on the Invasion of Cuba* (New York: New Press, 1998).

6. See Keith Bolender, *Voices from the Other Side: An Oral History of Terrorism Against Cuba* (London: Pluto Press, 2010). In 1976, Oriente Province was divided into five provinces, with the village of Boca de Samá becoming part of Holguín Province.

7. Charlie Hill, interview by author, Havana, May 31, 2018.

8. For one account, see Joan Didion, *Miami* (New York: Vintage, 1987), 99–108.

9. Arboleya, *Cuban Counterrevolution*, 160.

10. Charlie Hill, interview by author, Havana, June 27, 2019.

11. Charlie Hill, interview by author, Havana, May 30, 2018.

12. Rodolfo Rodríguez Cruz, "Cuba: Mass Polio Vaccination Program, 1962–1982," *Reviews of Infectious Diseases* 6, no. S2 (1984): 408–412.

13. "Tesis sobre la lucha ideoldgica," in *Tesis y Resoluciones del Primer Congreso del PCC* (Havana, 1976): 223–24, quoted in José Luis Rodríguez, "The So-Called Cubanology and Cuban Economic Development," *Cuban Studies* 16 (1986): 211.

14. Charlie Hill, interview by author, WhatsApp, February 30, 2025.

15. Pavón Tamayo headed the Consejo Nacional de Cultura. Ambrosio Fornet, "El quinquenio gris: Revisitando el término," *Criterios* 5 (2006); Carrie Hamilton, *Sexual Revolutions in Cuba: Passion, Politics, and Memory* (Chapel Hill: University of North Carolina Press, 2014), 117–19; Isabel Story, *Soviet Influence on Cuban Culture, 1961–1987: When the Soviets Came to Stay* (Lanham, MD: Lexington Books, 2020), 122–25.

16. Raúl Castro, "El diversionismo ideológico, arma sutil que esgrimen los enemigos contra la Revolución," *Verde Olivo*, July 23, 1972, 4–15.

17. Anne Luke, *Youth and the Cuban Revolution: Youth Culture and Politics in 1960s Cuba* (Lanham, MD: Lexington Books, 2018), 59–60. For culture in Havana during the period, see Antoni Kapcia, *Havana: The Making of Cuban Culture* (Oxford: Berg, 2005), 149–66; Jennifer L. Lambe, *The Subject of Revolution: Between Political and Popular Culture in Cuba* (Chapel Hill: University of North Carolina Press, 2024), 217–26. For a retrospective analysis by Cuban scholars, see Centro Teórico-Cultural Criterios, *La política cultural del período revolucionario: Memoria y reflexión* (Havana: Centro Teórico-Cultural Criterios, 2008).

18. Charlie Hill, interview by author, WhatsApp, August 6, 2020.

19. Karen Lee Wald, "Lennonism in Cuba at Last," *Z Magazine*, June 2001, 56–60. See also Ernesto Juan Castellanos, ed., *Los Beatles en Cuba: Un viaje mágico y misterio* (Havana: Unión de Escritores y Artistas de Cuba, 1997).

20. Charlie Hill, interview by author, Havana, June 24, 2019. For a useful summary of this period, see Kapcia, *Havana*, 149–68.

21. There is now a very large body of scholarship examining US involvement in political violence and counterinsurgency in Latin America. See, for instance, Lesley Gill, *The School of the Americas: Military Training and Political Violence* (Durham, NC: Duke University

Press, 2004); Gilbert M. Joseph and Greg Grandin, eds., *A Century of Revolution: Insurgent and Counterinsurgent Violence During Latin America's Long Cold War* (Durham, NC: Duke University Press, 2010); Greg Grandin, *The Last Colonial Massacre: Latin America in the Cold War*, 2nd ed. (Chicago: University of Chicago Press, 2011); Stephen G. Rabe, *The Killing Zone: The United States Wages Cold War in Latin America*, 2nd ed. (Oxford: Oxford University Press, 2015).

22. Gregory Randall, *To Have Been There Then: Memories of Cuba: 1969–1983*, trans. Margaret Randall (Brooklyn: Operating System, 2016), 102.

23. Tanya Harmer, "Refuge in Revolution: Chilean and Uruguayan Exiles in Cuba, 1973–1990," *Cold War History*, July 8, 2024, 13.

24. Harmer, "Refuge in Revolution," 13–14.

25. These are likely pseudonyms. Charlie will not even reveal the pseudonym of the Brazilian, a leftist who traveled to Nicaragua—with Cuban support—to join the Sandinista National Liberation Front.

26. Charlie Hill, interview by author, Havana, July 23, 2019.

27. Hill, interview, July 23, 2019.

28. Julius K. Nyerere, *Ujamaa: Essays on Socialism* (Dar es Salaam: Oxford University Press, 1968), quoted in Edward Onaci, *Free the Land: The Republic of New Afrika and the Pursuit of a Black Nation-State* (Chapel Hill: University of North Carolina Press, 2020), 55.

29. Hill, interview, July 23, 2019. For information on the Tricontinental movement, see Anne Garland Mahler, *From the Tricontinental to the Global South: Race, Radicalism, and Transnational Solidarity* (Durham, NC: Duke University Press, 2018).

30. See, for instance, Harmer, "Refuge in Revolution," 18.

31. Hill, interview, July 23, 2019.

32. ICAP declined to comment on this matter to the author during the research for this book.

33. William Lee Brent, *Long Time Gone: A Black Panther's True-Life Story of His Hijacking and Twenty-Five Years in Cuba* (New York: Times Books, 1996), 225.

34. One of those who refused was Margaret Randall, who worked for many years at the Instituo Cubano del Libro. Randall, *To Have Been There Then*, 31; Margaret Randall, "The Cuba I Knew Was Always Alive in Color," interview by María A. Cabrera Arús, *No Country Magazine*, April 12, 2021.

35. Charlie Hill, interview by author, Havana, July 21, 2019.

36. Kutty Hookham, quoted in Pia Koivunen, *Performing Peace and Friendship: The World Youth Festivals and Soviet Cultural Diplomacy* (Berlin: De Gruyter, 2022), 1.

37. Koivunen, *Performing Peace and Friendship*, 1. For the history of the youth festivals, see Margaret Peacock, "The Perils of Building Cold War Consensus at the 1957 Moscow World Festival of Youth and Students," *Cold War History* 12, no. 3 (2012): 515–35.

38. Anne Luke, "Within the Revolution, Everyone: Cuba, Youth, and Interrogating the 1970s Paradigm," in *Cuba's Forgotten Decade: How the 1970s Shaped the Revolution*, ed. Emily J. Kirk, Anna Clayfield, and Isabel Story (Lanham, MD: Lexington Books, 2018), 232–34.

39. Brent, *Long Time Gone*, 237–38.

40. Charlie Hill, interview by author, WhatsApp, December 4, 2023.

41. Brent, *Long Time Gone*, 238.

42. Brent, *Long Time Gone*, 238.

43. One foreign exile who was relocated during this time was Basilio José Mazor, a member of Argentina's People's Revolutionary Army, who hijacked a plane from Buenos Aires to Cuba in 1973. Mazor was sent to rural Pinar del Río Province to wait out the youth festival. Basilio José Mazor, interview by Daniel Van der Beken, *La Opinión*, July 14, 1991.

44. Brent, *Long Time Gone*, 239–41.

45. Charlie Hill, interview by author, WhatsApp, July 9, 2020.

46. Charlie Hill, interview by author, WhatsApp, April 24, 2025.

47. Harmer, "Refuge in Revolution," 14–15. See also Darío Croc Ures, *La colonia tupamara en Cuba: Un testimonio* (Montevideo: Argumento, 2019).

48. See Francisca Mercedes Diego-Olite, *Memoria viva: Destacamento Pedagógico Universitario Manuel Ascunce Domenech en la antigua provincia de Las Villas* (Santa Clara: Editorial Samuel Feijóo, 2022).

49. Charlie Hill, interview by author, WhatsApp, July 23, 2020. For more on La Escuela al Campo, see Denise F. Blum, "Cuba's School to the Countryside Program," in *Cuban Youth and Revolutionary Values: Educating the New Socialist Citizen* (Austin: University of Texas Press, 2011); John J. Cogan, "Cuba's Schools in the Countryside: A Model for the Developing World?," *Phi Delta Kappan* 60, no. 1 (1978): 30–32; Luke, *Youth and the Cuban Revolution*, 41–42.

50. Charlie Hill, interview by author, WhatsApp, July 9, 10, 11, 2020.

51. "Solidaridad Antimperialista, Paz y Amistad," *Granma*, July 29, 1978, 3–5; Luke, "Within the Revolution, Everyone," 234–36; Randall, *To Have Been There Then*, 107–8.

52. Hill, interview, April 24, 2025. The author's attempts to interview James Cherry, incarcerated during the time that research for this book was conducted, were unsuccessful.

53. Hill, interview, July 23, 2020.

54. Charlie Hill, interview by author, WhatsApp, July 24, 2020.

55. Hill, interview, July 24, 2020.

56. See Carmelo Mesa-Lago, *Cuba in the 1970's: Pragmatism and Institutionalization* (Albuquerque: University of New Mexico Press, 1974); Max Azicri, "Crime, Penal Law, and the Cuban Revolutionary Process," *Crime and Social Justice*, no. 23 (1985): 51–79.

57. For overviews of the Cuban legal system, see Julio César Guanche, "Cuba," in *The Oxford Handbook of Constitutional Law in Latin America*, ed. Conrado Hübner Mendes, Roberto Gargarella, and Sebastián Guidi (Oxford: Oxford University Press, 2021); Julienne E. Grant, Marisol Florén-Romero, Sergio D. Stone, Steven Alexandre da Costa, Lyonette Louis-Jacques, Cate Kellett, Jonathan Pratter, Teresa M. Miguel-Stearns, Eduardo Colón-Semidey, Jootaek Lee, Irene Kraft, and Yasmin Morais, "Guide to Cuban Law and Legal Research," *International Journal of Legal Information* 45, no. 2 (July 2017): 76–188.

58. A detailed analysis of the Cuban criminal justice system, with an extensive review of the scholarship, can be found in Deborah M. Weissman and Marsha Weissman, "The Moral Politics of Social Control: Political Culture and Ordinary Crime in Cuba," *Brooklyn Journal of International Law* 35, no. 2 (2010): 311–67.

59. Weissman and Weissman, "Moral Politics of Social Control," 311–67. For analyses of the 1979 Penal Code and of the Cuban legal system broadly during that period, see Harold J. Berman and Van R. Whiting Jr., "Impressions of Cuban Law," *American Journal of Comparative Law* 28, no. 3 (1980): 475–86; Raul Gomez Treto, "Thirty Years of Cuban Revolutionary Penal Law," *Latin American Perspectives* 18, no. 2 (1991): 114–25; Azicri, "Crime,

Penal Law," 51–79. For rehabilitation and the Cuban prison system, see Institute for Policy Studies, "Cuban Prisons: A Preliminary Report," *Social Justice* 15, no. 2 (1988): 55–62.

60. Azicri, "Crime, Penal Law," 71.

61. Berman and Whiting, "Impressions of Cuban Law," 482; for a short overview, see Cindy G. Buys and David S. Rodriguez, "Primer on the Cuban Legal System," August 9, 2017, https://doi.org/10.2139/ssrn.3016066.

62. Berman and Whiting, "Impressions of Cuban Law," 482.

63. Institute for Policy Studies, "Cuban Prisons," 56–57.

64. Berman and Whiting, "Impressions of Cuban Law," 483.

65. Berman and Whiting, "Impressions of Cuban Law," 485.

66. Berman and Whiting, "Impressions of Cuban Law," 483.

67. Charlie Hill, interview by author, WhatsApp, July 25, 2020.

68. Hill, interview, July 25, 2020.

69. Hill, interview, September 25, 2020.

70. Randall, *To Have Been There Then*, 94.

71. Hill, interview, July 25, 2020.

72. For the Cuban economy during this period, see Carmelo Mesa-Lago, "The Economy: Caution, Frugality, and Resilient Ideology," in *Cuba: Internal and International Affairs*, ed. Jorge I. Domínguez (Beverly Hills: Sage, 1982), 113–40.

73. Drew Fetherston and John Cummings, "Cuban Outbreak of Swine Fever Linked to CIA," *Newsday*, January 9, 1977; Mesa-Lago, "Economy," 126.

74. Ada Ferrer, *Cuba: An American History* (New York: Scribner, 2021), 408–19; William M. LeoGrande and Peter Kornbluh, *Back Channel to Cuba: The Hidden History of Negotiations Between Washington and Havana* (Chapel Hill: University of North Carolina Press, 2015), 214–19.

75. Charlie Hill, interview by author, Havana, December 28, 2023.

76. For a broader discussion of these themes, see Louis A. Pérez Jr., *On Becoming Cuban: Identity, Nationality, and Culture* (Chapel Hill: University of North Carolina Press, 2008).

77. The most comprehensive recent account is Susan Eva Eckstein, *Cuban Privilege: The Making of Immigrant Inequality in America* (Cambridge: Cambridge University Press, 2022).

78. LeoGrande and Kornbluh, *Back Channel to Cuba*, 214–16; Schoultz, *That Infernal Little Cuban Republic*, 353–55.

79. Barry Sklar, "Cuban Exodus," in *The Cuba Reader: The Making of a Revolutionary Society*, ed. Philip Brenner, William M. LeoGrande, Daniel Siegel, and Donna Rich (New York: Grove Press, 1989), 339–47.

80. Quoted in Schoultz, *That Infernal Little Cuban Republic*, 355.

81. Jo Thomas, "Havana Releases 33 Americans, and All but Three Return to U.S.," *New York Times*, October 28, 1980.

82. Thomas, "Havana Releases 33 Americans."

83. Thomas, "Havana Releases 33 Americans."

84. Thomas, "Havana Releases 33 Americans."

85. Asked in 2024 about the *New York Times* article, Charlie did not deny the reporter's account, saying only that he had made the claim because "Antar had died." He reiterated his previous version of the events of Rosenbloom's shooting, naming Michael as the killer. Charlie Hill, interview by author, WhatsApp, January 25, 2024.

86. Two individuals, who declined to be formally interviewed for this book or to assist with it, informed the author separately that reports of Charlie's comments to the reporter had contributed to their view of him as duplicitous.

87. United States v. Fonseca Machado, 53 F.3d 1242 (11th Cir. 1995).

88. Will Lester, "Authorities: Rafter Was Wanted in 1980 Hijacking to Cuba," Associated Press, June 23, 1993.

89. Hill, interview, July 24, 2020.

90. Marília Guimarães, *Nuestros años en Cuba: Un exilio entre sinsontes y el sabiá* (Havana: Casa Editora, 2008), 160, 166 (author's translation).

Chapter 11

1. Susan Eckstein, "Why Cuban Internationalism?," in *Cuban Political Economy: Controversies in Cubanology*, ed. Andrew Zimbalist (Boulder, CO: Westview Press, 1988), 158.

2. Eckstein, "Why Cuban Internationalism?," 157–60, 169–74.

3. Hill, interview, Havana, May 31, 2018. For the solidaristic and material rewards of medical internationalism, see Julie M. Feinsilver, "Fifty Years of Cuba's Medical Diplomacy: From Idealism to Pragmatism," *Cuban Studies* 41 (2010): 85–104; Eckstein, "Why Cuban Internationalism?," 166–74.

4. Piero Gleijeses, "Moscow's Proxy? Cuba and Africa, 1975–1988," *Journal of Cold War Studies* 8, no. 4 (2006): 98.

5. For Cuba's role in African anticolonialism, see, especially, Piero Gleijeses, *Conflicting Missions Havana, Washington, and Africa, 1959–1976* (Chapel Hill: University of North Carolina Press, 2003); Piero Gleijeses, *Visions of Freedom: Havana, Washington, Pretoria, and the Struggle for Southern Africa, 1976–1991* (Chapel Hill: University of North Carolina Press, 2013); Isaac Saney, *Cuba, Africa, and Apartheid's End: Africa's Children Return!* (Lanham, MD: Lexington Books, 2023).

6. Isaac Saney, "Homeland of Humanity: Internationalism Within the Cuban Revolution," *Latin American Perspectives* 36, no. 1 (2009): 111.

7. Quoted in Gleijeses, "Moscow's Proxy?," 103–4.

8. Fidel Castro, quoted in *Cuba's Internationalist Foreign Policy, 1975–1980* (New York: Pathfinder Press, 1981), 110, 115 (italics added).

9. Fidel Castro, *Cold War: Warnings for a Unipolar World* (Melbourne: Ocean Press, 2003), 49.

10. Francisco López Segrera, introduction to *De Eisenhower a Reagan: La política de Estados Unidos contra la revolución cubana* (Havana: Editorial Ciencias Sociales, 1987), 13–14.

11. "South Africa President Nelson Mandela Addresses Cuba Solidarity Conference," *Militant* 59, no. 39 (1995).

12. Gregory Randall, *To Have Been There Then: Memories of Cuba: 1969–1983*, trans. Margaret Randall (Brooklyn: Operating System, 2016), 101, 158.

13. Tanya Harmer, "Refuge in Revolution: Chilean and Uruguayan Exiles in Cuba, 1973–1990," *Cold War History*, July 2024, https://doi.org/10.1080/14682745.2024.2329281, 28–29.

14. Harmer, "Refuge in Revolution," 28.

15. For an account of Hatuey, see Bartolomé de las Casas, *A Short Account of the Destruction of the Indies*, ed. and trans. Nigel Griffin (New York: Penguin, 1999).

16. For more on the Reeve Brigade, see Steve Brouwer, *Revolutionary Doctors: How Venezuela and Cuba Are Changing the World's Conception of Health Care* (New York: Monthly Review Press, 2011), 29–30.

17. Aran Shetterly, *The Americano: Fighting with Castro for Cuba's Freedom* (Chapel Hill, NC: Algonquin Books, 2007).

18. Bob Baldock, *Wild Green Oranges: An Autobiographical Novel* (London: Clapton Press, 2021).

19. Jonathan M. Hansen, *Young Castro: The Making of a Revolutionary* (New York: Simon and Schuster, 2020), 98–104.

20. For Herboldt, see *Brothers in Arms*, directed by Jack Lewis (Idol Pictures, 2007). For the Cuban role in hastening the demise of apartheid, see Saney, *Cuba, Africa, and Apartheid's End*, 5–6.

21. *Brothers in Arms.*

22. *Brothers in Arms.*

23. The creator of the Fiesta del Fuego and its sponsoring institute in Santiago, Casa del Caribe, was the noted anthropologist, writer, and internationalist Joel James Figarola. See Carlos A. Lloga Domínguez, "Alcance de la cubanía en Joel James Figarola," *Santiago*, no. 117 (September–December 2008): 42–65; Joel James Figarola, *Alcance de la cubanía* (Santiago de Cuba: Editorial Oriente, 2001).

24. Charlie Hill, interview by author, Havana, July 22, 2019.

25. Hill, interview, July 22, 2019.

26. Charlie Hill, interview by author, Havana, July 23, 2019.

27. Hill, interview, July 23, 2019.

28. The first English-language book about Isla de La Juventud was written by Bill Brent's partner, Jane McManus, and is based on oral histories. See McManus, *Cuba's Island of Dreams: Voices from the Isle of Pines and Youth* (Gainesville: University Press of Florida, 2000).

29. Some of these students would later be interviewed by Jane McManus, who spent several weeks on the island with Bill Brent in 1990. McManus, *Cuba's Island of Dreams*, 131–34.

30. Charlie Hill, interview by author, Havana, July 24, 2019.

31. Hill, interview, July 24, 2019.

32. Hill, interview, July 23, 2019.

33. Hill, interview, July 24, 2019.

34. Hill, interview, July 24, 2019.

35. Charlie Hill, interview by author, WhatsApp, October 5, 2024.

36. Gary Marx, "U.S. Radicals Find Haven in Havana," *Chicago Tribune*, June 4, 2006.

37. Author's correspondence with Merriam Ansara, February 2022; Charlie Hill, interview by author, February 2022. Information on Brewton's fate is scant. "Brewton shot and killed in Jamaica on 12/15/75" states one source. *Aircraft Hijackings and Other Criminal Acts Against Civil Aviation Statistical and Narrative Reports* (Washington, DC: Federal Aviation Administration, Office of Aviation Security, May 1983), 25.

38. Jeffrey Haas, interview by author, Zoom, October 12, 2022. According to Haas, the other individual who participated in the attempted heist—Haas requested that the individual's name not be used but confirmed that it was not Richard Dixon—returned to Chicago in early 1976 and knocked on his door to convey the news about Brewton. Associates

of Huey Newton also tried to locate press coverage of the killing while Newton was in Cuba, without success. Memo, February 9, 1976, box 2, folder 18, H.P.N./Personal, Servant: Post Exile [1 of 3], 1975–76, Subseries 1: Personal, Series 1, Huey P. Newton Papers, Dr. Huey P. Newton Foundation Inc. collection, 1968–1994, M0864, Dept. of Special Collections, Stanford University Libraries.

39. Charlie Hill, interview by author, WhatsApp, February 13, 2022.

40. Dennis Cogswell, "Accused Killer Recalls Shooting," *Herald-Palladium*, July 23, 1976.

41. Cogswell, "Accused Killer Recalls Shooting"; see also Dennis Cogswell, "Accused Slayer Claims Self-Defense," *Herald-Palladium*, July 21, 1976.

42. "Fears Dixon Is Possible Target," *Holland City News*, January 15, 1976.

43. Haas, interview.

44. United States v. Richard Frederick Dixon, 592 F.2d 329 (6th Cir. 1979). Dixon was paroled in 2021.

45. Charlie Hill, interview by author, WhatsApp, July 10, 2020.

46. Charlie Hill, interview by author, WhatsApp, July 18, 2020.

47. Hill, interview, July 18, 2020.

48. Ellen Hampton, "For Former Black Militant, Island Is End of the Road," *Miami News*, June 16, 1987.

49. Anne Marie O'Connor, "Michael Finney's Last Flight," *Miami New Times*, May 8, 1991.

50. Patrick Critton, *Lion in the Foliage, Full Moon in the Sky: The Autobiography of Patrick Critton* (pub. by author, 2009), 139–40.

51. Anonymous, Radio Havana Cuba, Havana, July 18, 2023.

52. For more on *técnicos extranjeros*, see David L. Strug, "Witnessing the Revolution: North Americans in Cuba in the 1960s," *International Journal of Cuban Studies* 4, no. 1 (2012): 68–87.

53. Eduardo Moises Peñalver, "Redistributing Property: Natural Law, International Norms, and the Property Reforms of the Cuban Revolution," *Florida Law Review* 52, no. 1 (2000): 126–28. See also Jill Hamberg, "Cuba Protects Private Housing, Not Capitalist Real Estate," *Progressive Planning*, no. 189 (Fall 2011): 37–41; Douglas E. Matthews, "Real Property Law Under the Current Cuban Regime," *University of Miami International and Comparative Law Review* 3, no. 1 (1995).

54. Charlie Hill, interview by author, Havana, June 29, 2019.

55. Charlie Hill, Contrato de Compraventa de Vivienda, Banco Popular de Ahorro, Arroyo Naranjo, Havana, Cuba, July 17, 1984.

56. Imari Abubakari Obadele, *Free the Land! The True Story of the Trials of the RNA-11 in Mississippi and the Continuing Struggle to Establish an Independent Black Nation in Five States of the Deep South* (Washington, DC: House of Songhay, 1984), 168.

57. Assata Shakur, *Assata: An Autobiography* (Chicago: Lawrence Hill Books, 1987), 144. For Shakur's arrival and initial years in Cuba, see Teishan A. Latner, *Cuban Revolution in America: Havana and the Making of a United States Left, 1968–1992* (Chapel Hill: University of North Carolina Press, 2018), 236–39.

58. Edward Onaci, *Free the Land: The Republic of New Afrika and the Pursuit of a Black Nation-State* (Chapel Hill: University of North Carolina Press, 2020), 52.

59. Ron Howell, "On the Run with Assata Shakur: From Cuba, an Interview with the Black Liberation Army's Fugitive 'Soul,'" *Newsday*, October 11, 1987.

60. William Potts, interview by author, Havana, September 13, 2012; US Attorney's Office, Southern District of Florida, "U.S. Citizen in Cuba Returns to the United States and Is Arrested for 1984 Air Piracy Charge," news release, November 6, 2013, www.justice.gov/usao-sdfl/pr/us-citizen-cuba-returns-united-states-and-arrested-1984-air-piracy-charge.

61. Michael Muskal, "Man Returns to U.S. from Cuba to Face Charges in 1984 Air Hijacking," *Los Angeles Times*, November 6, 2013.

62. Yusimi Rodríguez, "William Potts on His Life in Cuba," pt. 1, *Havana Times*, September 22, 2013.

63. Potts, interview, September 13, 2012.

64. G. A. Elmer Griffin, "Murder on the Green: The Politics of Golf in the Eastern Caribbean," *Transition*, no. 4 (1997): 8–9.

65. Jon Nordheimer, "Torture Alleged in St. Croix Case," *New York Times*, May 5, 1973.

66. "Five Get Life Terms in 1972 Virgin Island Slayings: Spectators Shout," *New York Times*, August 14, 1973.

67. Peter Kerr, "New York-Bound Flight Hijacked to Cuba by Convicted Murderer," *New York Times*, January 1, 1985; "Hijacker Had Accomplice, Correction Officials Say," Associated Press, January 3, 1985.

68. LaBeet, also known as Ishmael Muslim Ali, is the subject of the documentary *The Skyjacker's Tale*, directed by Jamie Kastner (Cave 7, 2016). See also Michael A. Joseph, *Fountain Valley 1972* (Houston: Strategic Book, 2014).

69. Charlie Hill, interview by author, WhatsApp, November 3, 2024.

70. Hill, interview, November 3, 2024.

71. Charlie Hill, interview by author, Havana, June 5, 2018.

72. Charlie Hill, interview by author, Havana, July 1, 2018.

73. Charlie Hill, interview by author, Havana, August 1, 2019.

74. Hill, interview, August 1, 2019.

75. Charlie Hill, interview by author, WhatsApp, April 12, 2023.

76. Institute for Policy Studies, "Cuban Prisons: A Preliminary Report," *Social Justice* 15, no. 2 (1988): 61.

77. Institute for Policy Studies, "Cuban Prisons," 56.

78. Institute for Policy Studies, "Cuban Prisons," 58. For rehabilitation, see Mark S. Hamm, "Political Rehabilitation in Cuban Prisons: The Plan Progresivo," *Journal of Correctional Education* 40, no. 2 (1989): 72–79.

79. Institute for Policy Studies, "Cuban Prisons," 58–59.

80. Institute for Policy Studies, "Cuban Prisons," 59.

81. Institute for Policy Studies, "Cuban Prisons," 60.

82. UN General Assembly, *Convention Against Torture and Other Cruel, Inhuman or Degrading Treatment or Punishment*, December 10, 1984, www.hrweb.org/legal/cat.html.

83. Institute for Policy Studies, "Cuban Prisons," 59.

84. Charlie Hill, interview by author, WhatsApp, April 13, 2023.

85. Alejandro de la Fuente, *A Nation for All: Race, Inequality, and Politics in Twentieth-Century Cuba* (Chapel Hill: University of North Carolina Press, 2001), 314–15.

86. Hill, interview, April 13, 2023. Bill Brent's visit to a Cuban prison in the 1980s as a journalist for Radio Havana Cuba is similarly mixed. Describing acceptable living conditions, food, and medical care for prisoners, he nonetheless writes revealingly that prisons

anywhere in the world are "vivid proof that a society cannot live up to the hopes and dreams of its people." Brent, *Long Time Gone*, 265.

87. As of 2021 and likely earlier, Charlie had no criminal record in Cuba. Certificación de Antecedentes Penales, Registro de Sancionados, Ministerio de Justicia, República de Cuba, December 11, 2021.

88. "Journey to Cuba Began with New Mexico Killing," *Albuquerque Journal*, May 14, 1985.

89. "Journey to Cuba Began with New Mexico Killing."

90. Hill, interview, August 1, 2019.

91. Hampton, "For Former Black Militant."

Chapter 12

1. Isabel Story, *Soviet Influence on Cuban Culture, 1961–1987: When the Soviets Came to Stay* (Lanham, MD: Lexington Books, 2020), 23–25. The 1986 effort was known as the campaign to "rectify errors and negative tendencies." For the 1980s and state planning, see Andrew Zimbalist, "Interpreting Cuban Planning: Between a Rock and a Hard Place," in *Cuban Political Economy: Controversies in Cubanology*, ed. Andrew Zimbalist (Boulder, CO: Westview Press, 1988), 66–82. For more on "rectification," see Susan Eva Eckstein, *Back from the Future: Cuba Under Castro*, 2nd ed. (London: Routledge, 2003), 59–86.

2. Philip Bennett, "From Cuba, an Exile Looks Homeward," *Boston Globe*, February 27, 1989.

3. Bennett, "From Cuba."

4. Bennett, "From Cuba."

5. Bradford Martin, *The Other Eighties: A Secret History of America in the Age of Reagan* (New York: Hill and Wang, 2012).

6. Anne Marie O'Connor, "Michael Finney's Last Flight," *Miami New Times*, May 8, 1991.

7. Bennett, "From Cuba."

8. Bennett, "From Cuba."

9. O'Connor, "Michael Finney's Last Flight."

10. O'Connor, "Michael Finney's Last Flight."

11. R. v. Critton (P.D.), [2002] O.T.C. 451 (SC), 12.

12. Patrick Critton, *Lion in the Foliage, Full Moon in the Sky: The Autobiography of Patrick Critton* (pub. by author, 2009), 172.

13. C. J. Chivers, "Traced on Internet, Teacher Is Charged in '71 Jet Hijacking," *New York Times*, September 11, 2001.

14. R. v. Critton (P.D.), [2002] O.T.C. 451 (SC), 12–13.

15. Carlos Alzugaray Treto, "Cuban Foreign Policy During the 'Special Period': Interests, Aims, Outcomes," in *Redefining Cuban Foreign Policy: The Impact of the "Special Period,"* ed. H. Michael Erisman and John M. Kirk (Gainesville: University Press of Florida, 2006), 54–55.

16. Quoted in Louis A. Pérez, *Cuba: Between Reform and Revolution*, 5th ed. (Oxford: Oxford University Press, 2014), 316.

17. Hope Bastian, *Everyday Adjustments in Havana: Economic Reforms, Mobility, and Emerging Inequalities* (Lanham, MD: Lexington Books, 2018), 7.

18. Charlie Hill, interview by author, Havana, July 1, 2018.

19. For concise summaries of the Special Period, see Bastian, *Everyday Adjustments in Havana*, 2–7; Ariana Hernandez-Reguant, "Writing the Special Period," in *Cuba in the Special Period: Culture and Ideology in the 1990s* (New York: Palgrave Macmillan, 2009), 3–7.

20. State Department, memorandum, "The Decline and Fall of Castro," *Secret*, April 6, 1960, https://nsarchive.gwu.edu/document/27400-document-1-state-department-memorandum-decline-and-fall-castro-secret-april-6-1960.

21. Hill, interview, July 1, 2018.

22. Tod Robberson, "Story of Tug's Sinking Incited Cubans," *Washington Post*, September 11, 1994.

23. "Castro Threatens to Unleash Refugees After Riot Follows Ferry Hijackings," *Washington Post*, August 6, 1994.

24. Charlie Hill, interview by author, Havana, May 30, 2018.

25. "Cuban Officer's Alleged Killer Gets Asylum," *Tampa Bay Times*, February 3, 1995; William M. LeoGrande and Peter Kornbluh, *Back Channel to Cuba: The Hidden History of Negotiations between Washington and Havana* (Chapel Hill: University of North Carolina Press, 2015), 280–81.

26. "Havana Never Returned Hijackers to Albuquerque," *Albuquerque Journal*, August 13, 1994.

27. The *New York Times*, for its part, acknowledged that the United States had not returned Cubans who hijacked boats, "even when they used force." Steven Greenhouse, "U.S. Lets Cubans from Hijacking Stay, Detaining One," *New York Times*, August 11, 1994.

28. Bastian, *Everyday Adjustments in Havana*, 33–35.

29. See, especially, Andrew Zimbalist and Claes Brundenius, *The Cuban Economy: Measurement and Analysis of Socialist Performance* (Baltimore: Johns Hopkins University Press, 1989).

30. Charlie Hill, interview by author, Havana, June 28, 2019.

31. Esteban Morales Domínguez, *Race in Cuba: Essays on the Revolution and Racial Inequality*, ed. and trans. Gary Prevost and August Nimtz (New York: Monthly Review Press, 2013), 67–68.

32. See Amalia L. Cabezas, *Economies of Desire: Sex and Tourism in Cuba and the Dominican Republic* (Philadelphia: Temple University Press, 2009); Noelle M. Stout, *After Love: Queer Intimacy and Erotic Economies in Post-Soviet Cuba* (Durham, NC: Duke University Press Books, 2014).

33. Hill, interview, June 28, 2019.

34. "Man Killed in Havana as Blasts Hit 3 Hotels," *New York Times*, September 5, 1997.

35. Gail Epstein Nieves, "Basulto Testifies on Role as Anti-Castro Operative," *Miami Herald*, March 13, 2001.

36. LeoGrande and Kornbluh, *Back Channel to Cuba*, 304–13.

37. Joelle Attinger, Cathy Booth, and Reginald K. Brack Jr., "Interview: Fidel's Defense," *Time*, March 11, 1996.

38. Charlie Hill, interview by author, WhatsApp, October 10, 2024.

39. LeoGrande and Kornbluh, *Back Channel to Cuba*, 307.

40. Lars Schoultz, *That Infernal Little Cuban Republic: The United States and the Cuban Revolution* (Chapel Hill: University of North Carolina Press, 2011), 481–83.

41. United Nations, "Downing of Planes Sovereign Act in Defence of Borders, Cuba tells General Assembly," March 6, 1996, news release, https://press.un.org/en/1996/19960306.ga9052.r1.html.

42. Stephen Low, National Security Council, to Henry Kissinger, memorandum, "SR-71 Overflights of Cuba," Washington, March 10, 1975, in *Foreign Relations of the United States, 1969–1976*, vol. E–11, pt. 1, *Documents on Mexico; Central America; and the Caribbean, 1973–1976*, ed. Halbert Jones and Douglas Kraft (Washington, DC: Government Printing Office, 2015), doc. 295, https://history.state.gov/historicaldocuments/frus1969-76ve11p1/d295. See also Schoultz, *That Infernal Little Cuban Republic*, 358–59.

43. Kevin Fedarko, "This Cold War Is Back," *Time*, March 11, 1996.

44. Charlie Hill, interview by author, Havana, July 26, 2019.

45. Hill, interview, July 26, 2019.

46. Charlie Hill, interview by author, WhatsApp, August 1, 2023.

47. Josh Barbanel, "3 Killed in Armored Car Holdup," *New York Times*, October 21, 1981; Alexander Reid, "F. B. I. Captures a Key Fugitive in Brink's CASE," *New York Times*, February 13, 1986. For more on the Black Liberation Army, see Akinyele Omowale Umoja, "Repression Breeds Resistance: The Black Liberation Army and the Radical Legacy of the Black Panther Party," *New Political Science* 21, no. 2 (1999): 131–55. For Mutulu Shakur's biography and significance, see Akinyele Umoja, "Straight Ahead: The Life of Resistance of Dr. Mutulu Shakur," *Souls: A Critical Journal of Black Politics, Culture, and Society* 23, nos. 1–2 (2022): 4–35.

48. For more on Nehanda Abiodun in Cuba, see Teishan A. Latner, *Cuban Revolution in America: Havana and the Making of a United States Left, 1968–1992* (Chapel Hill: University of North Carolina Press, 2018), 242–51.

49. Hill, interview, August 1, 2023.

50. O'Connor, "Michael Finney's Last Flight."

51. Ron Ridenour, *Backfire: The CIA's Biggest Burn* (Havana: Editorial Jose Marti, 1991).

52. Ron Ridenour, "Reflections on Fidel, Cuba, Internationalism and Tamils," *Havana Times*, November 29, 2016; Nancy Nusser and Annie O'Connor, "For Political Exiles, Cuba Can Be Refuge, Island Prison," *Austin American Statesman*, February 3, 1991.

53. For the Puerto Rican independence struggle, see Nelson A. Denis, *War Against All Puerto Ricans: Revolution and Terror in America's Colony* (New York: Nation Books, 2015); Michael González-Cruz, *Militant Puerto Ricans: Migrants, Armed Struggle and Political Prisoners* (pub. by author, 2020).

54. Robert D. McFadden, "4 Killed, 44 Injured in Fraunces Tavern Blast," *New York Times*, January 25, 1975; "Text of Note Found Near Blast," *New York Times*, January 25, 1975; "Puerto Rico Bomb Kills 2, Injures 11," *New York Times*, January 13, 1975.

55. Selwyn Raab, "A Maimed Terrorist Flees Cell at Bellevue," *New York Times*, May 22, 1979.

56. Storer H. Rowley, "U.S. Angry at Mexico," *Chicago Tribune*, June 29, 1988.

57. Extradition Treaty, U.S.-Mex., May 4, 1978, U.N.T.S. No. 19462, at 191, https://treaties.un.org/doc/Publication/UNTS/Volume%201207/volume-1207-I-19462-English.pdf.

58. Dan Williams, "Mexicans Cool to U.S. Protest over Terrorist," *Los Angeles Times*, July 1, 1988.

59. Figure for Nicaraguan teachers is from Susan Eckstein, "Why Cuban Internationalism?," in *Cuban Political Economy: Controversies in Cubanology*, ed. Andrew Zimbalist (Boulder, CO: Westview Press, 1988), 158.

60. Bryna Brennan, "2 Killed in Contra Attack on Boat, Nicaragua Says," *Washington Post*, August 3, 1988.

61. Gail Walker, interview by author, New York, April 24, 2019.

62. Douglas Friedman, "Popular Education and Politics in Cuba: The Centro Memorial Dr. Martin Luther King Jr. and the Gramscian Civil Society Ideal," *International Journal of Cuban Studies* 4, no. 1 (2012): 36–52.

63. Hill, interview, July 26, 2019.

64. Stokely Carmichael, *Ready for Revolution: The Life and Struggles of Stokely Carmichael (Kwame Ture)*, with Michael Ekwueme Thelwell (New York: Simon and Schuster, 2003), 762–64.

65. Charlie Hill, interview by author, Havana, July 22, 2019.

66. Peniel E. Joseph, *Stokely: A Life* (New York: Basic Civitas, 2014), 213–25, 289–317.

67. Frantz Fanon, *The Wretched of the Earth* (New York: Grove Press, 1963), 99.

68. Hill, interview, July 22, 2019.

69. Hill, interview, July 22, 2019.

70. Charlie Hill, interview by author, WhatsApp, March 2, 2024.

71. For more on Fulani Sunni-Ali, see Asantewa Sunni-Ali, "Fulani Sunni-Ali (1948–2016)," in *Black Power Encyclopedia: From "Black Is Beautiful" to Urban Uprisings*, ed. Akinyele Umoja, Karin L. Stanford, and Jasmin A. Young (Santa Barbara, CA: Greenwood, 2018), 767–71.

72. Charlie Hill, interview by author, Havana, July 23, 2019.

73. Hill, interview, July 26, 2019.

74. Hill, interview, March 2, 2024.

75. Charlie Hill, interview by author, Havana, August 1, 2019.

76. Hill, interview, August 1, 2019.

77. Hill, interview, March 2, 2024.

78. Asantewa Sunni-Ali and Ayana Sunni-Ali, interview by author, Zoom, January 25, 2023.

79. Asantewa Sunni-Ali, interview, Zoom, January 25, 2023.

80. Latner, *Cuban Revolution in America*, 244–45.

81. Quoted in Geoffrey Baker, *Buena Vista in the Club: Rap, Reggaetón, and Revolution in Havana* (Durham, NC: Duke University Press, 2011), 369.

82. I borrow this framing from Devyn Spence Benson, *Antiracism in Cuba: The Unfinished Revolution* (Chapel Hill: University of North Carolina Press, 2016). For the significance of hip-hop on the island from a Cuban perspective, see Roberto Zurbano, "El Rap Cubano: Can't Stop, Won't Stop the Movement!," trans. Kate Levitt, in *Cuba in the Special Period: Culture and Ideology in the 1990s*, ed. Ariana Hernandez-Reguant (New York: Palgrave Macmillan, 2009), 149.

83. Hill, interview, July 22, 2019.

84. Hill, interview, July 22, 2019.

85. Hill, interview, July 22, 2019.

86. Hill, interview, July 22, 2019.

87. Hill, interview, July 22, 2019.

88. "Hijackers Admit to Shooting," Associated Press, November 11, 1999.

89. Dirk Johnson, "Puerto Ricans Clinton Freed Leave Prisons," *New York Times*, September 11, 1999; President Bill Clinton to Representative Henry A. Waxman, "Clemency

for FALN Members," read by Waxman to House Committee on Government Reform, September 21, 1999, C-SPAN, www.c-span.org/video/?152246-1/clemency-faln-members.

Chapter 13

1. The author recalls this practice while flying on Cubana de Aviación flights. The phrase references Fidel Castro's La Primera Declaración de La Habana speech of September 2, 1960, in which Castro proclaimed, "¡Cuba es el territorio libre de América!"

2. Jane McManus, *Getting to Know Cuba: A Travel Guide* (New York: St. Martin's Press, 1989), back cover.

3. Brett Skakun, "N. M. Fugitive Pursues Life of Freedom in Havana," *Albuquerque Journal*, March 8, 1981.

4. Skakun, "N. M. Fugitive Pursues Life of Freedom."

5. Tim Golden, "U.S., Avoiding Castro, Relaxes Rules on Cuba," *New York Times*, July 7, 1999; Cuban Assets Control Regulations: Sales of Food and Agricultural Inputs; Remittances; Educational, Religious, and Other Activities; Travel-Related Transactions; U.S. Intellectual Property, Rules and Regulations, Department of the Treasury, OFAC, 64 Fed. Reg. 25808 (May 13, 1999).

6. Charlie Hill, interview by author, Havana, July 21, 2019.

7. Eugene Robinson, *Last Dance in Havana: The Final Days of Fidel and the Start of the New Cuban Revolution* (New York: Free Press, 2004), 200.

8. Ellen Hampton, "For Former Black Militant, Island Is End of the Road," *Miami News*, June 16, 1987.

9. Doug Grow, "'Thug' or Revolutionary, He's a Fugitive in Havana," *Star Tribune*, February 6, 2000.

10. Grow, "'Thug' or Revolutionary."

11. Margaret Randall, *I Never Left Home: Poet, Feminist, Revolutionary* (Durham, NC: Duke University Press, 2020), 183.

12. Charlie Hill, interview by author, Havana, May 28, 2022.

13. Nehanda Abiodun, interview by author, Havana, July 17, 2018.

14. Brett Sokol, "Exiled in Havana," *Miami New Times*, September 7, 2000.

15. Abiodun, interview, July 17, 2018.

16. Charlie Hill, Certificate of Birth, State of Illinois, Division of Vital Statistics and Records, Primary Distribution No. 3593; Scott Simons, "Weber Family Supplied Medical Care for All," *Herald and Review*, October 30, 1983.

17. Simons, "Weber Family Supplied Medical Care."

18. Helen Yaffe, *We Are Cuba! How a Revolutionary People Have Survived in a Post-Soviet World* (New Haven, CT: Yale University Press, 2020), 168–69; Julie Feinsilver, "Fifty Years of Cuba's Medical Diplomacy—from Idealism to Pragmatism," *Cuban Studies* 41 (2010).

19. Charlie Hill, interview by author, Havana, June 28, 2019.

20. Robert Huish, "No Secret Cure: Why the 1970s Hold the Mystery to Cuba's Health Paradox," in *Cuba's Forgotten Decade: How the 1970s Shaped the Revolution*, ed. Emily J. Kirk, Anna Clayfield, and Isabel Story (Lanham, MD: Lexington Books, 2018), 99.

21. Hill, interview, June 28, 2019.

22. For racial discrimination, see Danielle Pilar Clealand, *The Power of Race in Cuba: Racial Ideology and Black Consciousness During the Revolution* (Oxford: Oxford University Press, 2017), 149–67.

23. "Ron Howell, "Tourism Reviving Racism in Cuba," *Newsday*, May 18, 2001.

24. Anecdotes of such experiences in later years are related in Jafari S. Allen, *¡Venceremos? The Erotics of Black Self-Making in Cuba* (Durham, NC: Duke University Press, 2011), 22–24; Tanya L. Saunders, *Cuban Underground Hip Hop: Black Thoughts, Black Revolution, Black Modernity* (Austin: University of Texas Press, 2015), 43–46; Mark Q. Sawyer, *Racial Politics in Post-Revolutionary Cuba* (Cambridge: Cambridge University Press, 2005), 102–3.

25. Hill, interview, July 21, 2019.

26. Fidel Castro, speech, Plaza de la Revolución, February 4, 1962, published in English as *The Second Declaration of Havana: Cuba's Answer to the OAS* (New York: Pioneer, 1962); Fidel Castro, interview by Lee Lockwood, in Lockwood, *Castro's Cuba, Cuba's Fidel* (New York: Macmillan, 1967), 128.

27. Fidel Castro, speech to Cuba solidarity rally, Riverside Church, New York, September 8, 2000, www.cuba.cu/gobierno/discursos/2000/ing/f080900i.html.

28. Esteban Morales Domínguez, *Race in Cuba: Essays on the Revolution and Racial Inequality*, ed. and trans. Gary Prevost and August Nimtz (New York: Monthly Review Press, 2013), 87, 99.

29. Charlie Hill, interview by author, WhatsApp, October 17, 2024.

30. Hill, interview, October 17, 2024.

31. Marc Frank, "Cubans Allowed to Stay at Tourist Hotels," *Reuters*, March 31, 2008.

32. Hill, interview, July 21, 2019.

33. For Cuban approaches to criminal justice, see Mark H. Kruger, "Community-Based Crime Control in Cuba," *Contemporary Justice Review* 10, no. 1 (2007): 101–14; Raul Gomez Treto, "Thirty Years of Cuban Revolutionary Penal Law," *Latin American Perspectives* 18, no. 2 (1991): 114–25; Deborah M. Weissman and Marsha Weissman, "The Moral Politics of Social Control: Political Culture and Ordinary Crime in Cuba," *Brooklyn Journal of International Law* 35, no. 2 (2010): 311–67.

34. Charlie Hill, interview by author, WhatsApp, August 6–7, 2025.

35. Hill, interview, August 6–7, 2025.

36. Hill, interview, October 17, 2024.

37. "Speech given by Dr. Fidel Castro Ruz, President of the Republic of Cuba, the day of the tragic events that occurred in the United States, *Portal Cuba*, September 11, 2001," www.cuba.cu/gobierno/discursos/2001/ing/f110901i.html.

38. Quoted in Lars Schoultz, *That Infernal Little Cuban Republic: The United States and the Cuban Revolution* (Chapel Hill: University of North Carolina Press, 2011), 535.

39. "Nabbed After 30 Years: Teacher Seized in Broadway Bank Heist and Shootout," *New York Daily News*, September 11, 2001; R. v. Critton (P.D.), [2002] O.T.C. 451 (SC), 12.

40. "Nabbed After 30 Years."

41. Corey Kilgannon, "Teacher Is Sentenced for Hijacking Past," *New York Times*, June 16, 2002.

42. Kilgannon, "Teacher Is Sentenced."

43. Teishan A. Latner, "Assata Shakur Is Welcome Here: Havana, Black Freedom Struggle, and U.S.-Cuba Relations," *Souls: A Critical Journal of Black Politics, Culture, and Society* 19, no. 4 (2018): 455–77.

44. This section draws on a long profile on Abiodun written by the author and more recent interviews with her. Teishan A. Latner, *Cuban Revolution in America: Havana and the Making of a United States Left, 1968–1992* (Chapel Hill: University of North Carolina Press, 2018), 242–51; Nehanda Abiodun, interview by author, Havana, July 17–18, 2018.

45. Janet Hill King, interview by author, WhatsApp, August 1, 2022.

46. Charlie was visited in Havana by a sister and a brother in May 2024.

47. City of Fairbanks, Police Department, Unsolved Murders, accessed July 2023, www.fairbanksalaska.us/police/page/unsolved-homicides (site discontinued).

48. Charlie Hill, interview by author, Havana, June 2019.

49. Antara Finney declined to be interviewed for this book. A May 1991 article by reporter Anne Marie O'Connor states Antara's age as two years old in May 1991. "Michael Finney," *Miami New Times*, May 8, 1991.

50. Anne Marie O'Connor, "Michael Finney's Last Flight," *Miami New Times*, May 8, 1991.

51. Charlie Hill, interview by author, WhatsApp, March 2, 2024.

52. Charlie Hill, interview by author, WhatsApp, November 5, 2024.

53. Charlie Hill, interview by author, Havana, June 5, 2018.

54. Charlie Hill, interview by author, WhatsApp, March 16, 2022.

55. Office of the Attorney General of the State of New Jersey, "Reward Increased to $1 Million on Escaped, Convicted Killer, Joanne Chesimard," news release, May 2, 2005.

56. Office of the Attorney General of the State of New Jersey, "Reward Increased to $1 Million."

57. For an examination of Shakur's life in exile, see Latner, *Cuban Revolution in America*; Teishan A. Latner, "Assata Shakur: The Political Life of Political Exile," in *Black Power Afterlives: The Enduring Significance of the Black Panther Party*, ed. Diane Fujino and Matef Harmachis (Chicago: Haymarket Books, 2020).

58. Charlie Hill, interview by author, Havana, July 23, 2019.

59. Charlie Hill, interview by author, WhatsApp, May 22, 2020.

60. Sanjay Gupta, "The Doctrine of Pre-Emptive Strike: Application and Implications During the Administration of President George W. Bush," *International Political Science Review* 29, no. 2 (2008): 181–96.

61. Charlie Hill, interview by author, WhatsApp, November 9, 2024.

62. William M. LeoGrande and Peter Kornbluh, *Back Channel to Cuba: The Hidden History of Negotiations Between Washington and Havana* (Chapel Hill: University of North Carolina Press, 2015), 368–69; Review and Disposition of Individuals Detained at the Guantánamo Bay Naval Base and Closure of Detention Facilities, Exec. Order No. 13492, 74 Fed. Reg. 4897 (January 22, 2009), www.govinfo.gov/content/pkg/DCPD-200900005/pdf/DCPD-200900005.pdf.

63. Assembly Concurrent Resolution No. 61, State of New Jersey, 214th legislature (prefiled for introduction in the 2010 session).

64. Tracey Eaton, "U.S. Fugitive Charles Hill Reflects on His 38 Years in Cuba," *Cuba News*, September 2009, 9.

65. Eaton, "U.S. Fugitive Charles Hill."

66. DeWayne Wickham, "Fugitives Have Good Reason to Fear Closer Ties to Cuba," *USA Today*, October 6, 2009.

67. Wickham, "Fugitives Have Good Reason to Fear."

68. DeWayne Wickham, "Testimony Could Change Course of Black Revolutionary's Trial," *Gannett News Service*, October 15, 2009.

69. Wickham, "Testimony Could Change Course."

70. John I. Gilderbloom, "Cuba," *Encyclopedia of 20th-Century Architecture*, vol. 1, *A–F*, ed. R. Stephen Sennott (Dearborn: Fitzroy Dearborn, 2004), 330. See also Michael Z. Wise, "The Architectural Importance of the U.S. Embassy in Havana, Cuba," *Architect*, December 23, 2014.

71. Charlie Hill, interview by author, Havana, June 22, 2018.

72. Hill, interview, June 22, 2018.

73. Hill, interview, June 22, 2018.

74. Shaunely de la Mercedes Hill Pedroso, interview by author, Havana, July 4, 2023.

75. See LeoGrande and Kornbluh, *Back Channel to Cuba*.

76. Hill, interview, June 22, 2018.

Chapter 14

1. A transcript of Castro's address was published online by the *Washington Post* an hour later. "Speech by Cuban President Raul Castro on Re-Establishing U.S.-Cuba Relations," *Washington Post*, December 17, 2014.

2. For the story of the Cuban intelligence agents, see Stephen Kimber, *What Lies Across the Water: The Real Story of the Cuban Five* (Halifax: Fernwood, 2013); Fernando Morais, *The Last Soldiers of the Cold War: The Story of the Cuban Five* (New York: Verso, 2015).

3. "Speech by Cuban President Raul Castro," *Washington Post*.

4. Dagoberto Rodríguez Barrera, quoted in Esteban Morales Domínguez and Gary Prevost, *United States-Cuban Relations: A Critical History* (Lanham, MD: Lexington Books, 2018), 16.

5. For US sanctions on Cuba and the issue of extraterritoriality, see Helen Yaffe, "US Sanctions Cuba 'to Bring About Hunger, Desperation and the Overthrow of the Government'", in Stuart Davis and Immanuel Ness, eds., *Sanctions as War: Anti-Imperialist Perspectives on American Geo-Economic Strategy* (Leiden: Brill, 2021) 129–47; Joy Gordon, "The U.S. Embargo Against Cuba and the Diplomatic Challenges to Extraterritoriality," *Fletcher Forum of World Affairs* 36, no. 1 (Winter 2012): 63–79.

6. Michael Weissenstein and Andrea Rodríguez, "Cuba Says It Has a Right to Grant Asylum to US Fugitives," Associated Press, December 22, 2014.

7. "A Conversation with Gov. Chris Christie and Steve Adubato," *NJ Spotlight News*, December 22, 2014.

8. Charlie Hill, interview by author, Havana, June 4, 2018.

9. Michael Coleman, "Udall Will Lead U.S. Delegation to Cuba," *Albuquerque Journal*, May 22, 2015.

10. Hill, interview, June 4, 2018.

11. Hill, interview, June 4, 2018.

12. Mark Oswald, "Lawyer Wants Charges Against Suspect in Officer's Death Tossed," *Albuquerque Journal*, March 11, 2015.

13. Patrick Oppmann, "Admitted Hijacker Dreams of Home After 43 Years Hiding Out in Cuba," CNN, April 9, 2015.

14. Oppmann, "Admitted Hijacker."

15. Oppmann, "Admitted Hijacker."

16. Oppmann, "Admitted Hijacker."

17. Oppmann, "Admitted Hijacker."

18. Oppmann, "Admitted Hijacker."

19. Jason Flores-Williams, statement to Alexander Zaitchik, "How I Hijacked a Plane and Spent the Next 44 Years Living in Cuba," *Thrillist*, January 27, 2016.

20. Carlos Álvarez Rodríguez, "The Long Read: The Story of Charlie Hill, an FBI Fugitive in Havana," *Huck*, March 25, 2016.

21. Álvarez Rodríguez, "Long Read."

22. *I Am Rebel*, season 1, episode 1, "Jacked," directed by Lance Edmands, premiered June 4, 2016, *National Geographic*.

23. *The Skyjacker's Tale*, directed by Jamie Kastner (2016).

24. Joy Blackburn, "Filmmaker Discusses Fountain Valley Documentary," *Virgin Islands Daily News*, September 20, 2017.

25. Blackburn, "Filmmaker Discusses Fountain Valley Documentary."

26. Certificación de Nacimiento, Registro de Estado Civil, Arroyo Naranjo, Ciudad de La Habana, República de Cuba, August 21, 2006.

27. Yeskenia Cardona Mauricio, interview by author, Havana, July 4, 2023.

28. Charlie Hill, interview by author, Havana, July 4, 2023.

29. *Charlie*, directed by Kadri Koop (2016), 13 min.

30. The author viewed these selections (and others like them) on Cuban television in 2016 and 2017: *The Black Power Mixtape, 1967–1975*, directed by Göran Olsson (2011); *The Black Panthers: Vanguard of the Revolution*, directed by Stanley Nelson Jr. (2015); *Nina*, directed by Cynthia Mort (2016).

31. Oppmann, "Admitted Hijacker."

32. Shaunely de la Mercedes Hill Pedroso, interview by author, Havana, July 16, 2018.

33. Charlie Hill, interview by author, Havana, January 3, 2022. Charlie was eventually granted permanent residency status in 2023.

34. See, for instance, Robin Hemley, "Why My Students and I Met with a Potentially Violent Fugitive in Cuba," *Observer*, February 7, 2015.

35. Oscar Ferrer, "Political Prisoners in the United States," *Granma*, December 31, 1978, English edition; John Rice, "Castro Defends Fugitive Sought by U.S.," Associated Press, May 11, 2005.

36. Álvarez Rodríguez, "Long Read."

37. Nehanda Abiodun, interview by author, Havana, July 18, 2018.

38. Abiodun, interview, July 18, 2018.

39. This perception of Charlie appears to be widely shared, both in Cuba and among foreigners who have encountered him there. Anonymous, interview by author, June 30, 2019.

40. Quoted in Robert Siegel, "Calif. Congressman Pushes Cuba to Extradite Man Who Hijacked Plane in 1971," NPR, March 18, 2016.

41. "Eldridge Cleaver: 'I'm Turning into a Patriot,'" *Kansas City Star*, September 28, 1975. For Cleaver in Algeria, see Justin Gifford, *Revolution or Death: The Life of Eldridge Cleaver* (Chicago: Lawrence Hill Books, 2020), 183–229.

42. "Speech by Cuban President Raul Castro," *Washington Post*.

43. Rick Fuentes, "Meet the Fugitive U.S. Terrorists Sheltered by Cuba," *New York Post*, March 16, 2016.

Chapter 15

1. "Fidel Castro, Cuba's Leader of Revolution, Dies at 90," BBC, November 26, 2016. English translation in original.

2. Various accounts attempted to capture the significance of this moment in Cuba. See, for instance, Ned Sublette, "Fidel Castro: A First-Person Account of the Day the Music Stopped in Cuba," *Billboard*, December 2, 2016.

3. Charlie Hill, interview by author, WhatsApp, October 4, 2023.

4. White House, Office of the Press Secretary, "Statement by the President on Cuba Policy Changes," December 17, 2014.

5. "Remarks by Ambassador Josefina Vidal at 'The Cuban Revolution at 60' Conference, Dalhousie University, Halifax, October 31, 2019," *Cuban International Relations at 60: Reflections on Global Connections*, ed. Mervyn J. Bain and Chris Walker (Lanham, MD: Lexington Books, 2021), 18.

6. Charlie Hill, interview by author, Havana, June 5, 2018.

7. William LeoGrande, "Coercive Diplomacy or Constructive Engagement: Sixty Years of US Policy Toward Cuba," in *Cuban International Relations at 60: Reflections on Global Connections*, ed. Mervyn J. Bain and Chris Walker (Lanham, MD: Lexington Books, 2021), 39–44.

8. Cuba's pre-1959 battle for self-determination is vivid in Ada Ferrer, *Cuba: An American History* (New York: Scribner, 2021).

9. See Louis A. Pérez Jr., "More Than Six Decades of Sanctions on Cuba," *NACLA*, October 24, 2022.

10. See Pérez, "More Than Six Decades."

11. The National Endowment for Democracy and the United States Agency for International Development "democracy promotion" programs in Cuba are woefully understudied by scholars. See William I. Robinson, "Pushing Polyarchy: The US-Cuba Case and the Third World," *Third World Quarterly* 16, no. 4 (1995): 643–59. For the National Endowment for Democracy's goals and methods, see "Case Study: NED Programs Focus on Long-Term Effort to Open up Cuba," accessed August 24, 2025, www.ned.org/about/how-we-work/case-study-ned-programs-focus-long-term-effort-open-cuba/.

12. Fidel Castro's address was made during the May Day celebration of 2000. Presidencia y Gobierno de Cuba, "Concepto de Revolutción," www.presidencia.gob.cu/es/noticias/concepto-de-revolucion/.

13. Anonymous, commentary to author, Havana, December 21, 2018. For World Bank study, see Barbara Bruns and Javier Luque, *Great Teachers: How to Raise Student Learning in Latin America and the Caribbean* (Washington, DC: World Bank, 2014).

14. Charlie Hill, interview by author, Havana, July 22, 2019.

15. The phrase, well known in Cuba, is a reference to Fidel Castro's June 1961 "*Palabras a los intelectuales*" (Words to intellectuals). In a speech clarifying the parameters of intellectual debate following the censorship of the documentary film *PM*, the Cuban leader proclaimed "dentro de la Revolución, todo; contra la Revolución, nada" (inside the Revolution everything [is permissible], against the Revolution, nothing), noting that the revolutionary process had its own rights, first among them the "right to exist." "Discurso pronunciado por el Comandante en Jefe Fidel Castro Ruz como conclusión de las reuniones con los intelectuales cubanos, efectuadas en la Biblioteca Nacional el 16, 23 y 30 de junio de 1961," *Portal Cuba*, June 30, 1961, www.cuba.cu/gobierno/discursos/1961/esp/f300661e.html.

16. Much critical commentary has been devoted to these questions in the context of the 2019 Cuban Constitution. See, for instance, Ailynn Torres Santana, "Socialism from Above: Assessing the Cuban Experience," *Dissent*, Winter 2019.

17. Dayana Rojas, Jorge Saavedra, Mariya Petrova, Yue Pan, and José Szapocznik, "Predictors of COVID-19 Fatality: A Worldwide Analysis of the Pandemic over Time and in Latin America," *Journal of Epidemiology and Global Health* 12 (2022): 150–59; Mary Anne Powell, Paul C. Erwin, and Pedro Mas Bermejo, "Comparing the COVID-19 Responses in Cuba and the United States," *American Journal of Public Health* 111, no. 12 (2021): 2186–93; Pedro Mas Bermejo, Lizet Sánchez Valdés, Lorenzo Somarriba López, Nelly Cristina Valdivia Onega, María Josefina Vidal Ledo, Ileana Alfonso Sánchez, Armando Seuc Jo, Yudivian Almeida Cruz, and Roberto Morales Ojeda, "Equity and the Cuban National Health System's Response to COVID-19," *Pan American Journal of Public Health* 45 (June 2021): 1–9.

18. The clothing line, BarbarA's Power Cuba, was founded in June 2016 in Havana.

19. Charlie Hill, interview by author, Havana, December 19, 2023.

20. One resource for understanding the July 11, 2021, protests in Cuba is a symposium organized by William M. LeoGrande, John M. Kirk, and Philip Brenner containing essays from Cuban and foreign commentators, which have been compiled into *The Road Ahead: Cuba After the July 11 Protests*, published online by the Center for Latin American and Latino Studies at American University, www.american.edu/centers/latin-american-latino-studies/the-road-ahead-cuba-after-the-july-11-protests.cfm. See also Alexander Hall Lujardo (coordinator), *Cuba 11J: Perspectivas contrahegemónicas de las protestas sociales* (Creative Commons, 2023); Editorial de La Tizza, "Tendremos que volver al future," *La Tizza*, July 15, 2021; Ailynn Torres Santana, "J-11 in Cuba," *NACLA*, July 22, 2021.

21. Carla Gloria Colomé, "11 de julio en San Antonio de los Baños: Lo que se ve/lo que no se ve," *El Estornudo*, July 22, 2021.

22. Nora Gámez Torres, "Cuba Admits to Massive Emigration Wave: A Million People Left in Two Years amid Crisis," *Miami Herald*, July 24, 2024.

23. Hope Bastian, *Everyday Adjustments in Havana: Economic Reforms, Mobility, and Emerging Inequalities* (Lanham, MD: Lexington Books, 2018), 12–13.

24. Hill, interview, December 19, 2023.

25. *Brothers in Arms*, directed by Jack Lewis, Idol Pictures, 2007.

26. *Brothers in Arms*.

27. *Brothers in Arms*.

28. Marcus Toerien, "John Nkadimeng and the Cuban Boy from the Cape," *Journalist*, August 25, 2020.

29. Carmen Lira Saade, "Soy el responsable de la persecución a homosexuales que hubo en Cuba: Fidel Castro," *La Jornada*, August 31, 2010.

30. "Discurso pronunciado por el Presidente de los Consejos de Estado y de Ministros de la República de Cuba, General de Ejército Raúl Castro Ruz en la clausura de la Asamblea Nacional del Poder Popular, en el Palacio de Convenciones, el 20 de diciembre de 2009," *Portal Cuba*, www.cuba.cu/gobierno/rauldiscursos/2009/esp/r201209e.html.

31. Hill, interview, July 22, 2019.

32. Hill, interview, July 22, 2019.

33. Fidel Castro, speech to the third congress of the PCC, February 7, 1986, published in the *Black Scholar* 20, no. 5/6 (1989): 9.

34. Esteban Morales Domínguez, *Race in Cuba: Essays on the Revolution and Racial Inequality*, ed. and trans. Gary Prevost and August Nimtz (New York: Monthly Review Press, 2013), 22.

35. Morales Domínguez, *Race in Cuba*, 76–77.

36. Jean Stubbs and Pedro Peréz Sarduy, "The Rite of Social Communion," in *AfroCuba: An Anthology of Cuban Writing on Race, Politics and Culture* (Melbourne: Ocean Press, 1993), 11.

37. Stubbs and Peréz Sarduy, "Rite of Social Communion."

38. Charlie Hill, interview by author, Havana, July 21, 2019.

39. Alejandro de la Fuente and Stanley R. Bailey, "The Puzzle of Racial Inequality in Cuba, 1980s–2010s," *Du Bois Review* 18, no. 1 (2021): 82–83; Frances Robles and Azam Ahmed, "More Black Officials in Power in Cuba as Leadership Changes," *New York Times*, April 22, 2018.

40. For Valdés Mesa, see Asamblea Nacional Poder Popular, Salvador Antonio Valdés Mesa, accessed August 24, 2025, www.parlamentocubano.gob.cu/salvador-antonio-valdes-mesa-0; for Chapman Waugh, see Asamblea Nacional Poder Popular, Inés María Chapman Waugh, accessed August 24, www.parlamentocubano.gob.cu/ines-maria-chapman-waugh; for Johnson Urrutia, see Asamblea Nacional Poder Popular, Beatriz Johnson Urrutia, accessed August 24, 2025, www.parlamentocubano.gob.cu/beatriz-johnson-urrutia.

41. De la Fuente and Bailey, "Puzzle of Racial Inequality in Cuba," 79.

42. Hill, interview, July 21, 2019.

43. De la Fuente and Bailey, "Puzzle of Racial Inequality in Cuba," 80–85.

44. Hope Bastian, *Everyday Adjustments in Havana: Economic Reforms, Mobility, and Emerging Inequalities* (Lanham, MD: Lexington Books, 2018), 7–16.

45. De la Fuente and Bailey, "Puzzle of Racial Inequality in Cuba," 85–91.

46. Hill, interview, July 21, 2019.

47. Nathan Schneider, "The Revolutionary Life and Strange Death of a Radical Black Mayor," *Vice*, April 17, 2016.

48. Hill, interview, July 22, 2019.

49. For twenty-first-century political descendants of the RNA, see, especially, Kali Akuno and Ajamu Nangwaya, eds., *Jackson Rising: The Struggle for Economic Democracy and Black Self-Determination in Jackson, Mississippi* (Québec: Daraja Press, 2017); Kali Akuno and Matt Meyer, eds., *Jackson Rising Redux: Lessons on Building the Future in the Present* (Binghamton, NY: PM Press, 2023).

50. The author was in Havana at the time and offered to make an introduction between the Jackson Rising delegates and Charlie. For an event overview, see https://cooperationjackson.org/events-calendar/yearofreturnreportback.

51. "Trump to Cuba: Return Woman Convicted in Trooper's Murder," Associated Press, June 16, 2017.

52. Shakur was also the stepfather of hip-hop artist Tupac Shakur. For more on Mutulu Shakur, see Akinyele Umoja, "Straight Ahead: The Life of Resistance of Dr. Mutulu Shakur," *Souls: A Critical Journal of Black Politics, Culture, and Society* 23, nos. 1–2 (2022): 4–35. For more on the views of the Cuban Five on the US prison system, see Mary-Alice Waters, ed., *It's the Poor Who Face the Savagery of the US "Justice" System: The Cuban Five Talk About Their Lives Within the US Working Class* (College Park, MD: Pathfinder Press, 2016).

53. Charlie Hill, interview by author, Havana, July 23, 2019.

54. Janet Hill King, interview by author, WhatsApp, August 2022. According to Janet, the FBI later telephoned one of her personal friends seeking information about the Hill family.

55. Shaunely de la Mercedes Hill Pedroso, interview by author, Havana, July 4, 2023.

56. Antar Charles Hill Cardona, interview by author, Havana, July 4, 2023.

57. *Charlie*, directed by Kadri Koop (2016), 13 min. Charlie would later say that the letter was authored by an associate of the filmmaker, not him. However, it is unlikely that he would have consented to read it on camera had it not resonated with him.

Epilogue

1. Edward W. Said, *Reflections on Exile and Other Essays*, 3rd ed. (Cambridge, MA: Harvard University Press, 2002), 173.

2. Charlie Hill, interview by author, June 29, 2018. Hill is unable to recall from which text this characterization of Lenin's sense of exile comes.

3. Teishan A. Latner, "Assata Shakur: The Political Life of Political Exile," in *Black Power Afterlives: The Enduring Significance of the Black Panther Party*, ed. Diane C. Fujino and Matef Harmachis (Chicago: Haymarket Books), 28.

4. Nehanda Abiodun, interview by author, Havana, July 17, 2018.

5. William Lee Brent, *Long Time Gone: A Black Panther's True-Life Story of His Hijacking and Twenty-Five Years in Cuba* (New York: Times Books, 1996), 276.

6. Gary Moore, "'Man Without a Country' Adjusts to Cuba Exile," *Miami Herald*, October 31, 1980.

7. Said, *Reflections on Exile and Other Essays*, 186.

8. Charlie Hill, interview by author, Havana, July 23, 2019. Hill was visited in Havana by two of his siblings in May 2024. It was the first visit that he received from members of his US family since his arrival in Cuba in 1971.

9. Charlie Hill, interview by author, Havana, June 5, 2022.

10. Carlos Álvarez Rodríguez, "The Long Read: The Story of Charlie Hill, an FBI Fugitive in Havana," *Huck*, March 25, 2016.

11. Hill, interview, July 23, 2019.

12. Hill, interview, July 23, 2019.

13. *The Return*, directed by Jon Fish (ESPN, 2019), 27 min.; "ESPN Documentary Shows Bleier's Emotional Return to Vietnam," Associated Press, August 17, 2019.

14. Hill, interview, July 23, 2019.

15. Charlie Hill, interview by author, May 31, 2018.

16. Hill, interview, May 31, 2018.

Index

Italic page numbers refer to illustrations.

www.ingramcontent.com/pod-product-compliance
Lightning Source LLC
LaVergne TN
LVHW101544020926
846999LV00029B/230

* 9 7 8 1 4 6 9 6 9 3 4 8 4 *